THE

MINERAL SPRINGS

OF THE

UNITED STATES AND CANADA,

WITH

ANALYSES AND NOTES

ON THE

PROMINENT SPAS OF EUROPE,

AND A LIST OF

SEA-SIDE RESORTS

BY

GEO. E. WALTON, M. D.,

LECTURER ON MATERIA MEDICA IN THE MIAMI MEDICAL COLLEGE, CINCINNATI; COMMITTEE OF THE MEDICAL ASSOCIATION OF THE STATE OF OHIO ON "THERAPEUTICS OF MINERAL SPRINGS."

NEW YORK:
D. APPLETON & COMPANY,
549 & 551 BROADWAY.
1873.

THE MINERAL SPRINGS

OF THE

UNITED STATES AND CANADA.

"Whatever may be said of them, mineral waters are not simple medicaments; whatever may be the predominant mineralizing agent, as demonstrated by analysis, it acts not alone. Nature, in combining with the more or less notable elements which chemistry may isolate, other exceedingly variable ingredients and principles, which have not yet been discovered, has done for this mineralized agent that which we seek to imitate each day in our prescriptions, when we endeavor to reënforce or diminish the effect of a medical substance by associating others with it."—Trousseau, *Clinique Médicale*, tome iii., p. 58.

"All substances administered in powder are active in proportion to the fineness of their division. Hence solutions, which are only minuter divisions of substances than powders, act more rapidly and energetically on the system at large than the latter, while their local action is less intense. On these accounts natural mineral waters are much more active than artificial solutions containing the same ingredients."—Stillé, *Therapeutics and Materia Medica*, vol. i., p. 75.

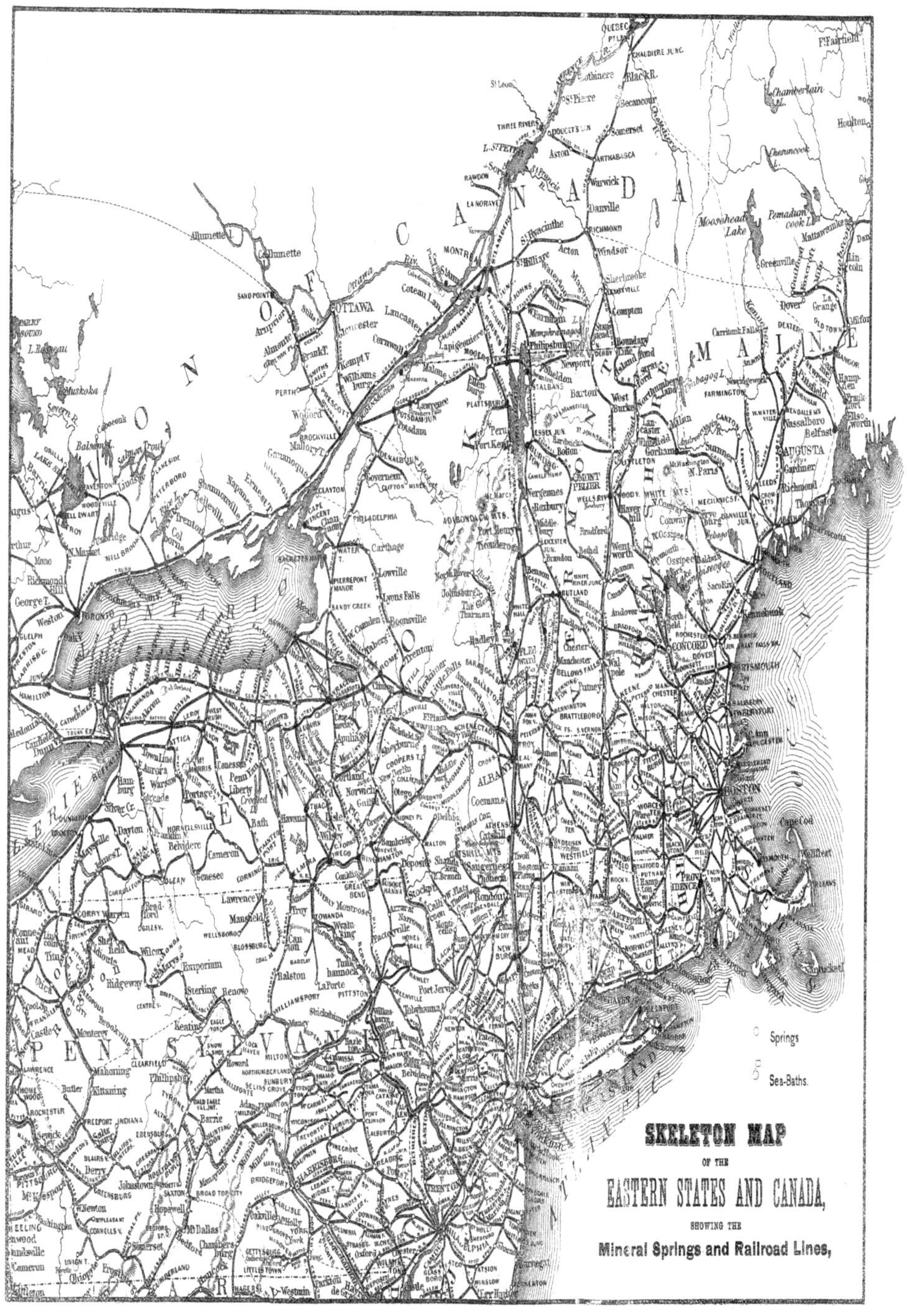

SKELETON MAP
OF THE
EASTERN STATES AND CANADA,
SHOWING THE
Mineral Springs and Railroad Lines,
Springs
Sea-Baths.
DOMINION OF CANADA
MAINE
NEW YORK
PENNSYLVANIA
ONTARIO
ERIE
QUEBEC
OTTAWA
MONTREAL
TORONTO
BOSTON
CONCORD
AUGUSTA
ALBANY
HARRISBURG

PREFACE.

FOR many years the author has desired to know whether there are any medicinal virtues in mineral waters. He has been accustomed to hear mineral springs mentioned with a smile by the majority of the members of the medical profession in the United States, while, on the other hand, patients are continually seeking springs without consulting their physician. Occasionally he has known medical gentlemen admit that patients afflicted with inveterate chronic diseases have resorted to mineral springs, and much to their surprise returned cured. Between this incredulity of the profession, and credulity of the public, he has thought there may be a medium of truth. He knew that medical men of experience abroad frequently recommended their patients to visit certain spas for the relief of their maladies. That very eminent French physician, Trousseau, devoted much time to writing a work, in company with Lasèque, entitled "Études Thérapeutiques sur les Eaux Minérales des Bords du Rhin," and, throughout his clinical work, as well as the able work of Prof. Niemeyer, mineral waters are assigned an important place in the treatment of many chronic diseases. With impressions derived from such facts, the author sought libraries and book-stores for information concerning the mineral springs of the United States, but found little or none.

In this volume the author has endeavored to arrange all the known facts concerning mineral waters, in such manner that they shall be readily accessible. For this purpose he has consulted the best European authors, their conclusions being drawn from hundreds of years of laborious investigation of the spas of Germany, France, Switzerland, and Italy. It has been interesting in the course of this study to note how closely the conclusions drawn by them, concerning the action of different classes of waters, agree with the observations made at springs in this country independent of any knowledge of foreign research. The portion relating to the springs of the United States is the result of a selection of credible evidence regarding them, gained by correspondence and personal observation. Acknowledgment should here be made to Stephen Powers, Esq., of California, who has so greatly aided in procuring information concerning the springs of that State.

To facilitate comparison, the analyses of all the springs have been reduced to the wine pint, the original analyses from which they are taken being based on the wine gallon, the imperial gallon, the litre, a thousand parts, etc. Wherever the alkaline carbonates were estimated as *bicarbonates* in the original analysis, they have been reduced to *carbonates.* The carbonate of iron is always understood to be the carbonate of the protoxide. In two or three of the analyses the uncombined elements were given, but the acids and bases have been combined according to approved methods, and the resultant salts appear. In some instances the springs were analyzed many years ago, previous to important discoveries in chemical science, and the water should be reanalyzed; for, although the analysis of a water does not indicate its absolute medical value, nevertheless, in many instances, it is an exceedingly important guide to its use. All waters of value should be thoroughly analyzed; and, though we cannot then account for their action, let us not close our eyes or ignore their efficacy, if such there be, but continue the search for the unknown quantities that elude our vision.

Although this country does not seem to present a complete list of the various classes of waters, still, for the treatment of many diseases, we have waters equal to any in the world, and one potent subdivision, the aluminous chalybeates (alum-waters), are found nowhere but in America of equal strength. However, when the waters of the Pacific coast shall be thoroughly analyzed, doubtless we shall find some of them equal the celebrated alkaline thermals of Vichy, and the muriated-alkaline thermals of Ems.

The list of springs is thought to be complete, but a few omissions may have occurred. The author will consider himself under obligations to any one who will favor him with information of springs not mentioned, however remote, provided they have been improved for public resort.

No. 224 Laurel Street,
Cincinnati, *December*, 1872.

CONTENTS.

CHAPTER I.

HISTORICAL.

CHAPTER II

MINERAL WATERS.

CHAPTER III.

CLASSIFICATION.

CHAPTER IV.

ACTION OF MINERAL WATERS.

CHAPTER V.

CHEMICAL CONSTITUENTS.

CHAPTER XI.

SALINE WATERS.

CHAPTER XII.

SULPHUR-WATERS.

CHAPTER XIII.

CHALYBEATE WATERS.

CHAPTER XIV.

PURGATIVE WATERS.

CHAPTER XV.

CALCIC WATERS.

CHAPTER XVI.

THERMAL WATERS.

CHAPTER XVII.

UNCLASSIFIED WATERS.

CHAPTER XVIII.

EUROPEAN SPAS.

CHAPTER XIX.

SEA-SIDE RESORTS.

MINERAL SPRINGS.

CHAPTER I.

HISTORICAL.

The pages of ancient authors frequently contain records of resorts where the sick bathed in healing waters or drank of medicinal fountains. In Greece the temples of Æsculapius were frequently erected near springs reputed to possess curative power. The ancient Athenians, during the summer months, sought the thermal—saline—sulphur baths of Ædipsus in the island of Eubœa, about sixty miles by sea from Athens. They have been known from remotest antiquity, and are a favorite resort at the present day. During the Mithridatic war, Sylla sought them, and Strabo tells us (book i., chap. iii., Proleg.) that, following an earthquake, these waters disappeared for three days, and reappeared at several different points. On the opposite side of the channel from Ædipsus, on the main-land, is the celebrated pass of Thermopylæ, so named from the hot sulphur-springs in the vicinity. They flow from the base of Mount Œta, and fall into the sea. Springs formed a favorite site for the establishment of temples. Near the Temple of Jupiter Ammon was an intermittent spring (Herodotus iv., 181). Delphi had its Fountain of Casotis (Pausanius x., 24, § 7), and these waters, now known as St. Nicholas, rise south of Lesche, and flow beneath the Temple of Apollo.

In the pages of Latin writers we frequently meet with allusions to medicinal springs, testifying the esteem in which they were held by the Romans. Horace, in describing the fictitious fame that the cold-water cure obtained at Rome, under the influence of a charlatan named Musa, speaks thus:

> "Of Velia and Salernum tell me, pray,
> The climate and the natives, and the way;
> For Baiæ now is lost on me, and I,
> Once its stanch friend, am now its enemy,
> Through Musa's fault, who makes me undergo
> His cold-bath treatment, spite of frost and snow.
> Good sooth, the town is filled with spleen to see
> Its steamy baths attract no company;
> To find its sulphur-wells, which found out pain
> From joint and sinew, treated with disdain
> By chests and heads, now grown so bold
> They brave cold water in the depth of cold;
> And finding down at Clusium what they want,
> Or Gabbi, say, make that their winter haunt."
>
> (Epist. i., 15. Conington's Translation of Horace.)

Unfortunately for Musa, the ill success of his mode of treatment soon caused a return to the mineral waters of Baiæ, which continued to be sought by multitudes, and are resorted to at the present day.

Pliny tells us in his Natural History (book xxxi., § 1) that all waters are gifts of the earth. He says: "They spring wholesome from the earth on every side and in a thousand lands; the cold, the hot, the hot and cold together, as at Tarbellum (Dax) in Aquitania, or in the Pyrenees, where they are separated only by a small interval, or yet the warm and tepid, announcing relief to the sick, and flowing from the earth only for man, of all living things. Under various names they add to the number of divinities, and establish villages." He also names the diseases for which certain waters were considered beneficial—the springs of Sineusa for sterility; those of Ænaria (Ischia, of to-day) for calculous affections. Of the latter, it is said by a late writer: "The attractions of this country and its waters are sufficient to merit with us the popularity they enjoyed with the ancients, and which is testified by numerous Latin inscriptions."

When the seat of the Roman Empire was transferred to the East, the well-known baths of Brusa, about sixty miles from Constantinople, were developed; and at this day they are the most celebrated baths in the Orient. Wherever the Romans penetrated the then Western wilds of Europe, they sought out the mineral springs of the country, and we find remains of their baths at Aix in Savoy, Aix in Provence; Bagnères de Bigorre and Bagnères de Luchon in the Pyrenees, Alhama and Caldas in Spain, Wiesbaden, Baden in Switzerland, and at Bath, or Aqua Solis, in England. The Latin word *aqua*, changed into Acqui, Aigues, Aix, Ax, and Dax, as applied to modern towns, remains to tell of their early celebrity as watering-places.

If there were historic records of the barbarous tribes of Germania, Gallia, and Hispania, we would doubtless learn that the same fountains were held in esteem by them which were subsequently resorted to by the Romans.

In the brilliant days of imperial Rome, bathing formed a chief enjoyment of patrician and plebeian. The luxury of warm bathing was indulged in to such excess that at one time eight hundred thermæ could be counted within the city, and several of these would accommodate three thousand bathers at one time. Many of these structures covered entire squares, and were adorned with every architectural beauty. An approach to them showed beautiful marble porticos supported by many-fluted columns, and entering and passing out might be seen orators, poets, senators, and sometimes the emperor. Within was a labyrinth of marble halls and colonnades decorated with statuary and mosaics by the masters, and in various spacious chambers scholars discoursed to an attentive auditory. Other apartments were devoted to athletic exercise, which was usually taken before entering the bath. After the bath, those who had leisure might pass an hour in the well-arranged library, or saunter in the gardens of rare flowers and exotic plants within the enclosure. The grandeur of these structures may be imagined when we are told that the baths of Diocletian were the repository of the famous Ulpian Library; that one of the halls of these baths forms the present magnificent Church of the Carthusians; and that the baths of Agrippa had for a vestibule that relic of antiquity so well described by Byron:

> "Simple, erect, severe, austere, sublime—
> Shrine of all saints and temple of all gods,
> From Jove to Jesus—spared and blest by time,
> Looking tranquillity, while falls or nods,
> Arch, empire, each thing round thee, and man plods
> His way through thorns to ashes—glorious dome!
> Shalt thou not last? Time's scythe and tyrants' rods
> Shiver upon thee—sanctuary and home
> Of art and piety—Pantheon! pride of Rome!"

Many traces of the Roman baths still remain, but the most familiar ruins are those of the baths of Caracalla. They were commenced by Antoninus Caracalla about the year A. D. 212. Subsequently they were enlarged by Elagabulus, and completed by Alexander Severus. They occupy an area nearly a mile in circuit, including the enclosure, and the bath-structure covered a space seven hundred and twenty feet long and three hundred and seventy-five feet wide. Within the enclosure were porticos, gardens, a stadium, and a large reservoir into which the Antonine Aqueduct emptied, and in front ran the Via Novo, one of the most magnificent streets in Rome during the time of the Antonines.

On page 5 we insert one-half of the ground-plan taken from Bell's work on baths, Dr. Bell having borrowed it from Cameron's "Baths of the Romans." The other half of the building corresponds to this in every particular.

Outside the bath-building, and within the enclosure, was a pavilion for spectators, whence they could see the exercises in the open air, apartments for those who had care of the baths, exedræ where gymnastic exercises were taught, retiring-chambers for those who exercised in the stadium, atrias to

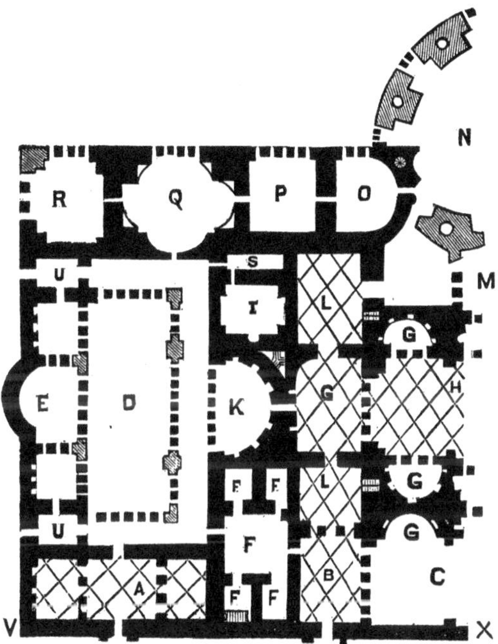

HALF OF THE PLAN OF THE BATHS OF CARACALLA. THE SIDE IN THE LINE V X FACING THE VIA NOVO; THE OPPOSITE SIDE OPENING UPON THE GARDENS.

A. Vestibule on entering the thermæ, on each side of which were libraries.
B. Vestibule for spectators and the clothes of those who were bathing.
C. Piscina, or large reservoir for swimming.
D. Peristyle, having a piscina in the middle for warm bathing.
E. Ephebium, or place for exercise.
F F. Rooms where the athletæ prepared for their exercises.
G G. Various halls or recesses for the use of those who frequented the baths.
H. Xystum, or portico for the athletæ to exercise under in bad weather.
K. Exedræ, or large recesses for the use of philosophers.
L. Rooms for conversation.
M. Aphodyterium, or undressing-room.
N. Cella solaris, one hundred and eleven feet in diameter, in which were the labra of the baths for ordinary bathing. Spartianus says this apartment could not be equalled by the architects of his age; that the window-lattices were overlaid with brass or copper, of which materials the whole vault was made, "and so vast was its extent that learned mechanicians declare it impossible to make one like it."
O. Laconicum, or hot-air bath.
P. Caldarium, or hot-vapor bath.
Q. Tepidarium, or tepid-water bath.
R. Frigidarium, or cold-water bath.
S. Elæosthesium, or room for oils.
T. Conisterium, or room where athletæ, after being anointed with oil, were sprinkled with dust so they might take surer hold in wrestling.
U U. Vestibules.

the academies, temples, piazzas for the masters to walk in, and covered baths for those who did not choose to exercise in the xystus.

It would appear from this description that the baths were divided into the warm-water baths—those apartments in which the piscinæ are located—and the hot-air and vapor-baths comprising the laconicum and the caldarium, which were heated to from 110° to 160° Fahr. Many bathers seldom entered these apartments. Those who frequented the baths disrobed in the contiguous vestibules, and placed their clothing in charge of servants, who received small sums of money for keeping guard. They then went to the elæosthesium and anointed the entire body with a cheap kind of oil, and afterward repaired to one of the many spaces devoted to gymnastic exercises. After exercising a sufficient time, they entered an adjoining warm-bath. Here numbers might be seen seated on the marble steps of the bath, which were just below the surface of the water. After ablution, they seated themselves on these steps and scraped the entire body with the *strigil*, a blunt instrument similar in shape to a small sickle, and made of bone, iron, bronze, or silver—most frequently of bronze. The wealthy had the operation performed by an attendant slave. It is said that it was not an agreeable proceeding, and that the Emperor Augustus was a sufferer by having it performed too roughly. Afterward the bather was washed by vases of water poured over him, and then thoroughly dried with cotton and linen cloths, and covered with a light shaggy mantle called *gausape*. Fastidious persons of wealth, in addition to the process described, had slaves go over their bodies with tweezers and pluck out every hair; the nails of feet and hands were then trimmed; and, finally, highly-perfumed oils in vases of alabaster or bronze were brought from the elæosthesium, and the entire body, not omitting the soles of the feet, was anointed. The clothing was then resumed, and they passed into the tepidarium, where they remained some time, so as not to be too suddenly chilled on going from the warm bath into the external air. The tepidarium in these baths, it seems, was only used for this purpose; water being employed only as a convenient method of regulating the temperature of the chamber. In smaller thermæ, however, and in provincial cities, this apartment was undoubtedly used for bathing. In this description of bathing the laconicum and caldarium are omitted. They were sought by those who desired, for the purpose of producing excessive perspiration in a similar way to the Turkish and Russian baths.

A word may be said concerning the oils and perfumes. They were of great variety, and universally employed, both by men and women. The rhodinium, extracted from roses, lirinium from the lily, myrrhinum from myrrh, baccarinum from foxglove, and cyprinum from the flowers of the privet-tree, were favorites. Also, cinnamomium, very costly, made from cinnamon, irinum, an oil made from the iris, balaninum, the oil of the nuts of the ben-tree found in India and Arabia, serpyillinum from wild-thyme, sysymbrium from water-mint, amaracinum from sweet-marjoram, nardinum from lavender. These scents and oils were used by preference for different parts of the body, some being considered best adapted to the head, face, and neck, others to the muscles and extremities.

A story of Hadrian, quoted by most writers on ancient baths, is told by Spartianus: "The Emperor Hadrian, who went to the public baths and bathed with the common people, seeing one day a veteran, whom he had known among the Roman troops, rubbing his back and other parts of his body against the marble, asked him why he did so. The veteran answered that he had no slave to rub him, whereupon the emperor gave him two slaves and wherewithal to maintain them. Another day, several old men, enticed by the good fortune of the veteran, rubbed themselves also against the marble before the emperor, believing by this means to excite the liberality of Hadrian, who, perceiving their drift, caused them to be told to rub each other."

In addition to the large number of public baths, there were many private baths in the residences of wealthy citizens. Seneca, when contrasting the luxuries of his own day with the simplicity of the republic, describes them thus: "That person is now held to be poor and sordid whose walls shine not with a profusion of the most costly materials, the marbles of Egypt inlaid with those of Numidia; unless the walls are set with mosaics in imitation of painting; unless the chambers are covered with glass; unless the Thracian stone, formerly a rare sight even in temples, surrounds those capacious basins into which we cast our bodies, weakened by immoderate sweats. And the water is conveyed through silver pipes. As yet, I speak only of plebeian baths; what shall I say when I come to those of freedmen? What a profusion of columns do I see supporting nothing, but placed as an ornament, merely on account of the expense! What quantities of water murmuring down steps! We are come to that pitch of luxury that we disdain to tread on any thing but precious stones."

When the thermæ first became public institutions, laws were passed regulating their use. They were placed in charge of the officials, called ædiles, whose duty it was to see that the rules concerning the baths were enforced. The hours of bathing were from two o'clock in the afternoon till dusk, between two and three being the hour most favorable. Notice was given that the baths were ready by ringing a bell, the warm water being then drawn into the various piscinæ. Hadrian forbade that any should bathe before two o'clock, and any who bathed after four o'clock were charged a hundred quadrantes, about equivalent to thirty cents of our currency. The usual price of a bath was one-third of a cent. Subsequently, to ingratiate themselves with the populace, the emperors permitted the baths to be opened earlier and closed later; and, under Alexander Severus, they were not only permitted to be opened before daybreak, but oil was furnished for lighting at the public expense. The baths were a place of general resort, and on public holidays it was customary to keep them open the entire day. They were then thronged by the lower classes. The emperors amused the people with baths, that their own derelictions might be forgotten.

There were separate thermæ for females, those most celebrated being the baths of Agrippina. However, with the degeneracy of public morals, it became necessary to pass most stringent laws forbidding women, under the severest penalties, from bathing with men, and, on the contrary, punishing those men with death who should be found in baths devoted to females.

It is difficult for us, living in this busy age, to understand how the people of Rome found time every day to frequent the baths. A bath, with all the accessories, must have occupied from one to two hours; and yet we read of citizens of distinction who bathed four and five times each day. Can we wonder that the degeneracy of public morals which permitted such excesses, was followed by effeminacy of the people, and finally by the downfall of Rome?

During the summer months the Romans resorted to Baiæ, ten miles from Naples, on the gulf. It was not only the wonderful mineral springs of hot and cold water, and the phenomena of extinct volcanoes, that were attractive. The surrounding country was charmingly beautiful, and was associated with the earliest epoch of Roman history. Near by was the most ancient city of Cumæ, with its sibyl; the Lake of Avernus, with its entrance to hell; the Forum Vulcani, the promontory of Misenum, the Phlegræan fields, and the Elysian plains. Amid these scenes the wealthy Romans erected elaborate villas and pursued the luxurious pleasures of the capital. A lively description of those baths is given by Seneca in Epistles 51 and 56: "He tells us that, while at Baiæ, he lived near the great bath-house, and was continually annoyed by the noise. Early in the morning the splashing of bathers greeted his ears, for they bathed at all hours. He was disturbed by the excited cries of those playing at ball, and by the deep-drawn sighs of those who swung heavy weights. Here one was trying his voice in song, there another was engaged in loud dispute, or perhaps a cry was raised at the detection of a thief caught stealing clothes of one of the bathers, no unusual occurrence. Then there were the shrill cries of the venders of eatables, especially the libum, or sweet-cake, long popular with bathers, and a remnant of which is still found in some of the German baths. He also tells us that it was common to see tipsy people wandering along the sea-shore, and to hear the shores of the Lucrine Lake resounding with the songs of pleasure-parties of men and women who skimmed about in gayly-painted boats of every variety of shape and color, decked out with crowns and chaplets of roses. All ancient writers describe these aquatic excursions as scenes of voluptuous pleasure; there was also abundance of gambling; and, on the whole, Seneca described Baiæ as a sort of vortex of luxury and harbor of vice."[1]

Passing over a period of a thousand years, during which we have no record of bathing-resorts, we come to the following description of Baden, in Switzerland, canton of Aargau, by Poggio Bracciolini, 1420: "Baden, though offering no great natural beauty, and nothing in the way of agreeable relaxation, presented such other pleasures that you might imagine Venus with her troop had deserted Cyprus and come to live at the baths. There were two public and about twenty-eight private baths attached to the hotels. In the public bath men and women bathe together in a state of entire nudity. In the private baths the men and women used at least partial clothing, and there was a partition between the men's and women's baths, with openings, however, which made it easy for them to talk to each other. People used often to bathe three or four times a day; indeed, to spend a great part of their time in the baths, to ask their friends to come and spend the day with them; they played at cards, and had their meals supplied to them on floating tables, and there was no lack of good eating and drinking."

The description of the same baths by Montaigne, one hundred and fifty years later, shows a decided change. He says: "Those who have ladies under their charge will do well to bring them here, where every lady has a bath to herself handsomely fitted up with a dressing-room, light and airy, with

[1] *London Quarterly*, July, 1870. "Baths."

rich windows, painted wainscoting and ceiling, and polished floors, and provided with small tables on which you may read or play while in the bath. . . . The people of this part of the country when they bathe usually have themselves so unmercifully cupped and bled that I have sometimes seen the two public baths almost full of blood. The houses are very handsome, and kept up on a grand scale. In that where we lodged there have been in one day three hundred mouths to provide for."

Some one hundred years later, in 1648, we have a description of the round of life at Bath, England, by the quaint court gossip, Pepys. It runs thus: "Up at four o'clock, being by appointment called up to the Cross bath, where we were carried one after another, myself and wife, and Betty Turner, Willet, and W. Hewer. And by-and-by, though we designed to have done before company came, much company came; very fine ladies; and the manners pretty enough; only methinks it cannot be clean to go so many bodies together in the same water. Good conversation among those that are acquainted here and stay together; but strange to see, when women and men here that live all the season in these waters, cannot but be parboiled and look like creatures of the bath. Carried away—wrapped in a sheet and in a chair, home; and then, one after another thus carried, I staying about two hours in the water, home to bed, sweating for an hour, and by-and-by comes music to play to me, extraordinary good as ever I heard at London almost, or anywhere, 5s. In the afternoon I went to make boys dive in the King's bath, 1s."

The only baths of the present day which resemble those of the middle ages are those of Leuk, in the valley of the Rhone, Switzerland. They are situated in a little mountain-nook, at the base of the perpendicular ascent of the Gemmi Pass. Here several hot springs, of large volume, issue from the earth, the waters of which are conducted to the various public baths. In the bath-houses there are several pools beneath the same roof, each of which is capable of accommodating between thirty and forty persons. On either side of each pool are dressing-rooms. From the "Guide Pratique" of Constantin James we translate as follows: "It is between four and five o'clock in the morning that they repair to the bath. The patients first dress in a long woollen tunic, then descend into the pool by a sort of inclined plane, in a stooping attitude, until they arrive at the desired depth. The basin is thus peopled with new arrivals, and is soon full. Let us penetrate for a moment in a bath-building, where the piscina is filled. What a singular sight! Imagine young girls, children, old men, priests, soldiers, sisters—what shall I say?—in fine, all conditions and all ages, assembled pell-mell in the same pool. Some sing, some read, others work or read; it is a crowded house, joyous with pleasantry and anecdote. Each bather has a floating table, a kind of little boat where he places his handkerchief, his snuff-box, or his luncheon. But what of the shipwrecks upon this little ocean? To see this multitude of heads agitating the surface of the water, we would call it a reunion of Tritons."

The method of bathing at Leuk is only tolerated at this day because of the number of hours required for the bath-cure. It is the custom to pass three or four hours of the morning, and one or two of the afternoon, in the water. Such a long time, alone, in a bath would indeed be irksome.

We will not lengthen this chapter by describing the baths of any of the celebrated spas of Europe; they are such as are met with at our American resorts, though usually far more elegant in accessories. In addition to amusements of every type, they are often the centre of gambling establishments of colossal dimensions. Those of Baden-Baden are well known to travellers. The Conversation-House, as it is politely termed, is of beautiful proportions, in the Grecian style of architecture, and built of solid stone. Within is a magnificent concert-room, ornate with frescoes and glittering with gilding, whence float strains of delicious music enticing the passer-by. Opening out from this saloon, on either side, are grand saloons, replete with elegant and luxurious appointments. These saloons are devoted to the fascinations of roulette and *rouge-*

et-noir. Around the tables may be seen the young, the beautiful, the middle-aged, and the gray-haired, the peasant and the nobleman, the countess and the count, the thoughtless and the statesman, each casting his five-franc piece or his thousands upon the table, and watching with intense interest the deft fingers of the dealer, as he rapidly shuffles the cards and throws forth the numbers that tell of the winning and losing of fortunes.

CHAPTER II.

MINERAL WATERS.

A MINERAL water, in the medical acceptation of the term, is one which by virtue of its ingredients, whether mineral, organic, gaseous, or the principle of heat, is especially applicable to the treatment of disease.

Water, as found in Nature, is never an unalloyed combination of its chemical constituents, hydrogen and oxygen. Pure water is a refinement of the laboratory, produced and retained with considerable difficulty. It is a colorless, inodorous, and tasteless fluid, nauseous when drank. Its solvent powers are unequalled by any known fluid.

As water falls from the clouds in the form of rain, it absorbs various gases, so that when obtained in this purest natural form it contains nitrogen, oxygen, carbonic acid, and sometimes traces of carburetted hydrogen, nitric acid, or ammonia. Having fallen upon the earth, its solvent power causes it to take up various salts and organic substances from the soil, so that when taken from rivers it frequently contains several grains of solid constituents to the gallon, or as much as a grain in a pint. The table (p. 15) shows the amount and number of these constituents to the pint in four rivers of this continent, and is interesting when compared with the analyses of mineral springs.

The origin of springs has been a subject of inquiry by philosophers of all ages. Aristotle taught that large caverns in the interior of the earth were filled with air which at the roofs was condensed to water by the cold, and thence made way to the surface of the earth by various outlets. Through the middle ages this was the received explanation, though

One Pint contains—	Schuylkill. B. Silliman, Jr.	Croton. B. Silliman, Jr.	Charles. B. Silliman, Jr.	St. Lawrence. T. Sterry Hunt.
SOLIDS.	Grains.	Grains.	Grains.	Grains.
Carbonate of soda	......	......	......	0.007
" magnesia	0.044	0.083	0.005	0.026
" manganese	......	traces.	......	.....
" lime	0.284	0.267	0.020	0.084
Chloride of potassium	......	......	......	0.002
" sodium	0.018	0.021	0.019	0.003
" magnesium	0.001	......	......	.....
" aluminum	......	0.021	......	.....
" calcium	......	0.047	0.005	.....
Sulphate of soda	......	0.019	0.048	0.018
" magnesia	0.007	......	......	.....
" lime	......	0.029	0.033	.....
Phosphate of alumina	......	0.104	0.012	.....
Silica	0.010	0.009	traces.	0.038
Oxides of iron and manganese	......	......	......	traces.
Alumina—phosphoric acid	......	......	......	traces.
Salts of soda with the nitric and organic acids	0.206	0.238	0.066	.....
Total	0.520	0.833	0.208	0.178
GAS.				
Carbonic acid	.05 cubic in.	2.18 cubic in.	0.006 cub. in.	not estimated.

Vitruvius believed springs to be due to rain and snow which penetrated the earth and accumulated in subterranean reservoirs.

In the early part of the seventeenth century, Descartes, who always impugned theories that possessed only the merit of being old, proposed a new explanation of the phenomena of springs. He imagined caverns to exist in the depths of the earth, into which water flowed from the sea. There the interior fires of the earth converted the water into vapor, which ascended to the upper part of the cavern, and by the low temperature was condensed to water; thence the water was forced upward through crevices in the rocks and escaped as springs.

Subsequently Mariotte and Halley demonstrated that the rainfall, including snow and dew, is sufficient to supply all the water that flows from rivers and springs. This view was promulgated by each of these philosophers about the same time, neither being aware of the observations and conclusions of the other. Mariotte estimated the mean fall of rain in the vicinity of Paris. He then compared this total with the quantity of water flowing away by the river Seine, and found it to be six times greater. From his experiments he concluded that all springs are due to meteoric water falling in the form of rain, snow, and dew, which permeates the earth till an impassable layer is met; it then courses along this layer till it escapes from a convenient outlet, or is forced upward by hydrostatic pressure.

Halley's conclusions were the same, though obtained in an altogether different manner. When making astronomical observations on the hills of St. Helena, 2,400 feet above the sea, his instruments became so wet with moisture, even under a clear sky, that he could use them with difficulty, and paper became so damp that the ink would blot. This phenomenon led him to experiment on the quantity of moisture exhaled from the sea. He procured a pan eight inches in diameter and four inches deep, which he filled with water salted to the same degree of salinity as sea-water. It was also heated to the temperature of the sea in summer. Having exposed the water to the open air, he found that in one hour's time the vessel lost 233 grains in weight, and at this rate there would be a loss of twelve ounces in twenty-four hours. He then estimated the surface of the Mediterranean Sea, and found it to be 160 degrees. If evaporation proceeded in the same manner over this entire surface as in the salted water of the pan, the loss in one day would be 5,280,000,000 tons. He next compared this quantity with the discharge of the rivers into the sea. The principal ones are the Ebro, the Rhone, the Dniester, the Danube, the Tiber, the Po, the Borysthenes, the Tanais, and the Nile, the remainder being small. He estimated that each of these rivers discharges ten times as much water into the sea in a day as the Thames, and the discharge of this river at Kingston Bridge he found to be 20,300,000 tons. Ten times this amount would give 203,000,000 tons as the discharge of each of the nine rivers named, and 1,827,000,000 tons as the total discharge of them all. But this enormous amount is only about one-third the quantity evaporated from the surface of the Mediterranean in a single day, leaving a remainder of 3,453,000,000 tons unaccounted for—

amply sufficient to supply all the springs for many miles from the coast.

It is, then, clearly established that the fall of water in the form of rain, snow, and dew, is large enough to supply all rivers and springs. We cannot, however, resist the impression that there is some truth in the theory of Descartes, and that certain springs derive their flow from the waters of the ocean. We know that volcanoes and earthquakes occur in its depths, and if large volumes of water are thus suddenly enchasmed, or if they slowly pass to the interior of the earth by devious channels, it is certainly probable that when superheated they may be forced to the earth's surface in the form of thermal waters or saline springs.[1]

But many of these springs contain ingredients in large quantities not found in rain-water or sea-water. Whence and how do they obtain these constituents?

It has already been stated that pure water possesses a solvent power unequalled by other fluids. No rocks, however dense, can resist its continued action. Even the glass vessels which we use are dissolved by it in minute proportions. And when, in addition, water contains large quantities of carbonic-acid gas, its solvent power on many substances is exceedingly increased. Every fissure of the earth is permeated by this solvent. It collects in the depths of mines, or drips from the roofs of caves. The railroad-tunnel through Mont Cenis—a mass of solid rock so dense that it soon turned the hardest steel—was so filled with water that a canal was dug through the centre to drain it away. When water has thus passed through thousands of feet of dense rock, and in the passage occupied years or centuries, it is not surprising that it frequently contains a large amount of ingredients. And when a stream of water thus impregnated becomes imprisoned between almost impermeable strata, it flows onward till a fissure

[1] Humboldt tells us: "When in September, 1759, Jorullo was suddenly elevated into a mountain 1,183 feet above the level of the surrounding plain, two small rivers, the Rio de Cuitimba and Rio de San Pedro, disappeared, and some time afterward burst forth again, during violent shocks of an earthquake, as hot springs, whose temperature I found in 1803 to be 186°.4 Fahr." ("Cosmos," Bohn's English edition, vol. i., p. 219.)

in the overlying strata is encountered, when by hydrostatic pressure it is forced upward and bursts from the earth as a mineral spring. Or, if an artesian well be sunk, and such a stream is penetrated, there is an outflow of water sometimes so strong as to be projected several feet above the earth.

An excellent illustration of the conditions under which mineral springs occur is found in Saratoga County, New York. The geological strata of this county from above downward are as follows: 1. Hudson River and Utica shales and slates. 2. Trenton limestone. 3. Calciferous sand-rock. 4. Potsdam sandstone. 5. Laurentian formation, of unknown thickness.

GEOLOGICAL SECTION AT SARATOGA SPRINGS.

The strata dip southward—elevated ranges of Laurentian rocks appearing in the northern portion of the county, and the superincumbent strata cropping out at intervals to the south, and running in parallel lines across the county: first, the Potsdam sandstone; next, calciferous sand-rock; then, the Trenton limestone; and lastly, in the southern half, the Hudson River and Utica slates and shales. However, at the village of Saratoga Springs, an unusual disarrangement of the strata has occurred. Doubtless by volcanic upheaval, the strata above the Laurentian rocks have been entirely fissured through; the southern section being considerably elevated, and the Potsdam sandstone on one side of the fissure corresponding with the calciferous sand-rock on the opposite. This condition is technically termed a *fault.* It is well illustrated by the accompanying plate,[1] on page 18.

The Laurentian rocks are composed of highly-crystalline gneiss, granite, and syenite, and are almost impervious to water, while the Potsdam sandstone and calciferous sand-rock, immediately overlying, permit it to pass freely. All the rain falling in the county north of the fissure, or fault, except that which passes off as surface-water, permeates the different strata till it meets the Laurentian rocks; thence it passes over the surface of these rocks till the fissure is reached, where it comes in contact with the uplifted ledge of rocks and accumulates. From the fissure in the Laurentian rocks, which penetrates to an unknown depth, carbonic acid doubtless arises, and thus, in addition to its mineral ingredients, the water becomes highly charged with this gas. The continual accessions of water and the pressure of the gas, together, force the water to the surface, where it breaks forth in the various springs of the Saratoga Valley. In one instance—the geyser spring or artesian well—the imprisoned water has been artificially liberated at a point where it is under great hydrostatic pressure, and it escapes with such force as to be projected twenty feet above the surface of the earth. The slightly different composition of the springs depends on accidental variations in the composition of the strata through which the water of each spring passes. These springs are a well-marked example of *ascending springs*, or those in which the water is elevated from a point below by hydrostatic pressure.

The Tuscan springs of California are another example of ascending springs, the water issuing from an interval between strata that have been upheaved by volcanic action. The diagram below illustrates the position of the strata on either side

[1] The plate is kindly loaned by Prof. C. F. Chandler, New York, from whose article in the *American Chemist*, December, 1871, the geological facts concerning Saratoga are taken.

of the spring.[1] The waters evolve a large quantity of carburetted hydrogen, which is purified and utilized for heating the water of the steam-baths.

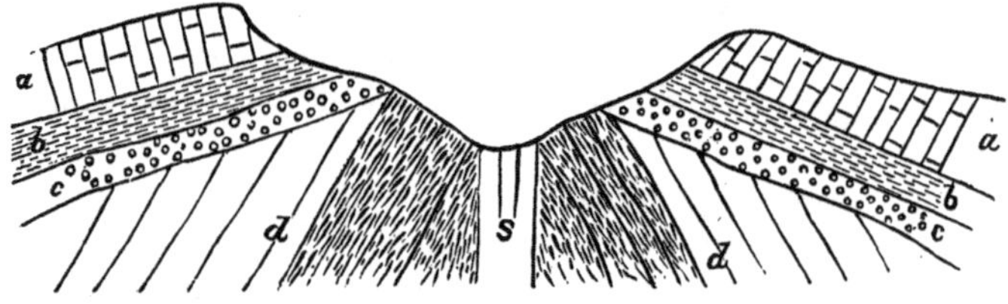

SECTION OF TUSCAN SPRINGS, CALIFORNIA.

a, *a*. Basaltic lava.
b, *b*. Volcanic ashes.
c, *c*. Conglomerate.
d, *d*. Cretaceous sandstone.
S. Springs.

Descending springs occur at the base of hills and mountains, and are seldom of such constitution as to be classed with mineral waters. They usually supply the purest drinking water. The water which they emit is the result of rain, snow, or ice, which falls or forms on the mountain. Owing to the direct way in which the water passes to them, they are more susceptible to variation in the flow than other springs. During and at the close of the rainy season, the volume will be considerably increased. In Switzerland many springs flow very freely during the summer, when the glaciers are melting, but are almost imperceptible at other times.

An excellent example of a descending mineral spring is found in the Rockbridge Alum waters of Virginia. These springs issue at the eastern base of a mountain-ridge, which rises almost perpendicularly above. The reservoirs in which the water collects are hollowed out of the mountain-base, which here consists of a stratum of clay-shale about eighty feet high, with a southeastern dip. This shale on analysis yields constituents similar to those found in the spring-water; that is, sulphate of iron, alumina, surphuret of iron, etc. The direct origin of these springs, from the descent of rain-water

[1] From "Geology of California," vol. i., p. 208.

through the shale, is further shown by the variable flow. In rainy weather there is an abundant supply, but during a dry season it is much reduced.

Intermittent springs form a curious feature in the phenomena of springs. There are springs that flow at regular intervals, once or twice a year, for a period of two or three months, or, it may be, once or twice a day, or even every hour. The cause of the first—those that flow at certain seasons of the year—has been mentioned in the description of descending springs. It is due to the irregularity of the fall of rain, or melting of snow and ice which supplies them. Many glacier-springs flow only in summer, while others emit water only during the middle of the day, while the heat of the sun is sufficient to melt the ice from which they are supplied. The Engstlebrunnen, in the Haslithal, canton of Berne, Switzerland, is of this kind. It flows from the middle of May to the middle of August, and, during this time, only from four o'clock P. M. to eight o'clock A. M. But, if the season is cold, it does not flow at all.

Other springs owe their intermittent character to their connection with the sea. Such springs are not far distant from the coast, and have several outlets, one of which empties into the sea. When the tide rises the outlet to the sea is closed, the water accumulates in the reservoir and finally overflows. Again, some of the intermittent springs are the discharges of a siphon. The spring is connected with a hidden reservoir by a siphon-like canal in the rock. When the reservoir fills, the siphon becomes charged till the water begins to flow; then it continues till the reservoir is emptied, and the process is to be repeated. The spring of the villa Pliniana, on the shores of Lake Como, is of this kind. It is thus described by Pliny:[1] "The nature of this spring, which falls into the Larian Lake, is extremely surprising; it ebbs and flows regularly three times a day. This increase and decrease is plainly visible, and very interesting to observe. You sit down by the side of the fountain, and, while you are taking a repast and drinking its

[1] Letter to Sura, Epist. iv., 30.

water, which is very cool, you see it gradually rise and fall. If you place a ring, or any thing else, at the bottom, when it is dry, the stream reaches it by degrees till it is entirely covered, and then again gently retires from it; and this you may see it do three times successively." Near Colmars, in France, is another spring of this kind. It flows every seven minutes. After the earthquake of Lisbon, in 1755, it lost this peculiarity, but it was restored by the earthquake of 1763.

But, the most remarkable intermittent springs are those which are the result of the tension of hot vapor. The most wonderful of these are the Geysers of Iceland, and those of Wyoming Territory. The outlet of these springs is the mouth of a silicious tube, reaching down some forty to sixty feet in the earth. This tube being full of water, the pressure exercised on the water at the bottom of the tube raises its boiling-point; that is, while water boils in the open air at 212° Fahr., the degree to which it must be elevated, under a pressure equal to that at the bottom of a tube sixty feet long, is 251° Fahr. When a layer of water at the bottom of the tube is elevated to this temperature, it evolves steam; but, as soon as the bubbles pass to the cooler layers above, they are condensed. When the succeeding layer above is heated to the boiling-point, the escaping steam-bubbles are condensed in turn in the superincumbent layers. After a time, however, the entire column of water to the surface reaches the boiling-point, when much of the water throughout the entire tube suddenly becomes steam, and the explosion immediately occurs. This is the explanation given by Prof. Bunsen, and that it is the correct one has been demonstrated by Prof. Tyndall, who constructed an iron tube, with a bowl surrounding the upper opening and an iron bulb at the lower end, in which all the conditions named were fulfilled, and on heating the water in the bulb he obtained the result indicated—a miniature geyser jetted steam and water into the air.

The physical characteristics of mineral waters differ in many respects from ordinary water.

Color.—Mineral waters, when examined in a glass, are usually clear and transparent. But when we look down upon them in the spring, or as they are accumulated in reservoirs, they frequently present a green hue, an optical effect depending on their density. In some instances, however, they present other colors, due to substances which they contain in impalpable division. The whitish color frequently observed in sulphur-water is caused by the precipitation of sulphur, the yellow by the change of a monosulphuret into a polysulphuret. A pure white color is often due to precipitation of carbonate of lime, while a blue color arises from the suspension of slate or clay in the water in minute subdivision. A red color is frequently seen in chalybeate waters, and results from the precipitation of the red oxide of iron. In some instances, however, a red color may be due to microscopic algæ of that color.

Odor.—Mineral waters, as a rule, possess a more or less marked odor.

In sulphur-waters a characteristic odor is always present, that of sulphuretted hydrogen. When waters are highly charged with this gas, the odor is perceptible for a considerable distance from the spring. However, in sulphur-waters containing the monosulphuret of sodium, the odor is but feeble.

Calcic waters, containing a large proportion of sulphate of lime, frequently disengage sulphuretted hydrogen by decomposition of the sulphate in presence of organic compounds.

Other waters emit odors depending on the soil through which they have passed.

Taste.—The character of a mineral water can seldom be determined by its taste, for this frequently depends on conditions which bear no relation to its medical properties.

Of the various waters, sulphur-waters possess a more decided taste than any others, depending on the presence of sulphuretted-hydrogen gas. This taste, however, is more properly an odor, rendered more perceptible in swallowing the gas. In addition, these waters are frequently bitter to the taste, due to sulphates of soda and magnesia, or chloride of magnesium; or they are salty, due to chloride of sodium.

Alkaline waters, when containing the alkaline carbonates

in large proportion, possess a peculiar taste which cannot be more definitely designated than by terming it alkaline. Waters of this class, however, frequently evolve large quantities of carbonic-acid gas, giving to them a pungent and agreeable taste, and entirely disguising the alkaline savor.

Saline waters necessarily possess the taste of table-salt, though this is sometimes entirely masked by large proportions of carbonic-acid gas.

Chalybeate waters usually present an inky or styptic taste, decided in proportion to the absence of other constituents.

Calcic waters are often sweet to the taste, especially if they contain considerable carbonate of lime. This taste is very marked in the Old Sweet Springs of Virginia.

Texture.—This word, as applied to water, is intended to represent the sensation of harshness, or smoothness, which it imparts when in contact with the skin. It is only when the feeling is peculiarly bland and soft that it has been noticed.

Certain waters possess a smooth texture in a remarkable degree. While immersed in them the entire surface of the body seems as though covered with a bland oil; the fingers, when rubbed together, are unctuous, as though they had been anointed, and this peculiar sensation of smoothness frequently remains for some time after leaving the bath. The Warm Springs of Virginia are notably possessed of this quality.

The cause of this unctuosity is unknown. It has been attributed to the presence of silicates in large proportion, to the monosulphuret of sodium, and to organic matter. Durand-Fardel thinks it is due to organic matter. He says: "It is worthy of remark that it is precisely those waters of the Pyrenees, richest in organic matter, which are the most unctuous."[1] Some authors suppose it arises from a combination, between the acid secretions of the skin and the bases of the water, forming a kind of soap.

Temperature.—Many theories have been proposed at different ages, explaining the elevated temperature possessed by many mineral springs. In the early part of this century,

[1] "Dictionnaire des Eaux Minérales," t. i., p. 591.

the chemical theory had many adherents. Philosopners who embraced this theory believed that within the interior of the earth, beneath each thermal spring, was a sort of chemical laboratory in which alkaline metals were being oxidized by water, and large volumes of heat thereby generated. Bischof, who persistently combated the chemical theory till it fell, showed that it would be impossible for such chemical action to continue, with perfect regularity, for thousands of years.

The theory uniformly received at the present day attributes the heat of springs to the interior heat of the earth, which pervades every portion of the globe. Springs proceeding from great depths partake of the heat of the point from which they arise; passing thence, by devious fissures, they break forth under the most varied circumstances—at the summits of mountains or in the depths of valleys, under a tropical sun or in the frigid zone. The borings of artesian wells supply indubitable proof of the correctness of this theory.

It has been found that at a certain point below the surface of the earth—varying according to the zone and constitution of the soil—the temperature is invariable throughout the year. At Paris this point is thirty feet deep; but, after this point is passed, the temperature of the earth steadily increases with the descent. The rate of increase is 1° Fahr. for every fifty or fifty-five feet. The artesian well of Grenelle, near Paris, is 1,600 feet deep, and the temperature of the water flowing from it 81.8° Fahr.; that of Passy is 1,731 feet deep, and the temperature of the water 82° Fahr.; that of Neusalzwerk, near Minden, in Prussia, is 2,094 feet, and the temperature 89° Fahr.; that of Mondorf, in Luxemburg, 2,278 feet, and the temperature 108.5° Fahr. In the United States, the artesian well at Louisville, Ky., is 2,086 feet deep, and the temperature at the bottom of the well is 86.5° Fahr.; the artesian well at Charleston, S. C., is 1,250 feet deep, and the temperature of the water is 87° Fahr.

It will be seen, from the figures given, that the temperature of water flowing from great depths is uniformly elevated. The temperature, however, is not always in proportion to the depth of the well. This arises from the fact that water flowing from the bottom of the well may intermingle with colder water from the strata above, producing a lower temperature than would be expected; or the vein of water supplying the well may arise from a much greater depth, giving an unusually high temperature, as is probably the case in the Charleston well.

It is worthy of note that the theory of hot springs now accepted was advanced as early as the third century by St. Patricus, probably Bishop of Pertusa. He was asked the cause of boiling water flowing from the earth, and replied: "Fire is nourished in the clouds and in the interior of the earth, as Etna and other mountains near Naples may teach you. The subterranean waters rise as if through siphons. The cause of hot springs is this: waters which are more remote from the subterranean fires are colder, while those which rise nearer the fire are heated by it, and bring with them to the surface which we inhabit an insupportable degree of heat."[1]

Having explained the origin of springs from meteoric water, it is needless to consider minutely the slight variations in the temperature of cold springs. They depend on the source or the water, whether from melting glaciers or summer showers, whether flowing superficially through alluvial earth, or deeply through ledges of limestone or masses of granite.

Electricity.—In seeking for an explanation of the remedial action of thermal mineral waters, it has been claimed that their efficacy is due to some mysterious electrical action. That hot water, and water containing a large proportion of saline ingredients, conducts electricity more readily than pure water has been clearly demonstrated by Prof. Kastner. According to Keller and Baumgartner, the mineral water of Gastein acts more powerfully on the magnetized needle of a multiplier than distilled or ordinary water.[2] Baumgartner and Roller state that the decomposition of Gastein water by the electrical current gives unusual results: while ordinary water separates into two volumes of hydrogen and one volume of oxygen, this

[1] Humboldt's "Cosmos," Bohn's edition, vol. i., p. 221.

[2] Althaus's "Spas of Europe," London, 1862, p. 65.

water yields three volumes of hydrogen to one of oxygen.[1] This result, however, is probably due to the salts contained in the water, and not to any peculiarity of the water itself. Perfectly pure water, in a vessel of pure gold, suffers hardly any decomposition under the action of a powerful battery; but, if a salt or acid be introduced, the separation takes place immediately. Griffin thinks that the salt forms the decomposing agent, not by increasing the conducting power of the water, but by being acted upon.[2] He further states that, "in certain cases, depending on the kind of salt that is submitted to electrolysis, and upon the concentration of the solution, there is found to be a deficiency in the quantity of oxygen. The reason of this deficiency is, that part of the water escapes complete decomposition. H,HO is converted into H and HO. The latter is the peroxide of hydrogen."[3] It is probable that this is the explanation of the peculiar decomposition of Gastein water (if any such peculiarity there be), and that, instead of an excess of hydrogen, there is really a deficiency of oxygen.[4]

Electricity in excessively minute proportions may be developed by the falling of a spout of hot-springs water on the surface of the body; but only to be detected by a wonderfully sensitive multiplier, one which would show electricity to be developed by every vito-chemical change that occurs in the human organism. Until something more definite can be discovered, it is necessary to reject all hypotheses attributing cures to the electrical action of waters.

Magnetism.—Within the past three years a number of artesian wells have been bored in Michigan, which are claimed by the proprietors to be magnetic, that is, the water is supposed to be impregnated with magnetism. A careful investigation of the question, however, reveals the fact that there

[1] Durand-Fardel's "Dictionnaire des Eaux Minérales," Paris, 1860, t. i., p. 591.

[2] "Chemistry of Non-Metallic Elements," London, 1860, p. 234.

[3] *Op. cit.*, p. 236.

[4] Althaus's "Spas of Europe," p. 85, says: "The assertion of Messrs. Baumgartner and Hessler has been shown, by numerous subsequent analyses, to be without any foundation whatever."

is no fixed magnetism in the water, but that the iron tubing of the well is highly magnetic. It is probable, however, that iron placed in a perpendicular position becomes more readily magnetic in Michigan than in many other portions of the earth, and the fact is worthy of investigation. An observation made by the author in August, 1871, at the Geyser Spring, Saratoga, an artesian well, 140 feet deep, showed no such evidence of magnetism as was found at St. Louis, Michigan.

The wells which first attracted attention as magnetic were St. Louis, Eaton Rapids, Alpena, and Spring Lake. The claim of magnetism for these waters was received with mingled credulity and incredulity. Thousands suffering with paralytic complaints journeyed hundreds of miles at great inconvenience, frequently to be disappointed. Some, however, improved and readily gave certificates of cure by the waters, the result being always attributed to magnetism.

During September, 1871, the author visited the famed St. Louis well. When thirty miles away, persons were readily found who would testify to the magnetism of the water, for they had magnetized knife-blades in their pockets that would pick up a pin, caused by holding the knife-blade for fifteen minutes in the flowing magnetic water. Arrived at the well, there were large numbers who would swear to the magnetism of the water. The following experiments were made:

Observation I.—I took my penknife and tested a blade with a compass, to discover whether it was magnetic. Placed on either side the north or south pole of a compass, it attracted the needle 1½°; it would not attract a needle. I then held it one-half hour, by the watch, in the water, as it flows from a horizontal tube attached to the main tube of the well. At the expiration of the time I tested it with the compass and needle, but found no perceptible change in its conditions. Result of this experiment, *negative.*

Observation II.—Descended a flight of steps, about six feet, to the point where the main tube of the well emerges from the ground. Here the joining of the tube is not perfect, and there is an overflow of water between the lower or encasing portion and the upper. Placed the same blade in this overflowing water, at a distance of four inches from the main tube, and let it remain for half an hour, the blade being in a horizontal position. At the end of that time tested it with the compass. It slightly repelled the north end of the compass-needle, and attracted the south end—moved it about 3°. Result favors magnetism of the water, *if* the tube itself is not magnetic; but, the tube being magnetic, the result is still *negative*, as it is well known that a strongly-magnetic body will cause magnetism by induction in steel, when placed in close proximity for that length of time.

Observation III.—Rubbed the same knife-blade on the main tubing for ten minutes. It was then powerfully magnetic, repelling the north end of the compass-needle, driving it half-way around the dial, and attracting the south end so that by a slight manœuvre the compass-needle would rotate in a circle. The conclusion is, that the *tube* is magnetic in a high degree.

Observation IV.—Took a quart-bottle of water fresh from the spring; removed it beyond the influence of the tube, where the compass-needle settled to the north. Then tested it with the compass on every side, but the needle was not perceptibly affected—I should have had a very sensitive needle. The inference, nevertheless, is that the *water* is *not* magnetic.

Observation V.—Placed the compass in different positions about the well, at the distance of seven feet, and found the north end sensibly deflected to the well; while, at a radius of three feet, the north end is powerfully deflected to the well in whatever position it is placed. When elevated above it, the north end of the needle dips downward. The inference is, that this effect is due to the *magnetism of the tube.*

The above experiments are not of themselves conclusive, but a report on the mineral springs of Michigan, by a committee of the State Medical Society, is exceedingly satisfactory. The committee consisted of Dr. H. O. Hitchcock, Prof. S. C. Duffield, and Prof. R. C. Kedzie. The duty of investigating the magnetism of the wells was assigned to Prof. Kedzie. In his report he first calls attention to the fact that water is a diamagnetic body. All substances have been divided by investigators into magnetic, or those susceptible of magnetism, and diamagnetic, or those possessed of a resistance to magnetism. Edmond Becquerel has found that if we represent the magnetic power of iron as 1,000,000, the diamagnetic power of water is 3; that is, it has a force 300,000 times less than iron, and thus one of *resistance to magnetism.*

To determine whether water flowing through a magnetic tube may carry magnetic force with it, Prof. Kedzie made the following experiment: He first magnetized an iron tube, by applying it to a strong horseshoe magnet. Through this tube he caused a stream of water to flow, and thence through a porcelain tube in which a steel bar was placed. The water flowed in this way, through a magnetized tube over a steel bar, for one hour, without developing any magnetic condition in the bar.

It was, however, objected that the water of these springs contains iron in solution, which may have an influence in producing a magnetic condition of the water, while the water, in the test made, contained no iron. To obviate this objection Prof. Kedzie repeated the experiment, substituting water containing four ounces of sulphate of iron to the gallon, and, instead of a single horseshoe magnet, he used a combination of horseshoe magnets known as a magnetic battery. In this way the iron tube was so strongly magnetized that iron filings, sifted over it, arranged themselves over the surface, standing out like stiff bristles; "yet, on passing the solution of sulphate of iron through a tube thus magnetized, and over a steel bar in a glass tube, for an hour, no development of magnetism in the steel bar could be detected."

Having reached the conclusion that the magnetism of the Michigan wells is confined to the iron tubing, Prof. Kedzie sums up the matter as follows:

"The question now arises, Does this magnetic property of these tubes arise from any magnetic quality or other peculiarity in the water flowing through these tubes? I answer,

No! Iron tubes of the same dimension, placed in a vertical position, whether sunk in the ground, or erected in the air, or suspended in water, would exhibit the same phenomena. Water, flowing through them or not, would have no appreciable influence in this magnetism. *This is well shown by the attempted artesian well at Charlotte, which has not reached flowing water, but is only a vertical tube sunk in the soil; yet, it is magnetic just the same as the flowing wells.*"[1]

The latter portion of the report is devoted to combating the statements in favor of magnetism of the waters made by other writers. The conclusion is, that these waters are not magnetic, are not susceptible of magnetism, and cannot produce magnetism. The phenomena of magnetism observed at the wells are entirely due to induction, caused by the highly-magnetic condition of the tube; and the magnetism of the tube is only a usual result of terrestrial magnetism.

These conclusions should not, however, detract from the actual value of the wells of Michigan. Many of the waters are strongly impregnated with active medicinal salts, and are exceedingly valuable therapeutic agents.

1 "Transactions of the State Medical Society of Michigan," 1871, p. 40.

CHAPTER III.

CLASSIFICATION.

IN the study of mineral waters a classification becomes necessary, in order that their application to the treatment of disease may be systematically considered. Several methods have been proposed. They have been classified according to their geological origin, their geographical location, their therapeutic action, and their chemical constitution. For medical purposes the geological or geographical classification is almost valueless, and the knowledge of the action of mineral waters is not so far advanced that they can be reliably grouped according to their therapeutic action. The chemical classification has met with most favor. Of this system there are two prominent ones, the German and the French. We give them below:

The German Classification.[1]

I. Alkaline	1. Simple carbonated. 2. Alkaline. 3. Alkali and common salt.
II. Glauber salt.	
III. Iron	1. Pure. 2. Alkaline and saline. 3. Earthy and saline.
IV. Common salt	1. Simple. 2. Concentrated. 3. With bromine, or iodine.
V. Epsom salt.	

[1] Macpherson's "Baths and Wells of Europe," London, 1869, p. 94.

VI. Sulphur.
VII. Earthy and calcareous.
VIII. Indifferent.

The French Classification.[1]

Sulphur waters..........	With salts of sodium. With salts of lime.
Chloride of sodium waters.	Simple. With bicarbonates. Sulphuretted.
Bicarbonated waters	Bicarbonate of soda. Bicarbonate of lime. Mixed bicarbonates.
Sulphated waters.........	Sulphate of soda. Sulphate of lime. Sulphate of magnesia. Mixed sulphates.
Ferruginous waters......	Bicarbonated. Sulphated. With salts of manganese.

A chemical classification, however, does not convey a definite idea of the medical action of a water. In the French classification, under sulphated waters, the sulphate of soda, sulphate of magnesia, and sulphate of lime waters, are grouped together, the first two being purgative in action, while the latter is not. The thermal waters, as a class, are ignored. In the German classification therapeutic requirements are more perfectly fulfilled, though there is the objection that the Glauber salt and Epsom salt waters are separated into distinct classes, whereas their action is almost identical—they are both purgative waters. The indifferent waters are all thermal.

In the classification arranged for this work I have endeavored to obviate these objections. It partakes both of the

[1] "Dictionnaire des Eaux Minérales," Paris, 1860, t. i., p. 468.

chemical system and the therapeutic system. The waters of each class have a similar action, varied however by minor differences, which are to a considerable degree indicated by the subdivisions. In the application of this or any other classificatlon, it is sometimes difficult to determine to which class a spring should be assigned, from the fact that none of its ingredients may especially predominate. Waters included under the subdivision Pure are only comparatively so, the ingredients, other than those distinctive of the class, existing in minute proportions. Thus a pure alkaline water may contain large quantities of the alkaline carbonates, but it can contain only very small proportions of chloride of sodium or other salts. The class Thermal waters may embrace waters which, as to their chemical constituents, belong to one of the other classes. The action of such waters, aside from their thermality, is indicated by the subdivisions to which they belong. It is rare, however, for thermal waters to contain a large proportion of mineral ingredients.

Classification.

I. Alkaline waters..	1. Pure. 2. Acidulous (carbonic acid). 3. Muriated (chloride of sodium).
II. Saline waters (chloride of sodium)	1. Pure. 2. Alkaline. 3. Iodo-bromated.
III. Sulphur waters...	1. Alkaline. 2. Saline (chloride of sodium). 3. Calcic.
IV. Chalybeate waters	1. Pure. 2. Alkaline. 3. Saline (chloride of sodium). 4. Calcic. 5. Aluminous.

V. Purgative waters.	1. Epsom salt (sulphate of magnesia). 2. Glauber salt (sulphate of soda). 3. Alkaline.
VI. Calcic waters....	1. Limestone (carbonate of lime). 2. Gypsum (sulphate of lime).
VII. Thermal waters..	1. Pure. 2. Alkaline. 3. Saline (chloride of sodium). 4. Sulphur. 5. Calcic.

CHAPTER IV.

ACTION OF MINERAL WATERS.

MANY, and, in this country, perhaps the majority of visitors at springs journey thither, not because of any specific malady with which they are afflicted, but to obtain relief and rest from the harassing cares of business, or the not less exacting demands of society. They go there for diversion; they wish to leave for a time the dusty and travelled highway of life, and wander in the shaded by-paths. After a month or two passed at the springs they return home refreshed and recuperated, possessed of a vigor they may not have known for years. Have the mineral waters produced this effect? No. The same renewal of life would have resulted had they sojourned anywhere amid pure air, beautiful scenery, and cheerful society.

The influences which thus prove restorative to those who are not the subject of disease, also contribute to the cure of those who are really sick. But, from acknowledging that change of air, scene, and exercise, take part in the salutary result in disease, we are apt to overleap this legitimate conclusion, and deny that spring-water has had any agency in benefits that have accrued. Nothing could be more unwise, and nothing more inconsistent with facts and the testimony of those who are regarded as the best authority in the practice of medicine.

The history of bathing-resorts, in the first chapter of this book, shows that mineral waters have been held in high esteem as remedies both by the civilized and uncivilized of every age. Are we to regard this as a mere whim of humanity, and affirm that in all past time they have but pursued a phantom? No.

It is our duty to investigate the question. Undoubtedly there is an atmosphere of quackery surrounding springs in this country, which is exceedingly repulsive to the scientific physician. The "cure-all" style of advertisement, pursued by many proprietors of springs, has contributed largely to bring odium upon mineral waters. Hopeless invalids have been induced to take long journeys to springs in no way adapted to their disease. Our obligations, however, are only increased by these abuses, and we should be prepared to give the sick reliable information.

In the study of mineral waters it is difficult to eliminate the causes which contribute to the cure of the patient. *Change of air* has a most remarkable effect in many diseases. The well-known disease, asthma, is an illustration of this fact. A physician, who is the subject of this harassing complaint, tells us that when he leaves the city he is relieved of the oppression which he continually experiences, but, on his return, it again fixes itself upon him. If atmospheric conditions have so great an influence in a disease which forms so clear an index, how many diseases are there, not so manifestly affected by these changes, but which are nevertheless in a great degree under their influence! We do not speak of pure and impure air as usually considered, but also of the many shades of difference produced by various kinds of vegetation, by exhalations from forests, by vapors from rivers and seas, and by the tenuity of the atmosphere at different heights above the surface of the earth. The extent to which vegetative exhalations pervade the atmosphere are clearly appreciated as we near the shores of America, in spring-time, after a transatlantic voyage. Long before land is in sight, the fragrance of woods and flowers is so strong that we can imagine ourselves within the precinct of a well-kept garden in full bloom. On the other hand, as we approach the sea-shore from inland, we can plainly detect the odor of salt-water long before the ocean is in view. The influence of mountain air in disease has never been closely studied. That it is peculiarly tonic and bracing, and purer than the air at lower levels, is undoubted; but, at the limited elevation of resorts in this country, the difference in density can have no appreciable effect. In Europe there is a tendency to regard great altitudes as favorable for consumptives, and persons affected with this disease are recommended to choose winter residences at elevations from two to five thousand feet above the level of the sea, care being taken, however, that the climate of such places is dry, and the sky bright and cheerful. They doubtless attain in this way the same object which we do in sending consumptives, in the early stages, to Minnesota.

Change of scene is another agency in the cure of certain diseases, which renders it difficult to estimate the actual influence of mineral waters.

Those who are well experience a lightness and buoyancy of spirit, a positive rest and recreation, when they exchange the monotonous routine of business for the always varying views of a pleasure-tour. How far the diseases of the hypochondriacal, the melancholic, and the overtasked, are favorably influenced by the journey to a summer resort, and the mirthful society congregated there, it is impossible to determine. But these auxiliaries of mineral-water treatment will never modify or eradicate the gouty or rheumatic diathesis, they will not arrest the formation of gall-stones, they will not cure catarrh of the bladder, or relieve diabetes, all of which the waters themselves will do.

It is objected by some that, when a mineral water is advised, we do not know exactly what was prescribed. In reply, it is only necessary to refer to the fact that all our remedies—of organic origin—are compound drugs of multiple ingredients, many of the constituents being unknown. Especially is this true, at the present day, of assafœtida, castor, and valerian; and yet we employ these medicines without hesitation. Previous to the present century the active principle of no vegetable drug was known, and yet many of them were used as skilfully as to-day. Opium was introduced into practice, and its value defined, by men who knew nothing of morphia, narcotine, codeia, thebaine, narceine, meconine, and meconic acid, its principal chemical constituents. Far be it from me to decry the value of these discoveries; let it only be remembered that there was a time when medical men knew nothing of them, and yet the virtue of the drug was the same as to-day. So, in the case of mineral waters, we may not be able to discover their exact ingredients, or decide the action of so many chemicals in one solution; but we should not, on this account, refuse to employ them if reliable evidence of their efficacy can be adduced.

In the study of mineral waters artificial preparations will not be considered. They may serve a good purpose in some instances, but, as a rule, they bear little resemblance to the natural waters. They are usually pleasant carbonated drinks, with a proportion of alkalies, iron, or Epsom salts, according as these ingredients may predominate in the water of the spring which they are supposed to represent. Chemists do not claim absolute accuracy for their analyses of waters; the combination of the elements is always empirical. How, then, even when the most scrupulous adhesion to details is observed (which seldom or never occurs), can manufacturers of these preparations produce an imitation identical in action with the spring-water?

Water is the most important inorganic constituent of the body.[1] It forms two-thirds of its substance, and is in more or less intimate combination with every organ, bone, or tissue. Chemically speaking, we are only so much water in combination with varied proportions of carbon, oxygen, hydrogen, nitrogen, chloride of sodium, phosphate of lime, carbonate of lime, carbonate of soda, etc. It is, however, an exceedingly mobile constituent; it is continually discharged from the body, and continually renewed, so that, while any given tissue or organ of the body maintains about the same proportion, it does not for any length of time retain the same particles of water.

When water is taken into the stomach it enters the circulation immediately. It is first absorbed by the gastric veins, and thence passes directly to the portal vein, and this blood-

[1] Flint's "Physiology of Man," p. 30.

vessel usually contains more water than any other. Certain conditions of the water, however, regulate the rapidity of this absorption. If an immoderate quantity is taken at once, a sensation of weight is produced, the absorbents are gorged by the excess of water, endosmosis is almost prevented, and the process proceeds but slowly. Again, the temperature of water influences its digestion. Water much warmer, or considerably cooler, than the blood readily penetrates the absorbents, while, if exactly the same temperature, it produces nausea and is frequently rejected. If, however, the temperature verges on the extreme in either direction, the water is not tolerated, for then the vitality of the mucous membrane is imperilled. When water entering the stomach is highly charged with mineral salts, it is absorbed but slowly.

When ordinary drinking-water is taken in large quantities, it acts principally as a diuretic. It largely increases the amount of urine discharged, and the quantity of urea, phosphates, sulphates, and chlorides, is also augmented.[1] If the temperature of the air is somewhat elevated, the water also acts as a diaphoretic. It seldom passes off by the intestines. These effects pertain to all kinds of water taken in large quantities, and are not peculiar to mineral waters, as is often imagined. Prof. Liebig tells us: "If a tumbler of about four ounces of ordinary water, which is poorer in salines than the blood, is taken every ten minutes before breakfast, a quantity of colored urine will be discharged after the second tumbler, which nearly corresponds to the quantity of water taken in the first tumbler; and, if twenty tumblers are taken one after another, there may be nineteen discharges of urine, which, at last, becomes almost colorless, and then contains hardly more salines than the water which was drunk."

A familiar illustration of the rapidity of the absorption and elimination of water is found in the tippler's ready method of sobering himself, after taking too much wine. He goes to the nearest fountain, and drinks one or two quarts of water. It enters the blood immediately, dilutes the alcohol there, and

[1] Althaus's "Spas of Europe," p. 160.

passes off freely by the kidneys, removing the alcohol with it, so that in ten minutes the man is perfectly sober.

It has been observed by Dr. Genth that, if large quantities of water are taken in twenty-four hours (four thousand cubic centimetres), the temperature of the body falls, the pulse becomes slower, and the number of inspirations per minute are diminished.[1]

The temperature of water drank also bears a relation to its action on the system as well as its absorption; thus, cold water increases the peristaltic motion of the stomach and intestines, while hot water does not produce this effect. For this reason certain mineral waters may purge when taken cold, but will not do so when hot.

Mosler,[2] who instituted a series of experiments relative to the action of water, found a difference of action at different ages. The effects were more decided and lasting in children than in adults. If water was administered for a considerable time, the metamorphosis of tissue proceeded much more rapidly in persons of feeble constitution than in the vigorous. He also found that in those instances in which the appetite was indulged (for it was usually increased), the waste of tissue was compensated, and the person did not lose in weight. In some cases the action of the water was more diaphoretic than diuretic.

The action of mineral waters may be divided into the *immediate* and the *remote.*

The *immediate* action is that which results within twenty-four hours after it is taken. It may present as a *stimulant, sedative*, or *eliminant*, according to the constitution of the water. The first impression of a mineral water is that which is exercised upon the stomach. Waters cold in temperature, containing considerable carbonic-acid gas and alkaline in constitution, will prove sedative, both to that organ and the arterial system, while hot waters and those highly charged with

[1] Althaus's "Spas of Europe," p. 161.

[2] "Untersuchungen über den Einfluss des innerlichen Gebrauches," etc. Gottingen. 1857. Quoted from Althaus.

sulphuretted hydrogen will prove stimulant. Certain sulphur-waters, containing considerable organic matter, are decidedly sedative in action, reducing the frequency of the pulse. The eliminant action results from the effect of the waters on the intestines, kidneys, and skin. Waters containing chloride of sodium, sulphate of soda, or sulphate of magnesia, in large proportion, act readily on the intestines. The alkaline and calcic waters prove diuretic, some of them stimulating the kidneys in a marked manner. Certain waters are cathartic or diuretic, according to the mode of administration. Thus, a water containing a comparatively small amount of purgative salts, with other constituents, such as sulphate of lime and carbonates, will prove actively cathartic if taken in doses of two or three glasses before breakfast; but, if the same quantity be equally distributed through the day in small portions, it will produce a copious flow of urine, while the intestines will be unaffected. Although pure water when taken in large quantities tends to produce diaphoresis, yet there are some mineral waters that affect the integumentary excretories in a marked degree. Such are the sulphur-waters. This action is promoted if the temperature of the surrounding atmosphere is high, and retarded if it is low.

Mineral waters also produce stimulation or sedation when applied externally. The results obtained in this way depend more on the temperature of the water than any action it possesses as a medicated agent. However, it is undoubted that water containing a large proportion of carbonic-acid gas is thereby rendered directly stimulant to the skin, and waters highly impregnated with organic constituents—those that are unctuous or oleaginous in texture—prove sedative.

The *remote action* of a mineral water is its *alterative* effect. And this, in the majority of diseases, is by far the most important quality.

Alteratives are medicines which, in appropriate doses, modify the nutrition of the body without producing any antecedent phenomena.[1] This is precisely the result obtained by the

[1] Stillé's "Therapeutics and Materia Medica," 1864, vol. ii., p. 629.

long-continued use of mineral waters in moderate doses. How this occurs is readily understood when we consider the constitution of the body. As has been before stated, we are only so much water in combination with varied proportions of carbon, oxygen, hydrogen, nitrogen, chloride of sodium, phosphate of lime, carbonate of lime, carbonate of soda, etc. The water thus combined may be termed the *water of constitution*, answering the same purpose in maintaining the body in form that the water of crystallization does in continuing a crystal in its integrity. But, although the amount of water in the body is about the same, it is continually being replaced, a portion being discharged and a corresponding portion received. For the ordinary purposes of quenching thirst we imbibe waters containing a very minute quantity of mineral ingredients; but when we repair to a mineral fountain for the cure of disease we drink freely of water containing double, treble, quadruple, and even a hundred times, the quantity and number of chemical constituents. The water thus introduced, slowly and regularly, penetrates every blood-vessel, capillary, and tissue of the bodily structure, gradually replacing the water of constitution, and by its different chemical affinities changing the molecular organism. It is not maintained that all of the constituents of the mineral water are retained; doubtless an almost infinitesimal quantity is incorporated each day; but in the course of weeks there is a decided and radical result—an alterative effect—manifested by increased metamorphosis of tissue, by elimination of poisonous elements, by the cure of disease. If too long continued, however, a cachectic state will result similar to that produced by the prolonged administration of other alterative agents after the full effect has been produced.

All mineral waters produce an alterative action. Is there any difference in this action as it results from various waters? We answer, unhesitatingly, Yes. The alterative effect of different classes of waters varies, just as the alterative action of iodine, arsenic, or mercury. Each acts on diverse portions of the blood and tissues. The alterative effect of alkaline waters exhibits itself in a reduction of the fibrinous element of the blood —in a modification of the processes which produce lithic acid. Saline waters exert their influence most decidedly on the glandular system. Sulphur-waters tend to the skin. Chalybeate waters affect the red globules of the blood. In like manner we may expect variations in the alterative action of the subdivisions of the different classes. And, although our knowledge in this direction is not as specific as desirable, still there is sufficient to amply establish the varied alterative action of mineral waters.

When mineral waters are taken in excessive quantities for some time, there is a kind of revolt of the system known as the *bad sturm*, or bath-fever. There is diminished appetite, a sense of excessive fatigue, excitement of the pulse, heat of the skin, and sometimes giddiness. While this feverish condition testifies the constitutional action of the water, it is in no way necessary or desirable in the treatment of disease. It corresponds to the ptyalism produced by hydrargyrum; the nausea dryness of the throat, and irritation of the eyelids, caused by arsenious acid, and the pustular eruption resulting from iodine. When this irritant action of a mineral water shows itself, it is necessary to diminish the quantity taken, or entirely suspend it for several days.

The action of thermal waters containing but a small proportion of mineral constituents is undoubtedly due to stimulation of the excretory function of the skin. A consideration of the process followed at these establishments enables us to understand how cures are produced in this way. In many of them the following or a similar routine is followed: The patient first enters a warm or hot bath, where he remains for some minutes until the capillaries of the skin are thoroughly congested. While there he places any painful or contracted joint or neuralgic portion of the body under a spout of hot water. From the warm bath he proceeds to the vapor-room, where he is surrounded with hot vapor of high temperature. During his stay in this apartment he drinks freely of hot water, and perspiration pours from the integument. Thence he passes to a retiring-room, where he reclines on a cot well wrapped in a blanket. There he remains for fifteen or twenty minutes, most of the time in a bath of perspiration, and the process is complete. A bath of this kind is repeated every day or every other day for weeks. Is it surprising that under these conditions the metamorphosis of tissue proceeds with excessive rapidity; that changes are wrought in a few weeks which in the ordinary course would occupy years? The entire system is drenched with warm water; it is thoroughly washed out, and in these copious sweats uric acid, syphilitic poison, and other materials of disease, are expelled.

Profuse warm and hot bathing is sometimes followed by an eruption on the surface of the skin known as *psydracia thermalis*, the *bad friesel*, or *la poussée*. It is accompanied with slight feverishness, fulness of the head, and other symptoms similar to those described above in bath-fever. These eruptions also occur in some instances as a result of the internal use of mineral waters. They were at one time thought necessary to the curative action of thermal waters. Experience, however, has proved the fallacy of this idea, unless it be in some instances of inveterate skin-disease, when these bath eruptions seem to *cure* the original malady *by substitution.*

We cannot close this chapter more appropriately than by quoting the words of the lamented Trousseau—a man possessed of a calm, judicial and philosophic mind—distinguished for accurate knowledge in every department of medicine—the most brilliant practitioner of this century:

"Whatever may be said of them, mineral waters are not simple medicaments; whatever may be the predominant mineralizing agent as demonstrated by analysis, it acts not alone. Nature, in combining, with the more or less notable elements which chemistry may isolate, other exceedingly variable ingredients, and principles which have not yet been discovered, has done for this mineralized agent that which we seek to imitate each day in our prescriptions when we endeavor to reënforce or diminish the effect of a medicinal substance by associating others with it. *In making due allowance always for the particular phenomena which may result from the action of such or such elements which enter into the composition of a mineral water, we should not attribute to a single principle, however dominant it appears in the chemical analysis, all the properties of the water, and clinical experience only can permit us to judge.*[1] This is so exceedingly true that dyspepsias allied to a grave cachectic state—I do not now speak of paludal cachexia—are admirably modified by very different waters, by those of Vichy or Pougues; by those waters in which the mineralizing principle escapes, so to speak, chemical analysis; such as the waters of Plombières and Bagnères-de-Bigorre. Although we range Plombières in the class of sulphated soda-waters and Bigorre in that of sulphated calcic, they have a mineralization so feeble in appearance that the predominance of such or such of their elements is lost, and renders their classification, so to speak, artificial. In comparing them with the waters of the Seine taken at different points near Paris, with those of Arcueil or those of the artesian wells of Grenelle, we find the advantage with the latter, relatively at least, to the waters of Plombières. But, considering the results of medical experience, we know that the waters of the Seine have no other effect than to occasion a slight diarrhœa in some individuals not habituated to their use, and which we know not how else to attribute than to the salts of soda, to the chlorides which they contain in very small quantity. They have never been, that I know of, inscribed in the very voluminous catalogue of mineral waters. In placing them thus in parallel with the waters of Plombières, of Bagnères-de-Bigorre—I will add, with the waters of Neris or of Mont Dore, which are hardly more mineralized than they—far be it from my thought of forgetting for an instant the efficacy of these justly-celebrated thermals.[2] Plombières and Bagnères-de-Bigorre, in the particular disease which occupies us, in virtue of an action which escapes us and which I know not how to

[1] The italics are not in the original

[2] These waters are used internally in dyspepsias.

explain, triumph over rebellious dyspepsias. Under their salutary influence the appetite revives, the constitution is re-organized; patients affected with dropsy, with visceral en-gorgement, arrive at Plombières or at Bigorre in a deplorable state, and depart, after a single season, in a condition notably ameliorated, and are often cured in a manner altogether un-expected."[1]

[1] "Clinique Medicale," Paris, 1865, t. iii., pp. 58, 59.

CHAPTER V.

CHEMICAL CONSTITUENTS.

Some writers on mineral waters almost entirely ignore their chemical constituents, finding in the fact that, when analyzed, we cannot explain all of their effects—an argument against any consideration of this portion of the subject. Fortunately, those who would thus place a seal on investigation are but a small minority. Although it will readily be conceded that an analysis, however accurate, in the present state of science, will not always indicate the diseases to which the water is applicable, still, in the majority of instances, it forms an exceedingly valuable guide—one which cannot be overlooked. And, if we are ever thoroughly to comprehend the action of mineral waters, the discovery lies in this direction. Since the discovery of iodine and its virtue in scrofula, its salts have been detected in many mineral waters which had long been considered valuable in that disease.

It is nevertheless true that the combinations of the elements, as shown in analyses, are altogether empirical. The chemist first determines the bases—the amount of magnesia, soda, potassa, lime, alumina; then the acids and gases—the carbonic acid, sulphuric acid, silicic acid, chlorine, iodine; and, after each of these elements is separated, he combines them according to approved formulæ, giving the result in so many grains of carbonate of magnesia, sulphate of potassa, chloride of sodium, iodide of sodium, etc. Yet, although the chemist may have performed his work most faithfully, still there are unknown quantities that elude his search, appearing in the analysis under the designations loss, organic matter, or extractive matter. These facts, however, only show that chemical science is not perfect.

The process by which rain-water dissolves salts from rocks

in passing through the earth, was alluded to in a previous chapter. Sulphates and chlorides, which form a large part of many rocks, are readily dissolved by pure water. When water becomes largely impregnated with carbonic acid and oxygen, its solvent power is exceedingly increased; so much so that there are no rocks that can altogether resist its action. Quartz, granite, and basalt, are decomposed by carbonated water. It has been shown by M. Struve that carbonated water, by driving out silicious acid, decomposes silicates under a moderate pressure. He effected a decomposition of silicates of soda and potash by treating Bohemian basalt, phonolite and felspar with carbonated water.[1] Although iron and lime are insoluble as carbonates, they are soluble as bicarbonates; and, if the water contain a sufficient quantity of carbonic acid, these ingredients are dissolved. If water containing sulphate of lime meets carbonate of magnesia, the carbonic acid combines with the lime and the sulphuric acid with the magnesia, and thus a soluble sulphate of magnesia is formed. From such facts we readily comprehend how waters originally pure become impregnated with many foreign ingredients in passing through the earth. A most conclusive experiment, showing that the constituents of mineral waters depend on the strata through which they pass, was made by M. Struve. At Bilin, in Bohemia, there is an alkaline mineral spring, the composition of which is given below. Struve took a quantity of clink-stone from the same locality, pulverized it, and subjected it to the action of carbonated water, under a pressure of two atmospheres, with the following result:[2]

Bilin (Bohemia), One pint contains—	Natural Water.	Artificial Water.
	Grains.	Grains.
Carbonate of soda	22.7	21.9
" magnesia	1.1	1.1
" lime	3.0	4.4
Chloride of sodium	2.8	1.9
Sulphate of potassa	1.7	1.6
" soda	6.1	4.8
Silica	0.3	0.5
Total	37.7	36.2

[1] Althaus's "Spas of Europe," p. 69. [2] *Ibid*, p. 69.

3

As a rule, the quantity of ingredients in mineral waters continues the same from year to year.[1] An illustration of this fact is found in our own country in the Congress Spring, of Saratoga. The analysis of that water, given under Saratoga Springs, was made by Prof. Chandler, in 1871, and it entirely agrees in the essential points with an analysis of the same water made in 1832 by Dr. J. H. Steel—thirty-nine years ago. However, there are a few instances on record of remarkable variation. This is the case with the springs of Saxan, in the canton of Valais, Switzerland. These waters were analyzed in 1844 by M. Morin, who then reported that they contained no iodine. In 1852, however, they were analyzed by Baron Cesati and Dr. Pigaut, who found considerable iodine. M. Pyr-Morin then gave them closer investigation, and has discovered that, in regard to this constituent, they change not only from year to year, but from day to day, and from hour to hour. Thus, within the same day the amount of iodine was found at one time to be 0; at another, 0.17; and at another, 0.31 to 10,000 parts of water. On another occasion four different examinations were made in the same day, and the record was thus: 0.61, 0.57, 0.17, and 0; and at another day the record ran thus: 0.98, 0.47, 0.67, and 0. The largest amount ever found was 2.25 in 10,000 parts of water. And this same spring also varies in other constituents. Such a result as here described is, however, altogether exceptional.

Sudden changes are sometimes due to earthquakes, showing the immediate connection of springs with fissures in the earth. During the earthquake of Lisbon the water of Töplitz, in Bohemia, assumed a reddish-yellow appearance, which lasted for an hour and a half, and at the same time the springs of Clifton, in Gloucestershire, England, became turbid. At the time of the earthquake in 1690, the water of Gastein be-

[1] Humboldt says: "The hottest of all permanent springs (between 203° and 209°) are likewise, in a most remarkable degree, the purest, and such as hold in solution the smallest quantity of mineral substances. Their temperature appears, on the whole, to be less constant than that of springs between 122° and 165°, which, in Europe at least, have maintained in a most remarkable manner their *invariability of heat and mineral contents* during the last fifty or sixty years."—(Cosmos, Bohn's English edition, vol. i., pp. 218, 219.)

came white and clayey. In 1765, after an earthquake, the fresh-water well of Castel Alfieri, in Piedmont, became charged with sulphurous vapors and salines, and so remained till 1808, when, after another earthquake, its former freshness returned.

Many mineral waters precipitate a portion of their constituents when they issue from the earth, thus forming deposits. This result is due to the escape of gases from the water, to the cooling of hot waters, and to other chemical changes arising from contact with the air. Prominent examples of such deposits are seen in the cones about the orifices of the recently-discovered geysers in Wyoming Territory; at the Peubla Hot Springs, Humboldt County, Nevada; at the High Rock Spring, Saratoga, and the Red Sweet Springs, Virginia. They almost invariably consist of carbonates, sulphates, or silicates of earthy bases.

CARBONATES AND BICARBONATES.

Nearly all mineral springs contain a proportion of carbonates; and in some springs they are found in large quantity. In such instances they give to the water its characteristic properties. Thus, if the carbonates are those of potassa, soda, magnesia, or lithia, the water is alkaline; if the base of the carbonate is lime, the waters are calcareous, and frequently form large deposits of tufa on the rocks and material with which they come in contact. A remarkable example of the presence of this carbonate is found in the spring of the Alabaster Cave, near Sacramento, California. The alkaline carbonates are formed when carbonated waters pass over or through rocks containing alkaline silicates, as granite, syenite, basalt, etc. Many of the carbonates are but slightly soluble in the form of simple carbonates; but, when by the presence of a large quantity of carbonic acid bicarbonates are formed, they dissolve readily. However, in the analyses published in this work, the result is always given as carbonates, in order that uniformity may be secured for the purpose of comparison.

Carbonate of Soda.—This salt is in the form of transparent and colorless prismatic crystals, having a strongly alkaline taste. The *bi*-carbonate exists in the form of a white powder. They both render water alkaline in reaction. In medicinal doses the carbonate of soda first diminishes the secretions, but subsequently increases them, the urine being most susceptible to its influence. It appears that the action on the discharge of urine is to augment the watery portion without increasing the amount of urea. Under its use the uric acid almost disappears, subsequently to reappear, although the medicine be continued. The free acids of the urine, however, are replaced by earthy phosphates. This carbonate also increases the alkalinity of the blood. It should be remembered that the blood, the saliva, the bile, the milk, and the secretions from the mucous membrane, are normally alkaline. In some diseases, however, they become acid, and the alkaline carbonates are probably efficient in the treatment of these diseases by the tendency to neutralize this condition. It is also asserted that a continued use of the alkalies reduces the quantity of fibrine in the blood.

The diseases in which this medicine has been found useful are as follows: In dyspepsia accompanied with acidity of the stomach and intestinal secretions; in diabetes, bicarbonate of soda has in some instances caused sugar to entirely disappear from the urine, and has reëstablished the general health; in lithiasis, that condition which tends to the formation of uric acid, gravel, and calculus, the administration of the bicarbonate in highly-carbonated water has given good results.

Carbonate of potassa is white, inodorous, and crystallizes with difficulty; it is usually met with in a granular state, and has great affinity for water. In mineral waters it occurs in the form of a *bi*-carbonate. This salt forms colorless, transparent, octahedral crystals, of a saline and caustic taste, readily soluble in water. It is not found in mineral waters in large quantity, though there is reason to believe it is more frequently present than is usually reported.

In its action on the system the bicarbonate of potassa is antacid and diuretic, and is used in the same diseases as the carbonate of soda. It has most frequently been employed to prevent the formation of lithic-acid deposits in the urine.

Carbonate of magnesia is a fine white powder, possessing a slight earthy taste and no odor. It is more frequently found in waters originating in secondary and tertiary formations than in primitive. It is a mild laxative, and a good palliative in acid or sour stomach, heart-burn, and sick-headache, especially if the person is constipated. It has been used successfully to check the formation of acid gravel, and has been considered superior to the alkaline salts of soda and potassa.

Carbonate of Lime.—The most familiar form of this substance is chalk. It is found in great abundance in the south of England and north of France. As an ingredient in mineral waters it occurs most frequently in those having their source in the secondary and tertiary formations.

The action of the carbonate of lime is altogether different from the carbonates above described. They are evacuant, diuretic, and promotive of secretion; while the latter diminishes the secretions and causes constipation, though at the same time being alkaline in action. It is analogous in its effects to lime-water. This preparation has powers useful in chronic bronchitis and chronic diarrhœa. It is interesting to note that over a hundred years ago lime-water was vaunted as a remedy in calculous affections, and, according to the best testimony, with good reason.[1] Though not a curative, it is a valuable palliative in these disorders. Many springs in this country which have long possessed a merited reputation for the relief of calculous diseases are chiefly impregnated with carbonate of lime, associated with a large quantity of carbonic-acid gas.

Carbonate of lithia is deposited from a solution in the form of small prisms. It dissolves in one hundred parts of cold water, but more readily when the water is charged with carbonic acid. The solution is alkaline. This salt comports itself in most respects like the carbonate of soda. It has

[1] Stillé's "Therapeutics and Materia Medica," vol. i., pp. 803, 804, says: "There can be no doubt that it is a remedy too much neglected at the present time as a palliative for stone. . . . There is some reason to believe that uric-acid gravel may be dissolved and eliminated under its use."

been especially recommended in the treatment of uric-acid gravel and gout. It was brought to notice by Alexander Ure, who found that it united with uric acid much more readily than carbonate of soda or potassa, and that the urate of lithia is the most soluble of all the urates; hence, when the excess of uric acid in the body forms this salt with lithia, it passes off readily by the urine. It is not usually found in mineral waters in large quantities.

Carbonate of Strontia.—This salt is found in mineral waters only in small quantities, and in the form of bicarbonate. In action it is similar to the corresponding salt of magnesia.

Carbonate of iron is of a reddish-brown color, possessing a ferruginous taste. It is without smell. Iron is not found in this form in mineral waters, but as a protocarbonate or bicarbonate.

The salts of iron administered internally in small quantities are dissolved by the gastric juice and enter the blood. They increase the appetite, promote digestion, impart redness to the blood-globules and augment their number. The person who may have been depressed and languid recovers strength and spirit under their influence. In large quantities, and continued for a long time, digestion is impaired, constipation ensues, and the fæces are blackened.

If iron is diminished in the blood, the lips are pale, the face is white and anæmic, the mind is depressed, and energy fails. From this fact we can appreciate the value of chalybeate mineral waters in treating anæmic conditions. Owing to the minute subdivision of the iron in mineral water, it readily enters the blood.

Carbonate of manganese is of a rose-red or brownish color. In mineral waters it is found as a bicarbonate. It is not of frequent occurrence, and exists in but small proportion. Medicinally it comports itself much like the salts of iron.

CHLORIDES.

Nearly all mineral waters contain chlorides in greater or less proportion. The fact that they enter so largely into the composition of soil, rocks, and vegetable and animal life, readily explains their almost universal presence in mineral waters.

Chloride of sodium, or table-salt, is by far the most important of the chlorides. It exists in the blood, the bones, and the muscles, in large quantity, and is essential for their integrity; and there is no solid or fluid in the body, except the enamel of the teeth, that does not contain this chloride in some proportion. From this fact we readily appreciate why salt is such a universal condiment. It is consumed in large quantities, each person taking from a quarter of an ounce to an ounce each day, though there is considerable variation in this regard in different nations. Russians are said to consume two ounces and more per day. This large amount, which is continually introduced into the system, is voided with the urine, leaving the absolute quantity the same.

The necessity of table-salt is illustrated by the experiments of Wundt. After having eaten food for three days unseasoned with salt, he found the urine had become neutral, and contained albumen. On returning to salted food, the urine regained its normal condition in two days. Salt is an important element in cell-formation; it is found in all exudations; so much so that in pneumonia, when exudation is active, chloride of sodium disappears entirely from the urine, to reappear when the process ceases. It is also known to exercise a direct effect on the growth of the hair. When an animal does not receive a proper quantity of salt, the hair becomes rough and wiry, and the beast betrays signs of feebleness and ill-condition. So necessary is it to them, that in the wild state they frequent "salt-licks" (saline springs) to obtain a sufficient supply.

Chloride of sodium, in moderate quantities, increases the flow of the gastric juice and the bile; and, by its antiseptic properties, prevents putrefactive changes in the intestinal action of the intestines, producing fluid motions; it is aperient, but not cathartic. The quantity of urea in the urine is also augmented. Barral found that when larger amounts of salt than usual were taken, the weight of urea excreted increased from 2.84 grammes to 6.02, and even 9.42 grammes, in twenty-four hours, from which we may conclude that salt in large quantities hastens the disintegration of tissue. The result of the use of salt in large quantities is to cause considerable irritation of the stomach and intestines; to increase the flow of urine, which is accompanied with burning along the course of the ureters; and to excite the generative organs. The secretion of the mucous membrane of the bronchial tubes is also decidedly increased.

Chloride of potassium is analogous to chloride of sodium, both in its properties and medical qualities, but is found only in small quantities either in the body or in springs.

Chloride of magnesium occurs in many mineral waters. It forms one of the chief constituents of the waters of the Dead Sea. It is the bittern of salt-works. Medicinally, it has been used as a cholagogue cathartic.

Chloride of calcium is exceedingly soluble, and occurs principally in saline waters. In medicine, it has been used in scrofulous humors, glandular obstructions, and general debility.

Chloride of iron is a comparatively rare ingredient of mineral waters. It is astringent and tonic.

Chloride of cæsium is a chemical curiosity, detected in 1860, in the saline mineral waters of Dürckheim, by Kirchhoff and Bunsen. The discovery of this unknown compound was made by spectrum analysis. Having determined in this way the presence of an unknown element in these waters, they proceeded to isolate it by direct experiment. For this purpose they evaporated over 105,000 pounds of the water, and were enabled to procure a small quantity of the chloride. From this chloride they determined the physical character of cæsium. Cæsium is the most electro-positive element at present known; its atomic weight is 123.4. In the spectrum it is recognized by two sky-blue lines—hence the name.

Since its discovery it has been found in comparatively large quantities in the mineral waters of Baden-Baden and Bourbonne-les-Bains; also, in the mineral known as lepidolite, found at Hebron, Maine.

Chloride of rubidium is a similar chemical curiosity found in mineral waters. It is much like chloride of potassium in its properties.

SULPHATES.

The sulphates are frequently found in mineral waters. They are active medicinal agents; and the two known as Epsom and Glauber salts are familiar to every one. Occurring in mineral waters in considerable quantity, they give to them a bitter taste and purgative action.

Sulphate of soda, popularly known as Glauber salts, is found in a number of mineral waters. Next to chloride of sodium, it is one of the most abundant of native salts. The popular name is derived from a German chemist who first discovered its artificial mode of preparation. It is a white crystalline salt, bitter and nauseous in taste, and, taken in doses of half an ounce, produces watery purgation. It is derived from basalt, porphyry, felspar, mica, granite, and other rocks.

Sulphate of magnesia, usually known as Epsom salts, is a transparent crystalline salt, having a bitter, nauseous, and saline taste. The name—Epsom—is derived from a spring in England of that name, from which it was originally prepared. It is a mild and efficient watery purgative. When dissolved, however, in a large quantity of water, this salt, as well as the sulphate of soda, tends to act on the kidneys, increasing the flow of urine. As a mineral, it occurs in serpentine, marl, clay, slate, and limestone.

Sulphate of lime, or gypsum, is not found in large quantity in mineral waters, from the fact that not more than twenty grains will dissolve in a pound of pure water. It does not occur in crystalline rocks, but is found in red sandstone and the fissures of porphyry, basalt, and granite. It is not employed medicinally. Deposited from spring-waters, it forms a hard coating on foreign substances; and twigs and leaves thus covered are popularly termed petrifactions—an error, however, as the internal substance is not changed into stone.

Sulphate of potassa is a bitter, purging salt, similar to the sulphates of soda and magnesia. It is not a frequent constituent of mineral waters.

Sulphate of iron is found in the waters of springs flowing through rocks containing sulphuret of iron. It is a greenish crystalline salt, exceedingly astringent in action and to the taste. It is seldom present in mineral waters. Examples, however, are found in the Alum Springs of Virginia, and the Oak Orchard Acid Springs of New York.

Sulphate of alumina is usually found associated with the sulphate of iron. It is a crystalline salt, exceedingly soluble in water, and of a styptic taste. In medicine, the preparations of alumina are principally employed as astringents, though testimony is not wanting of their remedial value in diseases of a different type, such as chronic bronchitis, chronic diarrhœa, whooping-cough, and lead-colic.

IODIDES.

Although the iodides occur in mineral waters only in small quantity, they undoubtedly influence their curative properties in a marked degree. Indeed, certain springs were long celebrated for the cure of scrofula, goitre, and analogous affections, their efficacy being unexplained till the discovery of iodine, its effects in these diseases, and finally its presence in the waters. Rilliett, of Geneva, has described the effects of iodine in small and long-continued doses. The symptoms are rapid emaciation—the appetite, however, continuing good and even being increased—nervous palpitations of the heart, debility, depression of spirits, and sleeplessness. In this emaciation the various glands are most affected, and goitres have disappeared in a few days when the symptoms were fully developed. Such effects have resulted even from a sea-side residence and the iodic exhalations of salt-water, but more frequently from the minute proportions of iodine in certain mineral waters.[1]

Iodide of potassium usually appears in semi-transparent cubical crystals, of a saline, penetrating, and bitter taste.

[1] Stillé's "Therapeutics and Materia Medica," vol. ii., p. 788.

There is seldom more than a trace to be found in mineral waters. This is the preparation most frequently employed for procuring the alterative effects of iodine in various diseases, such as scrofula, chronic rheumatism, tertiary syphilis, goitre, etc., etc.

Iodide of sodium is the form in which iodine is most frequently found in mineral waters. There is seldom as much as one-fifth of a grain of the salt to a pint of water; but even this minute proportion is sufficient to produce the alterative effects of iodine. This salt in all its characteristics resembles the iodide of potassium above described, and is remedial in the same diseases.

BROMIDES.

These salts exist in somewhat larger proportion than the iodides. The combination which is most frequently found is that of *bromide of magnesium.* This salt occurs in strong saline waters. The bromides, when given in small doses and long continued, are alterative in their effect, and in some cases reduce enlargements of lymphatic glands, the spleen, liver, ovaries, and uterus, but are not equal to the iodides for this purpose.[1] They are principally used to allay nervous irritability.

PHOSPHATES.

These occur in minute proportion in many springs. The minerals from which they are derived are basalt, mica, granite, dolomite, slate, chalk, and many other formations. The phosphates vary in action according to the base with which the phosphoric acid is combined: thus the phosphate of soda is a mild cathartic, possessing but little taste; the phosphate of iron is a tonic, and the phosphate of lime is recommended in scrofulous affections.

SILICATES.

Silica is found in some proportion in almost all springs, but in much larger quantity in thermal than in cold springs. Silicates have been supposed to impart to certain waters the

[1] Stillé's "Therapeutics and Materia Medica," vol. ii., p. 759.

peculiar unctuous texture which they possess. The medical action of these salts has never been investigated.

BORACIC ACID.

This acid is sometimes found in considerable quantity in springs rising in volcanic districts. In Southern California there is a lake from which borax—borate of soda—may be obtained in unlimited quantity. *Borate of soda* is an alkaline salt used externally as a cosmetic; internally it has proved decidedly emmenagogue and ecbolic. It has also been recommended for the purpose of dissolving lithic-acid gravel.

FLUORIDES.

Salts of fluohydric acid have been found in mineral springs in minute quantities. They are derived from mica, lepidolite, and hornblende. Their medicinal action is unknown.

NITRATES.

Occasionally, salts formed by nitric acid are found in mineral waters. The nitrates of soda and potassa, in moderate doses, are diuretic in action; in large doses, purgative.

ARSENIC.

In a few mineral waters minute quantities of this substance are found. It may also be mentioned that traces of *antimony*, *zinc*, *copper*, *tin*, *lead*, etc., are sometimes detected. Arsenic, in very minute doses, is an alterative medicine of decided value. It is efficacious in the treatment of chronic rheumatism, intermittent fever, and scaly diseases of the skin.

ORGANIC ACIDS.

In a number of mineral waters crenic and apocrenic acids are found. They contain no nitrogen, and are the product of the decomposition of humus. In some instances they form soluble compounds with soda, potassa, and iron. Their medicinal action has not been studied.

ORGANIC SUBSTANCES.

In the sulphur-waters of the Pyrenees, in France, three peculiar organic substances have been discovered. They are interesting to us, from the fact that several springs in this country of marked properties contain similar ingredients. They are described as follows: [1]

Barègine, or Hydrosin, of Lambron.—If certain sulphur-waters be evaporated to dryness, a brownish-yellow residue is left which is blackened on the application of heat, and at the same time disengages a small quantity of ammonia. This substance is found to be an organic azotized matter, and is called *barègine* from the springs of Bareges, in which it was first detected. The name *hydrosin* is more appropriate, as disconnecting it from any particular spring or supposed quality. A solution of it precipitates the salts of lead abundantly, and gives a white precipitate with nitrate of silver, which almost immediately assumes a reddish tint. This substance corresponds to the *sulfurhydrine* of Cazin and the *pyrénèine* of Fontan.[2]

Glaisine.—This is an amorphous deposit, sometimes transparent and sometimes opaque. It is soft and unctuous to the touch, and is deposited in the reservoirs where the water accumulates. It is insoluble. Anglada thought it to be identical with barégine; but the solubility of the latter and the insolubility of the former is of itself distinctive. Glairine, though containing nitrogen, is not one of those neutral nitrogenized substances termed albuminoids. It contains more carbon and hydrogen, but less oxygen and nitrogen. Bouis, in burning certain specimens of glairine, has found as much as eighty parts of silicious residue in a hundred.

Sulfuraria.—This is a confervoid growth formed in sulphur-waters the temperature of which is below 122° Fahr. Examined under the microscope, it presents the appearance of smooth, transparent, cylindrical tubes, filled with roundish

[1] The description of these substances is mostly compiled from the "Nouveau Dictionnaire de Médecine et de Chirurgie." Paris, 1870, tome xii., p. 240.

[2] Lefort's "Traité de Chimie Hydrologique." Paris, 1859, p. 804.

globules, and often containing animalcules. Access of air to the water is indispensable to the formation of sulfuraria. In composition it is analogous to glairine, and when burned leaves a large amount of silicious residue.

Besides the above-named organic substances, a number of microscopic algæ have been described.[1] The *monas sulfuraria*, elliptical in form, from $\frac{1}{75}$ to $\frac{1}{100}$ of a millimetre in diameter, and spotted with red, are supposed to pertain especially to calcic sulphur-waters. The *oscillaires* are greenish filiform bodies, from 5 to 30 millimetres in breadth, and varying in length in the same proportion. Each filament is composed of a diaphanous and almost mucilaginous tube, enclosing a series of minute disks covered with green matter, and which appear susceptible of contraction and dilatation in the direction of the axis. The *gallionella ferruginea* are of rectilinear, cylindrical form, varying in dimensions from $\frac{1}{1000}$ to $\frac{8}{10000}$ of a line, of a rusty color, almost always homogeneous, though occasionally presenting at intervals cells of diverse forms. Sometimes they give a rusty color to the water in which they are found.

That the presence of these organic constituents—especially those first named, hydrosin and glairine—exercise an influence in the action of the mineral waters in which they occur in large proportion, we cannot well doubt; but precisely what this influence is, has not yet been determined. Durand-Fardel says: "It is probable they give to such waters a sedative action; but more by simple contact than by physiological action. Indeed, waters which contain the largest proportion of organic matter in solution are generally less exciting than others, and possess even sedative properties in humid and pruriginous dermatoses and in neuropathic conditions."[2] In this country, the Red Sulphur Springs of Virginia have long been reputed as sedative to the arterial system, when taken internally. They contain an unusually large proportion of organic matter.

[1] "Dictionnaire Générale des Eaux Minérales," tome ii., p. 159.

[2] *Op. cit.*, tome ii., p. 479.

CARBONIC ACID.

Carbonic acid is an exceedingly heavy gas, being one and a half times heavier than air. For this reason it accumulates in wells and mines, and in rooms gravitates to the floor. It will not support combustion. A light is immediately extinguished in an atmosphere largely impregnated with this gas.

Carbonic acid, in some proportion, is found in almost all spring-water, and even in rain and river water it is present. The bright sparkle of certain waters and wines, and the pleasant acescent taste, is due to this gas. Indeed, water entirely deprived of carbonic acid is altogether unpalatable. Some spring-waters are so strongly charged with it in the depths of the earth, that when they escape they are projected many feet in the air. The Geyser Spring, of Saratoga, is an example.

It is a singular fact that a gas, which, taken into the stomach in moderate quantities, is agreeable and healthful, should prove a deadly poison when inhaled. A mixture of forty parts of oxygen, forty-five parts of nitrogen, and only fifteen parts of carbonic acid, is sufficient to destroy life. The symptoms are as follows: First, a sensation of heat pervades the entire body, the face is flushed, and the forehead covered with perspiration. In a short time the heat becomes excessive, the face is intensely red or of a deathly pallor; dizziness follows, the person totters in movement, and falls asphyxiated.

The pleasant and cooling effects of carbonated water, when drunk, are familiar to nearly every one in this country, where drinking it in the form of soda-water is so universally practised during the summer months. In moderate quantities, it stimulates the flow of saliva, aids digestion, slightly accelerates the pulse, renders the mind clear and the person cheerful. The imbibition, however, of large quantities causes sickness, vomiting, headache, vertigo, a tottering gait, and even asphyxia. Liebig tells us such results have especially followed after drinking large quantities of fermenting white wine, which on being introduced into the stomach evolves large quantities of carbonic acid, which enters the blood immediately, and has produced death in some instances.

Bathing in water highly charged with carbonic acid produces peculiar effects. The first sensation observed, if the water is below 86° Fahr., is, that the water is colder than would be expected from feeling it with the hand before entering. When in the bath, millions of minute gas-bubbles cover the body, producing a pricking or burning sensation, especially noticed on the scrotum, the nipples, and the labia. Many persons feel this burning for several hours after the bath. During the bath, the pulse becomes fuller, but not accelerated. The generative organs are powerfully stimulated. A bath of this kind is said to have an especial effect on the bladder. Patients who may sit in an ordinary warm-water bath for half an hour without desire to pass the urine, are compelled to do so after a few minutes' stay in the carbonic-acid water bath.[1] On leaving a bath of this kind, persons in health feel exceedingly exhilarated, and the inclination for muscular activity is decidedly increased; those who are semi-paralytic are said to walk more briskly.

SULPHURETTED HYDROGEN.

Next to carbonic acid, this gas is most frequently found in the waters of mineral springs. It is an exceedingly important constituent, and possesses decided influence over the action of waters in which it exists in large proportion. It frequently issues from the earth in the neighborhood of semi-active volcanoes, and is probably evolved through the decomposition of sulphurets by hot water. In some springs its presence is due to the double decomposition of sulphates, in the presence of organic matter. When sulphuretted hydrogen comes in contact with the air, it is readily changed, the hydrogen combines with oxygen, and sulphur is precipitated, giving to the water a milky appearance.

Sulphuretted hydrogen is an irrespirable gas, quickly producing death if inhaled in considerable quantity. However, when largely diluted with air, it may be inhaled, and in this way has been used medicinally. The first symptom of the

[1] Althaus's "Spas of Europe," p. 190.

poisonous action of the gas is a small and feeble pulse, indicating depression of the heart's action, together with a sensation of excessive feebleness. Taken internally, in water, in moderate quantities, it increases the activity of the intestines and augments the perspiration. If the water is highly charged with the gas, agitation, sleeplessness, and nervous excitement, are produced in some persons, similar to that resulting from strong coffee. Small quantities of the gas, applied to the mucous membrane of the eyes, nose, and bronchial tubes, stimulate the secretions.

CARBURETTED HYDROGEN.

This is the ordinary burning-gas used in cities. It escapes from some springs in large quantity, and is utilized for lighting the premises and heating water for the baths. It is not used medicinally.

OXYGEN AND NITROGEN.

These gases exist in small quantities in nearly all springs, not, however, in such proportions as decidedly to affect their medicinal action.

CHAPTER VI.

THERAPEUTICS.

In pursuing this most important branch of our subject, we will treat separately of each disease in which mineral waters prove beneficial, and refer to the classes of water adapted to them. A large number of maladies are immediately eliminated from consideration when we state, as a rule always to be remembered, that *mineral waters are only applicable to the treatment of chronic diseases.*

In the course of many chronic diseases there are times when the malady is in abeyance, and the patient is apparently well; while at other periods it manifests itself in all its severity. The well-known disease, gout, is an illustration. During the paroxysms, it presents all the characteristics of an acute disease; but in the intervals the person seems to enjoy good health, though liable to be overwhelmed at any time with an attack. These intervals may be termed periods of inactivity. *The appropriate time for using a mineral water is during the inactivity of the disease.* However, this rule will not apply to all chronic diseases, for some of them present no intervals of this kind. But it is always to be remembered that mineral waters should not be given when the patient is feverish and the pulse excited; these symptoms should first be allayed.

CONSTITUTIONAL AND GENERAL DISEASES.

Under this title are embraced cachectic diseases, depending on a peculiar vice or condition of the fluids and solids of the body—diseases which are frequently hereditary; and zymotic diseases, due to a specific poison introduced into the blood from without, either by direct contact or by breathing an atmosphere charged with the infecting poison. Although they frequently present local manifestations, they do not uniformly affect the same portions of the body; and the person is in a condition in which it is impossible to say what part of the organism will testify to the morbid state of the body.

Rheumatism.—This is a disease so familiar to every one that little need be said concerning its peculiarities. It is well known that acute may eventuate in chronic rheumatism, and that those who in early life have been afflicted with the former are very liable, as years advance, to become subjects of the latter.

Of chronic rheumatism there are three varieties. That ordinarily met with is known as *chronic articular rheumatism.* In this malady, one or more joints are the seat of more or less intense pain, for months or years; a pain which is increased by motion or pressure. The joints may be swollen, but there is seldom heat or redness. After the disease has continued a long time, the joint may become stiffened—a result due not only to thickening of the adjoining structures, but also to want of motion.

A second form of rheumatism is called *deforming rheumatism*, the *rhumatisme noueux* of French authors. It is seldom a result of acute rheumatism, and is more frequently observed in females than males. It usually attacks the joints of the hand and foot, invading them one by one. The joint attacked is the seat of almost continuous pain, though it is not often severe. It becomes gradually enlarged, and, on close examination, it will be found that the extremity of the bone is increased in size, and, in some instances, a bony formation has occurred within the joint, uniting the opposite synovial surfaces. The fingers at the same time become permanently flexed, and frequently a slight dislocation occurs, which, when the hand is considerably involved, gives a distorted and knotty appearance. The joints of the hand most frequently attacked are those of the first, middle, and ring finger, while the thumb and little finger are frequently untouched. In the foot, the great-toe is especially the seat of the disease. The disease is not, however, limited entirely to the hand and foot. Sometimes the hip-joint is affected by preference. A peculiarity of the disease is, that it almost invariably attacks the corresponding joints on the opposite sides of the body at the same time.

This form of rheumatism should be distinguished from the enlargement of gout, with which it is often confounded. In malformation of the joint from gout there are chalky deposits of urates, while in this disease the appearance of the joint results from osseous enlargement of the extremity of the bone. In gout the lower extremities are chiefly affected, while in this disease it is the upper. Women are most frequently the subjects of this malady, while gout principally occurs in men.

A third form of chronic rheumatism may be mentioned, termed *muscular rheumatism*. This form, as its name implies, affects the muscles and sheaths. It is a much milder form than either of those described, and seldom occasions permanent stiffness or contractions.

The *treatment* applicable to the different forms of chronic rheumatism does not vary materially. In all, the *thermal waters* should be chosen. These waters act more by heat than by their constituents. The temperature of the baths need not be high; from 95° to 100° Fahr. is sufficiently warm, when the rheumatism is of the ordinary chronic articular kind. The duration of the bath should be about fifteen minutes at first; and the time may be gradually extended till, toward the termination of the treatment, the patient may remain an hour or more. A course of baths usually consists of thirty in succession; and, if these are insufficient, it is best to suspend their use, to be again resumed a few months later.[1] A blanket-sweat after the bath is an exceedingly valuable auxiliary. Particular care is necessary that cold be not taken after the bath.

In cases of deforming rheumatism and chronic articular rheumatism, complicated with *stiffening of the joints*, baths

[1] Niemeyer's "Text Book of Medicine," American edition, vol. ii., p. 489.

of the temperature mentioned should be used, but the use of the hot douche should be added. The temperature of this may vary from 106° to 120° Fahr., according to the case and the effect produced. In deforming rheumatism, Trousseau also recommends douches of hot sand as efficacious in promoting resolution and subduing pain. He says: "We should have the patient plunge the affected part in hot sand, or let the sand fall upon it at as high a temperature as possible. The patients complain of a painful sensation of burning; nevertheless we can always, by the aid of the thermometer, graduate the temperature according to the degree of heat tolerated by each patient. This temperature may be from 140° to 158° Fahr. The douches, or local baths of hot sand, should be repeated from two to three times per day, and during one or two hours. It is important that the sand be maintained at the same degree of temperature—a condition easy to obtain, as the sand cools slowly, and is always easily replaced when it commences to cool. In following this rule in the usage of hot sand, the patient soon obtains notable relief, and it is easy to perceive a rapid diminution in the articular engorgements." [1]

One distinction may be made in the use of thermal waters in rheumatism. It is this: Rheumatics are divided into two classes—those of the lymphatic temperament and those of the nervous. In the former, waters rich in the sulphurets have seemed to produce the best results, and baths of the higher temperature are usually indicated; while in the latter—the nervous temperament—waters containing but a small proportion of constituents, and of moderate heat, are preferable.

Gout is the malady of *bon-vivants*, those who indulge largely in the pleasures of the table, and inherit a tendency to the affection. There are several forms of the disease. In *acute gout*, the paroxysms are attended with excessive pain. In *chronic gout*, the attacks are accompanied with less pain and fever, but may continue for weeks and months, and several joints may be attacked at the same time. This form, also, is frequently accompanied with chalky deposits of urates in the

[1] "Clinique Médicale," Trousseau, tome iii., p. 381.

joints. The *anomalous* or *atonic* form is one into which persons, previously the subjects of acute gout, fall; an enfeebled condition, accompanied by muscular weakness, dyspepsia, excessive perspirations, and increased sensitiveness; and slight errors in diet, excitement, exposure to cold, or changes of weather, produce severe pains in one or more joints, resembling the beginning of an acute attack of gout, but which is never fully developed. There may also be gout in the stomach, in the heart, in the brain, and other internal organs, but such complications are rare.

An attack of acute gout is one of the most painful affections which the human body endures. "A person of full habit and easy circumstances, a free liver, complains for some days of diminished appetite, of somnolence, and of inaptitude of the mind; usually of jovial disposition, he becomes irascible, and the urine is found to deposit a red or brick-dust sediment. On the day of the attack, however, these precursory symptoms subside. He retires at night and sleeps tranquilly; but toward two or three o'clock in the morning he awakes with a sensation of pain in one of the great-toes. He changes the position of his foot, hoping to obtain relief, but no amelioration follows; the pain increases slowly but surely in severity, till, finally, the touch of the covering is unbearable, and the slightest jar of the room or bed aggravates the pain, which he compares to a nail being driven into the joint, to tearing asunder of the ligaments, to the clinching of a vice at the utmost pressure—in short, exhausts the vocabulary of painful comparisons. The skin is hot, the pulse bounding. Toward morning the pain moderates, and when day dawns he feels little or no pain, and passes a comparatively easy day. The seat of the pain is red and swollen. Toward evening, however, the pain recommences, and during the night the previous tortures are repeated, again to subside in the morning. And each night, for as many as eight nights it may be, these pains recur."

In this disease there is always a condition known as the "uric acid diathesis;" the blood is charged with uric acid, but whether it is the primary cause, or only a phenomenon in the course of the disease, is unknown. The burden of testimony points to the excess of uric acid as the cause, this excess, however, depending on a disturbance in the processes of assimilation. The patient seems to do well as long as the uric acid is freely excreted by the kidneys; but when the uriniferous tubules are plugged by deposits of urates, and the flow of urine is impeded, an attack of gout is the result.

In treating this malady by mineral waters, an imperative rule is, that *waters should only be used during intervals of the attack*, and as far distant from a preceding or succeeding attack as we can determine.

For the *acute* or *regular* gout, the *alkaline waters* are preferable to all others, those rich in carbonate of soda. Formerly, a chemical theory obtained that the alkalies neutralized the excess of uric acid present; but this has long since been abandoned. The tendency of these waters is to lessen the severity of the attacks and lengthen the interval between them; but, if continued too long, there is great danger that regular gout may be converted into the chronic form, or that some important internal organ may become the seat of the disease. Trousseau tells us: "I know of no medication more perilous than that of these waters" (Carlsbad, Vichy, Vals, etc.), "administered without reserve, without discernment, without regard to individual conditions of health, of the form of the gout, without attention whether the paroxysm has been long enough past, or whether a new attack is imminent. . . . Are you to understand by this that I proscribe their employment? Assuredly, no; and I believe, with M. Durand-Fardel, in their efficacious action, but within a restricted limit. As a general rule, alkaline waters should not be taken more than ten or twelve days in succession, and in very small quantities at a time. It is a good plan to return to the spring each month for the time that I have mentioned."[1] This method of using waters is, however, impracticable for most persons. It shows, at leaat, with how great circumspection their action should

[1] "Clinique Médicale," tome iii., p. 357.

be guarded in this disease. Authorities agree on this point: Whoever pursues a course of alkaline waters, should be cautioned not to deluge the system with the water, but to drink with great moderation; three ordinary glasses per day of the stronger waters being amply sufficient. Frequently, one or two seasons of these waters will render a gouty subject comparatively free from attacks, provided the person is exceedingly cautious in his table habits, eating meat but once a day, not partaking of wine or beer, and restricting his diet chiefly to vegetables and soups. While taking alkaline waters, it is not unusual for a moderate paroxysm of gout to be excited. In this, however, there is no cause for alarm, a temporary suspension of the water being all that is indicated.

In regular gout the use of baths is contra-indicated as a rule. Durand-Fardel says: "The treatment of acute gout is altogether internal; however, baths may be employed in the absence of all actual manifestations of gout, and provided there is no tendency to irregular manifestations of the malady toward the head or chest. . . . The usage of douches is always to be dreaded."[1]

In *chronic* gout *saline waters* are indicated, those rich in chloride of sodium. And in this condition the same care in the use of waters is to be observed as in regular gout. The saline waters are especially useful in lymphatic temperaments.

The favorable effects of the classes of waters named, in relieving gout, is supposed by Niemeyer to depend on the reduction of plethora due to a misproportion between supply and demand in the body, "whether the plethora depend solely on hypertrophy of the blood, i. e., an increase of its cellular elements, and a certain density of the intercellular substance (the serum of the blood), or on an accompanying absolute increase of the amount of blood contained in the body. It is very interesting to note that the beneficial effect of these natural mineral waters on plethora, which has been long known, and which far exceeds that of ordinary water, agrees with the observations of C. Schmidt and Vogel, according to which the

[1] "Dictionnaire des Eaux Minérales," tome ii., p. 89.

amount of albumen in the serum of the blood is inversely proportional to the amount of salt."[1]

In cases of *anomalous* or *atonic* gout, those presenting general cachexia, the reducing course of treatment should be abandoned. The patient may take more freely of nutriment, and a little wine may be permitted. The waters then indicated are the chalybeates, or the chloride of sodium waters, containing considerable iron. The author just quoted says: "It is always better to let the patient use the ferruginous alkaline-saline and alkaline-muriatic mineral waters, such as Eger, Kissingen, or Homburg, than to prescribe simple ferruginous waters or preparations of iron." He adds: "In the later stages of the disease, the akrato-thermal springs—Wildbad, Gastein, Pfäffers, etc. [hot waters, containing but a very small proportion of ingredients—W.], are very serviceable. We may have the patient drink of these waters and bathe in them; perhaps the infarctions obstructing the tubules may be carried away by the former, and the kidneys washed out, as it were; while the latter have the most beneficial effect on the inflammation of the joints."[2] In using these last-named waters in this stage of the disease, we should remember the tendency of the malady, when too much interfered with, to leave the joints and attack some more vital part, and their effects should therefore be closely scrutinized.

With the precautions mentioned, *thermal waters* in the form of baths and douches may be employed with great benefit for the purpose of removing gouty deposits.

Syphilis.—For this frightful disease, the ravages of which are so much to be dreaded, there is no absolute cure. If men knew the perils of the disease, they would perhaps more carefully guard against the contraction of a malady which often renders old age a burden, and manifests its effects even to children's children. We have said there is no absolute cure—no condition in which we can say the patient will never have symptoms of the virus which has penetrated his system; nevertheless, under the use of proper remedies, the patient may,

[1] "Text-Book of Medicine," American edition, vol. ii., p. 504. [2] *Ibid*, vol. ii., p. 505.

to all external appearance, be entirely cured, and may suffer little inconvenience from the disease.

What is the value of mineral waters in this disease? Ricord has affirmed that mineral waters are insufficient by themselves to arrest the progress of the syphilitic virus; and this view is sanctioned by the most competent observers—Vidal, Sigmund, Michaelis, Constantin James, and Durand-Fardel. All, however, agree that in many instances they are a valuable auxiliary; that in certain cases the action of anti-syphilitic remedies is thereby rendered more reliable; that while using mineral waters the system is much more tolerant of the action of these medicines; and that ill effects from the previous improper use of them are obviated. An additional value of mineral waters, especially the sulphur-waters, in this disease, is as a diagnostic criterion. While using them it frequently occurs that persons who considered themselves free from the disease, have observed with alarm the appearance of the old malady in the form of skin-disease. It seems that, however latent the disease, its manifestation is developed by sulphur-waters; and, as a rule, persons suspected of syphilis, who pursue a course of these waters without any symptoms supervening, may be considered free from the disease. But in this, as in many medical problems, we do not arrive at mathematical certainty. Ricord tells us there are instances of persons following a complete course of mineral-water treatment without any trace of the disease being manifested, and yet the following summer there has been a reappearance of the symptoms.

All classes of mineral waters have been used in the treatment of syphilis; and, doubtless, they have proved useful, in greater or less degree, by their alterative action, in conjunction with other medicines. Durand-Fardel says: "It appears beyond question that the association of mineral waters with specific medication is well adapted to overcome the resistance which the morbid constitution of some individuals oppose thereto. Most frequently this is a state of anæmia and general debility—a mingled consequence of the disease and the treatment, in face of which the mercurials and iodide of potassium are inactive or dangerous. . . . We will with difficulty find a better combination of agencies capable of restoring the organism enfeebled by the diathesis, or under the prolonged influence of alteratives. The adjoining circumstances of altitude—air and sunlight—add to the remedial efficacy of the *sulphurous* and *chloride of sodium* waters, already indicated. We exclude neither the marine treatment; neither mother-waters (concentrated saline waters); neither the processes of hydrotherapy. The internal use of chalybeate waters, and of those which, as Challes, Saxon, or Wildegg, are sensibly iodurated, recommends itself in certain conditions."[1]

The method of treatment which has received most favor in this country, when springs are resorted to, is that by hot baths. This manner of elimination, by exciting all the emunctories of the system in an unusual degree, highly commends itself. In this way changes of tissue are wrought in a few weeks that would otherwise require years; and, along with the *débris*, the syphilitic poison is expelled. And, when sulphur and saline waters are employed, the hot bath cannot well be dispensed with; indeed, at all springs where this disease is treated, it is an important auxiliary. The various highly-mineralized waters which are efficacious, probably act by the force that is imparted to specific medicines already absorbed in previous courses of treatment.

Metallic Poisoning.—Workers in various metals are subject to various symptoms, both of the digestive and nervous systems, due to the slow absorption of the metal through the skin and lungs, producing a condition of chronic poisoning. Painter's colic is an ordinary form of this poisoning by lead, while that form of paralysis, known as "wrist-drop," is a further development of the disease. We may also class certain cases of syphilis that have been overtreated by mercurials under this head.

The waters which prove most efficacious in these conditions are those of the *sulphur* class; and, if they be *thermal*, so that

[1] *Op. cit.*, tome ii., pp. 813, 814.

the elimination of the metal may be aided by hot baths, so much the more are they appropriate. As a subsequent measure in anæmic and debilitated patients, the *chalybeate waters* will frequently prove beneficial.

Diabetes Mellitus.—Not every case in which sugar is found in the urine is a true case of diabetes mellitus; for there are sometimes healthy persons in whom a small proportion of sugar in the urine is an occasional condition; but they present none of the early characteristics of the disease—such as increased thirst, passage of immoderate quantities of urine, exaggeration of appetite, and feebleness of vision.

When, however, we have to do with a clear case of saccharine diabetes, what is the value of mineral waters in the treatment? We answer that, in many instances, they are unequivocal, though, at the same time, it must be added that as far as observed they are but palliative. The waters which have given evidence of utility are the *alkaline* and *calcic* waters—those rich in carbonates of soda, magnesia, etc. The treatment by alkaline waters has been followed with much advantage for many years at Vichy, in France, and Karlsbad, in Germany. Of the alkaline-saline thermals of Karlsbad, Niemeyer says: "In our present state of knowledge, a course of waters at Karlsbad is the measure which should deserve the chief reliance as a remedy for diabetes mellitus."[1]

During the use of these waters the quantity of sugar excreted is remarkably diminished, and all trace sometimes disappears; the inordinate thirst is also relieved, and the patient improves in strength. By successive seasons at these springs, together with proper attention to diet and exercise, the course of the malady has been stayed for years. Neither should balneary measures be omitted—a course of baths stimulating the functions of the skin proves a valuable adjunct. In this country the same beneficial results have followed the use of alkaline and calcic waters; and this has led proprietors of recently-discovered springs to exaggerate their efficacy in this disease. Let it be understood, however, that positive relief may be ob-

[1] "Text-Book of Medicine," American edition, vol. ii., p. 759.

tained by alkaline waters more certainly than by any other remedy. But we should not forget that the administration of the alkaline remedies of the shops sometimes procures similar results, though not equally satisfactory.

These waters are only to be resorted to in the first and second stages of the disease, before pulmonary phthisis or other profound lesions complicate the case. When these supervene, the malady is beyond the resource of medical art.

Intermittent Fever.—There is no evidence showing that the paroxysms of intermittent fever can be arrested by the use of mineral waters. In cases of paludal cachexia, however, they may modify the general condition of the system, so that appropriate remedies will readily yield the desired result. Under their use the chronic engorgements of the liver and spleen, produced by repeated paroxysms, are often entirely relieved. The waters most highly recommended are the *alkaline*—those strong in alkaline carbonates [1]—and containing a certain proportion of iron. *Saline* waters also produce favorable results; hot baths, in some instances, change an obstinate quartan or septan into a tertian, which readily yields to the usual treatment.

Chronic Dysentery.—Probably no country has ever known more of this terrible disease than our own—a disease that, during the late war, decimated the forces by invalidism and death, and sent many home to linger through a life of anxiety and pain—some of whom are living at this day, continually harassed by the malady.

The disease in the army was due to exposure, fatigue, paludal miasm, and a diet devoid of fresh meat and vegetables. The effect of miasm and a scorbutic diet has been clearly demonstrated. But, after the patient is entirely removed from the influence of these productive causes, there remains an ulcerated, inflamed, and irritable condition of the colon, which continues almost indefinitely. This same irritable and ulcerated condition of the colon sometimes occurs in civil life as a sequel of acute dysentery. The milder forms, unaccompanied by ulceration, are known as *chronic diarrhœa.*

[1] Trousseau's "Clinique Médicale," tome iii., p. 57.

The treatment of this disease has proved exceedingly unsatisfactory; many drugs giving temporary relief, but a slight cold or error in diet bringing it back with its former force. The ulcerated and inflamed surfaces are in the condition of a chronic ulcer, externally, which may for a time be inactive, but does not heal. Many mineral waters in this country are claimed to be a remedy for this condition. Those, however, which possess the most unequivocal testimony in their favor are the so-called *alum-waters* of Virginia, which are well worthy of trial in a disease so difficult of cure.

Anasarca, or dropsy, not being a disease, but a symptom of disease, it is not necessary to treat of it separately. It may be remedied, in some instances, by waters that relieve the condition on which it depends.

Cancer.—There is no reliable record of cure of this disease by mineral waters, though there are undoubted instances of considerable amelioration of symptoms. Cases of lupus and chronic ulcers have no doubt healed under their use, and hence has arisen the claim of cure for cancer. The waters which have attracted most attention in this disease are those of Sheldon, Vermont. Under the description of these waters this question is discussed.

Scrofula.—In this malady, or class of maladies, the best authorities bear uniform testimony in favor of the value of mineral waters. There are two classes of scrofulous persons; those of slender frame, with accelerated pulse and overactive nervous system, and those who are clumsy and thick-set, with enlarged nose and upper lip, and in whom the adipose tissue is strongly developed, the heart-action slow, and the nervous system obtuse. It is to this last class that mineral waters are best adapted.

First among waters for the relief of scrofula are the *saline.* Durand-Fardel says: "It is necessary to thoroughly understand the following rule of practice. Whenever we wish to remedy profound and confirmed scrofulous affections, such as show the constitutional dyscrasia in the most unmistakable manner, it is to waters strongly mineralized by chloride of sodium that we must resort."[1] These waters are used both internally and in the form of baths. The strong brine-bath, formed by concentration of saline waters, is especially useful. Speaking of these baths, after giving the indications for cod-liver oil, Niemeyer says: "It is far more difficult to furnish definite instructions for the use of the brine-baths, whose anti-scrofulous virtues enjoy a reputation almost as great as that of cod-liver oil. We know too little about the action of these baths, and about the effect which they produce upon nutrition, and the advantages derived from the salt, iodine, and bromine, which they contain, to enable us to determine upon theoretical principles where they are indicated, and where they are unlikely to do good. . . . Hence there is no resource but to send persons who have in vain tried cod-liver oil, and other anti-scrofulous remedies, to Kreutznach, Ischel, Kosen, or Wittekind, or some similar watering-place, in the hope that they may be among those to whom the baths will exhibit their anti-scrofulous virtues, which are by no means illusory."[2]

Sea-bathing also enters appropriately into the treatment of certain conditions of scrofulous habit. Here the action is complex, for, adjoined to immersion in the saline waters of the ocean, we have the continuous inhalation of sea-air. Sea-baths seem best adapted to those conditions in which the scrofulous diathesis is not fully developed. When the dyscrasia is well marked, and inveterate local manifestations are exhibited, they do not answer so good a purpose.

Sulphur-waters are deemed especially applicable to those forms of scrofula accompanied by lesions of the skin, known as scrofulides. For these scrofulous diseases of the skin Hardy tells us, "in the form of baths mineral waters possess a happy influence; the sulphur-waters, and, above all, those which are very rich in sulphur; good success is also obtained by the bromo-iodated waters."[3]

In this country, besides waters of the classes named, the

[1] "Dictionnaire Générale des Eaux Minérales," tome ii., p. 749.
[2] "Text-Book of Medicine," American edition, vol. ii., p. 747.
[3] "Leçons sur la Scrofule et les Scrofulides," Paris, 1864, p. 91.

Rockbridge Alum and the Healing Springs of Virginia enjoy considerable and well-deserved reputation in the treatment of scrofula. The last-named is especially adapted to those cases accompanied with ulceration of the skin or mucous membrane.

In the cure of scrofula by mineral waters, a cure cannot be accomplished by a short season of two or three weeks. It is frequently necessary to remain at the springs for two or three months, and perhaps to return the succeeding season to complete the cure.

Anæmia is the condition in which the red globules of the blood are diminished in quantity, and the other constituents are altered in character. It is not a disease in itself, but the result of many morbid conditions, especially such as prevail in numerous chronic diseases. Whenever the treatment of anæmia is the prominent indication in the course of a chronic disease, *chalybeate waters* should be selected, choosing those which, because of the additional constituents besides the iron, are applicable to the cure of the disease by which anæmia has been induced.

Chlorosis.—This condition is to be distinguished from anæmia, associated with other diseases, such as phthisis pulmonalis, albuminuria, dyspepsia, syphilis, etc. The deficiency of the cellular elements of the blood—the red blood-globules—is the prominent characteristic, the number decreasing so that they may not amount to one-half the usual quantity, while the other elements of the blood remain normal. In anæmia, as a result of disease, not only is the number of globules reduced, but the constituents of the blood are altered in character and quantity. Chlorosis is essentially a disease of early womanhood, and is in some unknown way connected with the process of development. The skin and mucous membranes are of a pallid hue, accompanied in some instances by a yellowish or greenish tint. The remedy above all others is iron, and, when it is desirable to send patients suffering from this disease to the springs, the *chalybeate waters* are to be chosen, The change of scene, and air and exercise, associated with a season at the springs, contribute largely to the effect of the waters. *Sea-bathing* is also of marked utility in these cases.

DISEASES OF THE NERVOUS SYSTEM.

Hemiplegia, or paralysis of one side of the body from cerebral apoplexy, is one of the most frequent forms of paralysis. The recovery in these cases is a work of Nature, and not of medicine, though by the proper use of mineral waters the process may be aided in some instances. After an apoplectic attack, not severe enough to destroy life, the communication between the brain and muscles is interrupted by the blood-clot pressing upon the intervening nervous filaments, or one side of the brain itself may be so pressed upon that impulse is not generated, and, as a consequence, we have entire suspension of motion of that portion of the body over which the implicated structures preside. Sensation is also abolished. Soon after the first effects of the apoplectic seizure have passed away, including the inflammatory fever, which is a result of the injury to the brain-substance, the condition of the patient begins slowly to improve, the more fluid portions of the clot are gradually absorbed, the pressure on the nerve-filaments is lessened, and, as a result, sensation is perhaps altogether restored, and motion partially. This process occupies months. At a certain point, however, the improvement ceases, the fluid portions of the clot have been absorbed, and there remains a shrunken nodule which is but slightly susceptible of absorption. It is just at this point that mineral waters may prove useful. By promoting metamorphosis of tissue, they may still further advance the absorptive process. For this purpose *saline* waters are preferred, with common consent, for, while they promote the process of resolution, they do not stimulate the nerve-centres, as is the case with strong sulphur-waters.[1] Waters feebly mineralized, and of elevated temperature, also produce good results in hemiplegia. In commending these *thermal waters*, Niemeyer says: "We must not hope that the destroyed filaments of the brain will be restored by the use

[1] "Dictionnaire Générale des Eaux Minérales," tome ii., p. 498.

of these waters, but experience shows that, at these places (Wildbad, Gastein, Pfäffers), both cerebral and spinal paralysis often improve; probably this improvement is due to the favorable influence of the baths on the inflammation about the clot, and on that portion of the paralysis due to it."[1]

Mineral waters should not, then, be resorted to soon after an apoplectic seizure, but a certain length of time should elapse. As a general rule, about the fifth or sixth month after the attack is the most favorable time for the use of mineral waters.[2] In this disease waters are used both internally and externally. The nearer to the attack the stronger is the indication for the internal use of waters, and more especially the laxative salines. In this manner it may be hoped that absorption will be advanced. Later, however, when all that can be gained in this way has been obtained, warm douches should be employed, expecting thereby to stimulate the peripheric nerves and arouse the inactive muscles. Nothing, however, is to be gained when the hemiplegic paralysis is of some years' standing, and the muscles will not respond to the stimulation of the electric current.

Paraplegia, or loss of motion in the lower extremities, is due either to functional derangement or organic disease of the spinal cord. It is in the first form only that we are to expect favorable results from treatment by mineral waters. When paraplegia is a result of rheumatism, syphilis, venereal excess, or chronic metallic poisoning, we may expect some success from their use. In the paraplegia consecutive to accouchement, Prof. Siebold strongly recommends the waters of Töplitz, in Bohemia (thermal waters, from 100° to 120° Fahr.).

The waters which have proved most efficacious in paraplegia are those of the thermal class. They are used both as a bath and douche. The mode of employing the waters of Wildbad, in Austria (91° to 100° Fahr.), in paraplegia, is thus described by Constantin James: "They first administer baths of from ten to fifteen minutes; then they augment the dura-

1 "Text-Book of Medicine," vol. ii., p. 202.
2 "Guide aux Eaux Minérales," Constantin James, p. 410.

tion so as finally to arrive at baths of an hour, which, however, they shorten or suspend altogether the moment symptoms of reaction are manifest. It is usually between the first and second week that benefit commences to be experienced. At this period they sometimes begin the use of the douche, of which the volume and the fall should possess but a very feeble degree of percussion. By the discreet application of the douche, the good effects of the waters are much aided." [1]

In paraplegia due to syphilis, or chronic metallic poisoning, we may appropriately apply those thermal waters which, besides heat, contain ingredients that act directly in eliminating the original cause of the disease.

It is perhaps best to repeat that paraplegia is only benefited when there is no organic lesion of the spinal cord. If the muscles of a paraplegic do not respond on testing them with the electric current, and the limbs are diminished in size, we can hope for no remedial effect from mineral waters.

Locomotor ataxia is characterized by an inability to properly control the movements of the limbs in walking, though muscular force remains. It is due to organic changes in the posterior columns of the lower portion of the spinal cord, and is little influenced in its unfavorable course by treatment of any kind. Trousseau, however, recommends *sulphur-baths*,[2] and Niemeyer favors *thermal waters*, not with expectation of cure, but as giving relief. Niemeyer says: "There is no doubt that tabes patients have been decidedly benefited by the treatment at these places (Wildbad, Gastein, Ragaz, Pfäffers, Töplitz, etc.)." [3]

Neuralgia.—In the treatment of neuralgia we have frequently to do with what may be termed a neuralgic constitution—one in which the nerves are in an irritable state, and readily impressed by external influences. This nervous condition is almost invariably accompanied by an asthenic state of the system; and, that we may relieve the neuralgias to which

1 "Guide aux Eaux Minérales," p. 244.
2 "Clinique Médicale," tome ii., p. 550
3 "Text-Book of Medicine," American edition, vol. ii., p. 276.

these persons are subject, we must address our remedies to the general condition. For this purpose, light, air, and exercise, are exceedingly important. And to these we may add the use of baths and mineral waters, by no means second in importance. The *thermal waters* are those which most frequently produce favorable results; not those of a high degree of heat, but such as are of moderate temperature, and where there are facilities for taking prolonged warm baths and douches of varying temperature. It should be added, however, that in some atonic cases most benefit is derived from a sudden and short immersion in a cold bath, or by the use of transition douches. *Chalybeate waters* are also valuable in anæmic cases. *Sea-baths* prove exceedingly effective in many instances.

The various local neuralgias, such as facial, brachial, and sciatic, are often dependent on rheumatism, syphilis, or metallic poisoning. It is in rheumatismal cases that the best results are obtained; and indeed it is the cure of these cases that has given to many thermal springs the great reputation they possess in this disease. When the neuralgia is a result of syphilis, we treat this condition; and when it arises from metallic poisoning, the sulphur-waters are of decided benefit. A favorite and valuable method of treating sciatic neuralgia is by the warm or hot douche. Especially has this proved beneficial when there is chronic inflammation of the nerve or nerve-sheaths.

HYSTERIA.

This disease is too often considered by the laity as a whim of a foolish woman, instead of a derangement of the nervous system, which it really is. Of the many kinds of treatment to which we are frequently compelled to resort, that of a sojourn at an appropriate watering-place affords hope of relief. If the patient be chlorotic, she should be recommended to *chalybeate waters*, especially those where, by their elevated temperature, there are facilities for pursuing a course of baths. *Sulphur* waters also prove beneficial, by their reconstituent property, choosing those which are sedative in action and are adapted for bathing. The prominent advantages of a life at the sea-side and *sea-bathing* should not be forgotten.

HYPOCHONDRIA.

Those who have had occasion to treat this disease are well aware of the many dilemmas in which we are placed, in order to satisfy the craving of the patient for something new in the way of treatment, and at the same time to prescribe a remedy that may really tend toward removing the malady. Under such circumstances, we may recommend these patients to certain mineral springs with the expectation that they will be benefited, temporarily, at least. The waters that prove most useful are the *saline* and *purgative* waters. They should be rich in carbonic acid, so that they agree with the stomach. Their efficacy depends on their favorable influence on engorged abdominal viscera, which frequently occupy a causative relation to this disease. When dyspepsia forms a prominent feature, the saline waters are to be preferred. Niemeyer says: "The benefit often derived from the springs of Karlsbad, Marienbad, and Kissingen [purgative and saline waters—W.], in the treatment of this affection, is no doubt mainly due to the beneficial effect exerted by these waters upon diseases of the gastric organs, which so frequently prove a source of hypochondriasis." [1]

DISEASES OF THE HEART.

This class is named only to remark that organic lesions or changes of the heart are in no wise relieved by mineral waters; on the contrary, there is so much danger from their use that, as a rule, they should be avoided. Functional derangements, however, such as palpitation, are frequently relieved, not by any direct action upon the heart, but by their favorable influence on the malady on which palpitation depends, as dyspepsia, anæmia, chlorosis, etc.

DISEASES OF THE RESPIRATORY SYSTEM.

Chronic Laryngitis.—This disease is otherwise known as

[1] *Op. cit.*, vol. ii., p. 898.

clergyman's sore-throat, chronic laryngeal catarrh, etc. It is characterized by a chronic inflammation of the mucous membrane lining the pharynx and larynx. The secretion from this membrane may be increased in quantity, but vitiated, becoming an acrid and viscid discharge, or it may be almost entirely suspended, causing the throat to feel exceedingly dry and uncomfortable. The mucous membrane also becomes thickened, the vocal cords included, and a harsh and hoarse voice is produced, or it may be almost altogether lost. The disease usually commences in the pharynx, and extends to the larynx. It is, however, seldom noticed in the early stages, as, until the voice begins to be involved, the patient is seldom alarmed.

In this disease mineral waters occupy a deservedly high position as a curative agent. Those most frequently useful are the *sulphur-waters* rich in sodium, and the *alkaline waters* rich in chloride of sodium. In speaking of Eaux Bonnes, typical waters of the sulphuretted-sodium kind, Durand-Fardel observes: "A long experience has proved that their usage, almost exclusively internal, in doses progressively increasing, produces happy effects, especially in lymphatic subjects slightly impressionable, and when the affection assumes a passive character."[1] Gibb also testifies in favor of these waters, especially in very chronic cases.[2] The use of this class of waters, in the form of spray projected against the posterior wall of the pharynx or directly into the larynx, also exercises a beneficial effect.

Concerning the alkaline chloride-of-sodium waters, we cannot do better than quote the remarks of Niemeyer at length:

"The use of the alkaline muriatic mineral waters (Säuerlinge, Halloid salts) has an unmistakable influence upon the course of many cases of chronic laryngeal catarrh, which, unfortunately, cannot as yet be distinguished from the cases in which it fails. For this mode of cure it is better to send the patient to such places as Ems, Obersalzbrunnen, or Gleichenberg, and, only when his means will not permit him to do oth-

[1] "Dictionnaire des Eaux Minerales," tome ii., p. 247.

[2] "Diseases of the Throat and Windpipe." London, 1864, p. 14.

erwise, to allow him to use seltzer-water or one of the so-called mineral waters, as a cure at home. We may let him drink the Ems or Kesselbrunnen water, or the Krähnchen of Ems, on the spot, as they have respectively a temperature of 117° Fahr., and 90° Fahr., without the addition of warm milk or warm whey; in order to warm them, it is better to mix the Obersalzbrunnen or the imported Ems water, with equal parts of hot milk. That the far more customary addition of whey should have any real advantage over that of milk is at least doubtful. The 'well-prepared whey' at celebrated watering-places—furnished generally by a 'Swiss,' and, if possible, by an Apenzeller in his national costume—so much lauded in the newspapers and bath journals, and to which often more credit is given than the springs themselves, is merely milk *minus* cheese, and can hardly effect more than the milk from which the cheese has not been eliminated. It is only in the somewhat rare cases in which milk is not well borne by the patient, while the whey is borne well or better, that I allow the latter to be added to the mineral water instead.

"Several hypotheses have been advanced as to the action of the alkaline-muriatic mineral waters. The fact that the ashes of the mucus are richer in salt (chloride of sodium) than the ashes of the blood, and that mucus becomes less tenacious upon the addition of salt, seems certainly to indicate that salt plays an important *rôle* in the formation of mucus, but it by no means justifies the conclusion that the use of salt effects a cure or more rapid resolution of the catarrhal process.

"In other quarters (Sprengler) the principal importance has been attributed to the amount of alkaline carbonates contained in these mineral waters, and depending on an observation of *Virchow's*, according to which, very dilute solutions of alkalies are capable of exciting the ciliary movements in epithelium. They assert, in explanation of the beneficial action of the waters in question, that their use reëstablishes the extinguished or re pressed ciliary vibrations. Grave objections may be brought against this explanation of the action of the saline waters, which is not merely palliative, but in many cases absolutely curative, and we must be content with the empirical fact that the springs of Ems, Obersalzbrunnen, and Selters [alkaline and alkaline-saline waters—W.], have often alleviated or cured chronic laryngeal catarrh; the cold sulphur-springs, too (such as those of Weilbach, in the dukedom of Nassau, of Eilsen, in the principality of Schamburg-Lippe, of Langenbrücken, in the grand-dukedom of Baden), which we usually make use of like those of Obersalzbrunnen and Selters, mixed with warm milk or whey. The sulphur-springs, also, of the Pyrenees, above all Eaux Bonnes, are, with good reason, in repute in the treatment of chronic laryngitis. Our conjectures as to the *modus operandi* of these waters are as yet vague and untenable; a matter, however, far less to be regretted than the fact that we have no criterion whereby to predetermine the cases in which relief may be expected, and those in which they do no good."[1]

Associated with consumption there is sometimes a chronic laryngitis, frequently accompanied by ulcerations, known as *laryngeal phthisis.* In these cases temporary relief is sometimes obtained by the moderate use of the above-mentioned waters with warm milk. It should be remembered, however, that the use of mineral waters in large quantities is injurious in cases of phthisis pulmonalis.

Chronic Pharyngitis.—This is the same disease as that above described, the seat being, however, limited to the pharynx. The treatment by mineral waters is the same as indicated in chronic laryngitis.

Chronic Bronchitis.—When bronchitis has continued for a long time, assuming the form known as *chronic bronchial catarrh*, or *bronchorrhœa*, marked relief is frequently obtained by the use of appropriate mineral waters.

The persons, however, in whom chronic bronchitis occurs may be divided into three classes, the scrofulous, the lymphatic, and the dartrous, or those who have a constitutional tendency to non-specific skin-disease. All authorities agree that sulphur-waters are especially adapted to the catarrhs of lymphatic constitutions, and the more lymphatism is developed the more

[1] "Text-Book of Medicine," American edition, vol. i., pp. 10–12.

certainly are sulphur-waters indicated. But if the patient is not of the lymphatic type, and, on the contrary, is of a sanguine or irritable temperament, and the cough torments by its frequency, the calming or sedative waters, associated with temperate baths, are indicated. Of waters adapted to this condition, the Red Sulphur, in Virginia, may be mentioned. If the patient is of the decidedly scrofulous type, then sulphur-waters rich in chloride of sodium, the *saline sulphur-waters*, should find preference. When the catarrhal condition is allied to the dartrous, or herpetic diathesis, the indication is still to use sulphur-waters; but care should be taken to recommend those which are notably sulphurous, and, at the same time, a somewhat active course of bathing should be pursued.

Soon after commencing a course of sulphur-waters the malady is frequently aggravated, and some authorities have thought this necessary to the relief of the disease. It is probable, however, that this is but a result of the general excitement usually produced by sulphur-waters, and in no way necessary to the treatment. Indeed, when it appears, it is an indication for the temporary suspension of the water or diminution in the quantity taken. In this connection, Durand-Fardel says: "But we believe, in the generality of cases, it is more frequently a result of the treatment than a means of cure. That which tends to prove this is, that many catarrhal affections are cured without showing appreciable signs of excitation, and that the treatment is often successfully applied in the absence of catarrhal conditions at the time." [1]

Asthma.—The cases of this disease may be divided into two classes—the humid, accompanied by chronic catarrh, and the dry, or purely nervous. The last-named cases are not benefited by mineral waters, and the former only inasmuch as the disease is associated with chronic bronchitis. It is the favorable action of mineral waters on this conjoined condition that sometimes affords relief in these cases. It should, however, be remembered that no case of asthma should be subjected to the use of mineral waters, without a thorough exam-

[1] "Dictionnaire Générale des Eaux Minérales," tome i., p. 394.

ination to determine whether general emphysema, or organic disease of the heart or large blood-vessels exists, either of which is sufficient reason for advising against the use of mineral waters. It may be added that cases of nervous asthma are sometimes relieved on resorting to springs; this is due, however, to a change of residence.

Consumption.—True phthisis pulmonalis is so little amenable to treatment by mineral waters, that we only mention the disease in order to advise patients against cherishing extravagant hopes concerning the reputed virtues of certain advertised springs. In the majority of cases, more harm than good is the result of an attempt to use mineral waters. There are cases, however, complicated by chronic bronchitis, with profuse bronchorrhœa, which are somewhat alleviated by waters applicable to the latter malady. The relief of these cases, together with the cure of cases of chronic bronchitis, wrongly diagnosed as consumption, forms the only known foundation for the reputation of mineral waters in this disease.

DISEASES OF THE DIGESTIVE SYSTEM.

Dyspepsia.—In the proper acceptation of the term, this word designates a functional derangement of the stomach.

The stomach may be subject to inertia, the peristaltic movements being performed slowly and with pain; or, it may be overactive, the ingesta being forced forward into the duodenum before the necessary stomach digestion has taken place. There may be diminished secretion of the gastric juice, or there may be over-secretion of this fluid, known as acid dyspepsia. In each of these forms, mineral waters may prove of utility, but it is in the last named that they have proved signally efficacious.

Before considering the treatment of dyspepsia by mineral waters, it may be well to state that nearly every mineral spring in the country names dyspepsia as one of the diseases to which it is peculiarly adapted. The explanation of this fact is readily understood, when we remember that in many cases of this trouble a change from the close confinement of a city, and the harassing cares of business, to the open fields, the pure air, and the healthful exercise of the country, is sufficient for relief without drinking a drop of mineral water.

In *acid dyspepsia* the *alkaline waters* have proved of exceeding utility—those containing a considerable proportion of carbonate of soda and largely impregnated with carbonic-acid gas. Their efficacy in these cases is undoubted, and the prescription of them is of long standing. It may be noted, however, that their value does not depend, according to present belief, on a neutralization of the acid of the stomach by an alkali. This theory, which long prevailed, has been abandoned.

When acid dyspepsia is accompanied by the evolution of large quantities of gas, it is known as *flatulent dyspepsia.* Then the *saline waters* should be prescribed in preference. Why this should be so is readily understood. The alkaline waters, by the carbonic acid which they contain, and the evolution of this gas in the stomach, would tend to increase the flatulence. In considering this form of dyspepsia, Trousseau says: "Mineral waters are here equally of incontestable utility; but it is no longer to Vichy, Karlsbad, or Pougues, that we should send the patient; these waters are harmful; it is Niederbronn and Forbach, of which the predominating principles are the same as those which enter into the composition of sea-water, that we should recommend; it is to Nauheim, Soden, Kissingen, chloride of sodium waters, as the first."[1] Sometimes acid dyspepsia is allied to chlorosis in females. Then a *chalybeate water*, rich in carbonic acid, should be selected.

In dyspepsias allied to constipation and engorgement of the abdominal viscera—a not unusual complication—the mildly purgative *sulphur* or *saline waters* should be employed.

Gastritis.—The chronic form of this malady is limited to the mucous membrane of the stomach, and has received the name of *chronic gastric catarrh.* It is closely allied to dyspepsia; indeed, if this term is applied in its broad signification, it is a dyspepsia; and on this account it has been almost entirely overlooked by some writers.

[1] "Clinique Médicale," tome iii., p. 51.

The symptoms of this malady are the following: One of the principal complaints of the patient is of a sense of fulness and pressure in the stomach, which is increased by eating, but seldom amounts to severe pain. With this sense of fulness there is usually some prominence of the epigastrium, caused by accumulation of gas in the stomach and retention of food, owing to the slowness of the digestive process. There are also eructations of gas, accompanied with a sour and acrid fluid. Sometimes there is vomiting. If vomiting does occur, it is usually mixed with considerable mucus. This is especially the case in the chronic gastric catarrh of tipplers. The sensation of hunger is almost lost, although the body may be much emaciated. If hunger, however, does occur, it is satisfied by a few mouthfuls. The catarrh may extend upward to the mouth, or downward into the intestines; in the latter case, frequently producing diarrhœa. The disease is usually accompanied with mental depression, which, in some instances, develops into hypochondria.

The causes of chronic gastritis are varied; prominent among them are articles of food that over-stimulate the mucous membrane of the stomach—such as highly-spiced sauces and meats. But the most frequent cause is the abuse of spirituous liquors.

The waters best adapted to the treatment of this disease are the *alkaline waters*—those rich in carbonate of soda. In cases associated with obstinate constipation, we should choose waters which, besides the carbonate of soda, contain a moderate proportion of laxative sulphates or chloride of sodium.

In the treatment of this malady Prof. Niemeyer highly extols the alkaline purgative waters of Karlsbad and Marienbad. He says: "The use of the waters of Karlsbad and Marienbad has the most wonderful results," and adds: "The results from this treatment are the most brilliant that are ever obtained in medicine."[1] He also says: "The learned professors of the Vienna and Prague schools prize the use of the warm springs of Karlsbad as the best remedy for chronic gastric catarrh."[2]

[1] "Text-Book of Medicine," vol. i., p. 499. [2] *Op. cit.*, vol. i., p. 499.

It need hardly be added that the patient should subject himself to rigid dietetic rules during treatment. He should eat sparingly of meats and avoid stimulating sauces. Spirituous liquors must be entirely abandoned. The patient should eat but little at night, and drink the water in the morning, before breakfast. This meal should not be taken for an hour after the last glass of water.

Gastric Ulcer.—When this affection is diagnosed, the waters found preferable are the *alkaline*, rich in carbonates. The warm springs of this class are to be preferred, or, in absence of them, waters from springs of this class may be warmed. The waters should be taken in the same manner as indicated in chronic gastritis. The results from the use of the proper mineral water are exceedingly satisfactory.[1]

Gastralgia.—This disease is also known as cardialgia. The name, however, is frequently misapplied, and dyspeptic persons suffering from pain or burning in the stomach are said to have gastralgia; in its proper meaning a malady of much greater gravity is signified. It is a purely nervous disorder, characterized by excessive pain in the stomach, coming on in paroxysms, at intervals usually of two or three days. When free from pain the patient may feel well, digestion being normally performed. The following is a graphic description of a paroxysm, from Romberg:

"Suddenly or after a precedent feeling of pressure, there is severe griping pain in the pit of the stomach, usually extending to the back, with a feeling of faintness, shrunken countenance, cold hands and feet, and small, intermittent pulse. The pain becomes so excessive that the patient cries out. The epigastrium is either puffed out like a ball, or, as is more frequently the case, retracted, with tension of the abdominal walls. There is often pulsation in the epigastrium. External pressure is well borne, and not unfrequently the patient presses the pit of the stomach against some firm substance, or compresses it with his hand. Sympathetic pains often occur in the thorax, under the sternum, in the œsophagean

[1] *Op. cit.*, vol. i., p. 518.

branches of the pneumogastric, while they are rare in the exterior of the body.

"The attack lasts from a few minutes to half an hour; then the pain gradually subsides, leaving the patient much exhausted, or else it ceases suddenly, with eructation of gas or watery fluid, with vomiting, with a gentle soft perspiration, or with the passage of reddish urine." [1]

This description applies to the disease as it shows itself in the severest form. There are, however, many minor degrees which still bear the well-marked symptoms.

In the use of mineral waters, whether in the severe or mild forms of the disease, it should be remembered that they should be taken only in the intervals of the attacks.

The *alkaline waters* act most efficiently in this disease, the more certainly, according as they are used at a period distant from the attack. Under their influences the malady is frequently entirely relieved. In cases associated with chlorosis, alkaline waters, containing a proportion of iron, are indicated.

Constipation.—This condition depends, as a rule, either on deficiency of the intestinal secretion or inactivity of the muscular coat of the bowels. It is not, usually, a primary disease, but symptomatic of some other derangement. As a rule, the frankly purgative waters are not indicated; those, however, which are mildly aperient, gently stimulate the intestinal secretions, and prove beneficial. In obstinate constipation, associated with dyspepsia, Trousseau recommends *laxative waters*, after having tried his favorite remedy, belladonna and other correctives, without avail.[2] Durand-Fardel recommends the *alkaline* (carbonate of soda) *waters*, which, although sometimes constipating in themselves at first, tend to excite intestinal and biliary secretion, and thinks that enough attention has not been given to the use of alkaline-saline waters in this condition.[3]

Hæmorrhoids.—Mineral waters do not act directly in curing this disease, but indirectly they sometimes prove of decided

[1] From Niemeyer's "Text-Book of Medicine."
[2] "Clinique Médicale," tome iii., p. 61.
[3] "Dictionnaire des Eaux Minérales," tome i., p. 489.

utility. Hæmorrhoids frequently depend on a condition of the abdominal organs, termed by the old authors abdominal plethora, one in which the liver, spleen, pancreas, and mesentery, are unusually filled with blood, and the current moves slowly. By the action of waters in stimulating the abdominal circulation and diminishing engorgement, much relief may be given. The waters which have proved most beneficial are the *saline waters* and *saline sulphur*-waters. It is well to combine the employment of baths.

Engorged Liver.—In almost all chronic hyperæmic conditions of the liver, mineral waters prove curative. Although the fact that engorged conditions of the liver exist, and precede grave lesions, is undoubted, still it is difficult exactly to define or diagnose the condition. As a rule, the subject of engorged liver presents a dusky or muddy complexion, the tongue is coated, the bowels are constipated, the appetite is uncertain, there is a pappy taste in the mouth, and a feeling of fulness in the head, especially after eating. The causes which produce engorgement of the liver are continued excess in eating, combined with sedentary habits; repeated and long-continued attacks of malarial fever; excessive indulgence in malt liquors; and organic lesions of the valves of the right side of the heart.

The waters which prove most valuable, in engorgement of the liver from any of the causes named, are the *saline waters*, *alkaline purgative waters*, and *saline sulphur-waters.* These waters produce their effect by liquefying the bile, promoting its flow, and by the increased movement which they impart to the action of the intestinal tube.

Frerichs, an acknowledged authority on diseases of the liver, gives prominent place to mineral waters in the treatment. When giving the treatment in chronic hyperæmia from overfeeding, he names several remedies, but in conclusion says we can remedy the condition "still better by regulating the intestinal secretions by the use of the springs of Kissingen, Homburg, Marienbad, and Karlsbad."[1] And in hyperæmia from obstructed circulation, when the condition of the patient is not

[1] Frerich's "Diseases of the Liver," Sydenham edition, vol. i., p. 376.

threatening, he says, "We may often succeed in procuring permanent relief by the careful employment of the Ragoczy spring of Kissingen, or the Mill spring of Karlsbad."[1] He, however, adds that, if the disease of the valves is far advanced, or the muscular tissues of the heart are much enfeebled, the waters are inappropriate.

In the application of mineral waters for the cure of engorged liver, it is exceedingly desirable to add the employment of prolonged warm baths to the internal use of the water, and warm douches over the region of the liver also aid the action of the water.

Gall-Stones.—The passage of biliary calculi from the gall-bladder through the bile-ducts into the duodenum, often causes the most intense pain the human organism can endure. Under severe attacks of *hepatic colic* the patient writhes from side to side of the bed, and cold perspiration often covers the surface of the body. If asked to describe the pain, he compares it to the cutting of a knife—to the boring of a red-hot iron through the side. The cause of the suffering is the distension of the bile-duct by a gall-stone in its passage, and the intensity depends on the size of the calculus. Any remedy, then, that will surely mitigate or cure these terrible attacks, merits attention. This mineral waters will do more successfully than any known medicine.

The causes of the formation of gall-stones are obscure. The general impression is, that they result from a thickened condition of the bile, in which crystallization and concentration of its salts take place, and that this condition is usually associated with free living, a sedentary life, and corpulence.

The waters which prove of greatest utility are the *alkaline waters*, the *saline-sulphur waters*, and *saline waters*, those of the first class being preferable. These waters doubtless act by the fluidity of the bile, which they produce, thereby reducing the tendency to formation of the stones,[2] and by their alter-

[1] *Op. cit.*, vol. i., p. 367.

[2] Murchison, "Diseases of the Liver," p. 359, says, "In dogs, for instance, with biliary fistulæ, the mere drinking of large quantities of water will increase the amount of water in the bile."

ative action influencing the nutrition of the liver. Under the use of the waters the patient not unfrequently has slight attacks of biliary colic, passing large numbers of calculi, to be followed, however, by immunity from paroxysms. The spring selected varies according to the condition of the patient, whether in addition to alkalinity a tonic or laxative effect be required.

In recommending a treatment for gall-stones, Trousseau says: "What we should do is to endeavor to regulate the functions of the bile, so as to prevent the return of the colic. . . . It is in answering this indication that the waters of Pougues, Contrexville, Vichy, Karlsbad, and Vals, are of so incontestable utility in the treatment of biliary gravel. . . . Under the influence of this potent medication, properly directed, the patients lose the unfortunate aptitude which they have contracted."[1]

Niemeyer says: "We do not know whether their efficacy depends solely on the formation of a thin fluid bile, by which the gall-stones are readily washed downward, or whether the bile is rendered so strongly alkaline by the use of these waters as to dissolve the coloring-matter and lime, or the cholesterine; but we should not delay prescribing the treatment till its mode of action can be explained."[2]

Frerichs and Murchison both favor the use of waters. After recommending Karlsbad, Vichy, Ems, etc., Frerich says: "These mineral waters have certainly proved the most efficacious remedies against gall-stones. In many severe cases I have directed my patients to go to Karlsbad, and have known them to return cured. . . . I have known favorable results ensue under my own eyes from drinking the water brought from the Mill spring of Karlsbad, either cold or warm."[3]

Fatty Liver.—In cases of this disease, mineral waters are recommended by Frerichs and Murchison, the *alkaline waters*, *muriated alkaline waters*, and *saline waters*, the same that are

[1] "Clinique Médicale," tome iii., p. 237

[2] "Text-Book of Medicine," American edition, vol. i., p. 703.

[3] "Diseases of the Liver," London, 1861, vol. ii., p. 531.

employed in engorgement of the liver. These waters apply to the fatty liver as developed in corpulent persons, and not to the form which occurs in consumption.

Jaundice.—This is a symptom of disease, and not a disease. It arises from obstruction of the flow of bile from the liver and gall-bladder into the intestines, or from non-separation of the coloring-matter from the blood, owing to impairment of action in the liver. It is to cases of jaundice arising from obstruction that mineral waters are best adapted. The most prominent cause of jaundice from obstruction is the impaction, or inertia, of gall-stones in their passage through the bile-ducts. It has already been treated under gall-stones. The second cause is *catarrh of the biliary ducts.*

When jaundice arises from the last-named cause the *alkaline waters*, or *muriated alkaline waters*, should be prescribed. The *saline sulphur-waters* also answer well in these cases.

Frerichs, in speaking of the Karlsbad, Marienbad, Kissingen, etc., in these cases, says: "They are with difficulty replaced by any other remedies in cases where the jaundice owes its origin to chronic congestion of the liver, with obstinate catarrh of the bile-ducts and mucous membrane of the stomach and duodenum, to gall-stones," etc.[1]

In jaundice, as a sequence of constipation, those waters which act favorably on this condition will also remedy this symptom.

Gravel.—The formation of gravel within the kidneys or bladder is the result of a constitutional condition, and does not depend on derangement of the organs in which the deposit takes place. However, the deposit of gravel in these organs causes irritation, chronic catarrh, and inflammation. The disease frequently depends on functional disturbance of the digestive system. Mineral waters procure relief in two ways: primarily, by the soothing influence they produce on the irritation or chronic inflammation of the ureters and bladder; secondarily, by the correction of the constitutional vice which causes the excretion of gravelly urine.

[1] "Diseases of the Liver," vol. i., p. 124.

Gravel is divided into the uric-acid, the phosphatic, and the oxalic, according to the chemical constitution of the deposit. Or it is classed as acid gravel, i. e., the uric-acid and the oxalic-acid gravel; or alkaline gravel, i. e., the phosphatic. In cases of acid gravel the urine is acid to test-paper, while, in alkaline gravel, the urine is alkaline.

In prescribing mineral waters for gravel, these distinctions should be remembered: In *uric acid*, or red gravel, and in *oxalic gravel*, the *alkaline waters* or the *calcic waters* should be chosen. Under the use of these waters the urine loses its acidity and becomes neutral, and the pain in the lumbar region and in the bladder passes away. However, it is not unusual in the commencement of treatment for the patient to pass a considerable quantity of gravel, but without much pain, and, finally, he experiences complete relief, in which condition he may remain for eight or twelve months; or, by employment of the waters during several successive seasons, entire freedom from attack may be secured for many years, complete constitutional change being wrought in the system.[1] Combined with the internal use of the waters, it is advisable to employ warm baths and douches. If, under treatment, the attacks of gravel, or nephritic colic, are increased in frequency or severity, it is an indication to diminish the quantity of water administered, or resort to waters less strongly mineralized. In *phosphatic gravel* the strongly alkaline waters are not to be employed; the *calcic waters* then afford the greatest relief. In this variety of gravel the water acts more by its impression on the urinary organs, which are then the seat of catarrh, than by its effect on the general system.

How calcic waters relieve gravel is not understood. One hundred years ago, lime-water was a favorite and efficient remedy in this disease. (*See* "CARBONATE OF LIME.")

Calculus.—Stone in the bladder is only an aggregation of the deposit which constitutes gravel, into a solid mass of varying size. It depends on the same causes, may be separated into the same divisions, and is relieved by the same classes of

[1] Trousseau's "Clinique Médicale," tome iii., p. 48.

waters. In this condition, however, it is relief only that can be obtained. The irritation of the bladder, caused by the presence of the stone, will be palliated, the general system may be so acted upon that the diathesis will be corrected, and the stone will not increase in volume; but there is no evidence that solution of the calculus can be produced.[1] A calculus, subjected to the action of certain mineral waters in a test-tube, may be partially disintegrated; but the human body is not a test-tube, and no such saturation of the urine by a mineral water can be caused as to represent a similar condition.

After the calculus has been removed by surgical operation, it is advisable to use mineral waters for the purpose of correcting the morbid condition that led to its formation, and prevent a new concretion.

In cases of *renal calculus* and hæmaturia, mineral waters prove of decided utility. In these cases the waters applicable to gravel prove appropriate. In giving the treatment of these conditions Sir Henry Thompson says, "Of all medicinal remedies perhaps none are so valuable as mineral waters, especially those which have sulphate of soda largely diluted as the main ingredient. Take Karlsbad, Friedrichs-halle, and Marienbad, as an example,"[2] It will be perceived that he prefers alkaline purgative waters to pure alkaline.

Vesical Catarrh.—Catarrh of the bladder results from any cause which produces frequent and long-continued retention of urine, and hence is a frequent accompaniment of calculus, enlargement of the prostate, and stricture of the urethra. In some instances it proceeds from cold, or is essentially a disease of the mucous membrane of the bladder, without regard to extraneous causes.

When catarrh arises from the first-named cause, calculus, it is amenable to the treatment named under that head.

Resulting from other causes, the waters most favorable are mild *calcic* and *alkaline waters;* not that they exercise any influence on the cause of the disease, but, by modifying the

[1] Durand-Fardel, *op. cit.*, tome i., p. 351.

[2] "On the Urinary Organs," American edition, 1869, p. 202.

constitution of the urine, they often give decided relief. It should be mentioned, however, that in this disease the bladder is frequently very irritable, and, under the administration of waters, dysuria is readily produced. The action of the water should therefore be closely scrutinized.

Albuminuria.—Bright's disease is mentioned only to state that there is no reliable evidence of the utility of mineral waters in this disease.

DISEASES OF THE UTERUS.

Chronic Metritis.—For convenience of treatment, we embrace three separate conditions under this designation, i. e., *uterine engorgement*, *uterine catarrh*, and *cervical ulcerations.* This arrangement is made from the fact that these diseases frequently depend on a morbid constitution, and it is through the correction of this condition that the internal administration of waters proves curative. The constitutional conditions that most frequently dominate over the uterine malady are scrofulous, rheumatic, and herpetic (or dartrous).

When a scrofulous tendency predominates, the uterine malady usually assumes the form of engorgement. In these cases *saline waters* produce the best results, correcting the constitutional condition, and possessing a resolutive action in uterine and peri-uterine engorgement. They, however, dispose directly to uterine hæmorrhage, and therefore the stronger waters should not be selected, especially if the patient be subject to menorrhagia.[1]

If the rheumatic diathesis is dominant, *thermal waters*, containing a proportion of alkalies, should be directed. Alkaline waters, like saline waters, possess a resolutive action in engorgements, but, unlike them, do not tend to cause uterine hæmorrhage.

The herpetic or dartrous[2] constitution is most amenable to *sulphur-waters.* When this condition prevails, the uterine malady is most frequently accompanied by uterine and vaginal

[1] Durand-Fardel, "Bulletin Générale de Thérapeutique," 1872, tome lxxxii., p. 484.

[2] The dartrous constitution is described under diseases of the skin.

catarrh. When congestion and neuralgia are prominent, these waters are not applicable, neither are they in cases complicated by menorrhagia.[1] Those which are but little exciting should be selected.

In the treatment of chronic metritis by mineral waters, balneary measures occupy a prominent place. The swimming-bath of moderate temperature (82° to 93° Fahr.) is that best adapted. The patient should remain in the bath for a considerable time—as long as half an hour, or even an hour. The vaginal douche would seem to be indicated in this disease, but it has been found injurious, the percussion caused by the injection of a stream of water against the neck of the uterus tending to produce congestion. Neither have douches in the lumbar region, or parts in the vicinity of the uterus, proved beneficial. Durand-Fardel says, "Save for exceptional cases they should be banished from the treatment of this disease." If it is desirable to act directly on a catarrh or ulceration, irrigations of feeble temperature and devoid of impulsive force should alone be employed.

Amenorrhœa.—This condition is allied to various states of the organism. It frequently presents in young girls of delicate constitution and scrofulous or lymphatic temperament. They are almost always chlorotic. In cases of this kind there is much to be hoped from a resort to springs; more, probably, from change of air, scene, and exercise, than from the waters. However, *saline waters* and *sulphur-waters*, especially those containing a proportion of iron, aid the recovery. To the internal use of the waters it is well to join swimming-baths of moderate temperature. Sea-bathing also gives favorable results when the person reacts well after the bath.

Sometimes suppression of menstruation is united with a plethoric condition. In these cases waters of a different type must be selected, those containing but a small proportion of constituents and which possess a calming or sedative influence. This indication is most frequently met with in *thermal waters* of moderate temperature.

[1] Durand-Fardel, *loc. cit.*

Dysmenorrhœa.—Painful menstruation, in many instances, depends on the same causes which induce amenorrhœa, and the same waters are indicated. Occurring in anæmic, chlorotic, and scrofulous girls, as a result of delayed development, the *saline waters* or *sulphur-waters*, combined with tepid bathing, are beneficial. *Chalybeate waters* are also appropriate.

When plethora and erethism of the nervous system exist, *thermal waters* of moderate temperature and but little mineralized are preferable. Cases are also benefited by the continued use of alkaline waters of very moderate strength.

It need hardly be stated that cases of dysmenorrhœa, depending on displacement of the uterus or constriction of the cervical canal, are beyond the power of mineral waters, and require surgical treatment.

Leucorrhœa.—This disease is a frequent accompaniment of chronic metritis, and depends on similar general conditions of the system. It is, however, more frequently manifested when metritis occurs in the herpetic or dartrous constitution. The waters then most favorable are *sulphur-waters*—those but feebly mineralized, as a rule; though, in some instances, the stronger waters yield excellent results. The highly-mineralized waters should, however, be used guardedly, lest uterine congestion be produced.

Combined with the internal use of waters, the tepid bath (82° to 93° Fahr.) should be employed. The vaginal douche is of service, provided it be employed *only as an irrigation*, without any propulsion against the uterus.

In cases of leucorrhœa marked by anæmia or chlorosis, the mild *chalybeate waters* may be advantageously employed.

Sterility.—The inaptitude of the uterus for conception depends on such varied causes that no mineral water can be considered a specific remedy. Nevertheless, by the relief of the causes, some of which are named in the preceding pages, mineral waters may prove corrective.

When the origin is an enfeebled condition of the generative organs, without other complication, bathing in waters highly charged with carbonic-acid gas is an efficient stimulant, often leading to the desired result. Chalybeate waters and sea-bathing also exercise a favorable influence in certain cases.

DISEASES OF THE SKIN.

The reputation which mineral waters have obtained in the treatment of skin-disease is based almost entirely on their efficacy in a single well-defined class of those diseases; i. e., the *dartrous* or *herpetic*. These diseases, according to M. Hardy, are distinguished as follows: "We call *dartres* various non-contagious elementary lesions of the skin, often hereditary, reproducing themselves in an almost constant manner, presenting itching as a chief symptom, always disposed to invade new regions, habitually chronic, and in which there is no cicatrix left after cure, although there may have been ulcerations."[1] In persons who are subjects of the dartrous or herpetic diathesis the cutaneous surface is usually dry, and perspiration does not take place readily. They generally eat freely. The skin is often the seat of itching, even in the absence of eruption, and is exceedingly susceptible, slight excesses in taking liquor, drinking coffee, certain articles of food, as shell-fish, lobsters, or crabs, irritant frictions, or the application of a plaster, developing cutaneous eruptions. But not only is the skin the seat of dartrous maladies—there are also various affections of the mucous membrane, embracing granular sore-throat, dartre of the nose, certain asthmas, chronic bronchitic affections, and catarrhal disorders of the genito-urinary organs. It is a singular fact that in some cases the sudden disappearance of an external manifestation of this diathesis, eczema, for example, is followed by an attack of bronchitis, and on the subsidence of the bronchitis the eczema returns. In some women the cure of eczema is immediately followed by leucorrhœa. Similar results sometimes succeed the disappearance of psoriasis.

The skin-diseases which belong to this diathesis are eczema, lichen, psoriasis, and pityriasis. The different forms of eczema are sometimes called moist dartres, while the others are termed

[1] "Leçons sur les Maladies de la Peau," Paris, 1860, p. 19.

dry or scaly dartres. These eruptions are all chronic in character, perpetuating themselves indefinitely for months and years.

Eczema.—Humid scale or tetter is one of the most frequent skin-diseases. It is characterized by the development of small vesicles and vesico-pustules, or by a red and thickened epidermis, from which there is a more or less abundant serous or sero-purulent secretion, which may form crusts and terminate by a scaly desquamation. The eruption is accompanied by excessive itching. Though a chronic disease, it may sometimes run its course in six or eight weeks, to reappear, however, in a few months or a year—the person suffering from it never feeling sure of freedom from an attack. There are many varieties of the disease, named according to the aspect, configuration, and location of the eruption. *Impetigo* is one of the most frequent forms.

In the treatment of this malady *sulphur-waters* often prove efficient, especially those of the subdivisions known as *saline sulphur-waters.* In those cases, however, which present acute symptoms during the invasion, such as excessive fatigue, headache, pain in the back, and fever, mineral waters should not be employed. Those waters which are highly mineralized should always be used with care, because of the irritation frequently produced.

The waters are used internally and in the form of baths. After having taken a number of baths all the local manifestations of the disease are often increased; but, on suspending or moderating the baths, the irritation is allayed, to be again excited by their use. The patient may quit the baths despairing and discontented; the eczema is lighted up once or twice afterward, and thence ceases. In other cases, however, the eruption gradually disappears, under the use of the waters, without occurrence of irritative phenomena. In order to obtain permanent relief from this malady, it is usually necessary to resort to the springs for several successive seasons. Not all cases, however, are susceptible of cure, though amelioration may always be anticipated.

Lichen.—This excessively chronic malady is characterized at its commencement by clusters of papules, surrounded by a red halo. This halo finally disappears, leaving the skin rough, thick, and seamed. The seat of the eruption is usually intensely itchy, and upon it there are small crusts or minute scales.

The waters most suited to the treatment of this disease are the *sulphur* and *saline sulphur*. In certain cases complicated by gastralgia, *alkaline waters* prove valuable.[1] The continued use of the waters in the form of baths is a necessity, and, in some instances, it is desirable to push the treatment until the bath-eruption, *la poussée*, is established, and a cure by substitution inaugurated.

Psoriasis.—Dry scall, or scaly tetter, is characterized by thick, dry, white, shiny scales, the skin beneath being dry, much thickened, of a dull-red color, and the seat of more or less itching. When the eruption is of long duration, the skin is frequently seamed and cracked. The patches of the eruption are various in form; and on whatever part of the person they occur, they will also be found, as a rule, in the vicinity of the elbows and knees. In this, as in all dartrous maladies, the *sulphur-waters* are the most efficient, used internally and in the way of baths. On this point Hardy expresses himself thus: "In fine, there is a remedy which should serve to confirm the cure, and which sometimes alone suffices to produce a cure in cases where all other means have failed, in *psoriasis inveterata*, for example—I mean sulphur-waters."[2] Durand-Fardel counsels the *saline-sulphur* waters internally, and that prolonged warm baths be employed until the eruptions known as *la poussée* or *Bad Friesel* are produced. The *thermal* waters containing but a small proportion of ingredients are of decided value for this purpose.

Pityriasis.—The most frequent manifestation of this disease is that occupying the head, and known as dandruff. It is only when it exhibits itself on other parts of the body that

[1] Hardy, *op. cit.*, p. 100.
[2] "Leçons sur les Maladies de la Peau," Paris, 1860, p. 120.

mineral waters are of much avail. It is the mildest exhibition of the dartrous diathesis, but exceedingly rebellious to treatment. *Sulphur-waters* are those that should be employed.

We have given the dartrous maladies in which mineral waters are eminently beneficial. Besides these diseases, there are various affections of the skin, due to scrofula or syphilis, in which mineral waters prove efficacious. In those of *scrofulous* character, the *saline-sulphur* waters are preferable. In *syphilitic* diseases of the skin, we must choose between *sulphur* and *thermal* waters. Neither, however, are alone sufficient for cure. In addition, it may be noted that, in certain inveterate cases of *acne* and *prurigo*, *sulphur-waters* prove curative.

In the application of mineral waters to diseases of the skin, baths are more to be relied on than internal administration, though both should be combined. In certain inveterate chronic diseases of the skin, it is desirable gradually to prolong the duration of the baths, and continue them until the eruptions known as *la poussée* are fully established.[1] In this way, the original disease is replaced by a different eruption, which disappears without a return of the old malady. For the purpose of producing the bath-eruption, the *thermal waters*, containing but a small proportion of ingredients, are sometimes exceedingly efficient, and produce a cure without other agency.

SURGICAL DISEASES.

Anchylosis.—This term is applied to stiffness or immobility of a joint. There are two kinds, the true and the false. In the former, adhesions of bone form between the articular surfaces; in the latter, there are no adhesions, but the ligaments and tendons are thickened by deposits, or have lost the power of motion by want of use. The conditions which produce false anchylosis are met with when a limb has been confined in an apparatus for a long time after fracture. And the same result may follow after dislocation or sprain. In each instance, there is usually an inflammatory deposit, resulting from the

[1] Hardy, "Leçons sur les Maladies de la Peau," deuxième partie, p. 126.

original injury. The thickening of the fibrinous and tendinous structures, which accompanies rheumatism, frequently produces a similar anchylosis. The want of use, which follows paralysis, often leaves a joint in a condition of false anchylosis.

From whatever cause *false anchylosis* occurs, decided benefit or cure is always to be expected from the appropriate application of mineral waters. The waters to be preferred are *thermal waters*, of the sulphur or saline class. A high degree of thermality is essential. The waters are to be employed in the form of warm baths to the body, and hot douches to the joint. The douches should be accompanied with shampooing and friction. The internal use of waters at the same time probably aid in procuring absorption of exudations. It should, however, be stated that thermal waters, containing an exceedingly small proportion of constituents, seem to produce equally good results, showing that the benefits result almost entirely from the outward application. Mineral mud-baths are much used abroad in these cases, and are supposed to aid the absorptive process.

Contractions.—This term is here used to indicate the shortening and rigidity of muscles, often rendering a limb almost useless, and causing deformity. It arises from a variety of causes, such as rheumatism, scrofula, gout, syphilis, or external injury. In the treatment of this condition by mineral waters, regard is to be given to these causes; but the especial virtue of the waters depends on the warm baths and hot douches, such as are found at thermal springs. That *thermal water*, therefore, should be selected which by virtue of its constituents especially acts on the originating cause. Mineral mud-baths are also thought to aid in these cases.

Hydrarthrosis.—This term is applied both to dropsy of a joint and that severe tubercular disease known as white-swelling.

Dropsy of a joint may arise from external injury, or it may depend on a rheumatic, scrofulous, or gouty constitution. Sometimes it is a result of syphilis. When the condition is chronic, mineral waters prove valuable in the form of warm baths and douches. Those *thermal waters* are especially valuable which answer the constitutional indications.

White-swelling is an exceedingly formidable disease, affecting the joints. It occurs chiefly, if not alone, in scrofulous subjects. The malady is usually subacute in its progress, and therefore not adapted to treatment by mineral waters. When peculiarly chronic in its course, the general health may be improved by a resort to springs, and absorption may be aided by baths and douches. These applications should, however, be employed with extreme reserve, and by no means relied on alone.

Coxalgia.—*Hip-joint disease* is but a manifestation of white-swelling in that articulation, and the restrictions given regarding the subjection of white-swelling to mineral-water treatment are equally applicable.

Caries.—The ulceration of bone is usually the result of scrofula or syphilis, though there may have been some external injury as the exciting cause. During the inflammatory stage, mineral waters should not be used; but, when this has passed away, great benefit may be derived from the employment of appropriate waters. The *thermal sulphur-waters* produce the best results, especially those of the saline subdivision. The water is taken internally, applied locally in the way of fomentations, and injected into fistulous tracts. Baths and douches are also used. The treatment should be conducted with care, lest too great irritation be produced.

Necrosis, which is but a result of caries, is subject to the same treatment.

Ulcers.—By this designation we refer to chronic ulcers, which sometimes endure for months and years. It frequently occurs that these ulcers are healed under the use of mineral waters. When they depend on scrofula or syphilis we may readily expect such results from waters adapted to those conditions. In other cases, where there is no marked constitutional indication, such as varicose ulcers, the internal and local application of waters often has a marked influence, causing an irritable or indolent ulcer to form healthy granulations and finally heal, although in the case of varicose ulcers there is always probability of a return. The waters which are most noted for the cure of ulcers are the *saline* and *sulphur*. They are employed both internally, locally, and in the form of a bath. At some springs the *sulfurin*, or *barégine*, which forms in the reservoirs, is used as a local application, and is supposed to be of especial utility; but, as far as discovered, it acts only by the water with which it is saturated.

Old Wounds.—It often results from bullet-wounds, and those produced by pieces of shell, that the bullet, the piece of shell, or a portion of the clothing, passes deeply into the muscular structures, is embedded there, and cannot be withdrawn. Under these circumstances the superficial wound may heal and reopen repeatedly, or it may not heal at all, or the wound may heal, but the person may be conscious of some foreign body within the tissues which continually annoys. Again, the cause of irritation may be a spicula of necrosed bone.

Under any of these conditions remarkable benefit frequently results from mineral waters. They are employed in the form of hot baths, hot douches, and internally. For this purpose *thermal waters* of high temperature yield the best results. Under their action the exudations which imprison the foreign body are converted into pus; the ball, piece of shell, or clothing, is loosened from its lodgment and soon finds its way to the surface. During the course of treatment, care is to be taken that the stimulant action of the waters, and the suppuration produced, be not carried too far. The contractions of muscles and joints, following wounds, are likewise favorably influenced by *thermal waters.*

So much reliance is placed on mineral waters in these and other affections, that the military establishment of France possesses five hospitals, at as many different springs, for the benefit of soldiers. Austria has a like number. Prussia sends her sick soldiers, in need of mineral waters, to Töplitz.

CHAPTER VII.

SUGGESTIONS.

A CERTAIN disease being given, it is always a question which spring to select. In the answer a number of considerations are involved.

In the arrangement of this work each spring is grouped in a certain class, but, while the waters of the class possess marked properties, which pertain to each spring in the class, nevertheless these springs present a certain individuality depending on auxiliary constituents. Thus, an alkaline water may also contain carbonate and sulphate of lime in considerable proportion, or, it may be, chloride of sodium, which forms the principal secondary constituent; or, again, a small proportion of iron may be present. And the same remark will apply to saline waters, sulphur-waters, chalybeate waters, thermal waters, etc. Now, in each instance, the water not only possesses the action referable to the class, but, in addition, this action is modified or reënforced by these auxiliary constituents, some known and perhaps some unknown. Hence, in designating the water suitable for a certain person, we must consult his individuality, and also the individuality of the spring; to inquire, in the case of the patient, whether the disease is predominated by a particular diathesis, such as the rheumatic, gouty, scrofulous, or dartrous, and, in regard to the water, whether its constituents, both principal and auxiliary, meet the indications both of the disease and the diathesis. Thus in a case of catarrh of the bladder, in a rheumatic subject, waters frankly alkaline or calcic should be employed; in a scrofulous patient alkaline waters, containing considerable chloride of sodium, would be appropriate—the muriated alkalines; in a dartrous subject calcic waters, containing sulphuretted hydrogen, that is, a calcic sulphur-water; in a patient decidedly anæmic, an alkaline water containing a proportion of iron, a mild alkaline chalybeate. This is the theory of the prescription of waters, and it is always best to consider the question in this way; nevertheless it must be acknowledged that in our present ignorance of the exact entities of disease, and the definite physiological action of chemicals and combinations, we are not to rely too implicitly on this method.

Besides the constitution of a water, it is necessary in many instances to consider the location of a spring, its elevation, temperature, and climatology. While some diseases improve more readily at a resort from two to four thousand feet above the sea, others do not profit by a mountain climate.

Some diseases do well in a comparatively dry atmosphere, and are injuriously affected by one that is moist. An exceedingly cool climate is adapted to one, while another is relieved in a warm region. Unfortunately, the meteorological observations necessary to solve these problems have been taken at but few springs in this country.

The surroundings of a spring are also to be considered. For certain patients, nothing could be more unfortunate than to sojourn at one of the crowded, fashionable resorts, where continual excitement prevails and appropriate accommodations are obtained with difficulty; while others, by the gayety and conviviality that are found there, would be wakened from a despondent condition and led to forget their ills.

The *season*,[1] as it is termed, usually commences the 1st of

[1] Invalids will do well to correspond with the proprietor of the spring, or the hotel, previous to commencing the journey. A letter addressed thus, at the commencement of or during the season, will always receive attention:

If but one hotel at the spring:	If several hotels at the spring:
Proprietor of........(naming the spring) ......(naming the county) ....(naming the State)	Proprietor of.........(naming the hotel) ....(naming the spring) ......(naming the county) .....(naming the State)

If the name of the springs and post-office are not the same, the name of the post-office must be inserted. The average price per day at the hotels is three dollars; and, per month, from sixty to eighty dollars. For parties, and persons remaining a long time, special arrangements can be made. Rooms can usually be secured in advance.

June and closes the 1st of October, though there are some resorts that are prepared to receive visitors throughout the year. The best time, as a rule, to commence treatment is in June or July; these months, however, are named only as being convenient. Mineral waters can be taken, and their beneficial effects secured, at any time of the year. The old idea, that they were not admissible in winter, has been entirely abandoned. Many diseases do not admit of delay, and for this purpose the bottled waters are applicable. However, there is not the care used in bottling waters that should be observed. When waters contain considerable gas, the bottles should always be closely sealed. There are but few waters that are at all adapted to shipment in barrels. The gases escape, and some of the chemical ingredients are decomposed by contact with the wood; and when these objections do not obtain, owing to the absence of gas in the water or salts that are decomposed by contact with organic matter, still the water often partakes of the taste of the wood. At some springs an extract of the water is made; that is, the water is boiled down in an iron or porcelain-lined vessel till the salts are precipitated, then form the extract, or salts. A certain quantity of these salts, dissolved in a definite quantity of water, is supposed to represent the spring-water. Although they may answer a good purpose when the spring-water cannot be obtained, they do not represent it accurately. In boiling, all the gases contained in the spring-water are driven off, and several chemical changes occur: sulphurets are converted into sulphates, bicarbonates into carbonates, and the protoxide of iron into the peroxide; also, the proportion of the constituents to each other is not maintained. In Europe, medicated soaps are sometimes prepared with the precipitated salts. At Krankenheil, in Bavaria, so-called iodine-soda and iodine-soda-sulphur soaps are made, and are said to be successfully used in chronic diseases of the skin.

"What shall we do?" is a question always asked on arrival at the spring which has been chosen as a place of resort. The answer is simple: If you are well, if you are there only for rest and recreation, assimilate yourself as rapidly as possible with the pleasures and society of the place; remembering, however, and practising the trite maxim, "Temperance in all things." Here are assembled a large number of persons, whose desires are similar to your own, and the community of interests produces the following result: The morning is passed in repairing to the spring and drinking of the water, in cheerful conversation, and excursions; the afternoon, in croquet, games, lounging, and preparations for the dance; and the evening is given to promenading and the festivities of the ball. At many of the springs a band of musicians performs in the park during the after-dinner hours and at tea-time.

What is the best time for taking the waters? The morning hours before breakfast, and in the afternoon before tea. That one may take the water properly, he should cultivate the healthful virtue of early rising, and the not less laudable virtue of early retiring. It cannot be expected that the most potent water will antidote the dissipations of enormous dinners, imbibition of spirituous liquors, and continuous dancing till the morning hours.

The quantity of water that may be taken varies so much at different springs that no fixed rule can be given. It may be stated, however, in a general way, that from two to three moderate-sized glasses—tumblers—in the morning, and two or three more during the day, may be taken. In drinking the water, from fifteen to twenty minutes should elapse between each glass; and, during the interval, it is well to promenade through the neighboring groves, or, in damp weather, under the covered walks, which should be contiguous to the spring. From half an hour to an hour should pass before the succeeding meal is taken. The practice of deluging the stomach with water is extremely reprehensible, and sometimes produces serious results. I have known violent inflammation of the kidneys, followed by chronic disease, established in this way. The temperature of water preferable for a cure is from 50° to 88° Fahr. If excessively cold, it is not readily absorbed, and acts injuriously on the stomach and intestines.

The production of crisis is no longer considered necessary to the curative action of waters, neither is preliminary treatment required other than, in some instances, simple remedies to control slight febrile conditions, depending on the fatigue of a journey. In the olden time, the patient underwent an enormous amount of dosing before it was considered proper for him to take the water. Boileau, in a letter to Racine, dated 21st July, 1687, thus describes the process. He says: "I have been purged and bled, and nothing more remains for me to undergo of all the formalities considered necessary before taking the waters. The medicines which I have taken to-day have, as they tell me, done me all the good in the world; for they have caused me to fall down four or five times from weakness, and have thrown me into a state in which I can hardly stand upright. To-morrow I am to begin the great work—I mean to say, that to-morrow I am to begin to take the waters."

The use of mineral waters by old persons, children, and pregnant women, should be exceedingly guarded. Formerly it was thought that pregnancy was an absolute bar to the employment of mineral waters. That idea, however, is no longer entertained. Under some circumstances, they have a beneficial effect on both mother and child when taken at this period.

During the treatment by mineral waters excesses of the table should be rigidly avoided. The combination of mineral water, mountain air, exercise, and amusement, frequently gives an appetite to which the person may have long been a stranger. Especially is this so in cases of dyspepsia; and, although the return of appetite is an indication of the favorable action of the water, permanent relief may be entirely frustrated by gratification of the palate. As a rule, the diet should be plain and nutritious when the full alterative effect of the water is desired.

The number of days necessary for treatment cannot be designated. A conventional period of twenty-one days is frequently named, but many cases require treble and quadruple that time. In some maladies, where it is desired to eradicate a morbid habit of the body, it is best to return to the appropriate water for two or three successive seasons. Patients need not be alarmed if, shortly after commencing the use of the waters, their symptoms are somewhat aggravated. This perturbation of the system frequently occurs, only to be followed by relief. A suspension or diminution of the water for a short time is all that is required. Occasionally there may be no decided benefit at the time, to be followed by relief on return home. As remarked by Trousseau, mineral waters are remedies which act "*à longue portée.*"

After a patient has repaired to a spring which, according to the best obtainable information is suited to his malady, he should remain there until he has given the waters a fair trial, and not vacillate from one resort to another. There are valetudinarians—especially to be met with in the Virginia springs region—who go the rounds from one spring to another, drinking a few days of this water, then of that, apparently possessed of the idea that some mysterious spirit pervades the springs, and, if the suitable one is found, renewed life will thrill through the blood with the first draught. The search of Ponce de Leon for the fountain of perpetual youth was not more quixotic. Just as well might one enter an apothecary's and dose himself with each drug, *seriatim*, hoping thus to discover the medicine adapted to his malady.

Invalids should, as a rule, consult the resident physician on arrival at the springs, who should be familiar with the precise action of the water, and adjust the dose to the varying conditions. For this purpose, the patient should bring with him a statement of his case from his physician, which will enable the resident physician more readily to possess himself of complete knowledge of the course of the disease. Unfortunately, many of the physicians at springs in this country are there for a single season only, and therefore have not the inducement to become thoroughly acquainted with the action of the water, which is secured by permanence. Proprietors of springs will do well to give close attention to the medical efficiency of their resorts. We cannot refrain from suggesting the impolicy of proprictors or physicians encouraging or permitting patients to remain when the waters are manifestly inapplicable to the disease. Neither is it advantageous for proprietors to advertise their waters as curative of a large number of maladies for which they have no special application. The springs are thus reduced to the level of quack nostrums, and the trifling present gain of such a course is more than counterbalanced by the loss of reputation which the water suffers by failure to cure or relieve.

Baths, which are an essential element in the treatment of many diseases by mineral waters, are usually taken during the morning. If breakfast be taken before the bath, it should be light, and precede it at least an hour. In some instances, the bath may be taken just before bedtime. The form of bath desirable varies with the disease. For general purposes, however, the swimming or "piscina" bath is preferable, the patient having opportunity for exercise. All fear of contracting contagious diseases in these baths is proved without foundation. The flow of water, however, should be sufficient for frequent renewal of the entire volume, and the chamber should be well ventilated. As a proper summary of the course to be followed at the springs, I quote the words of Alibert:

"When you arrive at the waters, act as you would do if you were entering the temple of Æsculapius, and leave behind you at the door all the passions which have been tormenting your mind and agitating your soul. Once there, abstain from imprudence, and do not exceed the prescribed doses, as so many invalids have done at all times, for Pliny already complained of the evil. 'Many sick people,' he says, 'take a pride in having remained for hours together in very hot baths, or in drinking unmeasured quantities of mineral waters, which are both equally dangerous.' Lead a quiet, calm, tranquil life; bathe and drink with moderation, and the water will gradually exercise its beneficial influence over you. Your sufferings will insensibly pass away in the precious liquid, and your forces will become invigorated."

In Europe, it is customary at some resorts to join the internal administration of whey—the *whey-cure*—to the use of mineral water. Whey, as nearly every one knows, is the yellowish, watery fluid which remains after milk has been coagulated, and the solid portion separated by straining. It possesses a mawkish taste. The principal constituents of a pound of whey are as follows: chloride of potassium, 13 to 15 grains; cloride of sodium, two to three grains; carbonate of soda, three to four grains; milk-sugar, 380 to 500 grains. Besides, it contains phosphates, and small quantities of iodine and fluorine. Whey usually produces a laxative effect, and even diarrhœa, though there are exceptions, in which it causes constipation. It is distinctly diuretic. As a rule, it is easily digested, and improves the appetite, though, taken in large quantities, it causes dyspepsia and diarrhœa. It is recommended in chronic laryngitis, bronchitis, phthisis pulmonalis, and chronic gastric catarrh. It is customary to mix equal portions of warm whey and mineral water. It may be of some value as an adjuvant; but the entire subject of whey-cure is much in the dark.

Abroad it is not unusual for patients to seek the *grape-cure* in the fall, after a season at the springs. The favorite resorts for this purpose are Bingen, Dürkheim, Vevay, Montreux, and Meran. Whatever may be said of the utility of this medication, it is certainly a pleasant one, and, if of value, can readily be adopted in this country.

The composition of Clairette grape-juice, in 1,000 parts, is given as follows:

Water	824.00
Grape-sugar	140.00
Gum and dextrine	5.00
Albumen and nitrogenous matter	15.00
Iron	0.63
Potassa	1.00
Soda	2.50
Lime	1.80
Magnesia	0.90
Tartaric acid	4.30
Malic acid	2.90

From this analysis, it will readily be seen that, in one pound of the grapes named, there would be about forty grains of salts, formed by the union of the organic acids with the bases soda, lime, magnesia, potassa, and iron. The quantity of grape-sugar would be about two ounces. The proportion of these constituents varies, however, with the species of grape, and the soil on which it is grown. The juice usually contains a proportion of inorganic salts, in addition to the salts named.

A comparison of the inorganic constituents of grape-juice with the Grand Grille, at Vichy, has been made as follows:

In Ten Thousand Parts.	Grape-Juice.	Grand Grille.
Chlorine	0.26	3.24
Sulphuric acid	1.09	1.64
Phosphoric acid	4.71	0.70
Silicic acid	3.44	0.70
Potassa	17.94 } 23.76	1.82 } 24.12
Soda	5.82 }	22.30 }
Magnesia	2.76	0.97
Lime	5.09	1.69
Iron and magnesia	1.50	0.12
Total	42.61	33.18

The quantity of grapes usually consumed varies from one and a half pounds to six or eight pounds per day, the pulp and juice alone being taken.

The action of grapes consumed in this way is as follows: During the first few days a cathartic effect is produced, frequent fluid evacuations resulting. After some days the purgative action is more regular, and there are several evacuations each day. In some instances, however, there is no laxative effect. Usually the appetite is increased, digestion is improved, and the fæces are darker; the secretion of urine is also augmented. Sometimes there is considerable excitement of the system during the beginning of the treatment; the pulse is more frequent, and there is congestion of the head. This, however, soon passes off, although palpitation of the heart, epistaxis, and even hæmoptysis, are said sometimes to result. Grapes are said to be useful in abdominal plethora, scrofula, chronic catarrh, tuberculosis, and gravel.

CHAPTER VIII.

THE SKIN.

Introductory to treatment of the subject of baths we give a description of the skin, one of the most important emunctories for purification of the blood, and that which is directly subject to the influence of bathing.

Anatomically, the skin consists of two layers: the external, called the epidermis, cuticle, or scarf-skin, and the internal, known as the cutis vera, or true skin.

The true skin is a dense, elastic tissue, permeated in every direction by blood-vessels, nerves, and lymphatics. Within its substance are the sebaceous follicles, usually discharging their oily contents beside the point of emergence of the hair. The perspiratory glands are also seated here. The papillary layer of the true skin consists of numbers of small conical prominences, quite irregularly distributed. The papillæ, when aggregated in masses and arranged in rows, constitute the ridges and furrows that may be seen on the palm of the hand and the sole of the foot. The papillæ are supplied with a large number of nerves and blood-vessels, rendering them exceedingly sensitive. The true skin varies in thickness in various parts of the body, being most dense on the back, outer sides of the limbs, and the palms of the hands and soles of the feet. This thickness may arise from different causes, sometimes being due to an increase in the corion—the substratum of the true skin—at others, to an accumulation of papillary eminences, to subserve the sense of touch, when great delicacy of feeling is required. We may form an idea of the extreme vascularity of this tissue, and the infinite number of blood-vessels with which it is permeated, from the fact that the point of the finest needle can nowhere penetrate the surface without blood being drawn and a sensation of pain produced.

The epidermis, or cuticle, is a defensive covering for the sensitive surface of the true skin, being accurately moulded to the papillary layer. It varies in thickness. When it is exposed to continued friction or pressure and atmospheric influence, it becomes thick, hard, and horny in texture, while that which is in contact with the papillary layer is soft and cellular in structure. The cuticle is formed by the exudation of cells from the papillary layer, the outer cells falling off as scurf, in scale-like particles. The color of the skin is due to pigment-cells found in the deep layer of the epidermis. The color of this pigment varies in different nations, and gives the characteristic hue. The epidermis is pierced by the excretory ducts of the sebaceous follicles and sweat-glands, which discharge their secretions upon its surface.

The sweat-glands are small, round, reddish bodies, consisting of one or more exceedingly small convoluted tubes, twisted and wound together in the most intricate manner. These characteristics are only perceptible under the microscope. Surrounding these glands are numerous blood-vessels. From them proceed the excretory ducts, which terminate at the surface of the epidermis. It is these glands that secrete perspiration—a watery, saline fluid. Although each of these glands is so minute, when we consider them in the aggregate we shall arrive at surprising figures. Mr. Wilson tells us as follows: "To arrive at something like an estimate of the value of the perspiratory system in relation to the rest of the organism, I counted the perspiratory pores on the palm of the hand, and found 3,528 in a square inch. Now, each of these pores being the aperture of a little tube of about a quarter of an inch long, it follows that in a square inch of skin on the palm of the hand there exists a length of tube equal to 882 inches, or 73½ feet. Surely such an amount of drainage as 73 feet in every square inch of skin—assuming this to be the average for the whole body—is something wonderful; and the thought naturally intrudes itself, 'What if this drainage were obstructed?'

"On the pulps of the fingers, where the ridges of the sensitive layer of the true skin are somewhat finer than on the palm of the hand, the number of pores on a square inch a little exceeded that of the palm; and on the heel, where the ridges are coarser, the number of pores in the square inch was 2,268, and the length of tube 567 inches, or 47 feet. To obtain an estimate of the length of tube of the perspiratory system of the whole surface of the body, I think that 2,800 might be taken as a fair average of the number of pores in the square inch; and 700, consequently, as the number of inches in length. Now, the number of square inches of surface in a man of ordinary height and bulk is 2,500; the number of pores, therefore, 7,000,000, and the number of inches of perspiratory tube, 1,750,000—that is, 145,833 feet or 48,600 yards, or nearly 28 miles."

The sebaceous glands are small, sacculated, glandular organs, found in all parts of the skin, but most frequently occurring in the face. Their orifice opens most frequently into the hair-follicles. The purpose of the oily secretion which they discharge is to lubricate the surface of the body, keeping the skin soft and pliable, and protecting it from the external air; it also gives gloss and softness to the hair. This fluid is much more abundantly secreted by the races that live in warm climates than those that inhabit cold ones.

Within the orifice of the sebaceous tubes a curious parasite, called the entozoon folliculorum, is frequently found. It occurs in great numbers in the inhabitants of large cities, whose skin is inclined to be torpid in function.

Function of the Skin.—In order that we may more clearly comprehend this, it is well to remember that the skin is continuous with the mucous membrane at the various orifices of the body—the mouth, nose, etc.—and that there is a striking similarity in the formation of the two structures. Indeed, we may term the one the external lining, the other the internal; the being man, with the various tissues of blood, nerve, muscle, and bone, being formed and nourished between these two linings, the mouth, lungs, stomach, intestines, liver, and kidneys, being but adaptations of this mucous membrane to the offices of assimilation and depuration; and, in the same manner, the skin performs these offices, though not in such a multiplicity of ways.

Absorption.—Undoubtedly the skin acts more readily by exhalation and secretion than absorption; but that it is absorbent in action is certain, though the subject has been considerably discussed, and many have taken the negative side of the question. For most fluids and substances capable of solution by the liquids of the body the skin is absorbent. It is related by Theophrastus that the odor of strongly-scented cataplasms, when placed over the stomach, is detected in the eructations. The treatment of various diseases by inunction with medicated ointments is practised at the present day with perfect confidence and certainty as to absorption of the drug. And when the dry epidermis is removed by a blister, and the cutis vera exposed, "medicines applied produce similar effects in doses but little larger than when they are made to act directly upon the gastric mucous membrane."

There has been much doubt whether the skin absorbs water or medical substances dissolved in water. Dr. Dill, of Edinburgh, concluded, from a series of experiments, that the body generally, but not uniformly, increases in weight in a warm bath (86° to 102° Fahr.). Dr. James Murray obtained similar results in baths from 88° to 104° Fahr.—that is, the body usually gained in weight; and he showed by tests applied to the urine that gallic acid is absorbed by a person immersed in a bath containing infusion of galls. Westrumb found the prussiate of potassa in the blood and urine of persons who had used a foot-bath containing this salt; and the urine, as well as the serum of the blood, was colored brown when the arms were kept immersed in an infusion of rhubarb.

The more recent experiments of Durian and Clemens tend to reconcile the apparent contradictory results that have been sometimes obtained. Prof. Alfred Stillé, of Philadelphia, sums up the observations referred to in these words: "By these experiments it is rendered clear that for every person there is a temperature at which the body, immersed in water, neither gains nor loses in weight; while, on the one hand, above this point it exhales more than it absorbs, and therefore becomes lighter, and, on the other hand, below this point it absorbs more than it exhales and grows heavier. Thus, in a bath of from 72° to 77° Fahr., the skin *absorbs* on an average 248 grains in a quarter of an hour, 442 grains in three-quarters of an hour, and nearly 700 grains in an hour and a quarter.[1] On the other hand, in baths at an average temperature of 97° Fahr., the body *loses* weight at the rate of 744 grains in fifteen minutes, 1,271 grains in thirty minutes, and 2,054 grains in forty-five minutes. In a bath of 113° Fahr. the body lost more than a pound in weight in the course of fifteen minutes. By this simple statement it becomes evident that, even in the case of water, exhalation is a more active function of the skin than absorption."[2] It is quite probable, from the conflicting results of experiments as to absorption, that, on the one hand, the body loses a portion of fluid in a tepid bath, and, on the other, absorbs an equal or nearly equal quantity; that is, there is an interchange of fluids. It may be noted that experiments in warm baths show that the *urine becomes alkaline, as a rule*, even when nitric acid or sulphate of quinine is dissolved in the water.

Transpiration.—The secretion of oil by the sebaceous follicles, and its purpose of lubricating the skin, have already been mentioned. The office, however, most worthy of notice in connection with this subject is that of perspiration—the elimination of carbonic acid and perspiration by the sweat-glands. The ingenious calculation by which it is shown that the combined length of the sweat-tubes, in an individual, is about twenty-eight miles has already been noticed. It may be asked, if these glands are constantly active, continually conveying

[1] Recent researches of Jamin and De Laurés throw doubt on this point. They affirm that the loss is large between 75° and 82° Fahr.

[2] Stillé's "Therapeutics," vol. i., pp. 56, 57.

their burden of perspiration to the surface of the skin, why is not that surface continually moist? We answer, because the fluid is eliminated so gradually that it passes off imperceptibly in vapor as rapidly as it is formed. However, we all know how, during vigorous exercise and the heat of summer, it is immediately seen on the surface in large beads of fluid. This fluid is composed mostly of water, but, besides, we find carbonic acid, acetate of ammonia, phosphate of soda and lime, carbonate of lime, chloride of sodium, sulphate of soda, muriate of ammonia, and traces of iron and animal matter. The quantity thus exhaled has been estimated as about two and a half pounds per day—larger than the amount given off by the lungs. It must not, however, be understood that all of this quantity is exhaled by the sweat-glands and sebaceous glands; the larger proportion is the result of simple evaporation from the surface of the skin.

The amount of discharge from the skin varies at different periods of the day, and under the varied conditions of our systems. Immediately after taking food the process is checked, but when digestion is fully established it is most abundant. The conditions of the atmosphere exercise a marked influence; when it is hot and dry, then transpiration is exceedingly active, while a moist atmosphere has an opposite effect.

The skin also acts the part of a respiratory organ, by absorbing oxygen and giving off carbonic acid, thus aiding the lungs in this important interchange of the gaseous constituents of the blood. Indeed, respiration is performed by the skin alone in some of the inferior animals. If one of the higher animals, in which the skin resembles that of a man in function, be enclosed in a bag of caoutchouc, leaving the head only exposed, it soon dies, as though asphyxiated, the heart and lungs being found gorged with blood, and the temperature of the body sometimes as much as 30° Fahr. below the normal standard.

Reflection upon the offices of the skin, which are almost unknown to the multitude, will impress forcibly upon us the exceeding importance of the bath as a sanitary and medicinal agent. If this continual discharge of aqueous elements is checked, may it not throw upon the other eliminators—the kidneys, the lungs, and the intestines—an excess of labor that will cause inflammation? If the twenty-eight miles of drainage are obstructed, may not the pent-up effete matter engender disease and death?

Taking cold—the sudden arrest of the function of the skin—is almost always followed by irritation of the mucous membrane of the lungs, kidneys and intestines, manifested by bronchitis, an excessive discharge of urine, and even nephritis or diarrhœa. These results, from the sudden arrest of the functions of the skin, are only mentioned by way of illustration. There is a long list of diseases in which obstruction of the skin is an exciting cause. Bathing is not only essential to a healthy and prolonged existence, but, through the stimulation of the action of the skin, in this way we may remove various morbid products of the organism which, by their accumulation in the system, are the source of disease.

CHAPTER IX.

BATHS.

The Cold Bath (70° Fahr. and below). — The primary phenomena of immersion in cold water are those of *sedation;* the more decided as the water is colder. They are diminished temperature and paleness of the skin, slower respiration and circulation of the blood, accompanied by panting and shivering. If the cold be great or long protracted, a sense of suffocation and constriction at the pit of the stomach is experienced, the skin is corrugated, the breathing is labored and convulsive, speech difficult, the circulation is depressed, the lips and even cheeks become bluish, the muscles are painful and seized with cramps, and, unless relieved, the person will lose his life.

On coming out of the bath, and while exposed to the air, the sensation of cold is increased; but in vigorous persons, as soon as the skin is dry, *reaction* takes place, a warm glow spreads over the surface, the muscles play with ease and elasticity, the mind is clear, and the person exhilarated.

Since the times of Musa, who cured the Emperor Augustus Cæsar of a supposed hopeless malady by the use of cold water, there have been repeated periods in which this useful remedy has been exalted into a panacea. Such it is not; but there are certain conditions of the system in which it is an efficient remedy.

The cold bath is most frequently used as a *tonic*, and is only applicable to persons who have sufficient vigor to procure prompt reaction. In this way it is more often employed to perpetuate an already healthy condition than to relieve disease. For the anæmic and depressed, needing tonics, other resources must be sought. There seems an incompatibility between the tonic effect of a cold bath and the fact that the bath itself is actually a sedative. This inconsistency, however, is only apparent. When we speak of the tonic action, it is only as a result, not as the immediate effect.

Cold applications are employed in an infinite number of ways in the treatment of disease. In fevers, the cold sponge-bath is a palliative, so acting by abstraction of heat. Active hæmorrhage, both external and internal, may frequently be controlled by cold applications: in the former acting directly, by contraction of the blood-vessels and tissues; in the latter, by reflex action, the sudden chill produced, as in hæmorrhage of the lungs, by application of cold to the chest, causing contraction of the capillary blood-vessels. In acute diseases of the brain, the continuous application of cold is of great advantage, lessening temperature by abstraction of heat and contracting the blood-vessels by direct action. Gout and rheumatism have sometimes been treated, in the acute stage, by application of cold to the affected part; but, though sometimes securing relief, the practice is not to be recommended, the cause of the disease still remaining in the system, ready to explode its force at some other point. Quite opposite to this is the action of the hot bath in this disease, which, by stimulating the excretory function of the skin, removes the cause.

As a guide to the use of the ordinary cold bath, we insert the following rules:

1. The most favorable *time* of day for taking a cold bath is on rising in the morning, or about noon.

2. The stomach should be empty when the bath is taken.

3. Exercise moderately before entering the bath and while in the bath; but the body *must not* be overheated on going into the water.

4. A cold bath should not be taken when fatigued.

5. The *duration* of a cold bath should not exceed five minutes.

6. The cold bath should be succeeded by friction of the surface, with a coarse towel or flesh-brush, till reaction is established.

7. If the cold bath is not followed by reaction, the duration has been too long, or cold bathing is not fitted for the individual.

8. The cold bath is not adapted to feeble or aged persons and infants.

9. Persons whose extremities or skin are usually cold should not use the cold bath.

10. Persons affected with *organic disease of the heart* should not take cold baths.

Baths between 70° and 85° Fahr. are denominated *temperate*, and from 85° to 92° Fahr. they are termed *tepid*. The latter range is that usually selected for the purpose of ordinary ablution. These baths abstract heat and lessen the frequency of the pulse in the same manner as the cold bath, though in much less degree.

The Warm Bath (92° to 98° Fahr.).—This may be termed the luxurious bath, that which the weary or the invalid enters with pleasure and quits reluctantly. Under its influence a sense of calm enjoyment and perfect tranquillity is experienced. Granville, in his glowing description of a bath in the Wildbad waters of Germany, well describes these sensations:

"After descending a few steps from the dressing-room into the bath-room, I walked over the warm, soft sand to the farthest end of the bath, and I lay myself down upon it, near the principal spring, resting my head on a clean wooden pillow. The soothing effect of the water as it came over me, up to the throat, transparent like the brightest gem or aqua-marine, soft, genially warm, and gently murmuring, I shall never forget. Millions of bubbles of gas rose from the sand and played around me, quivering through the lucid water as they ascended, and bursting at the surface, to be succeeded by others. The sensation produced, as these with their tremulous motion just *effleuraient* the surface of the body, . . . is not to be described. *It partakes of tranquillity and exhilaration; of the ecstatic state of a devotee, blended with the repose of an opium-eater. The head is calm, the heart is calm; yet there is neither drowsiness, stupefaction, nor numbness.*"

The physiological effects of the warm bath are as follows: There is diminution in the frequency of the pulse and a lessened number of respirations. The experiments of Marcard show that in baths of 96° Fahr., and below that temperature, the rapidity of the pulse is uniformly diminished. Dr. Lockette, of Virginia, in baths of 98° Fahr., found the pulse always reduced in frequency. In rare instances it was slightly increased on first immersion, but in a short time it fell below the normal standard, and so continued. In this respect there is a difference in individuals as to the amount of diminution of the pulse-beats, those whose pulse is usually rapid and excited showing the most decided variation. From these facts, and those given under the remarks on cold baths, we deduce the law that *in all baths of a temperature below the normal heat of the body*, 98° Fahr., *the pulse is diminished in frequency.*

Warm baths act decidedly on the functions of the skin; absorption and exhalation are much increased. In baths the temperature of which ranges between 86° and 96° Fahr., the absorption of water and medicinal salts seems most active.

The prolonged use of the warm bath, for days and weeks in succession, produces an eruption on the surface of the skin and febrile conditions, continuing for several days, known among the Germans as the *Bad-sturm*, or bath-fever. Formerly it was thought that the production of this critical fever was necessary to a cure; but this idea has been relinquished, and it is now usually considered as an indication of misuse of the bath, and a guide for diminishing the temperature or lessening the duration.

The warm bath may be considered, therapeutically, as *calming* and *restorative.* The person worn out by prolonged mental or physical exertion experiences in the warm bath a sense of quiet and relaxation, which is followed on quitting it, if the person do not remain too long, with a restoration of energy.

A dividing-line may clearly be drawn between the warm and the hot bath. To place the prominent points more definitely before the reader, the respective effects are shown in the following table:

WARM BATH. From 92° to 98° Fahr.	HOT BATH. Above 98° Fahr.
1. Calming and sedative.	1. Exciting.
2. Pulse *decreased* in frequency.	2. Pulse *increased* in frequency.
3. Respirations *decreased* in number.	3. Respirations *increased* in number.
4. Skin neither red nor congested.	4. Skin red and congested.
5. *Absorption* and exhalation of the skin increased.	5. *Exhalation* of the skin increased, and little or no absorption.
6. No determination of blood to the head.	6. Determination of blood to the head.
7. Secondary effects restorative.	7. Secondary effects depressing

The warm bath is applicable to many diseases. It calms nervous excitement, and has been used advantageously in mania, chorea, and hysteria. In *nephritis*, it allays pain, and aids the passage of *calculi. Congestions* and inflammations *of the liver* are also much improved by its use, in conjunction with other treatment. Conjoined with frictions and moderate exercise, it is also palliative in albuminuria. *Dysmenorrhœa* and *amenorrhœa* have been treated by warm baths from time immemorial. *Chronic metritis* is also subject to favorable influence by the warm bath. Many diseases of the skin are thereby rendered amenable to treatment, which otherwise baffle our best efforts. *Subacute rheumatism* and *gout* may be treated by warm baths, and even the more decidedly chronic types may be subjected to them when the hot bath cannot be used.

The following rules are applicable to the warm bath:

1. The best *time* for taking a warm bath is during the morning hours, and in some instances before retiring to bed.

2. The stomach should be empty at the time of the bath.

3. The *duration* of the warm bath may be from fifteen minutes to an hour, and sometimes longer.

4. The warm bath is applicable to almost all conditions of health or disease, but persons affected with organic disease of the heart or lungs should be careful in its use.

The Hot Bath (above 98° Fahr.).—The physiological effects of the hot bath are very different from those of a warm bath. During immersion in a hot bath, the skin becomes red, the pulse is increased in frequency, the respirations are increased in number, perspiration breaks forth on the parts not immersed, exhalation of the skin is greatly stimulated, the mind becomes confused, and, if too long continued, vertigo or even apoplexy may result. Dr. Lockette, of Virginia, whose pulse was 77, in a bath of 98° Fahr., tells us that, in a bath of 111° Fahr., it rose to 153 beats in a minute, and that it produced confusion of thought, partial delirium, *tinnitus aurium*, an inability to speak, dimness of sight, an intolerable pain in his head, with a most painful desire to make water. His sensations were precisely such as they are in a violent state of fever. There were great redness of the skin and flushing of the face. On raising himself out of the water, he almost swooned, and, being now covered with blankets, sweated very profusely. The results of the experiments of M. Rostan and M. Loude coincide with those obtained by Dr. Lockette. Liebermeister found the bodily temperature augmented by the hot bath. The extent to which exhalation of the skin is stimulated has been well shown by the experiments of Mosler, who proved that, in hot baths of high temperature, from one to two pounds' weight may be lost in the course of an hour. During a course of hot bathing a bath-fever sometimes occurs, similar to that described in treating of warm baths. There are constipation, a coated tongue, loss of appetite, nervous irritability, disturbed sleep, perspiration, palpitations, and eruptions on the skin, and a temporary discontinuance of the baths is indicated.

The diseases in which the hot bath is remedial are *chronic rheumatism*, *gout*, and chronic diseases of the skin, especially those of a scaly nature, such as *psoriasis*, *pityriasis*, and *lichen*, occurring in phlegmatic temperaments. In *neuralgias*, *paraplegia*, and *paralysis*, it is curative in a marked degree, especially when employed in the form of a hot douche. Dysmenorrhœa and amenorrhœa, associated with atonic conditions, are also favorably influenced by hot baths and douches. *Enlarged* and *contracted joints* are relieved by the same treatment. Engorgement of the abdominal viscera may be properly subjected to hot baths, and frequently with decided relief. In *tertiary syphilis*, the hot bath often acts as an indispensable adjuvant to cure. The stimulant effect on the excretory function of the skin, combined with proper medication, seems to eliminate the venereal poison with great certainty and rapidity. When the hot douche acts favorably in neuralgia, paralysis, and affections of the joints, it seems to do so by its local effect entirely. The blood-vessels, nerves, and lymphatics of the affected part, are stimulated to renewed vitality, which, on the one hand, relieves pain, and restores sensibility and motion, and on the other absorbs exudations and concretions.

Although hot baths form so potent a remedy, they should be employed with circumspection, and the effect closely observed from day to day. Venel asserts that, at Cauterets, a Spaniard died of hæmorrhage, from prolonged stay in a hot bath, and Buchan relates the case of a man who was attacked with paralysis, after the use of an excessively hot bath. The following rules will serve as a guide in the use of this bath:

1. The best *time* for taking a hot bath is during the morning.

2. The stomach should be empty, free from irritation, and the tongue clean.

3. The *duration* may be from five to fifteen minutes, and sometimes longer, according to temperature and condition.

4. The hot bath is more applicable to the middle-aged and old, than to young persons.

5. Plethoric persons should be guarded in the use of hot baths.

6. Those suffering from organic disease of the heart or lungs, or subject to vertigo, *should not* use *hot* baths.

7. The temperature of the hot bath usually employed, ranges from 102° to 110° Fahr.

Vapor-Bath.—In this bath the atmosphere is loaded with hot vapor. It acts rapidly in increasing the heat of the body, inasmuch as the body is not only heated by the surrounding hot medium, but, when perspiration would afford relief, evaporation is impeded by the already moist atmosphere. Owing to these conditions a high temperature of vapor-bath is intolerable, while a dry, hot-air bath may be taken at 212° Fahr., and higher, with impunity. In a vapor-bath of 120° Fahr., Fordyce found the pulse 145 after twenty minutes' stay. At a higher temperature, the pulse becomes more frequent and smaller, and, when the temperature reaches 170° Fahr., it can be borne but for a few moments without injury.

The physiological effects of the hot vapor-bath are congestion and redness of the skin, increase in frequency of the pulse, fulness of the head, oppression of the chest, arising from congestion of the lungs, and tendency to perspiration. Persons are often deceived by the seeming large quantity of perspiration on the skin, which is, in great part, only the condensation of vapor on the body. There is increase in the temperature of the body. Wiegand found that in a vapor-bath of 106° Fahr. a thermometer placed in the mouth rose from 99° to 102° Fahr. in five minutes, and reached 104° Fahr., when the temperature of the bath was increased to 110° Fahr. These observations may not, however, be altogether accurate, as the hot vapor entering the mouth would influence the thermometer; and, placed in the axilla, it does not mark so great change. But that the temperature of the body is decidedly increased is undoubted; and it is from this fact that the body so well tolerates the sudden transition from hot vapor to a cool shower-bath. The change is grateful and soothing, and is followed by copious perspiration under favorable conditions.

Russian Bath.—This is but a form of the hot vapor-bath. Under various forms it is used by all the inhabitants of Northern Europe—the Germans, Swedes, Norwegians, Russians—and, we are told, by the Indians of this continent. As employed in this country, it consists of antechambers, or dressing-rooms, warmed from 70° to 95° Fahr., and the bath-chamber. The latter is constructed of wood, and on one side of the room are rows of benches, usually three in number, one above the other. The temperature of the bath is according to the elevation of the bench; on the lower it is about 96° Fahr., and on the upper one it may be as high as 160° Fahr. The bather disrobes in the anteroom, and then, lightly covered, enters the bath. He first reclines on the lower shelf, then on the middle, next on the upper, remaining five, ten, or fifteen minutes on each, the time varying as the person is accustomed to the bath. At certain stages of this process, when the skin is red and the body very hot, the person is taken to a side-room and showered with cool, or even cold water; the skin being so intensely hot the sensation is very agreeable, and no danger need be apprehended, provided the contact of cold be brief. In Russia the attendant also rubs the body vigorously with various irritating and cleansing substances, such as the inner bark of the lime-tree, previously soaked in soap-suds, a hempen wisp, bran and soap-suds, or flannel cloths, the selection being adapted to the condition of the patient. The body is also kneaded, and the various joints rubbed and twisted till they are perfectly supple. The hot vapor is usually admitted to the room from coils of steam-pipes, but in Russia it is produced by throwing water on red-hot shot or stones; and there the equivalent for the cold shower often consists in running out into the open air and rolling in the snow, immediately returning, however, to the hot vapor-room. The duration of the bath for those not habituated is about fifteen minutes; but, after becoming accustomed to it, it may be prolonged to a half-hour, or even an hour. After the bath the person retires to an adjoining room, and remains till cool, usually partaking of some warm drink. If, however, copious perspiration is desirable, the patient is wrapped in blankets and reclines on a couch, where he remains for some time.

Hot-Air Bath.—In the hot-air bath the body is surrounded by a medium which, although it tends to increase its heat, presents at the same time the best conditions for conveying the heat away. The skin is stimulated to increased activity, and perspiration exudes from every pore; but it is immediately converted into vapor, which, in the change, absorbs enormous quantities of heat, and thus the body remains about the normal temperature. Experiment has proved that a person may remain seven minutes in dry air at 210° Fahr., and the body-heat will not rise more than one degree in temperature. In the hot-air bath the loss by evaporation depends more on the length of time passed in it than the temperature. Ten minutes passed in a hot-air bath of 122° Fahr., and one of 212° Fahr., give rise to the same loss by evaporation, and this in a constant proportion.[1] The difference between the toleration of a hot-vapor bath and a hot-air bath has already been noticed. While in the one we cannot endure a heat above 160° or 170° Fahr., in the other we can readily remain for some time after it passes the point of boiling-water. It is related that the workmen of the sculptor, Sir F. Chantrey, were in the habit of entering a furnace in which moulds were dried when the floor was red-hot and the thermometer stood at 350° Fahr. Chabert, the "Fire King," frequently entered an oven at a temperature of from 400° to 600° Fahr.

The physiological effects of hot air are somewhat as follows: On entering a bath of 160° Fahr. persons not accustomed to it usually experience a slight smarting and itching of the entire body. The pulse becomes at first small and frequent, respiration is impeded, and there is a feeling of constriction about the forehead. After some moments the pulse becomes fuller, but still increased in frequency, and the temporal arteries throb.[2] The skin feels hot, and there is a pungent, burning sensation about the nostrils. A copious perspiration covers the body, and sometimes the mouth is dry.[3]

[1] Bell on "Baths," p. 525.

[2] In my own case, after thirty-five minutes passed in the Turkish bath, twenty-five of which I was subject to 120° Fahr., and the last ten to 176° Fahr., the pulse rose from 84 on entering to 144.

[3] The colored attendant whom I met in the Turkish bath made the following statement: He is in the bathing-chambers six hours each day, the temperature of the air with which

The immediate after-effect of a hot-air bath is depressing, though when properly used it may prove tonic.

The Turkish Bath.—This is the form of hot-air bath in general use both in this country and Europe. It consists of four apartments: First, the undressing-room, at a temperature of about 80° Fahr. Here you disrobe, receive a light gown, and place your feet in sandals with wooden soles. Leaving this room, the *tepidarium* is entered. This is a chamber usually about ten feet square and nine feet high, the floor of slate or marble, and the walls of tile. Within this apartment are couches, on which you recline, usually remaining fifteen minutes. Temperature of this room, 120° Fahr. From the tepidarium you are conducted into the shampooing-room, of larger dimensions; temperature about the same. In the centre of this chamber is an elevated marble table, on which you place yourself, and every portion of the body is rubbed thoroughly and kneaded by the bath-attendant. From this room you enter the *caldarium*, and recline on a couch. This apartment is similar in size and construction to the tepidarium, but the temperature is 176° Fahr., and the walls are burning to the touch. Here you remain for ten minutes, the perspiration breaking forth from every portion of the body, and a pungent, burning sensation being felt about the nostrils. Then you are again taken to the shampooing-room, where you are douched with water of about 98° Fahr., and rubbed with wisps of sea-grass or hemp; then douched again. The attendant then takes a wooden *strigil*, of the antique pattern, and scrapes the body and extremities. Next you are showered with water of 90° Fahr.; then douched with water of 70° Fahr., the latter giving considerable shock, and terminating the bath. You are then conducted to the dressing-room, where, after being thoroughly dried, you recline for

he is surrounded during that time varying from 120° to 200° Fahr., some persons taking baths at the last-named temperature. He has followed this occupation four years. He has lost considerable in weight, and has very little appetite. Tongue is white and furred. Suffers from constipation—a passage once in two days; previous to taking charge of baths, having been regular. Passes very little urine. Perspires freely in the bath. Feels stupid. Sleeps very soundly; and frequently feels numb in portions of his body when he wakes.

some time on a couch, enjoying the pleasurable "*dolce-far-niente*" condition in which you find yourself. The system is in a state of lassitude, with a pleasant inclination to repose, unaccompanied, however, by the slightest sensation of weariness or fatigue. During the entire process the pulse has ranged as high as sixty beats per minute above the normal standard; and considerable skill has been required on the part of the attendant in adjusting the cooling douches so as to leave you at the close with the body cooled to the natural temperature.

The Turkish bath in the Orient is the same as that described, excepting that the chambers are not heated so high, the caldarium not being above 105° Fahr. For the purpose of the bath in health this temperature is preferable.

In Persia, India, and Egypt, the baths are similar to those of Turkey; and it seems that in countries of a southern latitude preference is always given to the hot-air bath, while in northern countries the hot-vapor bath is most in vogue.

As a therapeutic agent, the Russian and Turkish baths are applicable to chronic skin-diseases of the dry kind, and all chronic diseases in which it is desirable to stimulate the functions of the skin and produce active elimination, as gout, rheumatism, albuminuria, diabetes, torpid liver, etc. Care, however, must be used in the selection of cases; and the feeble, or those suffering from organic diseases of the heart or lungs, should not be subjected to the excitement of these baths.

The Douche.—This is an arrangement for projecting a stream of water on any part of the body at will. It is an exceedingly active agent, stimulating the blood-vessels, nerves, and lymphatics of the part to which it is applied, and, through the nervous system, affecting the entire organism. It may be used of tepid, warm, or hot water, the effects varying in degree according to the temperature. The cold douche is seldom employed, except when the surface of the skin has been artificially overheated.

Douches are differently named, according to the mode of

projecting the water. The ordinary *shower-bath* is a descending douche.

An *ascending douche*, frequently employed in diseases of the vagina, uterus, and rectum, is formed by an elastic India-rubber tubing, of convenient length, attached to a reservoir of tepid water, and terminated by metal tips, which are perforated with many holes, or have but a single orifice, according to the effect desired.

The force of the column of water for the uterine or rectal douche should be within the following limits: For the uterus, from two to six feet pressure; for the rectum, from two and a half to ten feet. The temperature may range from 82° to 92° Fahr., though, in some cases, it may be as high as 98° Fahr.

The *fan-douche* is a metal tip, spreading out like an ordinary fan, with the perforations at the circumference of the fan.

The *ring douche* is a cylinder formed of coiled pipes rising one above the other to the height of six feet, and about two and a half feet in diameter. These pipes are all perforated on the inside, and, when the patient is within and the water turned on, he is showered from every point of the circumference.

The *universal douche* is a similar contrivance, by which the person is showered from every direction—above, below, and on all sides.

The *spout-bath* is a douche of great power. It is formed by an orifice of from one to two and a half inches in diameter, from which the water is projected, over and downward, from a height of five or six feet. The patient, usually reclining on a slab, places himself under this stream of water and permits it to flow on the diseased part.

The Sitz-Bath.—This is a bath in which the thighs and middle portions of the body only are immersed, in other words, the person sits down in the water. It may be cold, warm, or hot, and acts according to the temperature. The warm sitz-bath produces relaxation of the tissues of the pelvis and relieves irritation, thus giving relief in stricture of the urethra, nephritic colic, amenorrhœa, and dysmenorrhœa. The cold or hot sitz-bath should be employed with caution.

The *foot-bath* has the effects of the warm or hot bath, according to temperature, though in a modified degree. This distinction, however, should be made: the primary action of the hot foot-bath, by the turgescence of the blood-vessels of the feet, relieves slight engorgements in other parts of the body, especially when the head is the seat of the engorgement.

Mineral-Mud Bath.—This bath consists of mineral mud taken from the marshy ground about the source of the spring. This mud, having been previously thoroughly dried, is placed in a large vat and mingled with hot mineral water till of a plastic consistency. The patient immerses himself in this hot mineral mud, varying in temperature from 85° to 100° Fahr., and remains from one to several hours. He then passes from this vat to an adjoining warm-water bath, where he is cleansed, thoroughly rubbed and dried.

Although of recent introduction in this country, this bath is of ancient date, having been described by Pliny and Galen. The effect of the bath is to produce a lively excitation of the skin, followed by free perspiration. When the baths have been continued for some time, miliary and erythematous eruptions sometimes occur on the surface of the skin, unaccompanied, however, as a rule, by the feverish conditions which present in the eruptions from prolonged warm or hot bathing.

This kind of bath is chiefly employed in diseases of the skin, chronic rheumatism, and affections of the joints, such as engorgements, contractions, and concretions. The good results of these baths abroad, in diseases of this nature, are attributed by the best authorities entirely to the external and topical application of heat, and the irritation produced by the friction of the mud. No heed is given to the supposed absorption of the chemical constituents. I give, however, the chief constituents of the most celebrated mineral-mud bath in Europe, that of Franzensbad, as taken from an exceedingly accurate analysis by Radig:

One thousand parts of the dried mud consist of the following:

	Parts.
Sulphate of protoxide of iron	24
Sulphate of soda	38
Sulphate of lime	14
Chloride of sodium	10
Protoxide of iron	88
Alumina	29
Magnesia	14
Silica	42
Coarse sand	50
Humic acid and ulmine	180
Vegetable substances	62
Vegetable substances (undestroyed)	423
	974

The remaining substances are sulphates of alumina, magnesia, strontia, lithia, manganese, and phosphate of lime. The original analysis is carried out to five places of decimals.

As a curiosity, the *sand-bath* may be mentioned. It consists in burying one's body in the warm sand of the sea-shore and remaining for some hours. It is practised by the Tartars of the Crimea. By this process slight perspirations, followed by eruptions, are produced.

Medicated Baths.—All baths of mineral-spring water, containing considerable mineral constituents, may be placed in this class; also, those baths of ordinary water in which medicines are dissolved. The substances most frequently introduced are alkaline carbonates, with a view of imitating the baths of alkaline mineral waters—common salt producing a bath somewhat resembling that of saline waters; sulphuret of sodium forming a bath similar to that of sulphur-waters. Baths of the fumes of various medicines—termed *fumigations*—are also used; of these, those of sulphur and mercury are most frequently employed. The person to be subjected to this process is seated on a stool, within a close box, the head only projecting from an aperture. The fumes are introduced beneath the stool, and the body is thus enveloped in an atmosphere highly charged with the vapor of medicinal substances.

Carbonic-Acid Bath.—This bath can only be used advantageously at springs where there is an abundant escape of the gas. Over the spring, or a portion of the spring, a bell-shaped reservoir is placed, and from the upper part flexible tubing conveys the gas to the room in which baths are given, or to a second reservoir, which may be arranged like the ordinary gasometer, so that the gas may escape under pressure. The bathing apparatus consists of an impervious box, within which the patient is seated, the head being without the box, and care being taken that properly-adjusted rubber-cloth envelops the throat, so that the gas may not escape, and the patient respire a sufficient quantity to become asphyxiated. The patient may take the bath with or without his clothing, as he desires. The effect of this bath has been described by M. Rotureau as follows: He experienced a lively sense of warmth, with redness of the face and pricking of the skin, accompanied at first by coldness of the feet; the pulse diminished in frequency. The bath was followed by a sense of renewed vigor and activity. In one experiment which he made, completely undressed, he felt at first exceedingly cold, and the heat that succeeded was accompanied with insupportable itching. The gas has also been administered in the form of a douche. According to Althaus, when applied locally to the eye, carbonic acid produces a burning sensation in the conjunctiva, accompanied with congestion. The secretions are increased, and tears flow freely; but, if the application is long continued, the secretions may be suppressed; the eye becomes congested, and disturbance of vision follows. When a douche of carbonic acid is directed upon the ear, the sense of hearing becomes more acute, the secretions of the lining membrane are augmented, and sometimes drowsiness follows the operation. Applied to the mouth or fauces, an acidulous taste is experienced, together with an astringent sensation, and the uvula and root of the tongue become injected; the flow of saliva is also increased. If the application be long continued, there are loss of taste and a sense of heaviness in the tongue, and, when douched upon the abdomen, it is said to promote hæmorrhoidal and menstrual flow, and in pregnant women to cause abortion.

The diseases in which the carbonic-acid bath is said to have proved useful, are rheumatism, neuralgia, paralysis, and granular pharyngitis.

CHAPTER X.

ALKALINE WATERS.

WATERS thus classified contain, as prominent constituents, the carbonates of soda, potassa, lithia, lime, and magnesia, the carbonate of soda being usually in much greater proportion than other carbonates. They also frequently contain a small proportion of chloride of sodium, and sulphate of soda, and potassa. They generally contain a large quantity of carbonic-acid gas. The action of these waters depends on the alkaline carbonates above mentioned, varied, however, by their peculiar combination with other salts, and sometimes by undiscovered ingredients. They tend to stimulate the stomach, to increase the appetite, to render the urine alkaline, to increase its flow, and in a slight degree to promote the activity of the skin. These waters prove purgative only in exceptional instances, usually producing constipation. They especially act on the mucous membranes, lessening catarrhal discharges.

Waters of this class, when of high temperature, prove exceedingly beneficial in *gout*, and it is in this disease that the alkaline Vichy waters of Europe have attained so great celebrity. Why these waters prove more beneficial than the active ingredients, given in the usual way, is not well understood. The fact, however, is incontestable, that waters of this class frequently prove more valuable than any other remedy. The cases of gout to which they are especially applicable are those in which the patient is of full habit. Waters of this class also prove beneficial in cases of *uric-acid gravel*, though the decided curative effect that was once expected has not been realized.

In *catarrh of the bladder*, however, they frequently prove curative. *Icterus*, depending on catarrh of the hepatic ducts, is relieved by them. *Chronic bronchitis*, or catarrh of the respiratory organs, unaccompanied by organic disease of the heart, will be favorably influenced by their use. Care, however, should be taken that cases subjected to their action have no tendency to hæmoptysis. It is this class of waters that have so long been known in Europe as proving decidedly beneficial in cases of *diabetes mellitus*. In one of the Western States, a spring is advertised as a new discovery—a cure in this disease—and that it is of value is undoubted; but, curiously enough, we find that it also is an alkaline water—no discovery, after all. Under the use of alkaline waters, the diabetic patient gains in strength, the harassing thirst ceases, the skin becomes moist, the urine is reduced almost to normal specific gravity, and often every trace of sugar disappears. In some incipient cases, it is quite probable a cure has taken place; but, though this result be not attained, the disease is often stayed in its course, and Althaus tells us that, "in some instances diabetes has, by the use of the Vichy waters, been brought to a stand-still for years."[1] In cases of *gall-stones*, these waters frequently give relief, causing them to be passed with less pain, and, by a periodical use for several seasons, entirely removing the tendency to formation of them. *Dyspepsia*, accompanied with acidity, is favorably affected, and that somewhat vague disease, catarrh of the stomach, more properly *chronic gastritis*, is amenable to treatment by these waters.

It will be seen that these waters, and the *alkaline-saline* waters, are in several instances, recommended in similar cases. The distinction to be made in determining, for a given case, which is preferable, is based on the answer to the question, whether the patient is of constipated habit, and requires an aperient or cathartic medicine; if he does, then the *alkaline-saline* waters are superior to the purely alkaline. Waters which contain a considerable proportion of carbonic-acid gas

[1] "Spas of Europe," p. 320.

are preferable, because more readily absorbed, and more agreeable to the taste.

BLADON SPRINGS.

Location and Post-Office.—Bladon Springs, Choctaw County, Alabama.

Access.—From Mobile up the Tombigbee River, one hundred miles north, by steamboat, on Tuesdays and Fridays, to Bladon landing; thence three miles and a half by stage. Or go to Demopolis, on the Alabama Central Railroad, forty-two miles west of Selma; thence by steamboat, on Tuesdays and Fridays, south, on Tombigbee River, about fifty miles to the landing.

Hotel.—Bladon Springs.

ANALYSIS.

One pint contains—	Vichy Spring, 67° Fahr. Profs. J. L. and W. P. Riddell.	Branch Spring, 67° Fahr. Profs. J. L. and W. P. Riddell.	Old Spring. Prof. R. T. Brumby.	Sulphur Spring, 67° Fahr. Profs. J. L. and W. P. Riddell.
SOLIDS.	Grains.	Grains.	Grains.	Grains.
Carbonate of soda	5.791	5.151	4.111	4.867
Carbonate of magnesia	0.036	0.076	0.170	0.081
Carbonate of iron	[1] 0.062	[1] 0.029	....	[1] 0.095
Carbonate of lime	0.109	0.267	0.344	0.302
Chloride of sodium	....	....	0.962	....
Sulphate of lime	[2] 0.282	[2] 0.349	0.002	0.370
Sulphate of iron	....	....	0.030	....
Sulphate of manganese	trace.	....	....	trace.
Silica and alumina	....	....	0.263	....
Crenic acid	....	....	0.091	....
Hypocrenic acid	....	....	0.075	....
Organic matter	0.282	0.237	....	0.156
Loss	....	....	0.040	....
Total	6.562	6.112	6.088	5.871
GASES.	Cubic inch.	Cubic inch.	Cubic inch.	Cubic inch.
Carbonic acid	8.18	7.40	4.07	6.61
Sulphuretted hydrogen	trace.	trace.	undetermined.	0.07
Chlorine	[3] 0.23	[3] 0.23	....	[3] 0.23

Properties.—It will be seen from the analysis that these are nearly pure alkaline waters, charged with considerable carbonic-acid gas. The *sulphur* spring does not differ materially from the other springs, except in containing a small proportion of sulphuretted hydrogen. They are very valuable waters of the class, and will prove appropriate in the cases to which alkaline waters are applicable.

Remarks.—The surrounding country is rolling. In every

[1] Carbonate of iron and oxide of alumina.

[2] Sulphate of lime and silicic acid.

[3] (Probably combined with sodium, forming chloride of sodium.—W.)

direction the eye rests on the primeval forest, composed almost entirely of pine-trees, and appropriately called "Piney Woods."

These springs are much frequented, and possess the conveniences of such resorts.

CONGRESS SPRINGS.

Location.—Santa Clara County, California.

Access.—Go to Santa Clara, a station on the San José branch of the Central Pacific Railroad, about forty miles south from San Francisco; thence by stage. Or to San José, forty-seven miles south from San Francisco; thence twelve miles by stage.

Hotel.—Congress Springs.

ANALYSIS.

One pint contains at 50° Fahr.:

Solids.	Grains.
Carbonate of soda	15.418
Carbonate of iron	1.753
Carbonate of lime	2.161
Chloride of sodium	14.894
Sulphate of soda	1.517
Silica, alumina, and trace of magnesia	6.235
Total	41.978

Properties.—According to the analysis, the accuracy of which is doubtful, these are valuable waters of the *muriated-alkaline* subdivision, possessing at the same time chalybeate qualities. When highly charged with carbonic-acid gas they form an agreeable drink, and are largely bottled and sold in California.

Remarks—The hotel is located on the summit of a mountain-spur, overlooking the foot-hills, and giving a view of blue mountain-peaks in the distance.

The springs, one-half mile distant from the hotel, are reached by a winding mountain-road.

The taste of the water reveals the presence of iron, which is indicated as well by the rusty-colored deposit which settles where it flows.[1]

[1] *Overland Monthly*, June, 1870.

CALIFORNIA SELTZER SPRINGS.

Location.—Mendocino County, California.

Post-Office.—Sanel, Mendocino County, California.

Access.—From San Francisco by steamer to Petaluma, thence by California & Northern Pacific Railroad to Cloverdale; thence twelve miles by stage to the springs.

Hotel.—Fountain House.

ANALYSIS.

One pint contains (F. A. Bauer):

SOLIDS.	Grains.
Carbonate of soda	4.61
Carbonate of magnesia	5.65
Carbonate of lime	8.80
Carbonate of iron	trace.
Chloride of sodium	2.15
Silicic acid	trace.
Total	21.21

GAS—Carbonic acid, abundant. (1871.)

Properties.—According to the analysis, this is a very fine alkaline water, and we should expect it to act favorably in cases of dyspepsia and diseases of the liver and bladder, in which alkaline waters are indicated.

PERRY SPRINGS.

Location and Post-Office.—Perry Springs, Pike County, Illinois.

Access.—By Hannibal & Naples Railroad to Griggsville, thirty-six miles east of Hannibal; thence six miles and a half by stage.

Hotel.—Perry Springs.

ANALYSIS.

One pint contains—	No. 1. Middle Spring. H. Engelmann, M. D.	No. 2. Upper Spring. H. Engelmann, M. D.	No. 3. Lower Spring. H. Engelmann, M. D.
SOLIDS.	Grains.	Grains.	Grains.
Carbonate of potassa	0.199	0.181	0.157
Carbonate of magnesia	1.260	1.097	0.777
Carbonate of iron	0.051	0.040	0.025
Carbonate of lime	1.380	1.715	1.708
Sulphate of soda	0.055	0.187	0.173
Silicate of potassa and soda	0.380	0.285	0.431
Silicate of sodium	0.015	0.048	0.072
Silicate of alumina	....	....	0 034
Total	3.290	3.503	3.377

—(" Geology of Illinois," vol. iv., p. 41.)

The temperature throughout the year is from 48° to 50° Fahr.

Remarks.—These springs are situated in a beautiful valley, surrounded by wooded hills. They are located about two and a half miles southeast of Perry, on one of the tributaries of McGee's Creek. The springs issue from the upper part of the Keokuk limestone, which underlies the valley and outcrops along the bluffs of the creek below the spring.[1] They are about two hundred yards apart. The upper one is called the sulphur spring, the middle one the magnesium, and the lower one the iron spring. The flow of the springs is about as follows: No. 1, one and a half gallon per minute; No. 2, one; No. 3, two.

VERSAILLES SPRINGS.

Location and Post-Office.—Versailles, Brown County, Illinois.

Access.—Versailles is a station on the Toledo, Wabash & Western Railroad, forty-eight miles east of Quincy, and sixty-six miles west of Springfield; springs, one mile and three-quarters from station.

Hotel.—Springs.

ANALYSIS.

One pint contains—	Magnesia Spring. G. A Marriner.	Curry Spring. J. V. Z. Blaney, M. D.	Monitor Spring. J. V. Z. Blaney, M. D.
SOLIDS.	Grains.	Grains.	Grains.
Carbonate of potassa and soda	0.165	trace.	trace.
Carbonate of soda	....	0.953	0.953
Carbonate of magnesia	1.119	0.933	0.878
Carbonate of iron	0.008	....	[2] 0.267
Carbonate of lime	1.825	1.514	2.017
Chloride of sodium	trace.	trace.	trace.
Sulphate of lime	trace.	0.261	....
Potassa	....	....	....
Alumina and trace of iron	....	0.091	.....
Silica	0.175	0.102	0.213
Organic matter	....	trace.	trace.
Total	3.292	3.854	4.328
GAS.	Cubic inch.		
Carbonic acid	3		

Remarks.—The springs are situated in a valley surrounded by hills, composed entirely of loess and drift. The valley was originally a part of the ancient valley of the Illinois River, and was excavated one hundred feet or more into the carboniferous rocks, which were once continuous across the area now occupied by the valley.[3]

The temperature of the water is 58° Fahr.

[1] "Geology of Illinois." [2] Trace of alumina. [3] "Geology of Illinois."

ST. LOUIS SPRING.

Location and Post-Office.—St. Louis, Gratiot County, Michigan.

Access.—From Detroit, *via* Flint & Père Marquette Railroad, ninety-eight miles, to East Saginaw; thence thirty miles by railroad to the springs. Or from Detroit, *via* Detroit & Milwaukee Railroad, ninety-eight miles, to St. John's; thence thirty miles by stage.

Hotels.—Eastman House, McHenry Hotel, Union Hotel.

ANALYSIS.

One pint contains (50° Fahr. S. P. Duffield, M. D.):

SOLIDS.	Grains.
Carbonate of soda	7.684
Carbonate of magnesia	1.080
Carbonate of iron	0.091
Carbonate of lime	5.019
Chloride of lime	trace.
Sulphate of lime	6.925
Silicate of lime	0.700
Silica	0.299
Organic matter and loss	0.208
Total	22.006
GASES.	**Cubic inches.**
Carbonic acid	1.36
Sulphuretted hydrogen	trace.

Properties.—The above analysis shows these waters to be strongly alkaline, and at the same time containing a small proportion of iron. They also contain sufficient of the salts of lime to ally them to calcic waters. From the constituents we would expect the waters to prove beneficial in acid dyspepsia, biliary calculus, and diseases of the bladder. The results of treatment, as exhibited by Dr. Stiles Kennedy,[1] show the waters to have been especially beneficial in dyspepsia and neuralgia. From his report of cases treated at the St. Louis Spring we have compiled the following table. (*See* page 151.)

Many of these cases were doubtless of the severest type; and the above results certainly appear favorable. It must be remembered, however, that all cases treated by Dr. Kennedy are not reported, and that of all who visited the spring only

[1] "Magnetic and Mineral Springs of Michigan." By Stiles Kennedy, M. D. Wilmington, Del.: James & Webb, 1872.

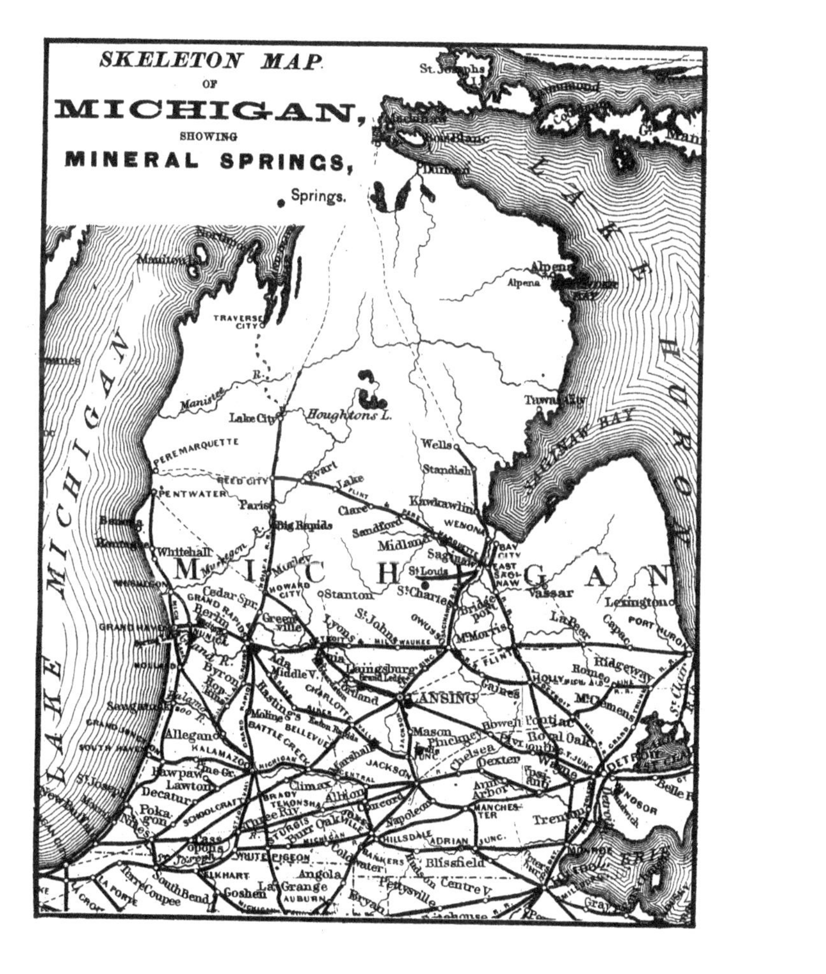
SKELETON MAP
OF
MICHIGAN,
SHOWING
MINERAL SPRINGS,
Springs.
LAKE MICHIGAN
LAKE HURON
SAGINAW BAY
MICHIGAN
Traverse City
Lake City
Houghtons L.
Alpena
Wells
Standish
Evart
Paris
Big Rapids
Clare
Kawkawlin
Midland
Saginaw
Bay City
St. Louis
St. Charles
Vassar
Lexington
Port Huron
Whitehall
Pentwater
Grand Haven
Muskegon
Stanton
St. Johns
Lansing
Greenville
Grand Rapids
Ionia
Hastings
Charlotte
Allegan
Kalamazoo
Battle Creek
Marshall
Jackson
Albion
Ann Arbor
Detroit
Pontiac
Mt. Clemens
Ypsilanti
Chelsea
Dexter
Mason
Owosso
Flint
Holly
Romeo
Royal Oak
Wayne
Trenton
Monroe
Adrian
Hillsdale
Coldwater
Three Riv.
Niles
St. Joseph
South Bend
Goshen
Elkhart
Angola
Bryan
Blissfield
Windsor
Lake Erie

Disease.	No. of Cases.	Cured.	Improved.	Not benefited.	Average duration of Treatment.
Dyspepsia	8	7	1	..	1 month.
Neuralgia	12	4	5	3	3 months.
Chronic rheumatism	6	2	4	..	2 months.
Subacute rheumatism	1	1	..	..	1 month.
Gonorhœal rheumatism	1	..	1	..	3 weeks.
Rheumatism "noueux"[1]	1	..	..	1	2 months.
Paralysis	4	..	4	..	2 months.
Paraplegia	1	..	1	..	2½ months.
Hemiplegia	1	..	1	..	2½ months.
Anæsthesia (partial)	2	2	..	..	2½ weeks.
Total	37	16	17	4	

a portion came under his observation. Again, the treatment was not limited to the internal use of the water, but all cases were subjected to the salutary influence of the bath; and, in the majority of instances, it was the warm bath that was prescribed. That the fact of the warm water, being that of the St. Louis Spring, had any bearing on the relief afforded, needs more complete demonstration. Especially in rheumatic and paralytic affections was the warm or hot bath and douche resorted to, and, in many instances, the additional aid of the continued electric current. In paralytic affections no cures are reported, though all seem to have improved. How much of this is due to the medical treatment, or how much to the water, is difficult to determine; our own impression is, that whatever was gained may be attributed to the combined effects of the warm bath and douche, shampooing, and electricity, regardless of the constitution of the water. As to its so-called magnetic power we are entirely skeptical, as may be seen in the treatment of this subject on another page. This water, however, is highly mineralized; and in cases of hemiplegia, depending on unabsorbed clot, some advantage may be expected from the resolutive action of the water. In cases of this nature alkaline waters have been recommended by the best European authorities, to be employed, however, only after some months have elapsed from the apoplectic seizure.

Although the report of Dr. Kennedy does not accurately determine the therapeutic value of this water, still it aids in

[1] The gouty rheumatism of some writers.

elucidating the subject. We cannot forbear complimenting him on his report of cases; and it is to be regretted that a similar method has not been pursued at the old-time resorts during the many years past.

Remarks.—The St. Louis Spring is situated in a town of the same name, the outgrowth of the lumbering interests of this portion of Michigan. On either hand it is surrounded by far-extending pine-forests, while near by flows Pine River. The well was the result of an attempt, in 1869, to procure a flow of salt-water, of which there is an abundance in many parts of Michigan. But when, at a depth of 200 feet, the water came from the artesian tube fresh and sparkling, it was abandoned, and received no further attention. However, as I was informed by the proprietor, after some months had passed by, a workman, engaged in constructing an extension of the neighboring mill, let his chisel fall near the tube, and it was immediately attracted toward it. Surprised at this, he called the attention of others to the fact, and soon numbers of people were found at the well magnetizing knife-blades on the tubing. It needed but a step in popular reasoning to transfer the magnetism of the tube to the water; and then the cry of "Magnetic water!" resounded through the village. It is said that an old paralytic, hopeless of cure, reasoned that if he could drink magnetism, and bathe in magnetism, his helpless limbs would move spryly again. So he commenced drinking the water and bathing vigorously, and, as the story goes, entirely recovered. The cry of "Magnetic water!" and the story of this cure were sounded through the State, and soon thousands flocked thither for relief.

Visitors at these springs are much attracted by the yellow-tinged articles of glass-ware that are sold at the spring. This color is the result of permitting a constant shower of the water to fall on the clear glass for many days. The yellow tinge is found to be a deposit "mainly of ferric oxide with carbonates of lime and magnesia."[1]

[1] "Magnetic and Mineral Springs of Michigan," p. 58.

LOWER SODA SPRING.

Location.—Linn County, Oregon.

Access.—By private conveyance from Salem, about thirty miles southeast.

Hotel.—Finlay's.

Analysis.—No accurate analysis of these waters has been made. They abound in carbonic acid and contain carbonates of soda and iron.[1]

Remarks.—These springs are situated on the Cascade Mountains, on the south fork of the Santiam, amid surrounding evidences of volcanic action. They escape from the base of a mountain-spur of porphyritic rock. The water flows from the springs with considerable force. It is somewhat affected in quantity by the varying seasons.

SHELDON SPRINGS.

Location and Post-Office Address.—Sheldon, Franklin County, Vermont.

Access.—Go to St. Albans, a station on the Vermont Central Railroad, in the northwest corner of the State; thence ten miles east, by Missisquoi Valley Railroad, to Sheldon. Persons going to the *Sheldon* Spring, one of the group, buy ticket to Congress Hall Station, eight miles east of St. Albans.

Hotels.—Bellevue, Central (at *the Sheldon Spring*, Congress Hall), Vermont House, Portland House.

Analysis.—No *reliable* quantitative analysis of these waters has ever been published. However, the prominent constituents are the alkaline carbonates, and silicic acid combined with

[1] The following extract is from the *Oregon Medical and Surgical Reporter*, September, 1870:

"On subjecting specimens of these several springs to a somewhat hasty analysis, the following result was given:

SOLIDS.	No. 1. In one ounce.	No. 2. In one ounce.	No. 3. In one ounce.
Bicarbonate of soda	1.25 grs.	5.02 grs.	10.02 grs.
Peroxide of iron	.40 grs.	.35 grs.	.98 grs.
Sulphur	....	trace.	....
Chloride of sodium	.25 grs.	1.25 grs.	.86 grs.
Carbonate of lime	....	....	.05 grs.
Organic matter	no trace.	....	....
Iodides and bromides	wanting.	wanting.	....

"Free carbonic-acid gas completely saturates the water of No. 1."

alkaline bases, forming silicates. There is also a small proportion of iron and some organic matter; also, traces of fluorides. It is exceedingly desirable that some chemist of acknowledged ability make a thorough analysis of these waters.

Properties.—All of the waters are alkaline to test-paper.

The water of the Sheldon Spring is pleasant to the taste, with an almost imperceptible odor of sulphuretted hydrogen. The Missisquoi water is limpid, without odor, and to the sense of taste does not differ from ordinary water. The Vermont water has a very slight taste of iron.

Aside from the known favorable action of alkaline waters in acid gravel, gout, and catarrhal disease of the bladder, the especial point to be considered in connection with these springs is their efficacy in cancer. It is claimed by the owners of the springs that they will cure true cancer. Is there a well-authenticated case of true cancer having been cured by these waters? I answer, No. But, while making this assertion, it must at the same time be stated that cases of true cancer have been palliated while using them. To confirm this we quote, by permission, from a paper read before the New York Academy of Medicine, February 17, 1870, by Prof. Fordyce Barker, on "Malignant Diseases of the Uterus." Under the head of constitutional treatment, he says: "The Missisquoi water of St. Albans, Vermont, has in some cases seemed to be of great benefit in arresting, for a time, the progress of the disease. In many, the use of these waters has seemed to produce no results. Many others, to whom I have suggested their use, have never reported to me, and it is therefore probable that the results in these cases were negative. But, in a few instances—one of cancer of the breast and four of uterine cancer—the apparent effect has been more striking than any results I have ever seen from any other agent. None were cured; but the ulcerated surface was cleaned off, as though it had been excised with the knife; the fetor, the discharge, and the pain, ceased for some time, and the health of the patient was greatly improved. One, a poor woman, whom I first saw in May, 1867, with ulcerated carcinoma, involving both the neck and body of the uterus, and exceedingly feeble, emaciated, and broken down by the profuse and horribly offensive discharges and repeated hæmorrhages, rapidly improved both in her local and general condition under the use of these waters. She is still alive, although the uterus is nearly destroyed; but her general condition is much better than when I first saw her. I will allude to another case, a patient of Dr. Sims. I first saw this lady with him in December, 1868. Dr. Sims informed me that when he examined her in Paris, in August, the whole surface of the enlarged cervix was one mass of rough, ragged ulceration. When I examined her, the diseased surface was as smooth as if it had been excised with a knife, and there was no discharge and no odor, although she suffered from horrible pains. She died a few months subsequently; but Dr. Sims expresses the strong conviction (and I concur with him) that her life was prolonged by the use of the Missisquoi waters. Although the general sentiment of the profession does not coincide with mine on this point, I cannot but avow the belief that the therapeutic effects of these waters are eminently worthy of careful investigation." A note appended to the above quotation runs thus: "In a letter which I have recently received from Dr. D. F. Fassett, of St. Albans, Vermont, a gentleman who is probably more competent than any one else to give an opinion based on extensive personal observation, as to the effects of these waters, he says: 'I have notes of four cases only of malignant disease of the uterus, under my own observation, all of whom used the water, one with marked benefit, and three with no benefit. But I have seen many cases of malignant disease located elsewhere, as in breast, face, and extremities, where the effect was to cause marked improvement in the general health and in the local manifestation of the disease; but there was no positive cure.'"

It may be added that during August, 1871, the author visited the Sheldon Springs, and while there saw a man suffering from epithelioma of the lower lip, the ulcer having eaten away to the level of the gum. His own statement was that he came to the springs in June, 1871, and remained for about six weeks. During this time he was continually improving. The discharge lost its fetid odor and almost ceased, and he gained much in general health. He then returned to his home in Massachusetts. Soon all his symptoms were as bad as ever. Again he went to the springs; and, at the time he was seen, some weeks after his return, had about regained what he had lost. This patient used the water of the Sheldon Spring.

Dr. G. S. Brigham had a patient suffering from cancer of the breast, who improved under the use of the Vermont Spring water.

What conclusion do we derive from these facts? Not that the water will cure cancer, but that sometimes it is *decidedly palliative*, and is worthy of trial in a malady so hopeless. It may also be stated that intractable ulcers (not cancers) have undoubtedly been healed under the use of these waters, as has been the case in the use of other waters.

The method of using the water is to drink a glass three or four times a day, or use it exclusively in the place of ordinary drinking-water, even making tea and coffee with it, if they be used. Besides, patients are in the habit of applying clay dug near the spring and moistened with the water as an epithem. The clay, no doubt, acts only by its cooling tendency; the water, however, as a lotion, may be an active agent. The waters of Celles, department of Ardèche, France, since 1837 have been claimed to cure cancer; and, very singularly, the Sheldon waters agree with them in the prominent constituents.

Remarks.—No springs are more delightfully situated than these, or could be more attractive to the invalid. They are four in number—the *Central*, within the village; the *Vermont*, half a mile from the village; the *Missisquoi*, one and a half mile northward; and the *Sheldon*, two miles from the village—all on the banks of the Missisquoi River. Within sight are Mount Mansfield and other of the Green Mountains. A cool, bracing, and pure air sweeps over the hills, and attractive excursions invite in every direction. The altitude is stated as two thousand feet above the sea.

MIDDLETOWN SPRINGS.

Location and Post-Office Address.—Middletown, Rutland County, Vermont.

Access.—From Albany, take Rensselaer & Saratoga Railroad to Poultney, sixty-eight miles north; thence eight miles, by stage, to springs.

Hotel.—Montvert.

Analysis.—No *accurate* analysis has ever been made.

WELDEN SPRING.

Location and Post-Office Address.—St. Albans, Franklin County, Vermont.

Access.—St. Albans is a prominent railroad-station on the Vermont Central Railroad, in the extreme northwest corner of the State.

Hotels.—Welden, Tremont, American.

Analysis.—By A. A. Hayes, M. D., Boston, 1867, gives the constituents as follows: Carbonates of soda, magnesia, and lime; chloride of sodium, sulphate of potassa and lime; iodide of magnesium, crenate of iron, silicate of soda, amounting to over three grains in a pint. The especial characteristics of this water are the crenate of iron and iodide of magnesium.

Remarks.—St. Albans is a delightful town, of five thousand inhabitants, overlooking Lake Champlain, two miles distant, on the west. The spring is situated on Edwards Street, south of Lake Street, about ten minutes' walk west of the depot.

ROCKBRIDGE BATHS.

Location and Post-Office.—Rockbridge Baths, Rockbridge County, Virginia.

Access.—From the north, to Washington; thence, *via* Orange, Alexandria & Manassas Railroad, to Goshen, one hundred and eighty-eight miles, southwest; thence, *via* stage, nine miles, to the springs. From Richmond, *via* Chesapeake & Ohio Railroad, to Goshen, one hundred and sixty-eight miles. From the southwest, *via* Virginia & Tennessee Railroad, Lynchburg, Charlottesville, and Chesapeake & Ohio Railroad. From Cincinnati, to Huntington, one hundred and sixty-five miles east, by river; thence, by Chesapeake & Ohio Railroad, two hundred and fifty-one miles southeast, to Goshen.

Hotel.—Rockbridge Baths.

Analysis.—An analysis before us shows these waters to contain a considerable proportion of magnesia and iron, with some iodine, though in what combinations is not stated. Temperature, 74° Fahr.

Properties.—These waters, as the name implies, are mostly used for bathing, and the large supply of water and elevated temperature render them well fitted for this purpose. There is a large pool for gentlemen, forty by sixty feet, and five feet deep, and one somewhat smaller for ladies. As a tonic bath, these waters are of deserved merit, and find their appropriate sphere.

Remarks.—These springs are delightfully situated on the banks of thė North James River, and the ride to them through the Goshen Pass affords views of some of the most picturesque scenery in Virginia. Two miles from the baths, on a little island in the North River, is a sulphur-spring, which is frequently resorted to by visitors.

CAPON SPRINGS AND BATHS.

Location and Post-Office Address.—Capon Springs, Hampshire County, West Virginia.

Access.—From north, south, and southwest, go to Baltimore; thence, by Baltimore & Ohio Railroad, eighty-one miles, west to Harper's Ferry; thence, thirty-two miles, south, on branch railroad, to Winchester; thence, twenty-three miles, by stage, to the springs. From the west, go to Harper's Ferry, on the Baltimore & Ohio Railroad; thence as above. From Chesapeake & Ohio Railroad, passengers may leave at Staunton; thence stage, twenty-four miles north, to Harrisonburg; thence sixty-eight miles, north by railroad, to Winchester.

Hotel.—Mountain House.

Analysis.—It is to be regretted that no *quantitative* analysis of this valuable water can be given. A *qualitative* analysis shows it to contain soda and magnesia, in the form of carbonates; also iodine, bromine, and silicic acid. This water is highly charged with carbonic-acid gas.

Properties.—The water has little taste or odor. Temperature, 66° Fahr. Flow, one hundred gallons per minute. The elevation is eighteen hundred feet above the sea. This water is efficacious in the treatment of acid forms of dyspepsia, gastric catarrh, *uric-acid gravel*, and catarrh of the bladder. It is one of the best carbonated-alkaline waters in Virginia. It may also be stated that, for many years, farmers have brought their horses to drink these waters, as a remedy for botts, large numbers of the larvæ being thereby discharged dead. As a deduction from this fact, they have been successfully prescribed for *intestinal worms* in children.

Remarks.—The location of these springs, in a gorge of the North Mountain, where cool, salubrious air may be breathed, and mountain-climbing, trout-fishing and deer-hunting indulged, renders it a most delightful resort. The hotel, five stories high, with its grand Doric portico, is faced by a large and tastefully-designed bathing establishment, which is complete in its appointments. Plunge, shower, douche, and warm baths, are at the option of the visitor.

There is also a fine chalybeate spring at Capon.

CHAPTER XI.

SALINE WATERS.

The word *saline* is here used in the ordinary acceptation of the term, meaning waters in which chloride of sodium (common salt) predominates. This designation has been thought objectionable by some authors, inasmuch as all the chemical salts contained in waters are included under the term saline; and, thus considered, the word is not distinctive. But the first impression presented to any one on hearing the words *saline water* is, that it contains a notable proportion of chloride of sodium; and, thus restricted, the name seems exceedingly appropriate.

When saline waters contain a very large amount of chloride of sodium, they are known as brines, and constitute true salt wells or springs. Besides the chloride of sodium[1] there are other chlorides, also sulphates of potassa, soda, lime, and magnesia; and, in a few instances, a considerable proportion of carbonates. It is in these waters that the rare ingredients, iodide and bromide of sodium, are most frequently found, on which, no doubt, their value in scrofula in a measure depends.

Many of these waters contain considerable carbonic-acid gas, imparting to them an agreeable taste, and causing them to rest well on the stomach. When waters contain a large proportion of this gas, they are sometimes called acidulous salines. When they contain much of the alkaline carbonates, they may be termed *alkaline-saline* waters.

Saline waters promote the action of the intestines—being

[1] See *chloride of sodium* in chapter on "Chemical Constituents."

aperient or cathartic—augment the flow of urine, increase the secretion of the mucous membranes, and promote epithelial desquamation. They also stimulate the glandular and lymphatic systems, and increase the flow of bile. Under their use the appetite and power of digestion are increased.

As a class, these waters are valuable in the treatment of *scrofula*, in which disease they should be used both internally and in the form of baths. They are also useful in *gout* and *chronic rheumatism*, in which diseases, however, thermal salines, or hot baths, are essential. Where *icterus* is due to catarrh of the biliary ducts, they often relieve the difficulty, and *gall-stones* are also favorably influenced by saline waters, especially if they be of the alkaline-saline class. Engorged conditions of the liver are especially amenable to their use. In *dyspepsia*, the mild alkaline-saline waters, containing considerable carbonic-acid gas, as those of Saratoga, are often of exceeding benefit. Strong salines should be carefully employed, as their protracted use sometimes proves debilitating.

Brines are chiefly used for bathing. When judiciously employed they prove valuable in scrofulosis, paralysis, and in chronic rheumatism. In these waters the iodides and bromides are sometimes found in comparatively large proportion, and it is quite probable that they contribute to their efficacy in no small degree.

Brine-baths act as a powerful stimulus to the cutaneous nerves, increasing the peripheral circulation, and, perhaps, by reflex action, influence remote organs, and even the nerve-centres. Elimination by the skin and kidneys is increased. Brine vapor-baths stimulate the mucous membrane of the respiratory organs and promote expectoration.

ST. CATHARINE'S WELLS.

Location and Post-Office Address.—St. Catharine's, Ontario, Canada.

Access.—St. Catharine's is a station on the Great Western Railroad of Canada, thirteen miles west of Niagara Falls, and two hundred and eighteen miles east of Detroit.

Hotels.—Stephenson House, Welland House, Spring Bank.

ANALYSIS.

One pint contains—	Stephenson-House Well. Prof. Croft.	Merritt's, or Welland-House Well. Prof. Croft.
SOLIDS.	Grains.	Grains.
Carbonate of iron	....	.880
Carbonate of lime	....	.060
Chloride of potassium	2.587	2.060
Chloride of sodium	217.234	275.868
Chloride of magnesium	24.760	29.644
Chloride of calcium	108.271	127.202
Chloride of ammonium and silicic acid	0.056	....
Sulphate of lime	15.981	14.429
Iodide of sodium	....	0.010
Iodide of magnesium	0.030	....
Bromide of sodium	....	trace.
Bromide of magnesium	0.045	....
Total	368.964	449.653

Temperature 60° Fahr.

A *concentrated water*, similar to the mother-lye of Kreuznach, prepared by evaporation, gives the following result on analysis:

One pint contains—	Grains.
Carbonate of magnesia and lime	2.08
Chloride of sodium	781.36
Chloride of magnesium	1,289.76
Chloride of calcium	2,950.40
Proto-chloride of iron	13.76
Sulphate of lime	16.32
Iodide of magnesium	2.11
Bromide of magnesium	2.01
Silica, alumina, and lithia	2.47
Total	5,060.27

—(J. R. Chilton, M. D., 1858.)

The large amount of proto-chloride of iron was probably formed from the surface of the iron vessel during evaporation.

Properties.—These celebrated waters are the most perfect type of iodo-bromated saline water known in this country. They very much resemble the celebrated waters of Krueznach, in Prussia, though containing the chloride of sodium, calcium, and magnesium, in much larger proportions. For this reason, when used internally, they are diluted with ordinary water—one-eighth to one-fourth of a glass of the well-water, and fill the glass with pure water. But they are especially employed in the form of warm baths, which are provided at all the hotels. They have been found beneficial and curative in *gout*, *rheumatism*, *scrofula*, and certain forms of neuralgia.

The *concentrated water* is used as an embrocation or diluted; a bandage is wet with it and applied to swollen joints from rheumatism or sprain, after the first inflammatory symptoms have subsided. It produces counter-irritation, which may be limited to simple redness, or carried to pustulation, according to the strength of the solution and the time it remains in contact with the surface. For baths, ten to twelve fluidounces, added to an ordinary bath-tub half full of hot water, affords a similar bath to that obtained at the springs. Internally, one or two teaspoonfuls to a glass of pure water.

Remarks.—St. Catharine's is pleasantly situated within three miles of Lake Ontario, whither visitors frequently drive. The air is pure, and the heats of summer are seldom felt. The wells are on the north bank of the Welland Canal—all within the distance of a mile. They vary in depth, from one hundred and fifty to five hundred feet. One of them—that at the Stephenson House—has been in use since 1812. At Spring Bank, the sanitarium of Dr. Theophilus Mack, every form of bath may be had, including the famed Oriental Turkish bath.

PLANTAGENET SPRINGS.

Location.—Prescott County, Province of Ontario, Dominion of Canada.

Access.—Plantagenet Springs are eighty-eight miles west of Montreal. Same route to Point Fortune as for Caledonia Springs, thence by stage.

Hotels.— ——

Analysis.—None—a cold saline.

Remarks.—The name of this spring, I am informed, has been changed to the "Caratraca."

CALEDONIA SPRINGS.

Location.—Prescott County, Province of Ontario, Dominion of Canada.

Post-Office Address.— ——

Access.—Caledonia Springs are seventy-two miles west of Montreal. From Montreal take Grand Trunk Railroad to Lachine, thence by steamer to Carillon; cross the Ottawa River to Point Fortune, thence by stage to the springs.

Hotels.— ——

ANALYSIS.

One pint contains—	Gas Spring. 44½° Fahr. T. S. Hunt.	Saline Spring. 45° Fahr. T. S. Hunt.	Intermittent Spring. 50° Fahr. T. S. Hunt.
SOLIDS.	Grains.	Grains.	Grains.
Carbonate of soda	.354	1.284	....
Carbonate of magnesia	3.834	3.769	6.294
Carbonate of iron	....	trace.	trace.
Carbonate of lime	1.078	.856	.921
Carbonate of manganese	....	trace.	....
Chloride of potassium	.225	.219	.222
Chloride of sodium	50.772	46.934	89.265
Chloride of magnesium	....	....	7.583
Chloride of calcium	....	....	2.091
Sulphate of potassa	.038	.035	....
Iodide of sodium	.003	.010	....
Iodide of magnesium	....	....	.015
Bromide of sodium	.109	.123	....
Bromide of magnesium	....	....	.173
Alumina	.082	trace.	trace.
Silica	.225	.309	.164
Total	56.670	53.539	106.678
GAS.			
Carbonic acid	5 cubic in.	4 cubic in.	
Flow per minute	4 gallons.	10 gallons.	

—(1847.)

Properties.—These are valuable iodo-bromated saline waters, very much resembling those of Dürkheim, in Bavaria. They are useful in *scrofula*, *gout*, *chronic rheumatism*, etc.

The Gas Spring evolves, besides carbonic acid, considerable quantities of carburetted hydrogen, estimated at three hundred cubic inches per minute. It is pleasantly saline to the taste. The Saline Spring, so called, is similar to the Gas Spring, but really *less* saline. It evolves very little carburetted hydrogen. The Intermittent Spring is two miles distant from the springs named. It is disagreeably bitter as well as saline. The reaction of these waters to test-paper is alkaline.[1]

LANSING WELL.

Location and Post-Office.—Lansing, Ingham County, Michigan.

Access.—Lansing is eighty-five miles west of Detroit, on the Detroit, Lansing & Lake Michigan Railroad. The well is one mile from the city, accessible by steamboat.

Hotels.—Lansing, Chapman, Everett, Edgar.

[1] "Geology of Canada."

ANALYSIS.

One pint contains (53½° Fahr. Dr. Jennings):

SOLIDS.	Grains.
Carbonate of soda	8.094
Carbonate of magnesia	1.421
Carbonate of iron	0.143
Carbonate of lime	7.782
Chloride of sodium	33.349
Sulphate of potassa	1.554
Sulphate of soda	3.131
Silica	0.413
Total	55.887
GAS.	Cubic inches.
Carbonic acid	24½

Properties.—This is a strong saline water, containing a sufficient quantity of alkaline carbonates to ally it to the alkaline waters; therefore it should be classed as an alkaline-saline water. In chemical composition it considerably resembles the celebrated Saratoga waters, though the presence of sulphates of potassa and soda in this water causes it to be more decidedly purgative in action. Taken in considerable quantity, they produce catharsis, but in moderate doses they act freely on the kidneys. The iron contained in this water is sufficient to modify the otherwise depleting effect they would produce if long continued.

These waters are applicable to cases of dyspepsia, accompanied with abdominal plethora, a class of cases usually produced by high living. We should also expect good results from their use in catarrh of the biliary ducts, gall-stones, and engorged liver.

Remarks.—Lansing, the capital of Michigan, located on Grand River, is necessarily the seat of many public institutions, and resorted to by the better classes from every part of the State. The population is about fifty-five hundred.

Adjoining the well, which is a mile up the river, is a good bath-house. The depth of the well is fourteen hundred feet, and the flow is nearly a gallon per minute.

SPRING LAKE WELL.

Location and Post-Office.—Spring Lake, Ottawa County, Michigan.

Access.—Spring Lake is a station on the Detroit & Milwaukee Railroad, one hundred and eighty-six miles northwest from Detroit, three miles east of Grand Haven. From Chicago to Grand Haven, by lake-steamer.

Hotels.—Magnetic Spring, Middlemist, Burnum's.

ANALYSIS.

One pint contains (52° Fahr. Prof. C. G. Wheeler):

SOLIDS.	Grains.
Carbonate of soda	0.005
Carbonate of magnesia	trace
Carbonate of iron	0.092
Carbonate of manganese	0.006
Carbonate of lime	0.012
Chloride of potassium	0.536
Chloride of sodium.	50.691
Chloride of magnesium	4.525
Chloride of calcium	14.177
Sulphate of soda	5.837
Bromide of magnesium	0.271
Alumina	traces.
Ammonia	0.002
Lithia	traces.
Silica	0.063
Organic matter	2.286
Total	78,503

Properties.—This water, strong in chloride of sodium, also contains an active proportion of the bromide of magnesium. In chemical composition this water much resembles the Edisenquelle of Kreuznach. These springs, however, contain a proportion of iodide of magnesium.

Remarks.—The town of Spring Lake is located on the shores of a beautiful sheet of water of the same name, five miles long and one mile wide. The resort owes its rise to the citizens of Chicago, who frequent it in considerable numbers. A good bath-house adjoins the hotel.

ST. LOUIS ARTESIAN WELL.

Location.—St. Louis, Missouri.

ANALYSIS.

One pint contains (73.4° Fahr. Dr. Litton):

Solids.	Grains.
Carbonate of magnesia	0.127
Carbonate of protoxide of iron. . . .	0.066
Carbonate of lime.	1.329
Chloride of potassium	1.126
Chloride of sodium.	43.826
Chloride of magnesium.	4.792
Chloride of calcium.	3.448
Sulphate of lime	5.709
Silica.	0.017
Total	60.440
Gases.	**Cubic inches.**
Carbonic acid	0.82
Sulphuretted hydrogen.	0.03

Properties.—It will be seen by the analysis that this is a good saline water. It contains a small proportion of sulphuretted hydrogen, but not sufficient of the gas to entitle it to the designation of a sulphur-water. The temperature is above the mean annual temperature of St. Louis, and it is, therefore, technically speaking, a thermal water.

Remarks.—This well is located at Belcher's sugar-refinery. It was bored in order to obtain water for manufacturing purposes, but the saline quality of the water rendered it useless. The total depth of the well is 2,199 feet; however, most of the water is said to flow from a depth of 1,515 feet. The analysis was made some fifteen years ago, since which time the flow of the water has considerably diminished.

FRUIT PORT WELL.

Location and Post-Office.—Fruit Port, Ottawa County, Michigan.

Access.—From Chicago, *via* Chicago & Michigan Lake Shore Railroad, to Fruit Port, a station one hundred and sixteen miles north; or from Chicago, by lake-steamer, to Grand Haven; thence nine miles, by railroad, to Nuncia; thence six miles, by railroad, to Fruit Port.

Hotel.—Pomona House.

ANALYSIS.

One pint contains (48° Fahr. C. G. Wheeler):

SOLIDS.	Grains.
Carbonate of soda	0.565
Carbonate of magnesia	0.308
Carbonate of iron	0.680
Carbonate of manganese	0.010
Carbonate of lime	0.443
Chloride of potassium	0.054
Chloride of sodium	58.003
Chloride of magnesium	5.851
Chloride of lime	13.888
Sulphate of soda	5.749
Bromide of magnesium	0.095
Silica and silicates	1.325
Alumina	traces.
Total	86.971

Properties.—This water, like that of the Spring Lake well, much resembles the celebrated waters of Kreuznach, in Prussia.

Remarks.—The village of Fruit Port is on the shores of Spring Lake. The town and surrounding country, to the extent of thirteen thousand acres, is owned by a Chicago company, engaged in the development of this fruit district. The well is a result of the mania for seeking "magnetic" wells, which has prevailed in this State since the discovery of the St. Louis well, in 1869. The resort is well patronized by citizens of Chicago.

SARATOGA SPRINGS.

Location and Post-office.—Saratoga Springs, Saratoga County, New York.

Access.—Saratoga is a station on the Rensselaer & Saratoga Railroad, thirty-seven miles north of Albany. Tourists from the North may pass over Lake Champlain, and at Whitehall take the cars south to Saratoga, forty-one miles.

Hotels.—Congress Hall, Grand Union, Clarendon, Everett, Waverley, Albemarle, Continental, American.

Boarding-Houses.—Vermont, Pitney, Washington Hall.

Properties.—It will readily be seen from the table of analyses that the principal constituents of these waters are chloride of sodium, the alkaline carbonates, and carbonic-acid gas,

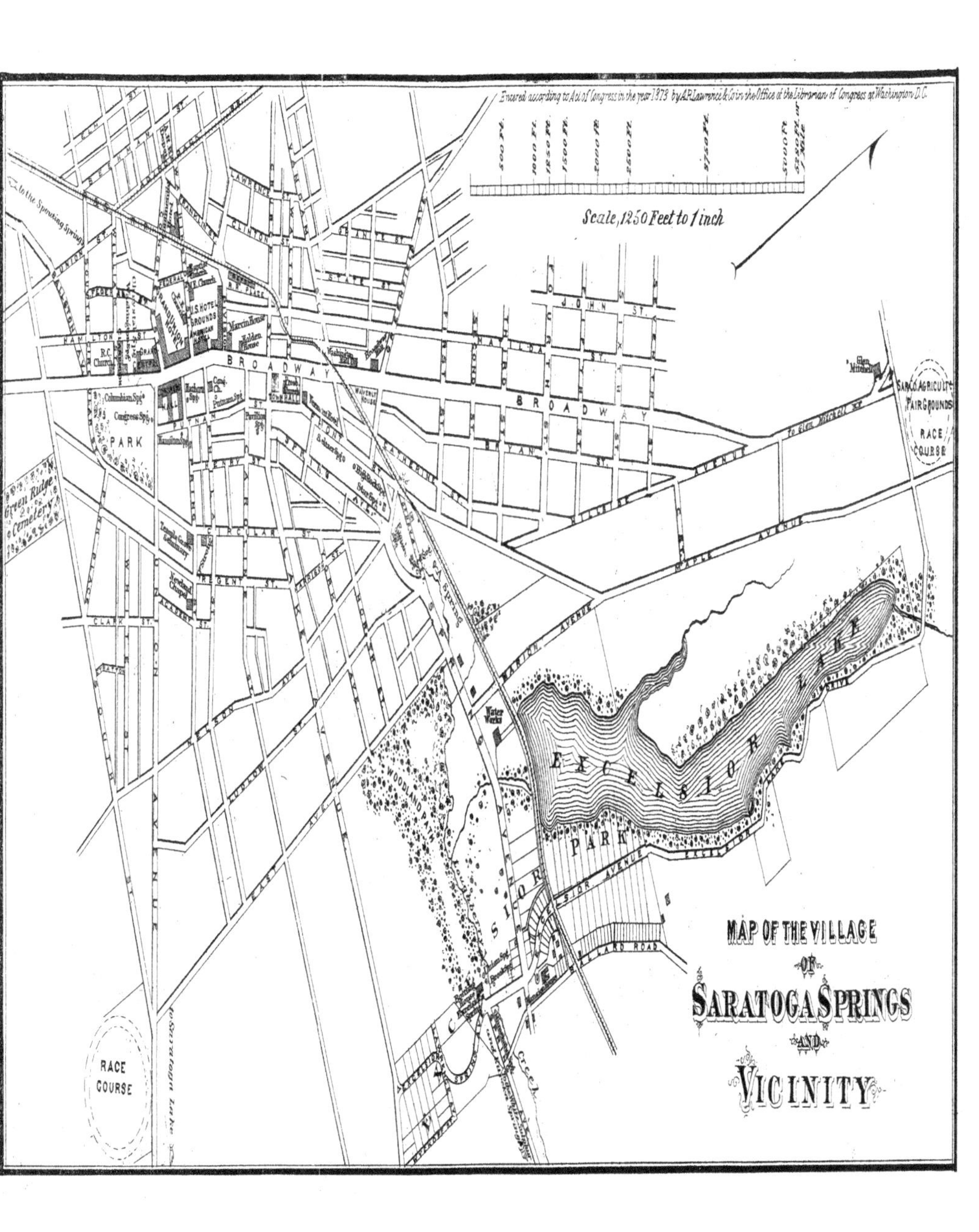

Entered according to Act of Congress in the year 1873 by A.R. Lawrence & Co in the Office of the Librarian of Congress at Washington D.C.
500 Ft.
1000 Ft.
1250 Ft.
1500 Ft.
2000 Ft.
2500 Ft.
3750 Ft.
5000 Ft.
5280 Ft. or 1 Mile
Scale, 1250 Feet to 1 inch
MAP OF THE VILLAGE
OF
SARATOGA SPRINGS
AND
VICINITY
BROADWAY
PARK
EXCELSIOR LAKE
EXCELSIOR PARK
EXCELSIOR AVENUE
WOODLAND PATH
Green Ridge Cemetery
RACE COURSE
SAR. CO. AGRICULT'L FAIR GROUNDS
Water Works
U.S. HOTEL GROUNDS
Congress Spg.
Columbian Spg.
Hamilton Spg.
MAPLE AVENUE
UNION AVENUE
CIRCULAR ST.
REGENT ST.
JOHN ST.
CLARK ST.
HAMILTON ST.
PUTNAM ST.
to Saratoga Lake
to the Spouting Springs

ANALYSIS OF SARATOGA SPRINGS.

One pint contains—	High Rock. 52° Fahr. Prof. C. F. Chandler.	Congress. 52° Fahr. Prof. C. F. Chandler.	Hathorn. Prof. C. F. Chandler.	Empire. Prof. C. F. Chandler.	Columbian. J. H. Steele, M. D.	Pavilion. Prof. C. F. Chandler.	United States. Prof. C. F. Chandler.	Seltzer. 50° Fahr. Prof. C. F. Chandler.	Geyser. 46° Fahr. Prof. C. F. Chandler.	Star. 52° Fahr. Prof. C. F. Chandler.	Red Spring. Prof. J. H. Appleton.	Eureka. R. L. Allen, M. D.	Excelsior Rock. R. L. Allen, M. D.	Hamilton. R. L. Allen, M. D.	Crystal. 50° Fahr. Prof. C. F. Chandler.
SOLIDS.	Grains.	Grains.	Grains.	Grains.	Grains.	Grains.	Grains.	Grains.	Grains.	Grains.	Grains.	Grains.	Grains.	Grains.	Grains.
Carbonate of soda	3.024	0.934	0.872	0.782	1.886	0.327	0.405	2.552	6.175	1.097	1.107	0.625	1.875	4.281	1.212
Carbonate of magnesia	4.069	9.019	13.072	3.182	3.461	5.650	5.899	2.988	10.322	4.586	2.618	3.667	4.042	4.883	5.568
Carbonate of iron	0.135	0.031	0.101	0.079	0.698	0.233	0.065	0.155	0.089	0.110	....	0.375	0.402	0.578	0.185
Carbonate of lime	11.443	12.449	14.815	9.520	8.500	10.432	8.084	7.804	14.793	10.795	7.324	5.165	9.625	12.249	8.845
Carbonate of lithia	0.154	0.374	....	0.163	....	0.744	0.380	0.071	0.549	0.124	0.016	....	....	....	0.339
Carbonate of strontia	trace.	trace.	trace.	trace	....	trace.	0.001	trace.	0.041	trace.	....	....	....	....	trace.
Carbonate of baryta	0.050	0.095	0.178	0.008	....	0.090	0.094	trace.	0.206	0.010	....	....	....	....	0.074
Chloride of potassium	1.122	1.006	1.199	0.536	....	0.958	1.078	0.167	3.079	1.212	0.686	....	....	....	1.040
Chloride of sodium	48.766	50.055	63.746	63.328	33.375	57.489	17.734	16.786	70.260	49.795	8.699	20.852	46.330	37.332	42.058
Sulphate of potassa	0.201	0.111	trace.	0.346	....	0.254	....	0.069	trace.	0.675	....	....	....	....	0.269
Sulphate of soda	...	....	....	....	....	....	....	....	....	....	....	....	0.165	....	....
Sulphate of magnesia	....	....	....	....	....	....	....	....	....	....	....	0.268	....	....	....
Phosphate of soda	trace.	0.002	0.001	0.003	....	0.001	0.002	trace.	trace.	trace.	trace.	....	....	....	0.001
Phosphate of lime	....	....	....	....	....	....	....	....	....	....	trace.	....	....	....	....
Iodide of sodium	0.011	0.017	0.025	0.001	0.320	0.009	0.006	0.004	0.031	0.015	....	0.583	0.529	0.449	0.008
Bromide of sodium	0.091	1.069	0.192	0.033	....	0.123	0.106	0.079	0.276	0.071	....	0.196	....	....	0.051
Fluoride of calcium	trace.	trace.	trace.	trace.	....	trace.	trace.	trace.	trace.	trace.	....	....	....	....	trace.
Biborate of soda	trace.	trace.	....	trace.	....	trace.	trace.	trace.	trace.	trace.	....	....	....	....	trace.
Alumina	0.153	trace.	0.016	0.052	....	0.041	0.012	0.047	trace.	trace.	[1] 0.219	0.029	....	....	0.038
Silicate of potassa	....	....	....	....	....	....	....	....	....	....	....	....	0.875	....	....
Silicate of soda	....	....	....	....	....	....	....	....	....	....	....	....	0.500	....	....
Silica	0.283	0.105	0.157	0.182	0.256	0.394	0.398	0.320	0.013	0.160	0.339	0.067	....	[2] 0.125	0.401
Organic matter	trace.	trace.	trace.	trace.	....	trace.	trace.	trace.	trace.	trace.	....	....	....	....	trace.
Total	69.502	75.267	93.874	78.215	47.946	76.745	33.764	31.042	105.834	68.650	21.008	31.827	64.343	59.897	60.089
GAS.	Cub. in.	Cub. in.	Cub. in.	Cub. in.	Cub. in.	Cub. in.	Cub. in.	Cub. in.	Cub. in.	Cub. in.	Cub. in.	Cub. in.	Cub. in.	Cub. in.	Cub. in.
Carbonic acid	51 (1866.)	49 (1871.)	47	43 (1872.)	34	41	30	40	57 (1870.)	50	....	29	81	40	39 (1870,)

[1] Alumina and sesqui-oxide of iron.

[2] Silica and alumina.

hence they may be termed *alkaline-saline* waters, of which the famed Seltzer Spring of Nassau is a typical example. In point of merit the Saratoga waters equal, if they do not surpass, any of the kind in the world. The large amount of carbonic acid which they contain, and the favorable combination of ingredients, render them very easy of digestion, and, to most persons, exceedingly pleasant to the taste. Many wonder why it is that during the hot months of the year such numbers crowd to Saratoga, thinking it only a whim of fashion; but, aside from social attractions or amusements, there is a positive value in the water, and pleasure in drinking it, which will always attract multitudes to its fountains.

These waters are especially adapted to cases of *dyspepsia;* those depending on high living, and an engorged condition of the abdominal viscera, are peculiarly subject to their beneficial influence. In *jaundice*, depending on catarrh of the biliary ducts, they are curative, and they would undoubtedly prove beneficial in cases of *gall-stones* with a tendency to their continual formation and passage. In *engorgement of the liver*, and all conditions of abdominal plethora, they are a valuable remedy. In catarrh of the bladder, they may also prove useful, but the decidedly alkaline or calcic waters are preferable.

High Rock.—On Willow Walk, near the Seltzer and Star Springs. This spring was known to the Mohawk Indians, as early as the fourteenth century, by the name of "The Medicine Spring of the Great Spirit." It was, however, unknown to white men till many years after the first settlement of the country, Sir William Johnson being the first white visitor. For many years after its discovery, the sick or curious might be seen following the trails from the settlements into the depths of the wilderness, there amid the solitude to drink silently of the mysterious water. In 1773, Dirick Scowton cleared a small portion of land on the summit of the hill, in the rear of High Rock Spring, and built a log-cabin, but misunderstandings with the Indians rendered it necessary to abandon the enterprise. In 1774, John Arnold, of Rhode Island, took possession of the house built by Scowton, and, having improved it, opened it as a tavern, and entertained visitors during two succeeding summers. This was undoubtedly the first pleasure-resort in the Northern States, that of Berkeley Springs, in Virginia, being the first in the Southern. Arnold was followed the next year by Samuel Norton, under the patronage of Isaac Law, who had purchased the land from Rip Van Dam. In this purchase Law was associated with Anthony Van Dam and Jacob Walton. Troubles with Great Britain now occurring, Norton abandoned the enterprise. In 1789, Gideon Putnam, of Sutton, came to the springs, leased three hundred acres of land, and was thereafter the pervading spirit of improvement. In 1802, he built seventy feet of the present Union Hall. The name High Rock is given from the concretions that have accumulated at the orifice of this spring for centuries, and formed a cone-like rock three feet in height, from the centre of which the water issues. The rock is composed of carbonate of lime, magnesia, and oxide of iron, precipitated from the water. Similar concretions form at many of the springs, but, owing to the direction of the flow of the water and other causes, do not assume the same form.

A few years ago, the proprietors, desirous of closing the lateral outlet of this spring, so that the water would again flow over the top of the rock, which it had ceased to do, had the rock undermined, and by means of a derrick lifted to one side. Just below the rock, four logs were found placed at right angles to each other, so as to form a curb. Under the logs were boughs of trees, resting on the black soil of a previous swamp. Undoubtedly, some ancient visitors of the spring had thrown brushwood over the swamp-ground at the orifice, and placed the logs around it. Below the rocks, the workmen followed the spring through four feet of tufa and muck; next, a layer of solid tufa, two feet thick, then one foot of muck, in which another log was found. Below this, three feet of tufa again; and there, seventeen feet below the apex of the rock, they found the embers of an ancient fire. By whom, and when, was the fire built?

DIMENSIONS OF HIGH ROCK.	Feet.	Inches.
Circumference at the surface of the ground .	24	4
Heights of rock above-ground . . .	3	6
Diameter of aperture, four inches below the top .	0	12
From the top of the rock to the water within .	2	2
Depth of spring from the top of the rock . .	10	0
Depth of water in the rock *above* the ground .	1	4

The accompanying section of High Rock conveys an idea of the formation:

GEOLOGICAL SECTION AT SARATOGA SPRINGS.

Congress Spring, in Congress Park, on Congress Street. In the year 1792, twenty-five years after Johnson's first visit to High Rock, a party of hunters on the return homeward discovered a trail which led them to a new spring. One of this hunting-party was John Taylor Gilman, a member of Congress at the time. On a subsequent visit, in honor of Gilman, they named it Congress Spring. The water proved exceedingly agreeable, and soon became the favorite spring, retaining its popularity to this day. In 1826, John Clarke, a native of Yorkshire, England, purchased the farm on which the spring was situated. Soon after the purchase he commenced bottling the water for exportation, and from that period is dated the large trade in bottled Saratoga-waters.

Columbian Spring, in Congress Park, a few rods southwest of Congress Spring.

This spring contains a larger proportion of *iron* than the other springs, rendering it a fine tonic in anæmic cases, but to be used with reserve by those who are plethoric or robust.

Hamilton Spring, on Spring Street, corner of Putnam, in the rear of Congress Hall.

This spring was first discovered by Gideon Putnam. It contains a large proportion of iron, and may be used in the cases to which the Columbian is adapted.

Pavilion Spring, in the valley, a short distance east of Broadway, between Lake Avenue and Caroline Street.

Star Spring, on Willow Walk, near the termination of Circular Street.

Empire Spring, in the north part of the village, a short distance above the Star Spring.

Washington, or *White Spring*, in the grounds of the Clarendon Hotel, South Broadway.

Putnam Spring, on Phila Street, near Broadway. A new shaft had been sunk here just previous to my visit, from which a water, highly charged with carbonic-acid gas, flowed quite rapidly.

Saratoga Seltzer, a short distance from High Rock Spring. The proprietors have attached a glass tube, some three feet long and one foot in diameter, to the orifice of this spring, through which the clear, sparkling water, filled with glittering bubbles of carbonic-acid gas, passes up rapidly. According to the analysis, this spring resembles the celebrated Seltzer, in Germany.

Saratoga A Spring, a few rods from the Red Spring.

Red Spring, on Spring Avenue, at the intersection of Geneva and Warren Streets, so named from the red deposit. This spring, though almost a century old, has never been properly developed until recently. Being less saline than any other spring at Saratoga, it will answer in some cases of dyspepsia, in which the other waters prove irritant. It is claimed that it is especially beneficial in cases of humid eczema, and other diseases of the skin, taken internally and applied as a lotion.

Excelsior Rock Spring, about one mile east of Broadway. One of the most delightful walks at Saratoga is along Spring Avenue, or Lake Avenue, through the woods, to this spring. This is one of the *Ten Springs*, the remainder, in the immediate vicinity, being yet undeveloped.

Eureka Spring, on Lake Avenue, one mile east of Broadway. The scenery in the vicinity of this spring is exceedingly attractive.

Hathorn Spring, on Spring Street, in the rear of Congress Hall. This spring was discovered in 1868, when clearing away the *débris* of the ruins of Congress Hall, preparatory to rebuilding. In taste and general character it resembles the Congress water, though stronger.

United States Spring, adjoining the Pavilion.

Crystal Spring, in Park place, Broadway, opposite Congress Park.

Indian Encampment.—A new spring was bored here in 1871.

Ellis Spring, on the Ballston road, near the Geyser.

White Sulphur Spring, immediately adjoining the Eureka Spring. The proprietors have erected a commodious bathing-house of fifty baths, with ample accommodations. Omnibuses run from the village to these springs.

Lake Sulphur Spring, on the east side of Saratoga Lake, about half a mile south of Snake Hill.

Geyser Spring, about two miles south of the village, on the Ballston road, and a short distance from the railroad.

This spring is one of the curiosities of Saratoga. It was discovered in February, 1870. During a dull season the owners of a bolt-factory, in which it is located, concluded to bore for mineral water. They chose the cellar of the factory in which to operate. Having sunk a tube to the depth of 154 feet, the water burst forth in such volume as to entirely inundate the premises. On attaching a tube of smaller calibre, the water was projected to the height of twenty-two feet, and continues spouting forth in a steady stream. It is highly charged with carbonic-acid gas, so much so that, when drawn from a faucet into a glass, it foams up like soda-water. It is also exceedingly rich in saline constituents.

The *dose of Saratoga water* is as follows: For a cathartic effect, drink two or three glasses leisurely, before breakfast, then walk for ten or fifteen minutes, and take another glass or two; breakfast half an hour afterward.

As an alterative, take a glass three or four times a day. An exception to this rule must be made in regard to the Columbian, Pavilion, Hamilton, and some other springs, as they contain a considerable proportion of iron, and should be used more guardedly. The use of these waters, however, as an alterative and tonic, would be in the quantity of one-fourth to a whole glass three times a day.

Remarks.—Saratoga Springs occur in a valley which runs north and south, for many miles, through a series of elevated table-lands. Mountain-ranges are seen in the distance, and lakes and rivulets are in the immediate vicinity of the springs. The village, with its magnificent hotels and elegant private residences, its densely-shaded streets and attractive walks, renders desirable what might otherwise be a very hot place in sultry July. The grounds of the different fountains are picturesquely adorned and shaded, and each hotel has its embowered court, where delicious music is frequently discoursed throughout the day. Congress Park, at the southern extremity of Broadway, is a favorite resort, where, during the morning hours, visitors congregate at the spring, drink of the waters, and stroll along the beautiful walks, beneath the shade of ancient forest-trees.

It is needless to say that here amusements of society, in every form, prevail; for the word Saratoga, whenever spoken, calls up visions of the dance, of walks and drives, of boating and fishing, and, unfortunately too often, of those dissipations which seem inseparable from civilization.

The principal drive is that to Moon's Lake House, four miles distant, on the shore of Saratoga Lake. From this point there is a pleasing view of this beautiful sheet of water. The lake is nine miles long and between four and five miles wide, opposite Snake Hill. A drive along the lake-shore is exceedingly attractive. An excursion steam-yacht, from the Lake House, makes frequent trips to interesting points. The avenue known as the "Mountain Drive," extending northward from Broadway, leads to Mitchell's Glen House, a famous resort. A drive of sixteen miles on the Mount Pleasant road brings one to Prospect or *Waring Hill*, said to be 2,000 feet above the sea, and commanding an extended view. At *Chapman's Hill*, a mile beyond the Lake House, there is a fine view. The hill is 180 feet above the lake. *Wagman's* Hill, three miles farther, is sixty feet higher. *Hagerty* Hill, six miles northward from the springs, on the road to Luzerne, gives a fine landscape view. *Bemis's Heights*, the scene of the famous engagement between Burgoyne and General Gates, is in the town of Stillwater, fifteen miles from the springs.

EXCELSIOR SPRING.

Location.—Syracuse, New York.

Analysis.—This is a pleasant saline water.

BALLSTON SPA.

Location and Post-Office.—Ballston, Saratoga County, New York.

Access.—From Albany, *via* Rensselaer & Saratoga Railroad, twenty-six miles north, to the springs. From the north and Lake Champlain, cars may be taken at Lake Champlain Junction, *via* Rensselaer & Saratoga Railroad; thence forty-five miles south.

Hotel.—Sans-souci.

ANALYSIS.

One pint contains—	United States. 50° Fahr. Geology N. Y.	Ballston Artesian Lithian Well. 52° Fahr. C. F. Chandler.	Franklin Artesian Well. 52° Fahr. C. F. Chandler.	Condo Dentonean Well. 49° Fahr. C. F. Chandler.
SOLIDS.	Grains.	Grains.	Grains.	Grains.
Carbonate of soda..........	2.11	1.084	8.200	2.982
Carbonate of magnesia......	0.72	18.378	18.175	11.729
Carbonate of iron	trace.	0.148	0.146	0.208
Carbonate of lime	3.65	20.675	17.565	15.494
Carbonate of lithia	....	0.701	0.613	0.950
Carbonate of strontia	....	0.083	trace.	0.018
Carbonate of baryta	....	0.397	0.125	0.484
Chloride of potassium	....	4.159	4.241	1.154
Chloride of sodium.........	53.12	93.753	82.418	80.685
Sulphate of potassa	....	0.065	0.095	trace.
Sulphate of soda	0.22	....	....	....
Phosphate of soda..........	....	0.006	0.001	trace.
Iodide of sodium...........	....	0.015	0.029	0.028
Bromide of sodium	....	0.455	0.583	0.296
Fluoride of calcium.........	....	trace.	trace,	trace.
Biborate of soda...........	....	trace.	trace.	trace.
Alumina....................	....	0.009	0.032	0.049
Silica	1.00	0.095	0.092	0.128
Organic matter.............	....	trace.	trace.	trace.
Total..................	60.82	134.968	127.315	114.205
GAS.	Cubic in.	Cubic in.	Cubic in.	Cubic in.
Carbonic acid	30.50	53.26	57.51	44.79

Properties.—These waters present the same properties as those of Saratoga. It will be noticed, however, that they are richer in mineral constituents, that of the Lithia well having the exceedingly large quantity of one hundred and thirty-four grains of solid matter to the pint.

Remarks.—The fame of Ballston Springs is almost coeval with that of Saratoga. The village spring, the analysis of which is not given, resembles closely the Red Spring of Saratoga. Low's Well is said to be similar to the United States Spring in composition.

During the coal-oil excitement, which swept over the country some years ago, a capitalist of New York conceived the idea of boring for oil at Ballston. He selected a site on the banks of the Kayaderosseras Creek, and commenced operations. After much labor, and when the well had attained a depth of five hundred and seventy-one feet, water flowed from the tubing in large quantity; but oil was the object, and the boring went on.

However, at the depth of six hundred and seventy-one feet, the steel rammer became immovably fixed in the rock, and the undertaking was abandoned. Then attention was turned to the water that flowed from the tube, and it was discovered to be the most highly impregnated with mineral ingredients of any in the county. The town of Ballston is an exceedingly pleasant one, where those who wish to avoid the excitement of Saratoga can live quietly, and drink equal, if not superior, water.

WILHOIT'S SODA-SPRINGS.

Location.—Clackamas County, Oregon.

Post-Office.—Salem, Marion County, Oregon.

Access.—From Salem go thirty miles northeast by road.

Hotel.—Wilhoit's Springs.

ANALYSIS.

One pint contains (J. H. Veach, M. D.):

SOLIDS.	Grains.
Carbonate of soda	10.946
Carbonate of magnesia	10.665
Carbonate protoxide of iron	0.750
Carbonate of lime	4.028
Chloride of sodium	25.125
Sulphate of soda	0.425
Sulphate of magnesia	0.810
Iodine	trace.
Total	52.749
GAS.	Cubic inches.
Carbonic acid	42

Properties.—According to the above analysis, these waters are of great value. They are of the alkaline-saline class, and closely resemble some of the finest waters of Europe, such as the Seltzer. "The water is strongly impregnated with carbonic-acid gas, constantly escaping from the surface, and giving a sparkling effervescence to the liquid. Very pleasant to the taste, it exhilarates fully as much as wine, on the first day, and on the second operates as a laxative and diuretic."[1] It will be observed that the water contains considerable iron, and should, therefore, be used somewhat guardedly.

[1] Prof. H. Carpenter, M. D., in the *Oregon Medical and Surgical Reporter*.

Remarks.—The springs are enclosed by groves of fir, pine, and oak, and all the surroundings contribute to enhance the beauty of the place.

ALBANY ARTESIAN WELL.

Location.—Ferry Street, Albany, New York.

ANALYSIS.

One pint contains (51° to 52° Fahr. Dr. Meade):

SOLIDS.	Grains.
Carbonate of soda	5.00
Carbonate of magnesia	2.00
Carbonate of iron (with a little silica)	1.00
Carbonate of lime	4.00
Chloride of sodium	63.00
Total	75.00
GAS.	Cubic inches.
Carbonic acid	28.00

The well is five hundred feet deep. —("Geology of New York.")

CHARLESTON ARTESIAN WELL.

Location and Post-Office.—Charleston, South Carolina.

ANALYSIS.

One pint contains (87° Fahr. Prof. C. U. Shephard, Jr.):

SOLIDS.	Grains.
Carbonate of soda	7.353
Carbonate of magnesia	0.001
Carbonate of lime	0.140
Chloride of sodium	9.459
Phosphates of lime, iron, and alumina	0.001
Silica	0.002
Organic matter	0.003
Total	16.959
GAS.	Cubic inches.
Carbonic-acid gas	0.28

Properties.—It will be seen from the analysis that this is an alkaline-saline water, chloride of sodium slightly predominating. The water is a *thermal*, but it seems better to class it here, as it is principally used internally. It is a good water of the class. The flow is estimated at twenty gallons per minute. The well is twelve hundred and fifty feet deep.

CHAPTER XII.

SULPHUR-WATERS.

THE prominent characteristic of these waters is the presence of sulphuretted hydrogen, hence the peculiar odor. Excepting the uniform presence of this gas, sulphur-waters vary exceedingly in composition. Some contain a large proportion of calcic carbonates, and hence may be termed calcic-sulphur waters; others, containing chloride of sodium in excess of other constituents, may be termed saline-sulphur waters; and, according to the proportion of these salts, will their action be modified. Those containing a considerable quantity of carbonate of lime and sulphate of lime will usually prove constipating, while those characterized by the presence of much chloride of sodium, or sulphate of soda or magnesia, will be cathartic. Still another element enters into the action of these waters, in many instances: organic matters, known by the names of barégine and glairine, undoubtedly differing in composition in different springs, and producing varied results. However, as a rule, the action of these substances seems to be sedative; as an illustration, see the Red Sulphur Springs of Virginia. Some sulphur-waters are exciting, others depressing, depending on the quantity of sulphuretted hydrogen, the salts, and temperature. Many of these waters are thermal. They all act as diaphoretics and alteratives. As a rule, they are decidedly diaphoretic, a result due to the sulphuretted hydrogen contained. Persons who take considerable quantities of sulphur-water are sometimes surprised to find articles of silver carried in the pockets decidedly blackened. This is due to the elimination of sulphuretted hydrogen in the perspiration, sulphuret of silver being formed.

Many sulphur-waters undergo chemical alteration after contact with the atmosphere. The principal agent in this change, according to Anglada, is oxygen. Under its influence the sulphurets are decomposed, sulphur is precipitated, and sulphites are formed. At the same time, the carbonic acid of the atmosphere unites with a portion of alkaline bases, forming carbonates.

The color of the white sulphur-waters is due to the precipitation of sulphur; the yellow, to the formation of polysulphurets; the blue is supposed to be due to slate held in suspension in the form of impalpable powder; and the red, to the development of algæ of this color, or precipitation of oxide of iron.

Sulphur-waters are especially applicable to the treatment of *diseases of the skin*, and, of these diseases, especially those falling under the class *dartrous*. (*See* "DISEASES OF THE SKIN.") They are also decidedly efficacious in cases of *chronic pharyngitis* and *laryngitis*.

The warm sulphur-waters are valuable in the treatment of *gout* and *chronic rheumatism*, more because of their elevated temperature than the saline constituents, unless they be of the alkaline-sulphur class, though their decidedly diaphoretic action may aid the elimination of uric acid. The warm waters also prove exceedingly serviceable in cases where exudations are to be absorbed, such as *stiff joints* and *old gunshot-wounds*. The natural warm or hot sulphur-waters are preferable; but properly-heated cold sulphur-waters will answer.

In *chronic poisoning by metals* sulphur-waters often prove exceedingly beneficial, by favoring elimination of the poison. In cases of *engorgement of the liver*, *abdominal plethora*, and *hæmorrhoids*, the *saline-sulphur* waters have long been justly esteemed as trustworthy remedies. In secondary and tertiary *syphilis*, sulphur-waters prove valuable as a means of diagnosis; and, in conjunction with other remedies, they aid in eliminating the venereal poison. Persons in whom syphilis is latent are often surprised to see external manifestations caused by the use of these waters.

It will be noticed that there is much variation in the quantity of sulphuretted hydrogen in the different springs. It is found desirable in some cases to let the water stand for some hours before drinking, in order that the superabundant gas may escape, and thus avoid the undue excitement of the system caused by ingestion of large quantities.

BLOUNT SPRINGS.

Location and Post-Office.—Blount Springs, Blount County, Alabama.

Access.—Go to Elyton, a station on the Alabama & Chattanooga Railroad, 144 miles southwest from Chattanooga; also, on the line of railroad (not finished) from Montgomery to Decatur, about eighty-five miles northwest from Montgomery; thence, about thirty miles northwest to the springs.

Hotel.—Blount Springs.

ANALYSIS.

One pint contains—	Red Sulphur. Prof. R. Brumby.	Sweet Sulphur. Prof. R. Brumby.
SOLIDS.	Grains.	Grains.
Carbonate of magnesia	0.55	0.45
Carbonate of iron	0.24	0.14
Carbonate of lime	0.85	0.56
Chloride of sodium	4.04	3.86
Chloride of magnesium	0.75	....
Sulphate of magnesia	0.20	0.30
Total	6.63	5.31
GASES.	Cubic in.	Cubic in.
Carbonic acid	0.75	0.75
Sulphuretted hydrogen	1.87	1.57

Properties.—A saline-sulphur water.

Remarks.—These springs are situated in a triangular valley, at an elevation of 1,580 feet above the sea. They are six in number. The present hotel was built in 1825; but many improvements are now in contemplation, among them the building of a new hotel.

SANDWICH SPRINGS,

Location and Post-Office.—Sandwich, Ontario, Canada.

Access.—From Detroit, cross the St. Clair River, by ferry, two miles to Sandwich.

Hotel.—Sandwich Springs.

ANALYSIS.

One pint contains (52° Fahr. Prof. S. P. DUFFIELD):

SOLIDS.	Grains.
Carbonate of potassa	trace.
Carbonate of soda	6.070
Carbonate of magnesia	1.618
Carbonate of lime	4.813
Chloride of sodium	0.070
Chloride of magnesium	19.220
Chloride of calcium	0.007
Sulphate of lime	15.479
Silica	0.014
Total	47.291
GASES.	Cubic in.
Carbonic acid	1.25
Sulphuretted hydrogen	4.72
Nitrogen	0.09

Properties.—This spring, it will be observed, is distinguished by the large amounts of chloride of magnesium and sulphate of lime which it contains; also, the enormous volume of sulphuretted-hydrogen gas.

CALEDONIA SPRINGS.

Location.—See these springs, described under "SALINE WATERS," p. 163.

ANALYSIS.

One pint contains (46° Fahr. T. STERRY HUNT):

SOLIDS.	Grains.
Carbonate of soda	3.321
Carbonate of magnesia	2.142
Carbonate of iron	trace.
Carbonate of lime	1.530
Chloride of potassium	.167
Chloride of sodium	28.004
Sulphate of soda	.133
Bromide of sodium	.073
Alumina	.019
Silica	.612
Total	36.001
GAS.	Cubic in.
Carbonic acid	2
Flow per minute	4 gallons

Properties.—T. Sterry Hunt, Esq., says of this water: "It has a feebly sulphurous taste and odor, and darkens the salts of lead and silver; but the quantity of sulphur existing, either as sulphuretted hydrogen or an alkaline sulphuret, is very inconsiderable, and cannot be quantitatively estimated by the ordinary processes. It is, however, sufficient to impart medicinal powers to the water; for the efficacy of this spring over all the others, in rheumatic and cutaneous affections, is well attested. According to Dr. Stirling, for many years a resident at the springs, the water was formerly more sulphurous than now."

PIEDMONT SPRINGS.

Location.—Contra Costa County, California.

Post-Office.—Oakland, Contra Costa County, California.

Access.—By omnibus, three miles distant from Oakland.

Hotel.—Piedmont Springs.

Analysis.—None.

Remarks.—From these springs there is a most extended view, embracing the bay and city of San Francisco, the Golden Gate, the bay of San Pablo, Tamalpais, and the coast-hills of Marin County. The climate is mild, and free from fogs. The waters possess the usual taste of waters of this class, and are said to prove aperient.

WHITE SULPHUR SPRINGS.

Location and Post-Office.—White Sulphur Springs, Napa County, California.

Access.—These springs are twelve miles distant, by rail, from Calistoga Springs, or an hour's drive by carriage.

Hotel.—White Sulphur Springs.

Analysis.—None has been made.

VALLEJO WHITE SULPHUR SPRINGS.

Location and Post-Office.—Vallejo Springs, Solano County, California.

Access.—From San Francisco, thirty miles, by steamer, to Vallejo; thence four miles, by stage.

Hotel.—Springs.

Analysis.—None.

GREEN-COVE SPRING.

Location and Post-Office.—Green-Cove Spring, Clay County, Florida.

Access.—From the north and west, by rail, *via* Charleston and Savannah, to Jacksonville; thence, by daily steamer, thirty miles south, on St John's River, to the spring. Or, from New York, by steamer to Charleston or Savannah; thence, by the connecting steamer, direct to the spring.

Hotel.—Clarendon House.

Analysis.—A partial analysis showed the water to contain sulphate of magnesia, sulphate of lime, chloride of sodium, iron, and considerable sulphuretted hydrogen. The water should be quantitatively analyzed. Temperature, 76° Fahr. The flow is exceedingly large.

Properties.—A water such as this proves exceedingly agreeable as a bath, in a southern climate, and is adapted to a number of diseases.

Remarks.—These springs are on the St. John's River, at a point where it is five miles wide, and affords every facility for boating, sailing, and fishing. The large flow of water is caught in a pool twenty-five by a hundred feet, and four feet deep, forming a magnificent swimming-bath, with dressing-rooms attached.

Florida will always be a popular resort for those who desire to escape the rigor of Northern winters; and certainly it is pleasant to live in a climate where spring follows close upon fall, and tropical fruits are abundant. During the winter many consumptives rendezvous at this and other points along the St. John's River.

RED SULPHUR SPRINGS.

Location and Post-Office.—Red Sulphur Springs, Walker County, Georgia.

Access.—From Chattanooga.

Hotel.— ———.

Analysis.—None.

Remarks.—Red Sulphur Springs, or "the Vale of Springs," are at the base of Taylor's Ridge. No less than twenty springs are found here in the space of half a mile. Near by, is Lookout Mountain.

CHARLOTSVILLE SPRINGS.

Location.—Charlotsville, near Simcoe, Norfolk County, Province of Ontario, Dominion of Canada.

Access.—A few miles from Port Dover, a landing on Lake Erie.

Analysis.—This water is notable for the large amount of sulphuretted hydrogen contained—over three and a quarter cubic inches to the pint. The amount of mineral ingredients is small.

FRENCH LICK SPRINGS.

Location and Post-Office Address.—French Lick Springs, Orange County, Indiana.

Access.—Going east or west, take Ohio & Mississippi Railroad to Shoals, one hundred and forty-nine miles west of Cincinnati, one hundred and ninety-one miles east of St. Louis; thence fifteen miles south, by stage, to springs. From the north or south, take New Albany & Chicago Railroad to Orleans, fifty-six miles north of Louisville, five miles south of Mitchell, a station on the Ohio & Mississippi Railroad; thence eighteen miles, by stage, to springs.

Hotels.—French Lick (West Baden, one mile distant).[1]

ANALYSIS.

One pint contains—	Pluto's Well. J. G. Rogers, M. D.	Proserpine. J. G. Rogers, M. D.
SOLIDS.	Grains.	Grains.
Carbonate of soda	....	1.816
Carbonate of magnesia	0.198	0.562
Carbonate of iron and alumina	trace.	0.812
Carbonate of lime	0.868	2.586
Chloride of potassium	....	0.626
Chloride of sodium	17.567	11.865
Chloride of magnesium	....	1.006
Chloride of calcium	0.668	....
Sulphate of soda	2.796	4.590
Sulphate of magnesia	2.264	8.666
Sulphate of lime	7.573	17.625
Silica	....	0.212
Total	31.934	48.816
GASES.	Cubic in.	Cubic in.
Carbonic acid	1.87	1.277
Sulphuretted hydrogen	3.18	2.125
Total	5.05	3.402

Chalybeate Springs not analyzed. (1870.)

Properties.—These waters are useful in all those diseases to which sulphur-waters are applicable, and, on account of the salines contained, especially to those associated with *engorgement of the liver* and abdominal viscera. In these cases it will be well to combine warm baths with the use of the water. Pluto's Well will be found best adapted to most diseases for which these waters are beneficial.

Remarks.—French Lick Springs are situated in the heart of a fine, rolling, agricultural country. They issue at the base of a hill immediately on the margin of French Lick Creek. Near by, flows Lost River, abounding in the choicest fish. Those who are inclined to sport, will find game near at hand.

WEST BADEN SPRINGS.

Location and Post-Office.—West Baden Springs, Orange County, Indiana.

Access.—Go to Shoals, a station on the Ohio & Mississippi Railroad, one hundred and fifty miles west of Cincinnati; thence by stage. Or, go to Orleans, a station on the Louisville, New Albany & Chicago Railroad, fifty-six miles north of New Albany; thence by stage.

Hotels.—West Baden (French Lick, one mile distant).

ANALYSIS.

One pint contains (E. T. Cox):

SOLIDS.	Grains.
Carbonate of potassa	0.078
Carbonate of soda	0.139
Carbonate of magnesia	4.895
Carbonate of lime	5.172
Chloride of sodium	9.748
Chloride of magnesium	1.425
Chloride of calcium	0.910
Sulphate of potassa	0.171
Sulphate of soda	0.388
Sulphate of magnesia	4.519
Sulphate of lime	1.398
Sulphate of alumina	0.569
Oxide of iron	0.011
Iodides and bromides	traces.
Silicic acid	0.055
Total	29.478
GASES.	Cubic in.
Carbonic acid	0.64
Sulphuretted hydrogen	0.61
Oxygen	0.21
Nitrogen	0.68

Properties.—It will be seen, from the analysis, that this is a saline-sulphur water, of much value in all those cases to which such waters are applicable.

Remarks.—West Baden is in the midst of a fine agricultural section. In sight of the hotel flows Lost River and French Lick Creek, which abound in choice fish.

INDIAN SPRINGS.

Location and Post-Office.—Indian Springs, Martin County, Indiana.

Access.—Go to Shoals, a station on the Ohio & Mississippi Railroad, one hundred and fifty miles west of Cincinnati; thence nine miles, by stage. Or, go to Bedford, a station on the Louisville, New Albany & Chicago Railroad, seventy-one miles north of Louisville.

Hotel.—Springs.

ANALYSIS.

One pint contains (53° Fahr. (E. T. Cox):

SOLIDS.	Grains.
Carbonate of potassa	0.315
Carbonate of soda	0.452
Carbonate of magnesia	2.368
Carbonate of lime	4.138
Chloride of sodium	4.921
Chloride of magnesium	0.007
Sulphate of potassa	0.300
Sulphate of soda	1.478
Sulphate of magnesia	3.799
Sulphate of lime	2.529
Sulphate of alumina	0.104
Oxide of iron	trace.
Iodides and bromides	trace.
Silicic acid	0.056
Total	20.467
GASES.	Cubic in.
Carbonic acid	1.19
Sulphuretted hydrogen	0.42
Oxygen	0.49
Nitrogen.	0.81

Remarks.—This is a good saline-sulphur water. The flow is large, estimated at four hundred gallons per minute, sufficient for all bathing purposes.

INDIAN SPRINGS.

Location and Post-Office.—Indian Springs, Butts County, Georgia.

Access.—Go to Forsyth, on the Macon & Western Railroad, twenty-five miles north of Macon; thence by stage. Or, to Griffin, on the Macon & Western Railroad, forty-four miles south of Atlanta; thence by stage.

Hotel.— ——.

Analysis.—None.

LODI ARTESIAN WELL.

Location and Post-Office.—Lodi, Wabash County, Indiana.

Access.—Lodi is a station on the Indianapolis & St. Louis Railroad, fifty-eight miles west of Indianapolis.

Hotels.—.

ANALYSIS.

One pint contains (Dr. Pahle):

Solids.	Grains.
Carbonate of magnesia	0.082
Carbonate of lime	0.252
Chloride of sodium	62.808
Chloride of magnesium	6.692
Chloride of calcium	5.991
Sulphate of potassa	0.100
Sulphate of soda	0 267
Sulphate of magnesia	0.407
Sulphate of lime	6.944
Phosphate of lime	0.150
Iodide of magnesium	trace.
Bromide of magnesium	0.110
Silicic acid	0.065
Sulphur (mechanically suspended)	0.625
Nitrogenous organic matter	0.100
Total	84.593
Gases.	**Cubic in.**
Carbonic acid	undetermined.
Sulphuretted hydrogen	0.99
Oxygen and nitrogen	undetermined.

Properties.—The above analysis, taken from the "Geology of Indiana," for 1869, shows this to be a very valuable saline-sulphur water. On comparison with the celebrated Blue Lick waters of Kentucky, it will be seen to possess a close analogy. It will prove useful in all those diseases to which saline-sulphur waters are applicable.

LAFAYETTE WELL.

Location and Post-Office.—LaFayette, Tippecanoe County, Indiana.

ANALYSIS.

One pint contains (55° Fahr. C. M. Wetherell, M. D.):

SOLIDS.	Grains.
Carbonate of magnesia	3.590
Carbonate of lime	1.044
Chloride of sodium	40.590
Chloride of magnesium	3.707
Chloride of calcium	0.465
Sulphate of lime	7.042
Iodide of magnesium	trace.
Alumina and oxide of iron	0.062
Silica	0.058
Total	56.558
GASES.	Cubic in.
Carbonic acid	1.52
Sulphuretted hydrogen	0.24
Nitrogen	0.61

Properties.—An excellent saline-sulphur water, principally used for exportation.

Remarks.—Flow, four gallons per minute. Depth of well, two hundred and thirty feet.

TRINITY SPRINGS.

Location and Post-Office.—Trinity Springs, Martin County, Indiana.

Access.—Go to Shoals, a station on the Ohio & Mississippi Railroad, one hundred and fifty miles west of Cincinnati, one hundred and ninety miles east of St. Louis; thence, eight miles by stage, to the springs.

Hotel.—Trinity House.

Analysis.—From the report of Dr. E. T. Cox, State Geologist of Indiana, 1871, page 110, we extract the following: "The temperature of the water of the Trinity Springs was 57° Fahr.; and that of the air, 89° Fahr. Bubbles of gas escape through the water, and a whitish deposit is found on the inside of the curbing. The qualitative, chemical examination of this water gave the following result: Sulphuric acid, carbonic acid, sulphydric acid, hydrochloric acid, soda, potash, magnesia, lime. This is also a saline-sulphuretted water, and contains precisely the same constituents found in the Indian springs."

UPPER BLUE LICK SPRINGS.

Location and Post-Office.—Upper Blue Lick Springs, Nicholas County, Kentucky.

Access.—By steamboat to Maysville, Kentucky, on the Ohio River; thence by Maysville & Lexington Railroad to within six miles of the springs.

Hotel.—Boarding accommodations.

ANALYSIS.

One pint contains (62 Fahr., June J. F. Judge and A. Fennel):

SOLIDS.	Grains.
Carbonate of magnesia	0.018
Carbonate of lime	3.133
Chloride of potassium	0.225
Chloride of sodium	64.567
Chloride of magnesium	4.716
Sulphate of potassa	1.622
Sulphate of lime	5.517
Iodide of magnesium	0.019
Bromide of magnesium	0.476
Alumina: phosphate of lime and peroxide of iron	0.246
Silicic acid	0.125
Loss	18.60
Total	82.524
GASES.	Cubic in.
Carbonic acid	6.02
Sulphuretted hydrogen	1.02

(1870.)

Properties.—These are exceptionally fine waters of the saline-sulphur class. They are aperient and alterative in action, proving efficacious in *engorgements of the liver* and abdominal organs, *gall-stones*, *gastric catarrh*, *granular pharyngitis*, and, combined with warm baths of the water, are valuable in chronic diseases of the skin.

Remarks.—These springs are located on the margin of the Licking River. The water has been deservedly popular with the people of the West ever since the early settlement of the country, and bottled and barrelled water is sold largely in all of the leading cities of the Ohio and Mississippi Valleys. The flow of the waters is large. The locality is well adapted for a summer resort; and it is to be hoped such arrangements will be made as will permit of employing the waters in every form of bath at the fountain-source.

LOWER BLUE LICK SPRINGS.

Location and Post-Office.—Lower Blue Lick Springs, Nicholas County, Kentucky.

Access.—From Maysville, Kentucky, a point on the Ohio River, sixty-five miles above Cincinnati, *via* Maysville & Lexington Railroad, and stage.

Hotel.—Blue Lick House.

ANALYSIS.

One pint contains (62° Fahr. Robert Peter, M. D.):

SOLIDS.	Grains.
Carbonate of magnesia	0.017
Carbonate of lime	2.957
Chloride of potassium	0.174
Chloride of sodium	64.107
Chloride of magnesium	4.049
Sulphate of potassa	1.117
Sulphate of lime	4.249
Iodide of magnesium	0.006
Bromide of magnesium	0.030
Alumina: phosphate of lime and oxide of iron	0.045
Silicic acid	0.138
Loss	2.216
Total	79.105
GASES.	Cubic in.
Carbonic acid	12.35
Sulphuretted hydrogen	2.28

—"Geology of Kentucky," vol. iii., pp. 361–368.

Properties.—These are exceptionally fine waters of the saline-sulphur class, exceedingly valuable in *engorgements of the liver* and abdominal viscera, and all diseases arising therefrom. They may also be relied on in *gastric catarrh*, and, in the form of warm baths, prove efficacious in diseases of the skin.

Remarks.—This spring was well known to the early settlers of the West, and from its waters Boone and other pioneers obtained salt for curing their venison. While engaged in its manufacture they were surprised by the Indians, and one of the deadliest battles in the annals of border life was fought near the spring.

The principal spring is located on the banks of the Licking, about twenty feet above the water's edge. It rises in an hexagonal reservoir of stone, six feet in diameter and about five feet deep. The flow of the spring is so rapid that the removal of almost 2,000 gallons in three hours caused the water in the reservoir to fall but one foot.

Besides the main spring there are others, on the opposite side of the river and in its bed, which on examination proved to contain the same ingredients.

It will be observed, on inspection of the analysis, that there is a striking similarity between these waters and those of the Upper Blue Lick.

BIG BONE SPRINGS.

Location and Post-Office.—Big Bone Springs, Boone County, Kentucky.

Access.—Go to Walton, a station on the Louisville & Cincinnati Railroad, eighteen miles west of Cincinnati; thence seven miles by stage to the springs. Or, by steamboat on the Ohio River to Hamilton Landing; thence one mile and a half to the springs.

Hotel.—Clay House.

Analysis.—No quantitative analysis of these waters has been made. The following is the statement in the "Geology of Kentucky," volume ii., page 62: "The quantitative analysis of these waters, at their fountain-head, indicated as their principal constituents: Sulphuretted hydrogen—which escapes in intermittent volume, proving the water to be saturated with this gas—chloride of sodium, sulphate of magnesia, sulphate of soda, sulphate of alumina, bicarbonate of lime, bicarbonate of magnesia, carbonate of soda. This water has an alkaline reaction." It is also stated that "these are truly fine sulphuretted-saline waters."

Remarks.—The supply of water is very abundant, several springs breaking forth in various directions, from the boggy flats forming the sources of Big Bone Lick Creek. The name "Big Bone" is derived from the fact that remains of mastodons are frequently found here, embedded in the bog. Some exceedingly fine specimens have been obtained.

There are three springs, known as the "Big Bone," the "Mastodon," and the "American Epsom."

PAROQUET SPRINGS.

Location.—Bullitt County, Kentucky.

Post-Office.—Shepherdsville, Bullitt County, Kentucky.

Access.—Go to Louisville; thence eighteen miles south on Louisville & Nashville Railroad to Shepherdsville; thence by stage.

Hotel.—Paroquet Springs.

ANALYSIS.

One pint contains (Prof. J. Lawrence Smith):

SOLIDS.	Grains.
Carbonate of soda	0.047
Carbonate of magnesia	0.188
Carbonate of iron	0.022
Carbonate of lime	0.300
Chloride of potassium	0.061
Chloride of sodium	38.700
Chloride of magnesium	6.004
Chloride of calcium	8.464
Sulphate of soda	0.302
Sulphate of alumina	0.062
Sulphate of lime	0.285
Iodide of sodium	0.019
Iodide of magnesium	0.031
Bromide of sodium	0.022
Bromide of magnesium	0.039
Silica	0.488
Organic matter	0.267
Total	55.301
GASES.	Cubic in.
Carbonic acid	0.75
Sulphuretted hydrogen	3.75

—"Geology of Kentucky," vol. ii., p. 74.

Properties.—These are valuable saline-sulphur waters, containing a large proportion of sulphuretted hydrogen.

ESCULAPIA SPRINGS.

Location.—Lewis County, Kentucky.

Access.—About twenty miles from Maysville and twelve miles from Vanceburg, on the Ohio River. Maysville is sixty-five miles east of Cincinnati.

Hotel.— ———.

Analysis.—No quantitative analysis of this water has been made. According to Dr. L. J. Frazee,[1] an analysis by Dr. Peter showed it to contain free sulphuretted hydrogen gas, bicarbonate of lime, bicarbonate of magnesia, chloride of sodium, chloride of magnesium, sulphate of soda, and sulphate of magnesia.

Properties.—Dr. Frazee adds: "It is proper to remark that most of these saline ingredients are in very minute quantities, so much so that the chloride of sodium, the sulphate of soda, and the sulphate of magnesia it contains, render it very slightly if at all aperient. Sulphur, in the form of sulphuretted-hydrogen gas, with which this water is impregnated, may be considered by far its most important ingredient. . . . The principal effect of the water appears to be to stimulate the secretory action of the system generally, but more especially that of the skin and that of the kidneys."

Remarks.—The Esculapia Springs are situated between two lofty ranges of hills, lying almost parallel. At the base of one occurs the sulphur spring, and at the base of the other a *chalybeate* spring.

GRAYSON SPRINGS.

Location and Post-Office.—Grayson Springs, Grayson County, Kentucky.

Access.—From Louisville, *via* Louisville & Nashville Railroad, forty-two miles south to Elizabethtown; thence twenty-six miles west, *via* Elizabethtown & Paducah Railroad, to Grayson Springs Station; thence two miles and a half by stage to the springs.

Hotel.—Grayson Springs.

Analysis.—These waters contain, according to Dr. Peter,[2]

[1] "Transactions Kentucky State Medical Society," 1872; report on "The Mineral Waters of Kentucky," by L. J. Frazee, M. D.

[2] Frazee, "The Mineral Waters of Kentucky."

chloride of sodium, sulphate of magnesia, phosphate of soda, sulphuretted-hydrogen gas, and carbonic-acid gas.

Remarks.—These springs rise in a valley, and within a circuit of a few hundred feet there is a number of sources, differing but little in constitution. A *chalybeate* spring is said to have been discovered on the grounds. Since the completion of the Elizabethtown & Paducah Railroad, this resort has been considerably patronized.

OLYMPIAN SPRINGS.

Location and Post-Office.—Olympian Springs, Bath County, Kentucky.

Access.—Go by rail to Lexington, Kentucky; thence, by Lexington & Big Sandy Railroad, about thirty-five miles east, to Mount Sterling; thence by stage. During 1873 the Lexington & Big Sandy Railroad will probably be finished to within three miles of the springs.

Hotel.—Olympian Springs.

ANALYSIS.

One pint contains (Salt Sulphur, Dr. Peter):

SOLIDS.	Grains.
Carbonate of magnesia	0.904
Carbonate of iron	trace.
Carbonate of lime	1.742
Chloride of potassium	1.334
Chloride of sodium	20.752
Chloride of magnesium	6.924
Sulphate of lime	trace.
Bromine and iron	trace.
Alumina	trace.
Silica	0.131
Water and loss	9.825
Total	41.612
GASES.	
Carbonic acid	not estimated.
Sulphuretted hydrogen	not estimated.

Properties.—This is a fine saline-sulphur water, seldom cathartic, promptly diuretic. The flow is six gallons per minute.

Remarks.—These springs are situated in the eastern portion of the State, where the surface is exceedingly rough and picturesque, approaching mountainous. Besides the water of which the analysis is given, there is also a so-called black-sulphur spring, and a chalybeate. The chalybeate tastes decidedly of iron, according to Dr. Drake.

FOX SPRINGS.

Location.—Fleming County, Kentucky.

Access.—Fox Springs are about ten miles from Flemingsburg, which place is twelve miles south of Maysville, a town on the Ohio River.

Hotel.— ———.

Analysis.—Dr. Frazee, in his report on "The Mineral Waters of Kentucky," says these are sulphur-waters similar to the Esculapia Springs.

Remarks.—This is said to be a pleasant resort. There is also a *chalybeate* water here.

ESTILL SPRINGS.

For location, etc., *see* "Estill Springs, Purgative Waters."

ANALYSIS.

One pint contains (Red Sulphur, Robert Peter, M. D.):

Solids.	Grains.
Carbonate of soda	0.168
Carbonate of magnesia	0.605
Carbonate of lime	1.472
Chloride of sodium	0.612
Sulphate of potassa	0.670
Sulphate of soda	1.254
Sulphate of magnesia	0.073
Silica	0.044
Organic and volatile matters	0.292
Total	5.190
Gases.	**Cubic in.**
Carbonic acid	5.01
Sulphuretted hydrogen	0.07

Properties.—It will be seen that this is a light sulphur-water, the sulphuretted hydrogen arising, in all probability, from decomposition of a sulphate. There are two other springs, the white and black sulphur, containing almost the same ingredients in about the same proportion. The black sulphur, however, contains one-half grain (0.502) of carbonate of iron to the pint.

LOUISVILLE ARTESIAN WELL.

Location and Post-office.—Louisville, Kentucky.

ANALYSIS.

One pint contains (76½° Fahr. Prof. J. Lawrence Smith):

Solids.	Grains.
Carbonate of soda	0.237
Carbonate of magnesia	0.204
Carbonate of iron	0.032
Carbonate of lime	0.520
Chloride of potassium	0.528
Chloride of sodium	77.690
Chloride of magnesium	1.847
Chloride of aluminum	0.151
Chloride of calcium	8.216
Chloride of lithium	0.013
Sulphate of potassa	0.403
Sulphate of soda	9.037
Sulphate of magnesia	9.667
Sulphate of alumina	0.225
Sulphate of lime	3.679
Phosphate of soda	0.193
Iodide of magnesium	0.044
Bromide of magnesium	0.058
Silica	0.111
Organic matter	0.089
Loss	1.015
Total	113.959

Gases.	Cubic in.
Carbonic acid	0.77
Sulphuretted hydrogen	0.25
Nitrogen	0.17

Properties.—It will be seen that this is a saline-sulphur water, and a valuable one.

Remarks.—This well is located at the paper-mill of A. V. Du Pont & Co., on Tenth Street, near Main. It is 2,086 feet deep, and occupied sixteen months in boring. The temperature of the water, as given in the analysis, is as it issues from the orifice of the well. A self-registering thermometer, sunk to the bottom of the well, indicated 86½° Fahr. Considering the point of constant temperature below the surface at Louisville as 53° Fahr., we have an increase of one degree of temperature for every sixty-seven feet below that point.

The water is bottled for exportation.

DRENNON SPRINGS.

Location.—Henry County, Kentucky.

Access.—Go to Newcastle, Henry County; thence about ten miles northwardly.

Hotel.—None.

Analysis.—No quantitative analysis has been made.

Properties.—"This is a very fine mineral water, acting not only on the skin, but as a mild aperient, diuretic, and diaphoretic."—(*Geological Survey of Kentucky*, vol. iii., p. 52.)

Remarks.—Twenty-five or thirty years ago this was one of the most fashionable resorts in the West. During one of the most prosperous seasons the cholera appeared at the springs, and the guests—panic-stricken—departed precipitately. During a following year the property was burned.

BEDFORD SPRINGS.

Location and Post-Office.—Bedford Springs, Trimble County, Kentucky.

Access.—Go to Sulphur Station, on the Louisville & Cincinnati Short Line Railroad, thirty-six miles east of Louisville, seventy-one miles west of Cincinnati; thence, six miles by stage, to the springs.

Hotel.—Bedford Springs.

Analysis.—In the "Geological Survey of Kentucky," vol. ii., page 79, the constituents of this spring are noted as follows: Chloride of sodium, sulphate of soda, sulphate of magnesia, bicarbonate of lime, bicarbonate of magnesia, carbonate of soda—alkaline to test-paper. The Epsom Spring, in the same vicinity, contains the same ingredients, except that sulphate of magnesia is in larger proportion.

WHITE SULPHUR AND TAR SPRINGS.

Location.—Breckenridge County, Kentucky.

Post-Office.—Cloverport, Breckenridge County, Kentucky.

Access.—Take daily steamers from Louisville, on the Ohio River, to Cloverport, one hundred and ten miles southwest; thence four miles south by carriage.

Hotel.—White Sulphur Springs.

Analysis.—No quantitative analysis has been made.

Remarks.—The springs, four in number, issue at the base of a high cliff. Their general character is that of sulphur-waters. One spring, however, is peculiar: on its surface a black substance floats, similar in appearance to tar; hence the name. Observations as to the therapeutic value of this substance are wanting.

The surrounding country is rough and the scenery picturesque.

DE SOTO SPRINGS.

Location.—De Soto Parish, Louisiana.

Post-Office.—Mansfield, De Soto Parish, Louisiana.

Access.—By steamboat on the Red River to Shreveport; thence, forty miles by stage, to Mansfield.

Hotel.—At Mansfield.

Analysis.—Within a radius of thirty miles of Mansfield are several valuable sulphur and chalybeate waters.

Remarks.—At some of these springs cabins have been erected, and, during the summer months, they are a popular resort for the neighboring inhabitants. The hotel at Mansfield is on the site of a spring.

WHITE SULPHUR SPRINGS.

Location and Post-Office.—White Sulphur Springs, Catahoula Parish, Louisiana.

Access.—By steamboat to Harrisonburg, on the Washita River, or Alexandria, on the Red River; thence, from the first point thirty-five miles by coach; from the second, twenty-five miles. Each of these places is between seventy-five and one hundred miles northwest from the junction of the Red River with the Mississippi.

Hotel.—Springs.

Analysis.—No quantitative analysis of the springs has been made. A qualitative one shows them to contain the usual ingredients of sulphur-waters, with a trace of iron.

Properties.—These waters are said to be useful in diseases of the skin, hepatic engorgements, and dyspepsia.

Remarks.—The springs are situated in the midst of that portion of Catahoula Parish known as the "piney-woods region." The surrounding country is undulating and covered with the long-leaf Southern pine. Near by is Trout Creek, a crystal-clear stream, the waters of which abound in large brook-trout.

ALPENA WELL.

Location and Post-Office.—Alpena, Alpena County, Michigan.

Access.—Go to Bay City, one hundred and eleven miles north of Detroit, on the Detroit & Milwaukee Railroad; thence by steamer, on Tuesdays, Thursdays, and Saturdays, about one hundred and ten miles north to Alpena.

Hotels.—Alpena House, Union House, Star Hotel.

ANALYSIS.

One pint contains (52° Fahr. Prof. S. P. Duffield):

SOLIDS.	Grains.
Carbonate of potassa	trace.
Carbonate of soda	1.364
Carbonate of magnesia	4.661
Carbonate of iron	0.170
Carbonate of lime	4.787
Chloride of sodium	8.532
Sulphate of lime	3.757
Alumina and silica	0.386
Total	23.657
GASES.	Cubic in.
Carbonic acid	1.05
Sulphuretted hydrogen	4.42
Nitrogen	0.03

Properties.—These waters abound in sulphuretted hydrogen, and, according to the analysis, there are but few springs in this country or Europe equally rich in this ingredient. (As to magnetism of the waters, *see* remarks on this subject.)

Remarks.—Alpena is situated on the shores of Thunder

Bay, an inlet of Lake Huron. It is but seventy-five miles south from Mackinaw. From its northern latitude and situation on the lake-shore, the temperature is cool and refreshing during the hot months of summer. The village numbers some 3,000 inhabitants, and is the outgrowth of a large lumber business which centres there. The waters flow from an artesian well 900 feet deep.

SHARON SPRINGS.

Location and Post-Office Address.—Sharon Springs, Schoharie County, New York.

Access.—Take Albany & Susquenanna Railway direct to the springs, fifty-nine miles west of Albany. Coming from the west, take Erie Railway to Binghamton; thence, by Albany & Susquehanna Railway, one hundred and eleven miles to springs. Or, New York Central Railroad to Palatine Bridge, fifty-five miles west of Albany; thence nine miles by stage.

Hotels.—Pavilion, Union Hall, Eldridge.

ANALYSIS.

One pint contains	White Sulphur Spring. 48° Fahr. J. R. Chilton, M. D.	Red Sulphur. 48° Fahr. Prof. Lawrence Reed.	Gardner Magnesia. 48° Fahr. Prof. Lawrence Reed.
SOLIDS.	Grains.	Grains.	Grains.
Carbonate of soda	....	0.043	0.042
Carbonate of magnesia	....	0.051	0.100
Carbonate of lime	....	1.122	0.842
Chloride of sodium	0.28	0.041	0.154
Chloride of magnesium	.80	0.091	0.054
Chloride of lime	....	0.008	0.020
Sulphate of magnesia	5.30	2.870	2.460
Sulphate of lime	13.95	12.080	11.687
Hydrosulphuret of sodium and hydrosulphuret of calcium	0.28	....	....
Hydrosulphuret of calcium and magnesium	....	0.111	0.781
Silicic acid	....	0.056	0.050
Total	20.11	15.973	16.190
GASES.	Cubic in.	Cubic in.	Cubic in.
Carbonic acid	....	0.57	0.277
Sulphuretted hydrogen	2.	1.31	0.750
Atmospheric air	....	0.50	0.375
Total	....	2.38	1.402

Chalybeate Spring, *see* page ——.

Properties.—As will be seen by the analysis, these waters are comparatively light, and for this reason may be taken in considerable quantities. In most instances, however, from two to four glasses will be found to answer. To produce the alterative effect, one or two glasses should be taken an hour before meals and on retiring, and continued for some weeks. When a cathartic effect is desired, and the water does not act readily, the action may be aided by taking a Sedlitz powder, or from half to a tablespoonful of Epsom salts, and afterward rely alone on the water.

The bathing arrangements are ample. The flow of water is abundant, estimated at 120 gallons per minute.

Remarks.—In describing Sharon Springs, we cannot do better than quote from a writer in *Harper's Monthly*, June, 1856, though with slight transposition of the sentences:

"The mineral springs at Sharon gush out from the bed of a small brook, and from a steep, wooded slope on its margin. For more than half a century their healing virtues have been known, and parents often took their children, who were afflicted with cutaneous disorders, and dipped them in the waters. Upon the slope from which the fountains gush, a curious phenomenon is exhibited: within the space of a few rods are five different springs—chalybeate, white sulphur, red sulphur, magnesia, and pure water. The two principal springs are the white sulphur and magnesia; the first on the margin of the brook, the other higher up on the slope.

"Although the village and the springs lie in a ravine, they are 900 feet above the Mohawk Valley. The eye, turned to the north and east, comprehends one of the grandest and most beautiful prospects imaginable. The hilly country seems subdued into a gently-rolling plain; and the woods, fields, villages, farm-houses, and brooks like silver threads, have the appearance of a gorgeous piece of tapestry, excelling, in richness of conception, form, and color, any thing the looms of Gobelin ever produced. Beyond, stretches the great valley, whose northern slopes, and the hills of Herkimer, Fulton, and Saratoga, fade away in mysterious, aërial perspective of azure, vermilion, and gold. And far beyond all, in dim, spectral mass, loom up the loftier peaks of the Adirondack Mountains."

Besides the charming scenery immediately at the springs, there are delightful rides to Cherry Valley and Cooperstown, the latter place commanding a view of Otsego Lake, nine miles in extent, and celebrated for salmon and trout-fish. Two miles distant from Cherry Valley are the *Tekaharawa Falls* (*see* CHERRY VALLEY SPRINGS). Twenty miles distant, by railway, is *Howe's Cave*, one of the most wonderful natural curiosities. The cave has been explored for seven miles, and, during the season, is illuminated for a distance of three miles from the main entrance, so that the visitor is relieved of the annoyance of smoking torches.

MASSENA SPRINGS.

Location and Post-Office Address.—Massena Springs, St. Lawrence County, New York.

Access.—From the east and south, *via* New York Central and Rome & Watertown Railroads, to Potsdam Junction, twenty-five miles east of Ogdensburg; thence fourteen miles northeast, by stage, to the springs. Or, go to Rouse's Point (outlet of Lake Champlain); thence eighty-two miles west, by Ogdensburg & Lake Champlain Railroad, to Brasher Falls; thence ten miles northwest, by stage, to springs. From the west, *via* New York Central and Rome & Watertown Railroads, to Potsdam Junction. Or, through Lake Ontario and down the St. Lawrence, to Ogdensburg, whence a boat runs during the season to Dodge's Landing, within three miles of the springs. Or, continue down the river to Cornwall, whence by ferry and carriage to the springs.

Hotels.—Harrowgate, Hatfield House.

ANALYSIS.

One pint contains (Prof. Ferd. F. Meyer):

SOLIDS.	Grains.
Carbonate of iron	0.045
Carbonate of lime	0.422
Chloride of potassium	0.063
Chloride of sodium	9.961
Chloride of magnesium	3.741
Sulphate of soda	0.437
Sulphate of lime	7.616
Hyposulphite of soda	0.526
Phosphate of soda	0.165
Bromide of magnesium	0.084
Sulphuret of sodium	0.176
Silicate of soda and organic compounds	1.397
Total	24.633
GAS.	Cubic in.
Sulphuretted hydrogen	0.663

Properties.—These are *saline-sulphur* waters, much resembling those of Eilsen, in the principality of Schaumburg-Lippe, but much richer, however, in chloride of sodium. I need not add that they are exceedingly valuable waters of this class. They have proved of decided utility in *dartrous diseases of the skin*, *scrofula*, *catarrh of the bladder*, and *gravel*. Their use should be combined in most cases with the tepid and warm bath.

Remarks.—The springs are delightfully situated on the banks of the Raquette River, a broad and rapid stream, flowing into the St. Lawrence, and affording fine opportunity for fishing. As early as the close of the last century these waters were discovered by surveyors, who noticed the oozy ground around them filled with the hoof-prints of the moose and deer, these animals visiting the spot to drink of the water. The Indians had used them as remedies for ulcerations, it is said, as long as tradition tells; and, as early as 1815, white people occasionally sought them for the relief of cutaneous diseases.

The quantity of water taken during the day should not, as a rule, exceed three or four tumblers. Bathing facilities are ample.

The drives in the vicinity of Massena are very attractive. A favorite visit is to the Indian village of St. Regis, about twelve miles distant.

DRYDEN SPRINGS.

Location and Post-Office.—Dryden, Tompkins County, New York.

Access.—From east, west, north, and south, go to Auburn, New York, on New York Central Railroad; thence by Southern Central Railroad to Dryden, thirty-six miles south. Or, go to Owego on the Erie Railway; thence by Southern Central Railroad to Dryden, thirty-two miles north.

Hotel.—Dryden Springs House.

Analysis.—These waters have never been thoroughly analyzed, either quantitatively or qualitatively. However, it is known that they contain sulphate of magnesia and chloride of sodium in notable proportions. One is said to be so strongly impregnated with sulphate of magnesia "that you can readily imagine yourself taking a dose of Epsom salts." There are also *chalybeate* wells here. The waters are cold, varying in temperature from 48 to 54° Fahr.

Remarks.—Dryden Springs are elevated, cool in summer, and a pleasant resort.

CHITTENANGO SPRINGS.

Location.—Madison County, New York

Post-Office Address.—Chittenango, Madison County, New York.

Access.—Chittenango is a station on the New York Central Railroad, one hundred and thirty-three miles west of Albany, and fifteen miles east of Syracuse. From station, three miles south by stage or carriage to springs.

Hotel.—White Sulphur Springs Hotel.

ANALYSIS.

One pint contains—	White Sulphur. 49° Fahr. Prof. C. F. Chandler.	Cave Spring. 49° Fahr. Prof. C. F. Chandler.	Magnesia. 49° Fahr. Prof. C. F. Chandler.
SOLIDS.	Grains.	Grains.	Grains.
Carbonate of magnesia	1.631	1.776	1.439
Carbonate of iron	0.007	0.014	0.029
Chloride of potassium	0.019	0.029	0.041
Chloride of sodium	0.129	0.196	0.229
Chloride of lithium	trace.	trace.	trace.
Sulphate of soda	0.027	....	....
Sulphate of magnesia	0.244	0.948	1.589
Sulphate of lime	10.177	13.265	14.385
Sulphate of strontia	trace.	trace.	trace.
Hydrosulphate of sodium	0.014	0.043	0.094
Hydrosulphate of calcium	....	0.140	0.116
Hyposulphite of soda	....	0.082	0.002
Alumina	0.010	0.027	trace.
Silica	0.085	0.064	0.072
Total	12.293	16.534	17.996
	Prof. Collier.	Prof. Collier.	Prof. Collier.
GASES.[1]	Cubic in.	Cubic in.	Cubic in.
Carbonic acid	4.5	3.2	2.8
Sulphuretted Hydrogen	0.1	0.4	1.6

Properties.—These waters may be taken in the usual quantity of a glass three or four times a day, on an empty stomach. It will be noticed that, in solid constituents, they are closely allied to the calcic waters.

Remarks.—The traveller, leaving the station, follows the narrow valley of the Chittenango Creek a mile or more beyond the village, and the springs are seen, gushing out from a

[1] Analysis by Prof. Collier, in 1870.

shelving ledge of rocks on the eastern bank of the stream. Ascending a neighboring summit to the height of 200 feet, a most pleasing view is had of the entire valley, and Cazenovia and Oneida Lakes. About two and a half miles above the springs the valley terminates, and the stream falls perpendicularly 140 feet, forming, with the deep gorge and surroundings, a scene well worth a visit.

RICHFIELD SPRINGS.

Location and Post-Office Address.—Richfield Springs, Otsego County, New York.

Access.—From Utica, ninety-five miles west of Albany on the New York Central Railroad, take cars on Utica, Chenango, & Susquehanna Valley Railroad, direct to the springs, thirty-five miles. From Binghamton, two hundred and fifteen miles northwest of New York on the Erie Railway, by Utica, Chenango, & Susquehanna Valley Railroad, one hundred and three miles to springs. The first named is the direct route.

Hotels.—Spring House, Hosford House, American House.

ANALYSIS.

One pint contains (Prof. Reid):

SOLIDS.	Grains.
Carbonate of magnesia	1.480
Carbonate of lime	0.870
Chlorides of sodium and magnesium	0.187
Sulphate of magnesia	3.750
Sulphate of lime	2.500
Hydrosulphate of magnesia and lime	0.250
Undetermined	19.187
Total	28.224
GAS.	Cubic in.
Sulphuretted hydrogen	3.3

The above is an analysis made many years ago. A new analysis is much needed.

Remarks.—The village of Richfield Springs is delightfully situated upon a narrow plain near the head of Canaderaga, or Schuyler's Lake, which forms the chief attraction to the visitor. The lake is but one mile distant from the hotel, and conveyances pass to and fro every half-hour. The lake is five miles in length, and a mile and a quarter at its greatest breadth. High hills surround it on every side except to the northward.

The waters of these springs were sought by the Indians long before the advent of the white man, and tradition tells a story of one of their healing prophets, who dwelt on a beautiful island in the midst of the lake. Hither the Iroquois would come for the relief of their maladies. During the night he would glide silently to the shore in his canoe, seek the fountains, and return with the magic waters. He became proud and powerful, and at last assumed to be twin-brother to the Great Spirit. Such blasphemy was visited with dire punishment. One morning a bridal party went forth to receive the prophet's benediction, but on arriving at the lake-shore found the island had disappeared. The Great Spirit in his wrath had thrust it with the proud prophet so deep in the earth, that it is said the waters of the lake where it stood are unfathomable by human measurement.

AVON SPRINGS.

Location.—Livingston County, New York.

Post-Office Address.—Avon, Livingston County, New York.

Access.—Avon is a station on the Erie Railway, sixty-five miles east of Buffalo; eighteen miles south of Rochester; three hundred and sixty-seven miles northwest of New York.

Hotels.—United States, Avon Springs Hotel (at the depot), Congress Hall, Knickerbocker Hall.

ANALYSIS.

One pint contains—	Upper Spring, 51° Fahr. Prof. Hadley.	Lower Spring. J. B. Chilton, M. D.	New Bath Spring, 50° Fahr. Prof. Beck.
SOLIDS.	Grains.	Grains.	Grains.
Carbonate of lime	1.000	8.666	8.870
Chloride of sodium	2.300	....	0.710
Chloride of calcium	....	1.051	....
Sulphate of soda	2.000	1.716	4.840
Sulphate of magnesia	1.250	6.201	1.010
Sulphate of lime	10.500	7.180	0.440
Iodide of sodium	....	trace.	....
Total	17.050	19.814	10.870
GASES.	Cubic in.	Cubic in.	Cubic in.
Carbonic acid	0.70	0.49	....
Sulphuretted hydrogen	1.50	1.25	.050

Properties.—It will be seen by analysis that these are valuable sulphur-waters, resembling in many respects the celebrated Spa of Neudorf, in Electoral Hesse. The flow is large from the lower spring, being fifty-four gallons per minute. Bathing arrangements are extensive. Dr. Salisbury, quoted by Dr. Francis, of New York, deceased, says: "Generally speaking, four or six half-pint tumblers of the water drank during the day, prove mildly cathartic, and, under its long-continued use in this dose, no debility ensues, but appetite and strength are much increased. In doses of from ten to fifteen glasses, it acts powerfully on the bowels, kidneys, and skin."[1]

Remarks.—The location of these springs, in one of the most beautiful portions of Western New York, together with the efficacy of the waters, conspires to make this a most attractive resort. And the place is not without historical interest. Near the Avon railway-station, at the foot of the slope, is the battle-field of the French under De Nouville, in 1687, where the invaded Senecas drove them from their hunting-grounds. And eight miles distant, at the Geneseo, General Sullivan retaliated with severity upon the Indians for their crueltics at Cherry Valley and Wyoming.

LONGMUIRS WELL.

Location.—Rochester, New York.

ANALYSIS.

One pint contains (52° Fahr.):

SOLIDS.	Grains.
Carbonates of lime and magnesia, with trace of oxide of iron	1.48
Chloride of sodium	6.52
Sulphate of soda	6.99
Total	14.99

GASES.	Cubic inch.
Carbonic acid	small quantity.
Sulphuretted hydrogen	2.16

—"Geology of New York."

[1] Pamphlet on "Mineral Waters." By Dr. Francis. 1834. (Astor Library.)

CHERRY VALLEY SPRINGS.

Location.—Otsego County, New York.

Post-Office Address.—Cherry Valley, Otsego County, New York.

Access.—Take Albany & Susquehanna Railroad direct to Cherry Valley, sixty-eight miles west of Albany; thence two miles to the springs. From the west, take Erie Railway to Binghamton; thence by Albany & Susquehanna Railroad, one hundred and twenty miles to Cherry Valley; thence two miles to springs.

Hotels.—None at the springs, though one in contemplation. Several in the village of Cherry Valley.

ANALYSIS.

One pint contains—	Bath-House Spring. J. B. Chilton, M. D.	Spring North of Bath-House. Prof. Perkins.
SOLIDS.	Grains.	Grains.
Carbonate of magnesia	2.227	1.245
Carbonate of iron	....	0.306
Carbonate of lime	1.177	1.844
Chloride of potassium	....	0.311
Chloride of sodium	1.555	0.266
Chloride of magnesium	0.460	....
Chloride of calcium	0.350	....
Sulphate of soda	1.385	....
Sulphate of magnesia	3.070	....
Sulphate of lime	7.210	18.683
Hydrosulphate of soda	0.075	....
Silica and alumina	0.045	....
Silex	....	0.455
Organic matter	0.085	....
Total	17.589	23.110

Remarks.—The above analysis of the Bath-House Spring shows these waters to be worthy the improvements that are contemplated. At present there are facilities during the summer months for taking baths at the springs.

These springs are situated in a portion of New York rendered historical by conflicts with the Indians. Stories are told of fierce struggles, and of white men seized and carried into captivity. Not long ago Judge Campbell still lived here, who, in 1778, when six years of age, was captured, with his mother and family, and taken first to Niagara, thence to Caughnawaga, near Montreal, where they remained for two years, finally to return to Cherry Valley.

Near the springs are the *Tekaharawa* Falls, which were thus described fifty-four years ago by the late Alvan Stewart:

"At the distance of one mile northeast of the village a small brook takes its rise, and runs north about a mile and a half, when, passing into a dark wood of hemlock, it is precipitated down a fall of one hundred and fifty-two feet of perpendicular height, where it is lost in a dark gulf below. . . . In approaching from the south one advances to the very border of the gulf before he dreams, or fancies, from any feature of the ground, that such a yawning abyss is within five yards of his feet. If sublimity be in any measure allied to horror, or connected with the grandeur of objects, one must feel its full force the first moment his sight meets the rocks which pave the bottom of this tremendous chasm."

CLIFTON SPRINGS.

Location and Post-Office Address.—Clifton Springs, Ontario County, New York.

Access.—Clifton Springs is a station on the Auburn Branch of the New York Central Railroad, two hundred and eleven miles west of Albany; sixty-three miles west of Syracuse; thirty-nine miles east of Rochester; ninety-seven miles east of Buffalo.

Hotel.—Clifton Springs.

ANALYSIS.

One pint contains (Prof. J. R. Chilton):

SOLIDS.	Grains.
Carbonate of magnesia	1.64
Carbonate of lime	1.21
Chloride of sodium	1.16
Chloride of magnesium	0.51
Chloride of calcium	0.51
Sulphate of soda	0.97
Sulphate of magnesia	2.06
Sulphate of lime	8.65
Organic matter	trace.
Total	16.71

"Sulphuretted hydrogen and carbonic acid abounds, but the quantity having been materially lessened while conveyed to New York, the proper amount could not be ascertained."—(1852.)

Properties.—This is a good calcic-sulphur water, especially indicated when a case otherwise requiring sulphur-waters is complicated by disease of the bladder, to which calcic waters are applicable.

Remarks.—These waters were first utilized in 1806 by the erection of suitable buildings for the accommodation of those who resorted to them from the surrounding country. At that time the springs flowed out on the borders of a marsh in the midst of a forest. Now Clifton is an exceedingly popular resort.

COLUMBIA SPRINGS.

Location.—Columbia County, New York.

Post-Office.—Hudson, Columbia County, New York.

Access.—Take cars on Hudson River Railroad, or boat on the river, to Hudson, one hundred and fifteen miles north of New York, and twenty-seven miles south of Albany; thence four miles northeast to springs by carriage.

Hotel.—Columbia Springs House.

ANALYSIS.[1]

One pint contains (Atwood):

SOLIDS.	Grains.
Carbonate of lime	2.724
Chloride of potassium	0.149
Chloride of sodium	10.590
Chloride of magnesium	3.929
Sesqui-chloride of iron	0.427
Sulphate of lime	8.117
Phosphate of soda	0.267
Hyposulphate of soda	1.018
Loss	0.102
Total	27.323
GAS.	Cubic inch.
Sulphuretted hydrogen	0.56

This is an exceedingly pleasant resort, where quiet, salubrious air, and rural scenery, may be enjoyed.

WHITE SULPHUR SPRINGS.

Location and Post-Office.—Cairo, Greene County, New York.

Access.—Go to Catskill, one hundred and nine miles north of New York, on the Hudson River Railroad; thence ten miles.

Hotel.—White Sulphur Springs House.

[1] A new analysis is desirable.

Analysis.—None has been made.

Remarks.—These springs are situated in the Catskill Mountains, at an elevation of one thousand feet above the level of the sea.

SHOCCO SPRINGS.

Location.—Warren County, North Carolina.

Address.—Warrenton, Warren County, North Carolina.

Access.—From Raleigh, *via* Raleigh & Gaston Railroad, sixty-two miles north, to Warrenton; thence nine miles by stage.

Hotel.—Buildings mostly destroyed.

Analysis.—The waters are said to be of the saline-sulphur class. Dr. Jos. A. Drake, of Hilliardston, who has been familiar with them for many years, writes that "they are slightly aperient and decidedly diuretic."

WARREN WHITE SULPHUR.

Location.—Warren County, North Carolina.

Post-Office.—Ridgeway, Warren County, North Carolina.

Access.—Go to Ridgeway, a station on the Raleigh & Gaston Railroad, fifty-seven miles northeast of Raleigh, and forty miles southwest of Weldon; thence ten miles by private conveyance or stage.

Hotel.—Warren Springs.

Analysis.—None.

Remarks.—Springs closed since the war, except in 1866. It is, however, proposed to reopen them.

WHITE SULPHUR SPRINGS.

Location.—Delaware County, Ohio.

Post-Office.—Lewis Centre, Delaware County, Ohio.

Access.—Go to Delaware, a station on the Cleveland & Columbus Railroad, twenty-four miles north of Columbus; thence by stage.

Analysis.—These are very feeble sulphur-waters. Prof. E. S. Wayne, who made the analysis, informs me that there are about four grains of solid constituents to the gallon, composed chiefly of carbonate and sulphate of lime, with a trace of the chlorides.

Remarks.—A few years ago this was a fashionable resort,

but the positive value of the water was not sufficient to maintain its temporary popularity. The property was sold to the State, and is now the seat of an industrial reform-school for girls.

WHITE SULPHUR SPRINGS.

Location and Post-Office.—White Sulphur Springs, Catawba County, North Carolina.

Access.—From Baltimore by rail, *via* Richmond, to Salisbury, North Carolina; thence, *via* Western Railroad of North Carolina, to the springs.

Hotel.—White Sulphur Springs.

MINNEQUA SPRINGS.

Location and Post-Office.—Minnequa Springs, Bradford County, Pennsylvania.

Access.—Go to Minnequa, a station on the Northern Central Railroad, thirty-six miles south of Elmira, and one hundred and thirty-four miles north of Harrisburg.

Hotel.—Minnequa Springs.

ANALYSIS.[1]

One pint contains (Dr. Gregg):

Solids.	Grains.
Carbonate of soda	0.136
Carbonate of magnesia	0.159
Carbonate of lime	0.091
Chloride of potassium	trace.
Chloride of sodium	0.129
Sulphate of lime	0.062
Oxide of iron and alumina	0.462
Sulphur	0.167
Organic matter	0.098
Total	1.299
Gas.	**Cubic inches.**
Carbonic acid	0.50
Sulphuretted hydrogen	undetermined.

Properties.—According to the analysis the water appears to be a chalybeate-sulphur water. It is said to be agreeable to the taste, on account of the carbonic acid contained. The flow is estimated at six gallons per minute.

[1] From the *Medical and Surgical Reporter*, 1872.

Remarks.—The springs are located in the Towanda Valley, at an estimated elevation of several hundred feet above the sea-level. The cultivated hills surrounding the valley form an agreeable landscape, while neighboring woods and streams supply opportunities for huntsmen and fishermen.

YORK SULPHUR SPRINGS.

Location and Post-Office.—York Sulphur Springs, Adams County, Pennsylvania.

Access.—Go to Oxford Station, ten miles east from Gettysburg, on the Hanover Branch of Pennsylvania Central Railroad; thence nine miles by stage.

Hotels.—York Springs.

Analysis.—The old analysis is inaccurate.

Remarks.—These springs were discovered in 1790, and at that time attracted much attention. They have ever since been resorted to by the citizens of Baltimore and the adjoining country.

CARLISLE SPRINGS.

Location and Post-Office.—Carlisle Springs, Cumberland County, Pennsylvania.

Access.—From Philadelphia, *via* Pennsylvania Central Railroad, to Harrisburg, one hundred and six miles west; thence, *via* Cumberland Valley Railroad, eighteen miles southwest to Carlisle; thence four miles by stage.

Hotel.—Springs.

Analysis.—None. They are mild sulphur-waters.

Remarks.—The springs issue at the base of the Blue Mountain. Not far distant is Canodoquinnet Creek, furnishing opportunity for fine fishing. These springs are very pleasantly located, and are much resorted to by families from Philadelphia and Baltimore.

GLENN SPRINGS.

Location and Post-Office.—Glenn Springs, Spartanburg District, South Carolina.

Access.— ———.

Hotel.— ———.

Analysis.—No quantitative analysis of these waters has been made. A qualitative examination by Prof. C. U. Shepard, of Charleston, shows them to contain sulphate of magnesia, sulphate of lime, carbonate of lime, and sulphuretted hydrogen.

SITKA, ALASKA.

As a matter of curiosity more than utility, we insert the following passages from a letter to the author, from H. J. Phillips, M. D., Post-Surgeon U. S. A., at Sitka:

"Sitka may be reached in the following way: Steamers leave San Francisco weekly in summer for Portland, Oregon. Fare, thirty dollars, including meals. From Portland a small but safe steamer leaves for Sitka about the end of every month. Fare, seventy dollars, with meals.

"The route taken is from Cape Flattery through the Straits of Fuca, in among islands through narrow passes, bounded on either side by high snow-capped peaks, all the way to Sitka. It is the longest and most wonderful inland navigation in the world, extending over twelve hundred miles, and well repays the traveller for his trouble and time. There is no hotel in Alaska, but plenty of empty houses. All the Russians who could pay their fares have left, and only those who cannot, now remain, as the place is retrograding very fast.

"About twenty miles from Sitka there are two springs, called here 'Geysers' or Warm Sulphur. The height of these respectively above the sea is eighteen and twenty-two feet; the flow about one-half gallon per minute. The temperature of the first is 104° Fahr.; of second, 96° Fahr.

"These springs were much frequented and used by the Russians before the session of the Territory to the United States. Two log-houses erected by the old Russian Fur Company have been destroyed by the Indians, but the two large wooden tanks still remain. These springs were highly recommended for the cure of syphilis and rheumatism, with the former of which diseases the Russians and Indians here are actually eaten up.

"There is a chalybeate spring about half a mile from the city of Sitka, flowing from a rock on the side of a road called Davis Avenue. No analysis has ever been made of the water. It was used by the Russians, and since that period occasionally by visitors.

"There is a mountain eleven miles long, and twelve hundred feet above the level of the sea, on the main-land of Alaska, and on the western bank of the Chilchat River, which is supposed to be composed almost entirely of iron. From the sides of this mountain issue numerous chalybeate springs."

The following abstract from the hospital register at Sitka is interesting:

	Mean Fahr.
Warmest day of summer, August 9, 1870	67°
Coldest day of summer, June 2, 1870	44°
Warmest day of winter, December 1, 1869	46°
Coldest day of winter, March 11, 1869	3°
Mean annual temperature, 1870	44°

ALBURG SPRINGS.

Location and Post-Office.—Alburg Springs, Grand Isle County, Vermont.

Access.—From New York or Boston, purchase tickets *via* Vermont Central Railroad to Alburg Springs Station, sixteen miles northwest of St. Albans, and one mile distant from the springs. From the west, go to Schenectady or Troy; thence north, *via* Rutland & Burlington Railroad. Or go down the St. Lawrence River to Montreal; thence, *via* Rouse's Point, or St. Albans, to springs.

Hotels.—Alburg Springs House, Missisquoi House.

ANALYSIS.

One pint contains (C. T. Jackson, M. D.):

SOLIDS.	Grains.
Chloride of sodium	1.095
Chloride of magnesium	0.627
Chloride of calcium and carbonate of lime	0.601
Sulphide of potassium and sulphate of potassa	1.237
Sulphate of soda	0.887
Insoluble matters	0.100
Organic acid of the soil (crenic acid) and loss	0.250
Total	4.797

(The water gives off a large quantity of sulphuretted hydrogen, and is distinctly alkaline from excess of sulphide of potassium.—C. T. J.)

A qualitative analysis of these waters has been made by Prof. C. F. Chandler, of New York, who finds, in addition to the above ingredients, the bicarbonate of lithia and strontia.

Remarks.—These springs have been a favorite resort since the year 1816, when Timothy Sowles, Elisha Reynolds, and Stephen Sweet, farmers, were induced to take boarders. The springs are located on the shores of Missisquoi Bay, amid the beauties of lake and mountain scenery. There are two springs, the northern one being somewhat ferruginous in character. They are about eighty rods from the water's edge, and thirty feet above the level of Lake Champlain.

JORDAN'S WHITE SULPHUR SPRINGS.

Location.—Frederick County, Virginia.

Post-Office.—Stephenson's Depot, Frederick County, Virginia.

Access.—From the north, go to Harper's Ferry, on the Baltimore & Ohio Railroad, eighty-one miles west of Baltimore; thence, on Winchester Branch of Baltimore & Ohio Railroad, to Stephenson's Depot, twenty-eight miles southwest; thence, by stage to the springs, two miles southeast of the depot. From the south, *via* Orange, Alexandria & Manassas Railroad, to Strasburg; thence north, twenty-three miles, by Baltimore & Ohio Railroad, to Stephenson's.

Hotel.—Jordan's.

ANALYSIS.

One pint contains (T. Antisell):

SOLIDS.	Grains.
Carbonate of potassa	1.213
Carbonate of magnesia	0.360
Carbonate of iron	trace.
Carbonate of manganese	0.002
Chloride of sodium	0.095
Sulphate of potassa	0.262
Sulphate of lime	0.641
Alumina	0.001
Silicic acid	0.032
Total	2.606
GAS.	**Cubic in.**
Sulphuretted hydrogen	0.25

The proportion of sulphuretted hydrogen is much larger

than here given, this analysis only showing the amount in the bottled water after it had been standing for some time.

Properties.—These are light waters, and may be taken in considerable quantity. When the waters do not act as an aperient, and it is desirable to produce this effect, it is aided by adding a teaspoonful of table-salt to each glass of water for two or three doses.

Remarks.—The springs are located in the Valley of the Shenandoah, five miles distant from Winchester. The buildings and spring are embowered in a grove of tall aspens, on either side of a stream of running-water. From the hills, at the rear of the hotel, fine views may be had of the Blue Ridge and Alleghany Mountains. Immediately in the vicinity of these springs the contests between Jubal Early and Sheridan occurred, and Winchester is said to have changed masters eighty-seven times.

HIGHGATE SPRINGS.

Location and Post-Office Address.—Highgate, Franklin County, Vermont.

Access.—Highgate is three and a half miles from Swanton, a station on the Vermont Central Railroad, nine miles north of St. Albans.

Hotels.—Franklin House, Champlain House.

ANALYSIS.

One pint contains—	Champlain Spring. A. A. Hayes.	T. Sterry Hunt.
SOLIDS.	Grains.	Grains.
Carbonate of potassa	0.459	....
Carbonate of soda	0.158	1.718
Carbonate of magnesia	0.152	0.729
Carbonate of lime	0.127	0.175
Carbonate of ammonia	trace.	....
Chloride of potassium	0.093	....
Chloride of sodium	0.021	2.930
Sulphate of soda	....	0.306
Protoxide of iron	0.004	....
Potassa and boracic acid	....	....
Crenic acid	0.112	....
Silicic acid	0.102	....
Total	1.228	5.858

—"Geology of Vermont." (1867.)

These springs are situated on the Missisquoi River, amid exceedingly attractive scenery.

NEWBURY SPRINGS.

Location and Post-Office Address.—Newbury, Orange County, Vermont.

Access.—From New York, *via* New York & New Haven Railroad, New Haven, Hartford & Springfield Railroad, Connecticut River Railroad, and Connecticut & Passumpsic Railroad, to Newbury, two hundred and ninety-three miles northeast of New York.

Hotel.—Springs.

ANALYSIS.

One pint contains (Prof. Hall):

Solids.	Grains.
Carbonate of soda	0.50
Carbonate of magnesia	0.30
Carbonate of lime	2.20
Chloride of sodium	0.04
Sulphate of soda	0.30
Sulphate of magnesia	0.05
Phosphate of iron	0.05
Protoxide of iron	trace.
Nitrate of potassa	0.05
Hydrosulphate of soda	0.04
Silica and suspended clay	1.10
Organic matter and ammonia	0.03
Total	4.66

Gas.—Sulphuretted hydrogen, undetermined.

STRIBLING SPRINGS.

(For location, access, etc., *see* description of these springs under "Chalybeate Waters.")

ANALYSIS.

One pint contains (No. II., D. K. Tuttle, M. D.):

Solids.	Grains.
Carbonate of potassa	0.093
Carbonate of soda	0.780
Carbonate of magnesia	0.251
Carbonate of iron	0.016
Carbonate of lime	1.204
Chloride of sodium	0.080
Sulphate of lime	0.156
Silicic acid	0.080
Total	2.660
Gases.	**Cubic in.**
Carbonic acid	1.30
Sulphuretted hydrogen	0.03

YELLOW SULPHUR SPRINGS.

Location and Post-Office.—Yellow Sulphur Springs, Montgomery County, Virginia.

Access.—From the north *via* Washington: Orange, Alexandria & Manassas Railroad, and Virginia & Tennessee Railroad, to Christiansburg, two hundred and sixty-four miles southwest from Washington; thence, three and a half miles by stage, to the springs. From the south and southwest, strike the Virginia & Tennessee Railroad; thence to Christiansburg. From the west, *via* Huntington and Chesapeake & Ohio Railroad, to Charlottesville, junction with Virginia & Tennessee Railroad; thence to Christiansburg.

Hotel.—Yellow Springs.

ANALYSIS.

One pint contains (55° Fahr. Prof. W. M. Gilham):

Solids.	Grains.
Carbonate of magnesia	0.173
Carbonate of protoxide of iron	0.077
Carbonate of lime	1.080
Chloride of potassium	0.012
Chloride of sodium	0.009
Sulphate of potassa	0.013
Sulphate of soda	0.093
Sulphate of magnesia	2.637
Sulphate of alumina	0.397
Sulphate of lime	7.912
Phosphate of magnesia	0.001
Phosphate of lime	0.002
Organic extractive matter	0.466
Total	12.872
Gas.	**Cubic in.**
Carbonic acid	1.25
Sulphuretted hydrogen	undetermined.

Properties.—These are fine calcic-sulphur waters, with an active proportion of purging sulphates.

Remarks.—These springs are on the eastern slope of the Alleghany Mountains, at an altitude of over two thousand feet above the level of the sea. The mountain-top rises but sixty feet above them. Visitors dwell amid the most beautiful mountain scenery, and breathe a cool and bracing atmosphere, even during the heats of July and August. Although these springs have been established as a resort but a few years, they have met with the favor of the public. Bishop Madison, as long ago as 1810, highly commended them.

The proprietors have arranged for baths of any temperature desired.

BUFFALO SPRINGS.

Location and Post-Office Address.—Buffalo Springs, Mecklenburg County, Virginia.

Access.—From Richmond, take cars on Richmond & Danville Railroad, to Scottsburg Depot, one hundred and one miles southwest of Richmond; thence, fifteen miles by stage, to the springs.

Hotel.—Buffalo Springs.

ANALYSIS.

One pint contains:

SOLIDS.	Grains.
Chloride of sodium	trace.
Chloride of magnesium	trace.
Sulphate of soda	0.163
Sulphate of magnesia	1.000
Sulphate of protoxide of iron	0.325
Sulphate of lime	0.437
Total	1.925
GAS.	Cubic in.
Sulphuretted hydrogen	0.15

Properties.—Although the above analysis is very imperfect, still it enables us, in some measure, to estimate its properties.

COYNER'S SPRINGS.

Location.—Botetourt County, Virginia.

Post-Office.—Bonsacks, Roanoke County, Virginia.

Access.—Bonsacks is a station on the Virginia & Tennessee Railroad, two hundred and twenty-six miles southwest from Washington; two hundred and eighty-six miles northeast by rail from Knoxville, Tenn. Springs are one mile from Bonsacks. (By giving the conductor notice, passengers will be left at the springs-platform, only two hundred yards distant from the hotel.)

Hotel.—Coyner's Springs.

Analysis.—None has been made.

Remarks.—There are five springs here, the principal ones known as the White, the Black, and the Blue, the names being due to the color of the sediment deposited by the water. The proximity of these springs to the main line of railroad from the Southwest to Washington and the East, together with the agreeable surroundings, renders this a pleasant resting-place to the tired traveller.

EGGLESTON'S SPRINGS.

Location and Post-Office.—Eggleston's Springs, Giles County, Virginia.

Access.—From Washington *via* Orange, Alexandria & Manassas Railroad, and Virginia & Tennessee Railroad, to Central (?), two hundred and seventy-four miles southwest; thence forty-one miles north to the springs.

Hotel.—Eggleston's.

Analysis.—None.

Remarks.—These springs are located in one of the most attractive mountain districts of Virginia, far out of the ordinary course of travel, and on this account all the more interesting to the tourist. New River here bends in a wide, majestic curve, over which towering cliffs of gray-stone, two hundred and ninety-five feet high, cast their shadows. The river has a depth at this point of one hundred and fifty feet. A few miles distant is Peter's Mountain and the "Narrows," where the river forces its way through a ragged defile in the mountain.

An exceedingly novel and romantic way of reaching the springs, is to leave the Virginia & Tennessee Railroad at New River Bridge, and float twenty-five miles down the stream in one of the *bateaux* which ply on its waters.

BOTETOURT SPRINGS.

Location and Post-Office.—Botetourt Springs, Roanoke County, Virginia.

Access.—By Virginia & Tennessee Railroad to Salem; thence nine miles by turnpike.

Analysis.—There are two springs—one sulphur, one chalybeate.

Remarks.—Some thirty years ago this was a popular summer resort, and deservedly so, both on account of the value of the water, the beauty of the scenery, and salubrity of the climate. But in 1842 the property was purchased by a company, and converted into an institute for young ladies. From the name of its principal benefactor, it has been called the "Hollins Institute." It has had a prosperous career, and is now in charge of Prof. Charles L. Cocke, A. M.

COLD WHITE SULPHUR SPRINGS.

Location and Post-Office.—Cold White Sulphur Springs, Rockbridge County, Virginia.

Access.—From Washington *via* Orange, Alexandria & Manassas Railroad, and Chesapeake & Ohio Railroad, to Goshen, one hundred and eighty-eight miles southwest; thence by stage two miles to springs. From Richmond *via* Gordonsville, one hundred and sixty-eighty miles to Goshen. From West *via* Cincinnati to Huntington, one hundred and sixty-five miles east, on the Ohio River; thence, by Cincinnati & Ohio Railroad to Goshen, two hundred and fifty-one miles southeast.

Hotel.—Cold White Sulphur.

Analysis.—None. The temperature of the water is $57\frac{1}{2}°$ Fahr., and the flow five gallons per minute.

MONTGOMERY WHITE SULPHUR SPRINGS.

Location and Post-Office Address.—White Sulphur Springs, Montgomery County, Virginia.

Access.—Visitors from North or South should buy tickets to Big Tunnel, a station on the Virginia & Tennessee Railroad, two hundred and fifty-nine miles southwest of Washington; thence by tramway.

Hotel.—Montgomery White Sulphur.

Analysis.—None.

Remarks.—These are decidedly sulphurous waters, applicable to those diseases which are advantageously treated by waters of this class. They are well located, and are a desirable place of resort.

FAUQUIER WHITE SULPHUR SPRINGS.

Location.—Fauquier County, Virginia.

Post-Office.— ———.

Access.—From Washington *via* Orange, Alexandria & Manassas Railroad, to Warrenton Junction, forty-seven miles west; thence by Warrington Branch Railroad and stage, total distance about fifty-six miles.

Hotel.—(Burned during the war.)

Analysis.—No accurate quantitative analysis has ever been made. Temperature 56° Fahr.

Properties.—The water is purgative and diuretic.

Remarks.—Previous to the war this was an exceedingly fashionable resort. The waters seem to possess decided value, and it may again be improved by suitable accommodations.

HUGUENOT SPRINGS.

Location.—Powhatan County, Virginia.

Access.—Seventeen miles from Richmond.

Hotel.—Huguenot Springs.

Analysis.—No quantitative analysis has been made. Prof. Rogers found it contained the usual ingredients of sulphur waters in small proportion.

Remarks.—The springs are so named from the fact that they rise on a tract of land granted by the British Government to a band of Huguenot refugees in 1685. The waters are considerably resorted to by citizens of Petersburg and Richmond. On the same ground there is a chalybeate spring.

BURNER'S SPRINGS.

Location and Post-Office.—Burner's Springs, Shenandoah County, Virginia.

Access.—From Washington *via* Orange, Alexandria & Manassas Railroad, to Woodstock, one hundred and one miles west; thence *via* stage, eight miles, to the springs.

Hotel.—Burner's Springs.

Analysis.—None.

Remarks.—These springs, seven in number, and therefore sometimes called *Seven Fountains*, are situated at the western base of the Massanutten Mountain. The springs are known as the Blue and the White Sulphur-waters, the Willow, the Chalybeate, etc. The location of this resort is exceedingly beautiful.

ROANOKE RED SULPHUR SPRINGS.

Location.—Roanoke County, Virginia.

Post-Office.— ———.

Access.—From Washington *via* Orange, Alexandria & Manassas Railroad, and Virginia & Tennessee Railroad, to Salem, two hundred and thirty-eight miles southwest; thence ten miles by stage.

Hotel.—Red Sulphur.

Analysis.—None.

Remarks.—These waters deposit a red sediment, and were so named from this fact. In medical action they are supposed to resemble the old Red Sulphur-Springs of Monroe County.

DAGGAR'S SPRING.

Location and Post-Office.—Daggar's Spring, Botetourt County, Virginia.

Access.—From Washington, *via* Orange, Aléxandria & Manassas Railroad and Virginia & Tennessee Railroad, to Buford's, two hundred and fifteen miles southwest; thence by stage, twenty-eight miles.

Hotel.—Springs.

Analysis.—None. It is a mild sulphur-water.

Remarks.—This resort was opened forty years ago, by Mr. Daggar, from whose hands it passed to J. W. Dibrell, and is, therefore, sometimes called *Dibrell's* Spring. It is a favorite resort with the inhabitants of the surrounding country.

GRAYSON SULPHUR SPRINGS.

Location and Post-Office.—Grayson Sulphur Springs, Carroll County, Virginia.

Access.—From Washington, *via* Orange, Alexandria & Manassas Railroad and Virginia & Tennessee Railroad, to Wytheville, three hundred and thirteen miles southwest; thence, twenty miles southeast by stage, to the springs.

Hotel.—Grayson Sulphur.

Analysis.— ———.

Remarks.—These springs are situated to the west of the Blue Ridge, and on the banks of New River. The surrounding scenery is exceptionally beautiful. Many years before they were improved, the neighboring inhabitants resorted here during the summer season. Since the hotel was built, the springs have received considerable patronage.

GREENBRIER WHITE SULPHUR SPRINGS.

Location and Post-Office.—Greenbrier White Sulphur Springs, Greenbrier County, West Virginia.

Access.—White Sulphur Springs is a station on the Chesapeake & Ohio Railroad, two hundred and twenty-seven miles west from Richmond, and one hundred and ninety-two miles east from Huntington, a point on the Ohio River one hundred and sixty-five miles east of Cincinnati. From Washington, *via* Orange, Alexandria & Manassas Railroad and Chesapeake & Ohio Railroad, two hundred and forty-seven miles.

Hotel.—Springs.

ANALYSIS.[1]

One pint contains—	Prof. A. A. Hayes. 62° Fahr.	Prof. W. B. Rogers. 62° Fahr.
SOLIDS.	Grains.	Grains.
Carbonate of magnesia	....	0.146
Carbonate of lime	0.884	0.441
Chloride of sodium	....	0.065
Chloride of magnesium	0.125	0.020
Chloride of calcium	....	0.008
Sulphate of soda	....	1.169
Sulphate of magnesia	4.427	2.379
Sulphate of lime	9.794	9.148
Sulphate of alumina	....	0.003
Protosulphate of iron	....	0.019
Earthy phosphates	....	trace.
Iodine (combined with sodium or magnesium)	....	undetermined.
Organic matter	0.545	0.001
Silicates (silicate of potassa, of soda, of magnesia, and a trace of oxide of iron)	0.432	....
Total	16.207	13.394
GASES.	Cubic in.	Cubic in.
Carbonic acid	1.41	1.06
Sulphuretted hydrogen	0.03	0.37
Oxygen	0.06	0.05
Nitrogen	0.58	0.54

Flow, thirty gallons per minute.

Properties.—These waters, so well known in the United States, very much resemble the celebrated cold sulphur-waters of Nenndorf, in Electoral Hesse. The combination of the purging sulphates, the salts of lime, and sulphuretted hydrogen, in the same water, is a valuable one, and gives to the water a wide range of application; though its effects in a given disease may not be so decided as that of a water containing a larger proportion of one of the constituents, to the exclusion of the remainder. It is an excellent aperient and alterative sulphur-

[1] Five minutes' walk southward, from the sulphur-spring, is a chalybeate spring.

water, possessing certain action on the kidneys. The diseases to which it is applicable are, *engorgements of the liver*, *dartrous skin-diseases*, *chronic poisoning by metals*, diseases of the bladder, as catarrh and gravel; and, as an adjuvant, in the treatment of secondary and tertiary syphilis. As a result of its action on the liver, it relieves *dyspepsias* and *jaundice*, due to congestion of this organ. In dyspepsias associated with obstinate constipation it also proves valuable. In many of these diseases the warm or hot bath should be combined with the internal use of the water. For this purpose the proprietors have erected a number of well-arranged baths, the water being heated in the tub by steam, a method much preferable to that of heating in tanks and thence drawing to the bath.

In conversation with Dr. Moorman, resident physician at the springs, he informed me that the water is decidedly injurious in scirrhus of the stomach, organic disease of the heart, and phthisis pulmonalis. He also states that, in using the water in urinary affections, its action should be carefully scrutinized, in order that irritation be not produced, and copious diuresis should never be sought.

Usually this water decreases the number of beats of a rapid pulse, by allaying the diseased conditions on which the excited circulation depends; and it is a rule, that *it never proves beneficial when it perseveringly excites the frequency of the circulation.*[1]

For general use the water should be taken in the quantity of a glass three or four times a day. For the purpose of purgation, three glasses an hour before breakfast and three glasses an hour before dinner.

Remarks.—These springs are the Mecca of all Virginia tourists, the resort of the gay and fashionable, a place where pleasure-seeking reigns supreme. They are located in a beautiful valley, near the summit of the Greenbrier Mountains, nearly two thousand feet above the sea. Within this valley, overlooked by mountain-summits, we behold the magnificent hotel, with its extended, white-columned porticos. In front, the

[1] Moorman, "Mineral Waters of the United States and Canada," p. 119.

broad lawn spreads out before us, interwoven by various winding walks. Encompassing the lawn on either side are long lines of shining white cottages, embowered beneath the shade of ancient oaks; while, at the distant extremity, the famous spring bubbles beneath a pavilion. Taking one of the by-paths, to the right from the lawn, we soon find ourselves in the romantic "Lovers' Maze." Here, under a dense shade of forest-trees, obscurely-winding paths lead in every direction, amid a thick growth of laurel, till one is completely lost. At various points we find ourselves at the edge of a precipitous declivity, whence extended views may be had of the deep valley below, and the mountain-ranges in the distance. And over the natural beauties of the place the "season" throws a spell of life and revelry. Ladies and gentlemen throng the porticos, pass and repass across the lawns, and each embowered seat in the "Lovers' Maze" has its appropriate occupants. One wakes drowsily at morn, and lounges through the day, only to prepare for the brilliant scenes of the levee and ballroom.

SALT SULPHUR SPRINGS.

Location and Post-Office.—Salt Sulphur Springs, Monroe County, West Virginia.

Access.—From the north go to Washington; thence *via* Orange, Alexandria & Manassas Railroad, and Chesapeake & Ohio Railroad, to Alderson's Station, two hundred and forty-nine miles west from Richmond; thence about fifteen miles south. Or, leave Chesapeake & Ohio Railroad at Alleghany Station; thence *via* Sweet Springs, twenty-nine miles, to the springs. From the west, *via* Cincinnati to Huntington, a point on the Ohio River, one hundred and sixty-five miles east; thence by Chesapeake & Ohio Railroad to Alderson's, one hundred and seventy miles southeast. (*See* Analysis, page 230.)

Properties.—These waters are alkaline in reaction, and somewhat bitter to the taste. They contain an active proportion of purging sulphates, and are valuable waters. The Iodine Spring, according to the analysis, much resembles the waters of Challes, in Savoy, both containing similar salts, and the unusual ingredients, in sulphur-waters, of iodine and bromine. These waters are applicable to *engorgements of the*

ANALYSIS.

One pint contains—	Old Spring, 49° Fahr. to 56° Fahr. Prof. W. B. Rogers.	Iodine Spring, 65½° Fahr. D. Stewart, M. D.
SOLIDS.	Grains.	Grains.
Carbonate of potassa	....	0.291
Carbonate of soda	....	1.350
Carbonate of magnesia	0.414	0.875
Carbonate of lime	1.283	4.125
Chloride of sodium	0.197	0.188
Chloride of magnesium	0.033	0.035
Chloride of calcium	0 007	0.070
Sulphate of soda	2.795	3.000
Sulphate of magnesia	2.276	2.500
Sulphate of lime	10.613	8.500
Peroxide of iron	0.012	0.133
Iodine	trace.	0.079
Bromine	....	0.081
Silicic acid	....	0.220
Alumina	....	0.023
Earthy phosphates (soda and lithia)	trace.	0.091
Organic matter (with sulphur)	1.155	....
Total	18.785	21.561
GASES.	Cubic in.	Cubic in.
Carbonic acid	1.66	4.32
Sulphuretted hydrogen	0.43	2.30

liver, *dartrous skin-diseases*, and *chronic metallic poisoning*. The waters of the Iodine Spring are said to prove especially beneficial in cases of *scrofula* and *syphilis*.

There are facilities for employing the water in the form of warm baths.

Remarks.—North of the Iodine and Salt Sulphur Spring is another water known as the Sweet Sulphur Spring, the first discovered of the group, but for many years neglected. It is lower in temperature, and more pleasant to the taste than the other waters, and, when they prove too cathartic in action, may be temporarily substituted. The name salt applied to these waters is inappropriate, as it conveys a wrong impression of their constituents.

These springs are situated in a charming valley on the banks of the Indian Creek, and are shut in on every side by hills and mountain-summits. Eight miles distant to the southeast the graceful outlines of Peter's Mountain are seen, while Swope's Mountain is but two miles distant to the northwest.

RED SULPHUR SPRINGS.

Location and Post-Office.—Red Sulphur Springs, Monroe County, West Virginia.

Access.—From the North go to Washington; thence *via* Orange, Alexandria & Manassas Railroad, and Chesapeake & Ohio Railroad, to Alderson's, two hundred and sixty-nine miles west from Washington; thence —— miles southwest. From south and southwest, go to Dublin Depot, two hundred and eighty-two miles southwest from Washington, on the Virginia & Tennessee Railroad; thence thirty-eight miles north by stage. From west, *via* Cincinnati and Ohio River to Huntington, one hundred and sixty-five miles east; thence one hundred and seventy miles by Chesapeake & Ohio Railroad to Alderson's; thence —— miles south.

Hotel.—Springs.

ANALYSIS.

One pint contains, (54° Fahr. A. A. Hayes, M. D.):

SOLIDS.	Grains.
Carbonate of magnesia	0.602
Carbonate of lime	0.656
Sulphate of soda	0.518
Sulphate of lime	0.069
Sulphur compound (organic matter, W.)	1.049
Silicious and earthy matter	0.102
Total	2.996
GASES.	Cubic in.
Carbonic acid	1.00
Sulphuretted hydrogen	0.13

(1842.)

This analysis, having been made from water sent to Roxbury, Mass., is not an index of the quantity of gas as it exists at the spring. There it evolves considerable sulphuretted hydrogen.

The chemical character of the sulphur compound is given by Prof. Hayes,[1] as follows:

1. When separated from a solution by evaporation or by drying from a gelatinous state, it forms greasy films, which do not darken solutions of lead or copper.

2. In pure water they slowly dissolve, and the solution gives salts of the compound with the bases.

[1] Burke on the "Virginia Springs," p. 101.

3. Solution of carbonate of soda dissolves them, and a fluid results which froths by agitation.

4. In caustic solutions of alkalies the films dissolve, and the solutions are slightly yellow-colored. These solutions have the peculiar odor of soap-lyes. They do not blacken metals, nor color metallic solutions. Acids decompose the solutions, and the sulphur compound separates in the form of a bulky jelly generally; some oxyacids, giving flocks.

5. Nitric acid dissolves the films, and the salts of baryta and lead do not indicate the presence of sulphuric acid. On heating the solution a yellow matter separates, which resembles that produced by acting on azotized bodies by this agent; sulphuric acid is thus produced, and the yellow precipitate requires a large proportion of nitric acid for its complete oxidation. The result of this action is an acid which gives a deep-yellow color with ammonia in excess.

6. Chlorine in muriatic acid separates from the sulphur compound some white flakes, which are finally oxidized, and a colorless solution formed, in which sulphuric acid exists.

7. Alcohol did not dissolve the compound.

In another portion of his report, Prof. Hayes says: "The peculiar sulphur compound which forms a part of the saline contents of this water has never been described,[1] if it has ever before been met with; while in the natural state, and out of contact with atmospheric air, it is dissolved in the water, and forms a permanent solution. Air, acids, and other agents, separate it from the water in the form of a jelly, and alkaline carbonates, alkalies, water, and other agents, redissolve it. It has no acid action on test-fluids, but bears that character with bases, and forms compounds analogous to salts. In its decomposition ammonia is formed, and hydro-sulphuric acid is liberated; or, if heat be employed in the experiment, sulphur is separated. It combines with the oxide of silver, and forms a salt of a reddish-purple color, in the form of a flocculent precipitate, which dissolves in pure water; with the oxide of lead a yellowish-white powder, and with the oxide of copper a

[1] 1842.

pale-blue salt in fine powder. In these compounds it remains unaltered, and may be separated from them and transferred to other bases. Mixed with a small quantity of water, and exposed to a temperature of 80° Fahr., it decomposes, and emits a most offensive odor of putrefying matter with hydro-sulphuric acid."

The red deposit which occurs in the springs is considered by Prof. Hayes to be an algoid growth from the viscid deposit of the sulphur-compound.

Properties.—As will be seen from the analysis, this water contains but a small proportion of saline constituents, the chief ingredient being the sulphur-compound. This substance, in many of its reactions, resembles hydrosin or the soluble organic matter of sulphur-waters, though the number of corresponding tests are not sufficient to establish the identity.[1]

The action of these waters, taken internally, is decidedly *sedative.* In corroboration of this fact we may give the testimony of Dr. Jos. Scott. He went to the springs with a pulse which, for some months, had ranged from 100 to 110, accompanied with occasional cough and hæmorrhage from the lungs. He drank the first day four pints, the second day six pints, the third day eight pints. On the third day the pulse fell to 70 in the morning, and 80 to 84 in the evening, and so continued while using the water. Dr. Henry Huntt arrived at the springs with pulse 115, cough and pulmonary hæmorrhage. He confined himself to low diet, and drank six glasses of the water during the day—two before breakfast, one at eleven A. M., one at five P. M., and two at bedtime. In ten days the pulse was reduced to 78. Dr. Woodville, of the Sweet Springs, tells me he has experienced the sedative action of the water on the heart in his own person when in a state of health.

This water seems to possess a peculiar tendency toward the mucous membrane of the lungs, allaying irritation and

[1] Compare Henry, "Analyse Chimique des Eaux Minérales," p. 454, Paris, 1858. Also "Nouveau Dictionnaire de Médicine et de Chirurgie," tome xii., p. 240, Paris, 1870.

diminishing expectoration. It also acts on the intestines and kidneys. *In small quantities it is cathartic, in larger quantities diuretic.* According to Dr. Huntt, its beneficial effects are most decided when it acts freely on the kidneys. The water should first be taken in moderate quantities—two or three glasses each day—and gradually increased till diuretic action is produced. The time recommended for taking the principal draughts is at bedtime and before breakfast, an additional glass being taken once or twice through the day.

The water by its sedative action proves hypnotic in some cases.

The diseases in which the water proves decidedly beneficial are *chronic bronchitis, chronic pharyngitis,* and *chronic laryngitis.* In these diseases they equal, if not surpass, any known waters. It has also given temporary relief in cases of phthisis pulmonalis of the chronic form, not by any specific curative influence, but in its action in allaying congestion and irritation of the mucous membrane of the lungs.

Remarks.—These springs are beautifully situated on Indian Creek, at the edge of a mountain-enclosed plain. The mountains, rising on either side, are clothed to the summit with the pine. The approach is by roads that lead through most charming scenery.

BLUE SULPHUR SPRINGS.

Location.—Greenbrier County, West Virginia.

Access.—From Greenbrier White Sulphur Springs, a station on the Chesapeake & Ohio Railroad, twenty-three miles west by stage.

Hotel.—(Burned.)

Analysis.—None.

Remarks.—This was once a well-improved spring, and may at some future time again be a place of resort.

CHAPTER XIII.

CHALYBEATE WATERS.

These springs, as the name indicates, are strongly impregnated with iron, or iron is the principal active ingredient. This last clause is added, inasmuch as some waters may not contain an exceedingly large proportion of iron, yet, owing to absence of other salts, this is the predominant agent. In each class of waters, springs are found containing iron; indeed, there are not many that do not contain it in some proportion. The iron is usually found as a bicarbonate, though in some instances, in which sulphuric acid is in excess, it exists as a sulphate.

Waters of this class are usually limpid and devoid of odor. They have an astringent and inky taste if the iron is present in large quantity, but, if the water be highly charged with carbonic-acid gas, this taste is disguised.

The effect of iron-waters is to increase the appetite, promote digestion, stimulate the activity of the heart, and redden the blood.

The chalybeate waters which prove most valuable are those containing a large amount of carbonic-acid gas and but a small proportion of other constituents.

Pure acidulous chalybeates prove of exceeding benefit in cases of *anœmia* and *chlorosis.* And not only are they used in cases in which a deficiency in redness of the blood-globules is the prominent indication: they are also valuable as an adjunct to treatment by other waters. It is not unfrequent for patients, who have undergone a course of alterative treatment, to be sent to springs of this class as an appropriate termination. These waters are also useful in cases of indigestion, amenorrhœa, dysmenorrhœa, hysteria, paralysis, and sterility, in which anæmia is a prominent indication.

Many waters containing considerable iron are also strongly impregnated with saline (chloride of sodium) or alkaline constituents, and may be termed *saline-chalybeates* or *alkaline-chalybeates.* They will be found under the class Saline or Alkaline Waters. It need hardly be added that, in prescribing these chalybeates, we apply them to those anæmic cases in which the other constituents of the spring are especially applicable.

The so-called *Alum Waters* of Virginia have been included in this class, inasmuch as iron is one of the most prominent constituents. Of all the mineral waters these are among the most decided in the curative effect. The peculiarity of these waters consists in the large proportion of alumina and the presence of *free* sulphuric acid; the last-named ingredient occurring in only two or three places in this country outside of Virginia, as at the Oak Orchard Acid Springs, New York, and the Tuscarora Acid Springs, Canada. These waters are of a yellowish tint, and have a strongly astringent, accompanied with a styptic taste. In temperature they are cold.

In what manner these waters prove efficacious—whether by the peculiar combination of alum with other ingredients, or by some undiscovered agent—is unknown. It is worthy of notice that, while from the chemical character of the water we should expect an astringent action, the fact is that they frequently act as a mild cathartic. The diseases in which they are curative are *scrofula* in all of its forms, and *chronic diarrhœa,* except cases accompanied with considerable congestion of the mucous membranes and liver. They are also decidedly beneficial in chronic *eczema* and *leucorrhœa,* occurring in scrofulous individuals.

BAILEY SPRINGS.

Location and Post-Office.—Bailey Springs, Lauderdale County, Alabama.

Access.—Go to Tuscumbia, a station on the Memphis & Charleston Railroad, one hundred and forty-five miles east from Memphis, one hundred and sixty-four miles west from Chattanooga, fifty-two miles east from Corinth, and forty-three miles west from Decatur; thence, *via* Florence Branch, to Florence, forty minutes; thence, nine miles northeast, by stage.

Hotel.—Bailey Springs.

Analysis.—The following qualitative analyses have been made:

CHALYBEATE SPRING. (Dr. Curry.)	ROCK SPRING. (Prof. Tuomey.)
Carbonate of potassa.	Carbonate of potassa (traces).
Carbonate of soda.	Carbonate of soda.
Carbonate of magnesia.	Carbonate of iron.
Chloride of sodium.	Chloride of sodium.
Oxide of iron.	Sulphur, perhaps combined with soda.
Carbonic-acid gas.	
Sulphuretted-hydrogen gas.	

Accompanying his analysis, Prof. Tuomey says: "I regret that I had it not in my power to make a quantitative analysis of this far-famed water. My analysis was conducted, however, with as much care as possible; yet it is proper to state that, under favorable circumstances, an analysis in which a large quantity of water could be used might develop other ingredients in addition to those given.

"The iron is in greater abundance than would appear from the deposit below the outlet of the spring. It is even thrown down slowly during the process of concentration by boiling.

"The prominent ingredients are carbonic acid, iron, and soda."

Properties.—These waters are *alkaline-chalybeate*, and we would expect them to prove useful in a number of diseases. Dr. H. A. Moody informs me that they have proved especially beneficial in *scrofula* and *dropsy*, the latter more particularly when associated with disease of the kidneys, or enlargement of the liver or spleen. Dropsy being but a symptom of some other disease, they act in this respect as a palliative by diuresis. In *leucorrhœa*, *amenorrhœa*, *dysmenorrhœa*, and *irritability of the bladder*, they are said to prove of service.

Remarks.—These springs are situated in a fertile and rolling country. The hotel is on the summit of a semicircular hill, horseshoe in form; and in the valley, under cover of a shed, are the springs, five in number—the Rock, the Chalybeate, the Soda, the Alum, and the Freestone.

A short distance from the springs is Shoal Creek, where curious Indian remains may be seen; and those fond of sport may amuse themselves with fishing. Muscle Shoals, six miles distant, present a series of broken water-falls, the roar from which may be heard for several miles.

FRY'S SODA SPRING.

Location.—Siskiyou County, California.

Access.—Go to Sacramento; thence, by Oregon division of Central Pacific Railroad, to Red Bluff; thence by stage, about ninety miles, to the spring. The Oregon Railroad, when finished, will pass within half a mile of the spring.

Hotel.—Fry's Soda Springs.

Analysis.—"The water is a chalybeate, there being an extensive ferruginous deposit around the spring; it is also highly impregnated with carbonic acid, sparkling like soda-water. The temperature of the water was 52° Fahr. in September, 1862."[1]

Remarks.—These springs are located at the bottom of the cañon of the Upper Sacramento, at an elevation of two thousand three hundred and sixty-three feet above the sea. The sides of the gorge are studded to the summit with pine, fir, and cedar, while the banks of the river are beautiful with the "vivid incessant green" of the eternal spring which rules in California. Here we are but a short distance from the base of Mount Shasta, fourteen thousand four hundred and forty feet high, almost equal in altitude to Mont Blanc.

The *ascent of Mount Shasta* is most readily made from this side. Persons wishing to make the ascent, procure horses and guides at Sisson's Ranch, eight miles from the springs. "The best season of the year for the ascent is in July or August. Before July the snow is hardly gone from the camping-ground from which the ascent to the summit and return is to be made in one day, and after that month the in-

[1] "Geological Survey of California," vol. i., p. 331.

cessant fires in the surrounding forests fill the air with smoke, and take away all distinctness from the distant view. The plan adopted by those ascending the mountain is to pass the first night at Camp Ross, near the line of perpetual snow; and from that point to start sufficiently early to keep always on the hard-frozen snow, the heat of the sun by mid-day softening it nearly to the summit, so as to make climbing almost if not quite impossible; while the ascent on the frozen surface is quite easy, especially if one has the soles of his boots well provided with nails. Our party started at 3½ A. M., and reached the summit by 11½ A. M., but others, not encumbered as we were by barometers and instruments, would be able to make the ascent in considerably less time. Of course a night near the full of the moon is preferable, although the usual bright starlight of the summer will answer to enable one to pick his way over the snow. It is advisable to leave Strawberry Flat in season to camp early and comfortably at the base of the snow, and to have plenty of warm clothing, as the temperature at an altitude of seven thousand six hundred and twenty-nine feet will probably be pretty near the freezing-point before morning. There is abundance of wood and water at Camp Ross, and the trail from Strawberry Flats sufficiently good, to allow those wishing to save their strength, to ride the whole way."[1]

STAFFORD SPRINGS.

Location and Post-Office.—Stafford Springs, Tolland County, Connecticut.

Access.—Go to Willimantic, thirty-two miles east of Hartford, on the Hartford, Providence & Fishkill Railroad; thence twenty miles north to Stafford.

Hotel.—Stafford Springs House.

Analysis.—No quantitative analysis has been made. In Trumbull's "History of Connecticut" (1818), the following occurs: "The springs are two in number. The first discovered contains iron, held in solution by the carbonic acid, or fixed air, natron or native alkali, a small proportion of marine

[1] "Geological Survey of California."

salt, iodine, soda, magnesia, and some earthy substances. The other is charged principally with hydrogen gas of sulphur; it also contains a very minute portion of iron. The spring first discovered has been pronounced by chemists to be one of the best chalybeate springs in the United States." Prof. C. U. Shepard, in his report of the "Geological Survey" of the State, 1837, states that these springs are "the most important in the State. No escape of gas perceptible. Sides of reservoir were lined with a thick flocculent precipitate of oxide of iron caused by the decomposition of the carbonate of iron from access of air."

GREENCASTLE SPRINGS.

Location and Post-Office.—Greencastle, Putnam County, Indiana.

Access.—Greencastle is thirty-eight miles west from Indianapolis, by either Indianapolis & St. Louis Railroad, or St. Louis, Vandalia, Terre Haute & Indianapolis Railroad. Also one hundred and thirty-nine miles north from Louisville, by the Louisville, New Albany & Chicago Railroad.

Hotels.—Jones House, Centre House.

ANALYSIS.

One pint contains—	North or Daggy Spring, 56° Fahr.	Middle or Dew-drop Spring, 52° Fahr.
SOLIDS.	Grains.	Grains.
Carbonate of potassa	0.011	0.009
Carbonate of soda	0.012	0.008
Carbonate of magnesia	0.588	0.667
Carbonate of protoxide of iron	0.051	0.298
Carbonate of lime	1.819	1.485
Chloride of sodium	0.099	0.087
Sulphate of soda	0.017	0.012
Sulphate of magnesia	0.131	0.129
Alumina	0.020	0.009
Silicic acid	0.011	0.001
Loss, and undetermined	0.012	0.028
Total	2.771	2.733

Remarks.—There is another spring on the grounds, known as the South or Diamond Spring. It is similar to those of which the analysis is given.

CATOOSA SPRINGS.

Location and Post-Office.—Catoosa Springs, Catoosa County, Georgia.

Access.—Go to Ringgold, a station on the Western & Atlantic Railroad, twenty-two miles southeast from Chattanooga, one hundred and fifteen miles northwest of Atlanta; thence four and a half miles east, by stage, to the springs.

Hotel.—Catoosa Springs.

Analysis.—No exact quantitative analysis has been made. The waters, however, are reported as strongly chalybeate. There are also sulphur-waters here.

Remarks.—There are very many springs at this point, all rising within the space of two acres. They were much resorted to before the war, but the buildings subsequently needed repair. They are, however, open for visitors, and are being reimproved.

MADISON SPRINGS.

Location and Post-Office.—Madison Springs, Madison County, Georgia.

Access.—From Augusta *via* Georgia Railroad, to Union Point, seventy-six miles; thence, *via* Athens Branch, to Athens, three and a half hours; thence by stage.

Hotel.— ———.

Analysis.—None.

ESTILL SPRINGS, KENTUCKY.

(For location, etc., *see* "ESTILL SPRINGS, PURGATIVE WATERS.")

ANALYSIS.

One pint contains (Dr. Peter):

SOLIDS.	Grains.
Carbonate of magnesia	0.335
Carbonate of iron	0.233
Carbonate of lime	1.159
Chloride of sodium	0.066
Sulphate of potassa	0.080
Sulphate of soda	0.087
Sulphate of magnesia	1.224
Sulphate of lime	2.084
Alumina and trace of phosphates	trace.
Silica	0.233
Organic and volatile matter	1.028
Total	6.529
GAS.	Cubic in.
Carbonic acid	4.15

KNIGHTSTOWN SPRING.

Location and Post-Office.—Knightstown, Henry County, Indiana.

Access.—Knightstown is a station on the Indianapolis & Chicago division of the Pittsburg, Cincinnati & St. Louis Railroad, thirty-four miles east of Indianapolis.

Hotels.— ——.

Analysis.—No complete analysis of this water has been made. Dr. T. C. Fox, State Geologist of Indiana, in a letter to the author, remarks: "From a qualitative examination of some of the water sent to my office, it proved to be almost a pure chalybeate, having only about twenty-five grains of solid constituents in an imperial gallon, mostly calcic and magnesic salts."

SCHUYLER COUNTY SPRINGS.

Location.—Schuyler County, Illinois.

ANALYSIS.[1]

One pint contains (Dr. Blaney):

SOLIDS.	Grains.
Sulphate of magnesia	0.373
Sulphate of lime	9.242
Protosulphate of iron	8.745
Silica	0.164
Alkaline sulphates	0.979
Total	19,503

Dr. Blaney remarks that the water "has an acid reaction, a strong, styptic taste, a trace of organic matter, and an obscure trace of chlorides."

HOPKINTON SPRINGS.

Location and Post-Office.—Hopkinton, Middlesex County, Massachusetts.

Access.—From Boston to Westborough, a station on the Boston & Albany Railroad, thirty-two miles west; thence, about three miles southeast.

Hotel.— ———

Analysis.—The waters are said to contain carbonic acid, carbonate of lime, and iron.

[1] "Geology of Illinois," vol. iv., p. 89.

OWOSSO SPRING.

Location and Post-Office.—Owosso, Shiawassee County, Michigan.

Access.—Owosso is a station on the Detroit & Milwaukee Railroad, seventy-nine miles northwest from Detroit.

Hotel.—National.

ANALYSIS.

One pint contains:

Solids.	Grains.
Carbonate of magnesia	1.413
Carbonate of iron	1.443
Carbonate of lime	2.228
Chlorides of sodium and potassium	0.262
Silica and alumina	0.077
Total	5.423

Properties.—This is a strong chalybeate water; but, that the proportion of iron is as large as shown in the analysis, I very much doubt. It should be reanalyzed.

Remarks.—The town of Owosso is situated at the intersection of the Detroit & Milwaukee Railroad and the Jackson, Lansing & Saginaw Railroad. The population is over two thousand.

SCHOOLEY'S MOUNTAIN SPRINGS.

Location and Post-Office Address.—Schooley's Mountain, Morris County, New Jersey.

Access.—From New York *via* Morris & Essex Railroad to Hackettstown, sixty-two miles west, thence two and one-half miles by stage.

Hotels.—Belmont House, Heath House.

Analysis.—None. Said to be a pure chalybeate.

Remarks.—This is an exceedingly popular resort, on account of its accessibility and the beauty of the surrounding scenery.

The spring issues from the earth near the summit of the mountain, and is conveyed some distance to a convenient place by pipes. The temperature of the water is 50° Fahr., the taste strongly chalybeate. The water contains considerable carbonic-acid gas, and, for this reason, is acceptable to the stomach. The discharge is small—about one-half gallon per minute.

COOPER'S WELL.

Location and Post-Office.—Cooper's Well, Hinds County, Mississippi.

Access.—From New Orleans, one hundred and eighty-three miles north, *via* New Orleans, Jackson & Great Northern Railroad, to Jackson; thence, twelve miles west, by stage.

Hotel.—Cooper's Well.

ANALYSIS.

One pint contains, (50° Fahr. Prof. J. Lawrence Smith):

SOLIDS.	Grains.
Chloride of sodium	1.045
Chloride of magnesium	0.435
Chloride of calcium	0.540
Sulphate of potassa	0.076
Sulphate of soda	1.463
Sulphate of magnesia	2.910
Sulphate of lime	5.265
Sulphate of alumina	0.765
Peroxide of iron	0.420
Crenate of lime	0.039
Silica	0.225
Total	13.183
GASES.	Cubic in.
Carbonic acid	4.0
Oxygen	1.5
Nitrogen	4.5

Properties.—This is an exceedingly valuable chalybeate water, containing a proportion of purgative salts, and bearing considerable resemblance to the waters of Bocklet, near Kissingen, in Bavaria. This combination adapts the waters to numerous conditions in which *anæmia* is associated with constipation or abdominal plethora. It is found exceedingly valuable in certain dyspepsias, in dropsy, and in *chlorosis.* In *chronic diarrhœa* this water has long enjoyed high repute. The waters act as a diuretic or aperient, according to the quantity taken and the mode of drinking.

Remarks.—This is the most noted mineral water in Mississippi, and has long been a favorite with the people of the Southern country.

The artesian well whence the water flows is one hundred and seven feet deep, and the flow is exceedingly abundant.

OCEAN SPRINGS.

Location and Post-Office.—Ocean Springs, Jackson County, Mississippi.

Access.—Ocean Springs is a station on the New Orleans, Mobile & Texas Railroad, eighty-three miles east from New Orleans, and fifty-seven miles west from Mobile. Or the springs may be reached by coast-steamers from either New Orleans or Mobile.

Hotels.—Morris House, Egan House.

ANALYSIS.

One pint contains (J. L. Smith):

SOLIDS.	Grains.
Chloride of potassium	trace.
Chloride of sodium	5.971
Chloride of magnesium	0.621
Chloride of calcium	0.485
Protoxide of iron	0.589
Iodine	trace.
Alumina	trace.
Organic matter	trace.
Total	7.666
GASES.	Cubic in.
Carbonic acid	1.22
Sulphuretted hydrogen	0.16

—"Geology of Mississippi."

Properties.—This water is a *saline-chalybeate*, abounding in iron, which no doubt is held in solution in the form of a carbonate. The unusual combination of chloride of sodium, carbonate of iron, and sulphuretted hydrogen, especially adapts it to the treatment of diseases of the skin allied to a scrofulous diathesis.

Remarks.—The name of these springs is derived from their proximity to the ocean, the beach being but half a mile distant, and affording ample facility for sea-bathing. The springs are much resorted to by citizens of New Orleans and Mobile.

OAK-ORCHARD ACID SPRINGS.

Location.—Genesee County, New York

Post-Office.—Medina, Orleans County, New York.

Access.—Go to Medina, a station on the New York Central Railroad, forty miles west of Rochester, thence six miles south by carriage. Or go to

Batavia, a station on a branch of the New York Central Railroad, thirty-two miles west of Rochester, thence twelve miles north by carriage.

Hotel.—(Closed.)

ANALYSIS.

One pint contains (J. R. Chilton, M. D.):

SOLIDS.	Grains.
Sulphate of magnesia	1.035
Sulphate of alumina	1.210
Sulphate of lime	4.950
Protosulphate of iron	1.790
Silica	0.130
Organic matter	0.422
Free sulphuric acid	10.370
Total	19.907

Properties.—This spring is, in one respect, the most remarkable in this country. The occurrence of notable quantities of sulphuric acid in springs in a free state is exceedingly rare. Only two other springs of this character are known in this country, that of the neighboring town of Byron in the same county, and the Tuscarora Sour Spring in the county of Wentworth, Canada. None of the kind are known in Europe. "An earth somewhat similar to that found in Byron is said to exist in great quantities at a village called Danlakie, in the south of Persia, between three and four days' journey from Bushire, on the Persian Gulf. The natives employ it as a substitute for lemons and limes in making their sherbets." These, with Paramo de Ruiz and Rio Vinagre, New Granada, South America, comprise all the known springs containing free sulphuric acid in considerable quantity.

The Oak-Orchard water has been used with advantage in a number of diseases. Prof. J. H. Armsby, of Albany, says: "The diseases in which I have found it most useful are as follows: ill-conditioned ulcers, diseases of the skin, passive hæmorrhages, diarrhœas depending on an atonic condition of the mucous membranes, in depraved and impoverished conditions of the body from specific disease and from intemperance."

When drunk the water is diluted with an equal quantity

of pure water. From half a wineglass to a wineglass three times a day is thus taken. In treatment of ulcers the water is taken internally, and also applied directly, lint being saturated with the water and changed twice daily.

SHARON SPRINGS.

Location, etc.—See these springs, under Sulphur-waters.

ANALYSIS.

One pint contains (Maisch):

SOLIDS.	Grains.
Carbonate of magnesia	1.120
Sulphate of potassa	trace.
Sulphate of soda	.467
Sulphate of magnesia	1.019
Sulphate of lime	7.975
Protosulphate of iron	0.175
Organic matter	3.560
Total	14.316

(1861.)

MINERAL SPRING.

Location.—Monmouth County, New Jersey.

Access.—Near Oceanville, two miles' drive from Long Branch.

Analysis.—No accurate analysis has been made; one gallon is said to contain one and a quarter grain of carbonate of iron.

ADAMS COUNTY SPRINGS.

Location and Post-Office.—Mineral Springs, Adams County, Ohio.

Access.—From Cincinnati, seventy-five miles east, by steamboat on the Ohio River, to Rome; thence, nineteen miles north by stage.

Hotel.—Mineral Springs.

Analysis.—No accurate quantitative analysis has been made; a qualitative analysis, by Prof. E. S. Wayne, states that there are fifteen grains of solid matter to the pint, composed of chloride of magnesium, sulphate of lime, carbonate of lime, chloride of sodium, chloride of calcium, and oxide of iron. The flow of the spring is about one gallon per minute, and the temperature 56° Fahr.

Remarks.—These springs are located in that portion of Ohio which most nearly is entitled to the name of mountainous. The springs, two in number, are situated in a valley at the base of a high hill, several hundred feet in altitude, known as Peach Mountain. From the surrounding elevations, far extended and attractive views may be had, while the woodlands and streams supply amusement for the sportsman. "Point Lookout," three miles from the springs, is frequently visited by those who delight in an extended view.

CRESSON SPRINGS.

Location and Post-Office.—Cresson, Cambria County, Pennsylvania.

Access.—Cresson is a station on the Pennsylvania Central Railroad, two hundred and fifty-two miles west of Philadelphia, and one hundred and two miles east of Pittsburg.

Hotel.—Mountain House.

Analysis.—None. Principal spring said to be a chalybeate.

Remarks.—Cresson is resorted to more because of its mountain elevation than the value of the waters. The air is pure and bracing, and the thermometer seldom rises to 75° Fahr. in the hottest days of summer. Guests sleep under blankets the entire season. The mountains furnish abundant opportunity for excursions, while many delightful drives wind through the valleys. The springs are seven in number, the principal one being about a quarter of a mile distant, on the site of the old Alleghany Portage Railway, now abandoned, but still showing the manner of constructing railways many years ago.

BLOSSBURG SPRINGS.

Location.—Tioga County, Pennsylvania.

Access.—From New York, *via* Erie Railroad, to Corning, two hundred and ninety miles northwest; thence, *via* Blossburg & Corning Railroad, to Blossburg, forty-one miles south.

Hotel.— ———.

Analysis.—None. The waters are said to bear some resemblance to the alum-waters of Virginia.

FAYETTE SPRINGS.

Location and Post-Office.—Fayette Springs, Fayette County, Pennsylvania.

Access.—From Pittsburg, *via* Pittsburg, Baltimore & Washington Railroad, to Connellsville, fifty-seven miles south; thence, *via* Fayette County Branch Railroad, to Uniontown, fourteen miles south; thence, twelve miles by stage to the springs.

Hotel.—Fayette Springs.

Analysis.—None.

Remarks.—These springs are located in the Laurel Mountains, amid most romantic scenery, where cool mountain-air may be enjoyed.

MONTVALE SPRINGS.

Location and Post-Office.—Montvale Springs, Blount County, Tennessee.

Access.—Go to Knoxville on the Virginia & Tennessee Railroad; thence, *via* Knoxville & Charleston Railroad, to Maryville, sixteen miles northwest; thence, nine miles by stage to the springs.

Hotel.—Montvale Springs.

ANALYSIS.

One pint contains—	60° Fahr. Prof. J. B. Mitchell.	60° Fahr. J. R. Chilton, M. D.
SOLIDS.	Grains.	Grains.
Carbonate of iron	0.300	....
Carbonate of lime	1.657	....
Chloride of sodium	0.245	....
Chloride of magnesium	....	0.012
Chloride of calcium	....	0.018
Sulphate of soda	0.564	1.102
Sulphate of magnesia	1.500	2.184
Sulphate of lime	9.276	10.243
Oxide of iron	....	0,149 [1]
Alumina	0.062	....
Silica	....	trace.
Organic matter	....	0.005
Total	13.604	13.663

(1857.)

Properties.—These are *calcic-chalybeate* waters. They have considerable reputation in *chronic diarrhœa* and *scrofula.* In dropsy, associated with engorgement of the liver, they act favorably, both as a diuretic and by their effect on that organ.

[1] In a note accompanying his analysis, Dr. Chilton says: "The oxide of iron was deposited in the bottle; it was probably held in solution in the water by carbonic acid."

In large quantities, the waters are cathartic; in moderate quantities, laxative and diuretic.

Remarks.—These springs are situated in a mountain-glen, amid the heights of the Chilhowee Mountains. Here, amid the pleasures of mountain-rambles, the various sports of field and stream, and the luxury of cool, pure mountain-air, one may pleasantly pass the summer days.

Three miles distant is a *sulphur-spring.*

BEERSHEBA SPRINGS.

Location and Post-Office.—Beersheba Springs, Grundy County, Tennessee.

Access.—Go to Tullahoma, a station on the Nashville & Chattanooga Railroad, sixty-nine miles southeast from Nashville, and eighty-two miles northwest from Chattanooga; thence, thirty-four miles northeast by rail, to McMinnville; thence, about twelve miles by stage. Or, go to Cowan, a station on the Nashville & Chattanooga Railroad, sixty-four miles northwest from Chattanooga; thence by stage.

Hotel.—Beersheba Springs.

Analysis.—The water has never been analyzed, but is said to be a fine chalybeate. Temperature, 58° Fahr.

Remarks.—These springs are situated near the summit of a spur of one of the Cumberland Mountains. The scenery is wild and attractive. The temperature is cool during the summer months. A register of temperature taken at the hotel, from July 20 to August 1, 1872, gave the following result: Mean temperature for twelve days: 6 A. M., 72°; 12 M., 79.8°; 6 P. M., 78.8° Fahr.

Being convenient of access from Nashville and Chattanooga, the springs are much resorted to by the wealthy of those cities.

RAWLEY SPRINGS.

Location and Post-Office Address.—Rawley Springs, Rockingham County, Virginia.

Access.—From Washington, *via* Orange, Alexandria & Manassas Railroad, to Harrisonburg, one hundred and thirty-eight miles west; thence, twelve miles by stage, to the springs. Or, *via* Baltimore & Ohio Railroad, to Harper's Ferry; thence, by Winchester branch, to Harrisonburg (connections not good). Or, by rail to Staunton, Virginia; thence north, twenty-five miles by stage, to Harrisonburg.

Hotel.—Rawley Springs.

ANALYSIS.

One pint contains (51° Fahr. Prof. J. W. Mallet):

SOLIDS.	Grains.
Carbonate of magnesia	0.085
Carbonate of iron	0.203
Carbonate of manganese	0.002
Carbonate of lime	0.055
Carbonate of ammonia	trace.
Carbonate of lithia	trace.
Chloride of sodium	0.005
Sulphate of potassa	0.014
Sulphate of soda	0.068
Sulphate of lime	0.013
Alumina	0.005
Silica	0.085
Organic matter	0.036
Loss	0.073
Total	0.644
GAS.	Cubic in.
Carbonic acid	0.77

(1870.)

Properties.—This water is the best *pure chalybeate* in Virginia, and proves efficacious in *chlorosis*, *leucorrhœa*, *amenorrhœa*, and *menorrhagia*, when depending on anæmic conditions, and all maladies caused by an impoverished condition of the blood. It forms an admirable tonic after the alterative treatment by other waters.

Remarks.—These springs are delightfully situated on the southern slope of the North Mountain, amid salubrious air and pleasing landscapes.

SWEET CHALYBEATE SPRINGS.

Location and Post-Office Address.—Sweet Chalybeate Springs, Alleghany County, Virginia.

Access.—From Washington, *via* Orange, Alexandria & Manassas Railroad, and Chesapeake & Ohio Railroad, to Alleghany Station, two hundred and forty-one miles west; thence, by stage nine miles, to the springs. From

Richmond, *via* Gordonsville, two hundred and twenty-one miles, to Alleghany Station. From the west, *via* Cincinnati and Ohio River, to Huntington, one hundred and sixty-five miles east; thence, *via* Chesapeake & Ohio Railroad, one hundred and ninety-eight miles southeast, to Alleghany Station.

Hotel.—Sweet Chalybeate Springs.

ANALYSIS.

One pint contains (75° to 79° Fahr. Prof. W. B. Rogers):

SOLIDS.	Grains.
Carbonate of lime	0.337
Chloride of sodium	0.011
Chloride of magnesium	0.196
Chloride of calcium	0.003
Sulphate of soda	0.404
Sulphate of magnesia	0.897
Sulphate of lime	4.110
Sesquioxide of iron	0.092
Total	6.050
GAS.	Cubic in.
Carbonic acid	13.

Properties.—This is a fine *calcic-chalybeate* water, containing a proportion of purgative salts. The taste of the water is sweet and ferruginous. The water is beneficially employed in cases of *anœmia*, *chlorosis*, *leucorrhœa*, and other diseases associated with an impoverished condition of the blood. It has also proved decidedly efficacious in *neuralgia* and *gastralgia.*

Remarks.—These springs, formerly called the *Red Sweet Springs*, are situated in one of the most beautiful valleys of Virginia. They are four in number, and flow from the base of a curiously-incrusted ledge of rocks. Although there are four different sources, they do not differ essentially in chemical constitution, unless it be the upper one, which is somewhat similar to the Old Sweet Springs, one mile above. On the 19th of August, 1871, I found the average temperature of the four sources to be 76° Fahr. The flow of the springs is eight hundred gallons per minute. The red substance covering the bottom of the springs is not an oxide of iron, but an algoid growth.

Besides the use of the water internally, it is largely used

as a bath. Swimming-baths have been constructed, about twenty by thirty feet in area. Doubtless the good results obtained in many maladies treated here are principally due to the use of these baths. The temperature of the bath is 76° Fahr.

The temperature at this resort is usually cool and agreeable. A record taken at the office of the hotel gives the following results:

Average Temperature.	6 A. M.	12 M.	6 P. M.
From July 2 to September 5, 1870 . .	70½°	84½°	78° Fahr.
From July 24 to August 19, 1871 . . .	65	80	78

ROCKBRIDGE ALUM SPRINGS.

Location and Post-Office.—Rockbridge Alum Springs, Rockbridge County, Virginia.

Access.—From the North to Washington; thence, *via* Orange, Alexandria & Manassas Railroad, and Chesapeake & Ohio Railroad, to Goshen, one hundred and eighty-eight miles southwest; thence, by stage, to the springs. From Richmond, *via* Chesapeake & Ohio Railroad, one hundred and sixty-eight miles, to Goshen. From the southwest, *via* Virginia & Tennessee Railroad, Lynchburg, Charlottesville, and Chesapeake & Ohio Railroad. From the west, *via* Cincinnati and the Ohio River, to Huntington, one hundred and sixty-five miles east; thence, *via* Chesapeake & Ohio Railroad, two hundred and fifty-one miles southeast, to Goshen.

Hotel.—Rockbridge Alum.

ANALYSIS.

One pint contains—	No. 1. A. A. Hayes, M. D.	No. 2. A. A. Hayes, M. D.	No. 4. A. A. Hayes, M. D.
SOLIDS.	Grains.	Grains.	Grains.
Chloride of sodium	0.058	0.126	0.055
Sulphate of potassa	.....	0.221	....
Sulphate of magnesia	0.185	0.220	0.552
Sulphate of lime	0.180	0.408	0.418
Protoxide of iron	0.460	0.608	0.587
Alumina	1.846	2.288	3.011
Crenate of ammonia	0.175	0.088	0.153
Silicate of soda	0.318	....	....
Sulphuric acid (free)	2.347	1.908	0.689
Silicic acid (free)	....	0.355	0.218
Organic matter	....	....	0.127
Total	5.514	6.167	5.800
GAS.	Cubic in.	Cubic in.	Cubic in.
Carbonic acid	0.7	1.9	1.1

(1852.)

Properties.—These waters are clear and odorless. They possess a strongly astringent and styptic taste. In temperature they are cold. A mass or extract is prepared from the water by evaporation, which, when redissolved, is said to possess the virtues of the spring-water.

These are the best known of the alum-waters of Virginia. Their value in the treatment of disease is undoubted. In what diseases do they prove curative? The answer is simple and explicit. In every form of *scrofula*—scrofulous ulcers, scrofulous diseases of the skin, scrofulous discharges from the ears and nose, and scrofulous diseases of the bones. In *chronic diarrhœa* they have proved a most reliable remedy, except in those cases in which there is congestion of the mucous membranes and liver. They are also beneficial in leucorrhœa and chronic eczema.

Contrary to what we would expect, these waters occasionally prove purgative. In a letter to the author, Prof. H. R. Noel, of Baltimore, resident-physician at the springs, remarks: "It is true that the waters sometimes prove purgative, but I believe it to be true in two classes of cases. 1. Great atony of the digestive tract, especially of the small intestine. 2. When persons drink it in great excess because they are at the springs, and wish to reap rapidly the greatest possible benefit.

"The waters, in nine cases out of ten, should be used as a diuretic, and taken in doses of from one-fourth to one-half of a small tumbler, six, eight, ten, or twelve times a day, and afterward gradually increase the dose, and diminish the number of doses, to about six or eight glasses a day. The water does not act simply from its astringent character, but it is a most powerful agent in restoring perverted histogenesis. I have seen the worst forms of scrofula and some bad syphilitic eruptions cured in ten weeks by it, and not one grain of medicine used.

"The water should be taken, as a rule, from four to ten weeks, and but little improvement will occur under two, and in most cases not under three or five weeks; but, once inaugurated, its effects will last for months."

Remarks.—The springs are situated in a glen-like nook

formed by the spurs of the North and Mill Mountains, and break forth from a mass of shale-rock at the base of the ridge. This shale contains large quantities of alumina and the salts of iron, and the springs are formed by the percolation of water through this mass. Four different reservoirs have been formed, numbered respectively No. 1, No. 2, No. 3, No. 4. They differ somewhat, as is seen in the analysis, especially in the quantities of sulphuric acid.

The immediate surroundings of this resort are attractive. The hotel and brick cottages encircle a lawn embowered with trees, and sociability and amusement add their charms.

From a register of temperature at the hotel I made the following averages:

Average Temperature during	6 A. M.	12 M.	6 P. M.
June, 1869	60.3°	72.2°	71.8° Fahr.
July, 1869	72.2	76.9	76.4
August, 1869	64.8	76.9	75.9
June, 1871	62.1	72.6	70.3
July, 1871	62.9	73.5	71.5
August (to the 24th) 1871	64.9	79.1	77.3

Warmest days during summer of 1869—July 14th, 15th, 16th—87° Fahr. at 12 M.

Warmest days during summer of 1871 (up to 24th of August)—August 16th—89° Fahr. at 12 M.

PULASKI ALUM SPRINGS.

Location.—Pulaski County, Virginia.

Post-Office.—Dublin, Pulaski County, Virginia.

Access.—From Washington, *via* Orange, Alexandria & Manassas Railroad, and Virginia & Tennessee Railroad, to Dublin, a station two hundred and eighty-two miles southwest; thence, twelve miles by stage. From Richmond, *via* Burkeville, two hundred and twenty-nine miles southwest, to Dublin, and *via* Gordonsville two hundred and sixty-two miles. From the south and southwest, strike the Virginia & Tennessee Railroad; thence to Dublin.

Hotel.—Pulaski Alum.

Analysis.—These waters are similar to the Rockbridge Alum. According to an analysis before me, they contain a larger proportion of iron.

Properties.—These waters may be used in very much the same way, and in the same diseases, as the Rockbridge Alum.

Remarks.—The springs are very pleasantly situated on Little Walker's Creek, at the base of Walker's Mountain. The surrounding country abounds in minerals. In the immediate vicinity of the springs is a rich lead of plumbago.

BATH ALUM SPRINGS.

Location and Post-Office.—Bath Alum Springs, Bath County, Virginia.

Access.—From Washington, *via* Orange, Alexandria & Manassas and Chesapeake and Ohio Railroads, to Millboro', one hundred and ninety-six miles southwest; thence, ten miles by stage, to the springs. From Richmond, *via* Chesapeake & Ohio Railroad, one hundred and seventy-six miles northwest, to Millboro'. From the west, *via* Cincinnati and the Ohio River, to Huntington, one hundred and sixty-five miles east; thence, *via* Chesapeake & Ohio Railroad, 244 miles southeast, to Millboro.

Hotel.—Springs.

ANALYSIS.

One pint contains—	No. 1. A. A. Hayes, M. D.	No. 2. A. A. Hayes, M. D.
SOLIDS.	Grains.	Grains.
Chloride of sodium	0.022	....
Sulphate of potassa	....	0.032
Sulphate of magnesia	0.352	0.160
Sulphate of lime	0.476	0.317
Protoxide of iron	1.814	2.722
Alumina	1.286	1.536
Crenate of ammonia	0.232	0.222
Silicate of soda	0.253	0.394
Sulphuric acid (free)	0.726	0.985
Total	5.161	6.368
GAS.	Cubic in.	Cubic in.
Carbonic acid	1.4	1

Properties.—These waters very much resemble the Rockbridge Alum, and are valuable in similar diseases, as follows: *Scrofula, chronic diarrhœa,* eczema, and diseases depending on an impoverished condition of the blood. They contain a larger proportion of iron than the Rockbridge Alum.

Remarks.—The springs are very pleasantly located on the stage-road from Millboro' to the Warm Springs. The buildings, consisting of an hotel and cottages, are of brick, tastefully designed, arranged in the form of a crescent, and looking out upon a beautiful lawn of ten acres. The waters issue from a ledge of slate-stone, and are caught in pools formed in the rocks. Besides those of which the analysis is given, there are others varying in strength, but of the same general character. There are also one or two springs which bear no resemblance to those named, but which have not been sufficiently investigated for their medical properties to be assigned.

STRIBLING SPRINGS.

Location and Post-Office.—Stribling Springs, Augusta County, Virginia.

Access.—From Washington, *via* Orange, Alexandria & Manassas Railroad, and Chesapeake & Ohio Railroad, to Staunton, one hundred and fifty-six miles; thence, thirteen miles northwest by stage. From Richmond, *via* Chesapeake & Ohio Railroad, one hundred and thirty-six miles to Staunton. From the West, *via* Cincinnati and Ohio River, to Huntington, one hundred and sixty-five miles east; thence, *via* Chesapeake & Ohio Railroad, to Staunton, two hundred and eighty-three miles southeast.

Hotel.—Stribling Springs.

ANALYSIS.

One pint contains—	Alum Springs.		
	No. 4. D. K. Tuttle, M. D.	No. 5. D. K. Tuttle, M. D.	No. 6. D. K. Tuttle, M. D.
SOLIDS.	Grains.	Grains.	Grains.
Sulphate of potassa	0.067	0.113	0.126
Sulphate of soda	0.083	0.293	0.224
Sulphate of magnesia	0.066	0.043	0.822
Sulphate of alumina	2.086	2.244	4.801
Sulphate of iron	1.192	1.643	1.615
Sulphate of lime	1.832	2.118	2.389
Sulphuric acid (free)	0.631	1.227	0.817
Silicic acid	0.244	0.264	0.264
Organic matter	0.469	....	....
Total	6.670	7.945	11.058

ANALYSIS.

One pint contains—	Chalybeate Springs.	
	No. 1. D. K. Tuttle, M. D.	No. 3. D. K. Tuttle, M. D.
SOLIDS.	Grains.	Grains.
Carbonate of potassa	0.044	0.095
Carbonate of soda	0.095	0.123
Carbonate of magnesia	0.122	0.138
Carbonate of iron	0.009	0.014
Carbonate of lime	0.188	0.104
Sulphate of lime	0.028	0.386
Silicic acid	0.165	0.114
Total	0.651	0.974
GAS.	Cubic in.	Cubic in.
Carbonic acid	8	2

For analysis of No. 2, *see* Sulphur-Waters.

Properties.—The Alum Springs are beneficial in *scrofula, chronic diarrhœa*, eczema, and all skin-diseases depending on a scrofulous diathesis.

The Chalybeate Springs, containing as they do considerable carbonic acid, are agreeable to the taste.

Remarks.—This is a very old and well-known resort, dating back to 1811. It takes the name from Erasmus Stribling, who first drew decided attention to the value of the waters, and made many improvements for the accommodation of the public. They are sometimes called the *Augusta Springs.*

The springs are delightfully situated in a cool and salubrious locality. They enjoy the advantage of being protected to the northward by a range of mountains, which enables visitors to go earlier in the season, and remain later in the fall, than at many other Virginia watering-places.

CHURCH HILL ALUM SPRINGS.

Location.—Not far from Richmond, Virginia.

Post-Office.— ———.

Access.— ———.

Hotel.— ———.

ANALYSIS.

One pint contains (J. C. Booth, M. D.):

Solids.	Grains.
Chloride of sodium	0.578
Sulphate of potassa	0.305
Sulphate of soda	0.243
Sulphate of magnesia	10.758
Sulphate of lime	11.104
Sulphate of ammonia	0.080
Persulphate of sesquioxide of iron	6.408
Bisulphate of sesquioxide of iron	10.419
Sulphate of protoxide of iron	3.023
Persulphate of alumina	9.116
Silica	1.303
Phosphoric acid	trace.
Total	53.337

(1854, U. S. Dispensatory.)

BEDFORD ALUM SPRINGS.

Location and Post-Office.—Bedford Alum Springs, near New London, Bedford County, Virginia.

Access.—From Washington, *via* Orange, Alexandria & Manassas Railroad, and Virginia & Tennessee Railroad, one hundred and ninety-three miles southwest, to Forest Depot; thence, four miles by stage to the springs. From Richmond, *via* Burkeville, one hundred and thirty-six miles; *via* Gordonsville, one hundred and sixty-nine miles to Forest Depot.

Hotel.—Bedford Alum.

ANALYSIS.

One pint contains (Prof. William Gilliam):

SOLIDS.	Grains.
Sulphate of potassa	1.270
Sulphate of magnesia	1.583
Sulphate of lime	2.334
Sulphate of alumina	.905
Sulphate of protoxide of iron	2.932
Sulphuric acid (free)	2.497
Total	11.521

Properties.—This is another of the valuable alum-waters cf the same general character as the Rockbridge alum, though differing in containing a larger proportion of the salts of potassa, magnesia, lime, and iron, and a smaller amount of alumina. They have been found beneficial in *scrofula, chronic diarrhœa*, eczema, and diseases depending on an impoverished condition of the blood. A mass or extract is prepared from this water by evaporation, which, when dissolved in water in proper proportions, is said to possess the remedial qualities of the water.

Remarks.—This spring is located on the line dividing Campbell and Bedford Counties. It is within three hundred yards of the village of New London, of Revolutionary memory. Here stands the old court-house in which Patrick Henry made several of his finest efforts, among others the celebrated speech against the notorious Johnny Hook. These are the nearest springs to the *Peaks of Otter*, five thousand three hundred and seven feet above the sea—the highest peaks of the Blue Ridge, and by many considered the highest in Virginia. The ascent well repays the tourist.

VARIETY SPRINGS.

Location.—Augusta County, Virginia.

Access.—By Chesapeake & Ohio Railroad. The springs are a station during the summer season, one hundred and seventy-three miles west from Washington, and two hundred and sixty-six miles southeast from Huntington.

Hotel.—Variety Springs.

ANALYSIS.

One pint contains (Prof. Wm. Gilham):

SOLIDS.	Grains.
Chloride of sodium	0.037
Sulphate of potassa	0.036
Sulphate of magnesia	1.455
Sulphate of alumina	4.301
Sulphate of protoxide of iron	0.639
Sulphate of lime	1.666
Free sulphuric acid	0.171
Silica	0.142
Total	8.447

Properties.—This water, known as the "Alum Spring," bears a resemblance to the celebrated Rockbridge Alum, and may be used for the same diseases.

Remarks.—Besides the above spring there are others, termed the All-Healing, the Sulphur, and the Chalybeate. From the number of different waters here the name "Variety" is derived.

CHAPTER XIV.

PURGATIVE WATERS.

THESE waters are characterized by containing a large proportion either of sulphate of magnesia (Epsom salts), or sulphate of soda (Glauber's salts); and, as a consequence of these ingredients, they produce copious alvine dejections. They are bitter to the taste, and, in some classifications, are called *bitter waters.*

Although many mineral waters act as an aperient, or laxative, they do not produce active catharsis, and possess other qualities for which they are esteemed; while these waters are used almost exclusively for the purgative effect.

Waters of this class are useful in all cases requiring active saline purgation, and are especially applicable to persons of robust constitution, with tendency to abdominal plethora. They should be used with care, since constant use of saline purgatives produces decided derangement of the digestive organs.

It is perhaps needless to say that the familiar name, Epsom salts, is derived from the name of the purging-well—Epsom, or Ebbesham—near London, of which sulphate of magnesia is the active ingredient. These waters, as a rule, act much more mildly than a simple solution of the active ingredient; a result due to the other ingredients present, such as the salts of lime and chloride of sodium. Those purgative waters are preferable which contain a considerable quantity of carbonic-acid gas.

A subdivision of purgative waters, classed as alkaline-purgative waters, of which Carlsbad, in Bohemia, is a prominent example, does not readily produce purgation. The water, and those of like character, is applicable to a large class of diseases to which pure purgative waters are not adapted, such as functional and even organic disease of the liver, gastric catarrh, gout, gall-stones, etc. (*See* "CARLSBAD," under "EUROPEAN SPAS.")

ESTILL SPRINGS.

Location.—Estill County, Kentucky.

Access.—From Cincinnati, *via* Kentucky Central Railroad, to Nicholasville, one hundred and twelve miles south; thence, *via* stage, about forty miles east, to Irvine.

Hotel.— ———.

ANALYSIS.

One pint contains (Robert Peter, M. D.):

SOLIDS.	Grains.
Carbonate of magnesia	0.321
Carbonate of iron	0.166
Carbonate of lime	3.841
Chloride of sodium	2.201
Chloride of calcium	0.211
Sulphate of potassa	0.313
Sulphate of magnesia	32.910
Sulphate of lime	3.987
Silica	0.503
Loss	10.736
Total	55.189

Properties.—It will be seen that the Irvine Spring is largely impregnated with sulphate of magnesia, and therefore decidedly purgative.

(For sulphur spring, *see* "SULPHUR WATERS." For chalybeate spring, *see* "CHALYBEATE WATERS.")

CRAB-ORCHARD SPRINGS.

Location and Post-Office.—Crab Orchard, Lincoln County, Kentucky.

Access.—From Louisville, *via* Knoxville branch of Louisville & Nashville Railroad, to Crab Orchard, one hundred and fifteen miles southeast.

Hotel.— ———.

ANALYSIS.[1]

One pint contains—	Foley's Spring. R. Peter, M. D.	Sowder's Spring. R. Peter, M. D.
SOLIDS.	Grains.	Grains.
Carbonate of magnesia	0.955	2.734
Carbonate of iron	trace.	trace.
Carbonate of lime	6.648	8.689
Chloride of sodium	2.216	7.290
Sulphate of potassa	1.239	2.172
Sulphate of soda	7.384	2.900
Sulphate of magnesia	25.660	21.789
Sulphate of lime	1.349	11.416
Bromine	....	trace.
Silica	0.403	0.153
Loss and moisture	4.323	....
Total	50.182	52.143
GAS.		
Carbonic acid	Not estimated.	Not estimated.

Properties.—These waters are chiefly used for the manufacture of the *Crab-Orchard Salts*, produced by boiling down the water. Thousands of pounds of these salts are sold in the Western States. They prove much less irritant in their action than Epsom salts; and, when taken in small and repeated doses, are more likely to produce bilious evacuations. An analysis of a specimen is as follows:

ANALYSIS.

One hundred parts contain (R. Peter, M. D.):

	Parts.
Sulphate of magnesia	63.19
Sulphate of soda	4.20
Sulphate of potassa	1.80
Sulphate of lime	2.54
Chloride of sodium	4.77
Carbonates of lime, magnesia, iron, and silica	0.89
Bromine	trace.
Water of crystallization and loss	22.61
Total	100.00

Remarks.—The spring called Foley's, in the analysis, is usually termed Epsom. It is half a mile from the centre of the village, on the Fall Dick road. Sowder's Spring is about one mile and a half from Crab Orchard; flow, two hundred gallons a day.

[1] "Geology of Kentucky," vol. ii., pp. 233-239.

HARRODSBURG SPRINGS.

Location and Post-Office.—Harrodsburg Springs, Mercer County, Kentucky.

Access.—From Cincinnati, *via* Kentucky Central Railroad, to Nicholasville, one hundred and twelve miles south; thence, *via* stage, about twenty-five miles.

Hotel.— ———.

ANALYSIS.

One pint contains—	Grenville Spring. Raymond.	Saloon Spring. Raymond.
	Grains.	Grains.
Carbonate of magnesia	2.87	0.26
Carbonate of iron	....	0.86
Carbonate of lime	0.60	2.99
Chloride of sodium	trace.	1.24
Sulphate of magnesia	16.16	27.92
Sulphate of lime	11.06	10.24
Total	30.69	43.01

Properties.—The principal characteristic of these springs is the sulphate of magnesia. This salt is cathartic; but, in the presence of the almost equal amount of sulphate of lime, and, in the Saloon Spring, of the carbonate of iron, the action is considerably modified, and they are generally laxative.

Dr. Drake, a man of admirable judgment, stated that "these waters are very beneficial in chronic inflammations and obstructions of the abdominal viscera; in such cases of dyspepsia as are attended with subacute gastritis; and in almost every kind of hepatic disorder, except when the liver is indurated and consequently incurable. They are almost equally beneficial in chronic inflammations of many other parts of the system, especially of the serous and fibrous membranes."

BEDFORD SPRINGS.

Location and Post-Office.—Bedford Springs, Bedford County, Pennsylvania.

Access.—From Huntingdon, a station on the Pennsylvania Central Railroad, two hundred and three miles west of Philadelphia, and *via* Broad Top Railroad, fifty-two miles south to the springs. Or, from Cumberland, a station on the Baltimore & Ohio Railroad, one hundred and seventy-eight miles northwest from Baltimore, and *via* railroad lately finished, about forty miles north to the springs.

Hotel.—Bedford Springs.

ANALYSIS.

One pint contains (58° Fahr. Dr. Church):

SOLIDS.	Grains.
Carbonate of iron	0.625
Carbonate of lime	1.000
Chloride of sodium	1.250
Chloride of lime	0.375
Sulphate of magnesia	10.000
Sulphate of lime	1.875
Loss	0.375
Total	15.500
GAS.	Cubic inch.
Carbonic acid	9.25

Properties.—This valuable water is a *purgative-chalybeate*, bearing considerable resemblance in its properties to the celebrated springs of Franzensbad, in Bohemia. The cathartic action of the water is so much modified by the large proportion of iron contained, that it can be taken for a considerable time without producing other effect than that of a *laxative diuretic*, and *diaphoretic*. The diuretic action of the water is very marked.

The waters are decidedly valuable in all cases of *anæmia*, accompanied by abdominal plethora. In *engorgement of the liver* they give decided relief, and in gravel and calculus they are useful. *Dyspepsias*, accompanied with constipation in anæmic subjects, are subject to their remedial action.

Remarks.—These springs are beautifully situated in a valley of the eastern range of the Alleghany Mountains. The waters break forth from a fissure in the limestone-rock at the base of a mountain-spur. From the spring, terraced walks lead upward in every direction to the summit, whence a most beautiful and extended view of the valley and the town of Bedford is obtained.

The hotel accommodations are extensive, and the proprietors have made arrangements for supplying baths of every description. About two hundred yards distant from the main spring is a *sulphur-spring* which evolves considerable sulphuretted hydrogen. It is said to contain no iron.

BEER SPRINGS.

Location.— ———, Oregon.
Access.— ———.
Hotel.— ———.

ANALYSIS.

One pint contains—

SOLIDS.	Grains.
Carbonate of magnesia	1.61
Carbonate of lime	1.93
Chloride of sodium	1.12
Chloride of magnesium	0.56
Chloride of calcium	0.67
Sulphate of magnesia	6.05
Sulphate of lime	1.06
Vegetable extractive matter	0.42
Total	13.42

MIDLAND WELL.

Location and Post-Office.—Midland, Midland County, Michigan.

Access.—From Detroit, *via* Detroit & Milwaukee and Flint & Père Marquette Railroads, one hundred and twenty miles north, to Midland.

Hotels.—Empire, St. Nicholas, International.

ANALYSIS.

One pint contains (47° Fahr. S. P. Duffield, M. D.):

SOLIDS.	Grains.
Chloride of sodium	3.405
Chloride of magnesium	0.228
Chloride of calcium	0.647
Sulphate of potassa	8.559
Sulphate of soda	2.298
Sulphate of lime	0.464
Phosphate of alumina	0.180
Silica	0.308
Organic matter	0.257
Loss	0.334
Total	16.680

Properties.—This is a purgative water, its action being chiefly due to the sulphate of potassa, a laxative salt, not used in modern medicine, but known and much used in the middle ages as Polychrestus salt, or Paracelsus's Specific. The waters are valuable of the class, but observation is necessary to determine their special indications.

Remarks.—The well is located in the town of Midland, the county-seat of Midland County, on the Tittibawassee River. The flow is about two gallons per minute. Good facilities for bathing have been provided.

ELGIN SPRING.

Location.—Addison County, Vermont.

Post-Office.—Vergennes, Addison County, Vermont.

Access.—Go to Vergennes, a station on the Vermont Central Railroad, twenty-one miles south of Burlington, and ninety-nine miles north of Bellows Falls; thence, three miles south by stage.

Hotel.— ———.

A qualitative analysis by C. L. Allen, M. D., given in the "Geology of Vermont," is as follows: In one pint there are about thirty grains of solids, of which the principal element is sulphate of magnesia. There are also carbonate of soda, carbonate of lime, sulphate of soda, sulphate of iron, and carbonic-acid gas, five cubic inches to the pint. The water is a good cathartic.

CHAPTER XV.

CALCIC WATERS.

THESE waters contain the salts of lime as principal constituents, usually in the form either of the sulphate (gypsum) or the carbonate (limestone). In addition, the alkaline carbonates and carbonic-acid gas are sometimes found in considerable proportion. The waters are usually limpid, and possess but little taste, though an exception is met with in the Sweet Springs of Virginia.

Lime exists in the human body in considerable quantity. It is estimated there are two pounds of this substance in the bones of the adult, combined with phosphoric acid, forming a phosphate. It also enters into the composition of the blood, saliva, muscles, nerves, and other organs. It is eliminated by the kidneys as a carbonate or phosphate, and in certain diseases of the nervous system the quantity excreted is much increased.

No exact investigations have been made concerning the physiological action of calcic waters. As a rule, they increase the excretion of urine, and promote perspiration. They usually prove constipating, though, when taken in large quantities, they may cause purgation in some persons. On the skin and mucous membrane they seem to possess an astringent and exsiccating action, which Buchheim thinks is due to a chemical combination of lime with fatty acid. Upon the urinary apparatus they possess a sedative action.

These waters, especially those rich in carbonate of lime and carbonic acid, prove decidedly beneficial in diseases of the urinary apparatus, such as *catarrh of the bladder*, *gravel*, and *calculus*, and are even preferable to alkaline-waters. That waters containing a large proportion of the salts of lime should be useful in calculus, may seem paradoxical; nevertheless, such is the fact.[1] It is probably due to their diuretic action, and the influence of the lime on the inflamed mucous membrane of the bladder and urinary passages. They are not solvents of the stone. These waters are also useful in *gastralgic dyspepsia.* The waters included under this class, containing considerable alkaline carbonates, prove valuable in cases of *diabetes mellitus.*

BUTTERWORTH SPRINGS.

Location and Post-Office.—Grand Rapids, Kent County, Michigan.

Access.—Grand Rapids is a station on the Detroit & Milwaukee Railroad, one hundred and fifty-eight miles northwest from Detroit.

Hotels.—Rathbun, Eagle, Sweet's.

ANALYSIS.

One pint contains (54 Fahr.° S. P. Duffield):

SOLIDS.	Grains.
Carbonate of soda	0.434
Carbonate of magnesia	0.432
Carbonate of iron	0.088
Carbonate of lime	0.724
Chloride of potassium	1.227
Chloride of sodium	1.591
Chloride of magnesium	5.232
Chloride of calcium	0.763
Sulphate of lime	9.392
Silica	0.064
Alumina	0.051
Organic matter and loss	0.083
Total	20.081

Properties.—This calcic water much resembles, in chemical constitution, the waters of Bath, England, with the exception of the exceedingly large proportion of chloride of magnesium which it contains.

Remarks.—The city of Grand Rapids is at the head of navigation on the Grand River, about forty miles from its mouth. At this point the river is three hundred yards wide,

[1] *See* Carbonate of Lime.

and falls eighteen feet in a mile. The population is over sixteen thousand.

The spring is located on Huron Street, near the centre of the city. Adjoining is a commodious bath-house, with suites of rooms on separate floors for ladies and gentlemen.

EATON-RAPIDS WELLS.

Location and Post-Office.—Eaton Rapids, Eaton County, Michigan.

Access.—From the east take Great Western Railroad of Canada to Detroit; thence, Michigan Central Railroad to Jackson; thence, *via* Grand-River Valley Railroad, to Eaton Rapids, twenty-four miles northwest of Jackson. From east and south go to Toledo; thence, *via* Lake Shore & Michigan Southern Railroad, to Jackson; thence as above. From Chicago and the west take Michigan Central Railroad to Jackson; thence as described.

Hotels.—Vaughan House, Frost House, Eaton-Rapids House, Central Hotel.

ANALYSIS.

One pint contains—	Frost Well. Prof. S. P. Duffield.	Shaw Well. Prof. R. C. Kedzie.	Mosher Well. Prof. R. C. Kedzie.	Stirling Well. C. T. Jackson, M.D.	Bordine Well. Prof. R. C. Kedzie.
SOLIDS.	Grains.	Grains.	Grains.	Grains.	Grains.
Carbonate of potassa	....	0.159	0.144	....	0.284
Carbonate of soda	....	1.446	0.672	[1] 0.542	0.472
Carbonate of magnesia	0.949	0.480	0.565	....	0.622
Carbonate of iron	0.248	0.154	0.125	0.292	0.208
Carbonate of lime	4.816	2.592	2.429	....	8.518
Chloride of sodium	0.959	0.112	0.112	[1]	0.187
Sulphate of soda	....	....	....	1.811	....
Sulphate of magnesia	....	....	....	0.978	....
Sulphate of lime	0.488	6.016	5.645	5.748	7.187
Nitrate of ammonia	....	trace.	trace.	....	....
Silicic acid	....	0.175	0.817	....	....
Silica	1.689	....	....	....	0.250
Organic matter and loss	0.094	0.112	0.106	....	....
Total	9.188	11.246	10.115	8.871	12.718
GASES.	Cub. in.	Cub. in.	Cub. in.	Cubic in.	Cubic in.
Carbonic acid	2.82	2	1.92	2	2
Sulphuretted hydrogen	....	trace.	trace.	....	....

Properties.—These waters possess the usual qualities of calcic waters, and, at the same time, from the presence of a

[1] In this analysis, carbonate of soda and chloride of sodium together amount to 0.542 grains.

proportion of alkaline carbonates, partake of the properties of alkaline waters. In the French classification they belong to the *mixed bicarbonates.*[1] The analysis of these wells was made before the insertion of the final tubing, and it is supposed the water analyzed contained a notable proportion of surface-water.

Remarks.—The town of Eaton Rapids is pleasantly situated on Grand River, and, since the discovery of the wells in 1869–'70, has grown rapidly.

Every facility for baths in every form may be found here, several of the wells being directly connected with the hotels.

LESLIE WELL.

Location and Post-Office.—Leslie, Ingham County, Michigan.

Access.—From Detroit, *via* Michigan Central Railroad, seventy-six miles west, to Jackson; thence, fifteen miles north, *via* Jackson, Lansing & Saginaw Railroad, to Leslie.

Hotel.— ———.

ANALYSIS.

One pint contains (Prof. R. C. Kedzie):

SOLIDS.	Grains.
Carbonate of potassa	0.359
Carbonate of soda	0.380
Carbonate of magnesia	0.650
Carbonate of iron	0.171
Carbonate of lime	2.214
Sulphate of lime	0.733
Silica	0.216
Organic matter	0.067
Total	4.790
GAS.	Cubic in.
Carbonic acid	1.68

Properties.—This is a calcic water, containing almost sufficient iron to entitle it to be classed with the chalybeates, and, consequently, is especially applicable to those cases in which a calcic water is needed, and in which anæmia is an indication for the administration of iron.

[1] *See* Magnetism.

Remarks.—Leslie is an enterprising town of about one thousand inhabitants. The proprietors of the well have provided a bath-house adjoining.

HUBBARDSTON WELL.

Location and Post-Office.—Hubbardston, Ionia County, Michigan.

Access.—From Detroit, *via* Detroit & Milwaukee Railroad, to Pewamo, one hundred and thirteen miles northwest; thence, six miles and a half by stage.

Hotel.— ———.

ANALYSIS

One pint contains (Prof. P. H. Douglass):

Solids.	Grains.
Carbonate of magnesia	0.794
Carbonate of lime	2.067
Protoxide of iron	0.019
Silica	0.017
Total	2.897

Remarks.—The proprietors have erected a bath-house at the well.

YELLOW SPRINGS.

Location and Post-Office.—Yellow Springs, Greene County, Ohio.

Access.—Yellow Springs is a station on the Little Miami Railroad, seventy-four miles north of Cincinnati.

Hotel.—Neff House Park.

ANALYSIS.

One pint contains (52° Fahr. Wayne and Locke):

Solids.	Grains.
Carbonate of lime	2.446
Chloride of sodium	0.019
Chloride of magnesium	0.021
Chloride of calcium	0.193
Sulphate of lime	0.169
Oxide of iron	0.049
Organic matter	None.
Total	2.897

Properties.—This water is diuretic, and sometimes laxative. The union of a proportion of iron with the other ingredients imparts tonic qualities. The water is a good one, and popular in the section of country where it is located.

Remarks.—Yellow Springs are beautifully situated on the banks of the Little Miami River, which here clears a passage between precipitous banks, fifty feet high, known as the Cliffs. The surrounding country is undulating, and attractive drives lead in every direction; those to Cedars, Springfield, Xenia, and Clifton (which gives a charming view of the Falls of the Miami), are particularly delightful.

GETTYSBURG SPRINGS.

Location.—Gettysburg, Adams County, Pennsylvania.

Access.—From Baltimore, *via* Northern Central Railroad, forty-seven miles north, to Hanover Junction; thence, thirty miles west, to Gettysburg; thence, by street-railroad or omnibus, to the springs.

Hotel.— ———.

ANALYSIS.

One pint contains (Prof. F. A. Genth):

SOLIDS.	Grains.
Carbonate of soda	0.027
Carbonate of magnesia	0.041
Carbonate of iron	0.003
Carbonate of manganese	0.001
Carbonate of lime	0.627
Chloride of sodium	0.082
Chloride of lithium	trace.
Sulphate of potassa	0.026
Sulphate of soda	0.308
Sulphate of magnesia	0.847
Sulphate of lime	0.104
Phosphate of lime	0.001
Fluoride of calcium	0.001
Borate of magnesia	0.004
Silicic acid	0.254
Organic matter, with trace of nitric acid, etc.	0.088
Impurities suspended in the water, like clay, etc.	0.138
Total	2.552

In addition, minute quantities of carbonate of copper, sulphate of strontia, alumina, and traces of carbonate of nickel, carbonate of cobalt, and sulphate of baryta. (1873.)

Properties.—This water is clear, inodorous, and tasteless. As will be seen by the analysis, it partakes both of an *alkaline* and *calcic* character, though the salts of lime predominate. The combination is an exceedingly valuable one, and produces good results. The water has proved beneficial in *gravel*, *calculus*, *catarrh of the bladder*, *catarrh of the stomach*, and *dyspepsia.* It is said to be efficient in gout and rheumatism, and that *chalk-stone concretions* of the joints have been removed by its use. The dose of the water in the majority of cases is a gill three times a day, though in some instances it is recommended to commence with a very much larger quantity, and gradually diminish the dose. The water has been named *Katalysine water* by the proprietors of the spring.

Remarks.—These springs break forth in a picturesque valley, a few miles west of the town of Gettysburg. Within view are the Catoctin and South Mountains. The immediate vicinity of the springs was the scene of the commencement of the battle of Gettysburg. The value of the water was long known to the neighboring inhabitants, but it has only been brought to public notice within a few years. The bottled water is largely sold throughout the country.

CLARENDON SPRINGS.

Location and Post-Office.—Clarendon Springs, Rutland County, Vermont.

Access.—Go to West Rutland, a station on the Rensselaer & Saratoga Railroad, four miles from Rutland ; thence, four miles by stage, to the springs.

Hotel.—Clarendon House.

ANALYSIS.

One pint contains (50° Fahr. A. A. Hayes, M. D.):

SOLIDS.	Grains.
Carbonate of lime	0.38
Muriate of lime, Sulphate of soda, Sulphate of magnesia	0.34
Total	0.72
GASES.	**Cubic in.**
Carbonic acid	5.77
Nitrogen	1.20

Properties.—This is a water, the reputed efficacy of which is not accounted for by the solid ingredients shown by the analysis. The water is remarkable as containing a considerable proportion of free nitrogen gas, an unusual constituent. It also contains a large proportion of carbonic-acid gas, rendering it acceptable to the stomach. It is used as a remedy in *gravel*, *dyspepsia*, and *engorgement of the liver.*

Remarks.—These springs have been a favorite resort since the early settlement of the country, and are among the first ever visited.

An extract from the "Geology of Vermont" runs thus: "Tradition informs us that their medicinal virtues were first discovered in 1776 by one Asa Smith, who resided in the eastern part of the township. He is reported to have 'dreamed' of a spring in the western part of the town, and full of faith started through the wilderness, and over the high hills that separate the two portions of the town, in search of the spring that would furnish water that should restore him to health. Arriving at the spot, he recognized it as the one he had seen in his dream, and accordingly at once drank the water, and bound clay saturated with it on his swollen and inflamed limbs." The man is said to have been healed of his malady, and thenceforth the water has enjoyed considerable reputation.

The springs are delightfully situated amid the green hills of Vermont, at an elevation of eight hundred feet above the level of the sea.

SWEET SPRINGS.

Location and Post-Office.—Sweet Springs, Monroe County, West Virginia.

Access.—From Washington, *via* Orange, Alexandria & Manassas Railroad, and Chesapeake & Ohio Railroad, to Alleghany Station, two hundred and forty-one miles west; thence, ten miles by stage to the springs. From Richmond, *via* Chesapeake & Ohio Railroad, to Alleghany Station, two hundred and twenty-one miles west. From the west, *via* Cincinnati and Ohio River, to Huntington, one hundred and sixty-five miles east; thence, *via* Chesapeake & Ohio Railroad, one hundred and ninety-eight miles southeast, to Alleghany Station.

Hotel.—Sweet Springs.

ANALYSIS.

One pint contains (74° Fahr. Prof. W. B. Rogers):

SOLIDS.	Grains.
Carbonate of magnesia	0.103
Carbonate of lime	3.757
Chloride of sodium	0.017
Chloride of magnesium	0.039
Chloride of calcium	0.018
Sulphate of soda	0.793
Sulphate of magnesia	1.174
Sulphate of lime	1.646
Peroxide of iron	0.018
Iodine	trace.
Earthy phosphates	trace.
Silica	0.021
Total	7.586
GAS.	Cubic in.
Carbonic acid	11.00

Properties.—These are valuable calcic waters, containing a small proportion of purging sulphate, and a large amount of carbonic-acid gas. They are promptly *diuretic* and *diaphoretic* as a rule, and seldom purgative, the laxative action of the sulphate of magnesia being controlled by the salts of lime. The water much resembles that of Pougues, department of Nièvre, France.

The taste of this water is sweet, and the reaction alkaline. In August, 1871, I took the temperature of the drinking-fountain, and found it 74° Fahr. The temperature of the baths nearly corresponds. This water, therefore, is, strictly speaking, a thermal water. The flow of the water is about twelve hundred gallons per minute—quite a mill-race.

These waters are a valuable therapeutic agent. In *dyspepsia*, depending on atonic conditions, they will undoubtedly afford relief, especially in those cases attended with gastralgia. In *sterility* unaccompanied by obstruction, the water has frequently proved efficacious, no doubt by the stimulant effect exercised on the generative organs by the carbonic acid in the bath. But especially is the water valuable in *gravel.* Dr. Woodville, for many years resident at the springs, informed me that he had never known a case that was not benefited. Its efficacy in gravel appears reasonable, from the fact that the water of Pougues, which it resembles, has long had a well-merited reputation in this malady. It may be stated that the Pougues water is applicable by preference to phosphatic gravel accompanying catarrhal conditions of the urinary apparatus, and this water proves of especial service when catarrhal trouble predominates.

The waters are largely used in the form of a bath. The bath-building is a large brick structure, separated into two compartments. The baths are each about sixty by thirty feet, and continually replenished by the spring-water, which, fresh from the depths of the earth, breaks forth all over the sandy bottom. As before stated, the temperature of this bath is about 74° Fahr., but on first immersion it feels cooler. The first bath should not exceed three minutes. After becoming accustomed to the shock, one may remain from five to eight minutes, though long immersion is not desirable.

Remarks.—The springs are situated in one of the most charming valleys. Dr. Burke, in his work on "Virginia Springs," says: "This vale, about five miles in length, and of an average of about half a mile in width, bounded on the north by the Alleghany, and on the south by the Sweet Springs Mountain, may, without disparagement of other beautiful valleys, be denominated the *Tempe* of Virginia."

The hotel is large and commodious, and with the long line of villa-like brick cottages, sweeping around a semicircle of one-fourth of a mile, and terminated by the tasteful bath-building facing the hotel, forms a pleasing picture. The neighboring forests abound in delightful walks, and for the sportsman deer and trout are easily accessible. The society is of those who admire elegance more than display.

The Red Sweet Springs (chalybeate) are but one mile distant.

BERKELEY SPRINGS.

Location and Post-Office Address.—Bath, Morgan County, West Virginia.

Access.—Take cars at any point on the Baltimore & Ohio Railroad, and go to Sir John's Run, a station one hundred and thirty miles west of Baltimore, on the Baltimore & Ohio Railroad; thence, two and a half miles by stage, to the springs.

Hotel.—Berkeley Springs.

ANALYSIS.

One pint contains (74° Fahr. A. A. Hayes, M. D.):

SOLIDS.	Grains.
Carbonate of lime	0.625
Chloride of sodium	0.112
Chloride of calcium	0.026
Sulphate of magnesia	0.045
Crenate of lime	0.455
Crenate of iron	0.010
Silicate of iron	0.080
Loss	0.008
Total	1.361

Flow, twelve hundred gallons per minute.

Properties.—Strictly speaking, these are thermal waters, used chiefly in the form of baths. Employed in this way they have proved of decided value in neuralgia, and in cases of debility they are a most admirable restorative, when the system reacts well.

For the purpose of bathing every facility is presented. The flow of water is exceedingly abundant, the stream therefrom supplying several mills in its way down the valley. This large supply has been utilized so as to furnish baths of every description. There is a gentlemen's and a ladies' bath-house, with numerous private baths; a gentlemen's swimming-bath, sixty by twenty feet, and five feet deep, containing over fifty thousand gallons of water; a ladies' swimming-bath, thirty by sixteen feet, and four and a half feet deep. Also, a separate establishment for warm, spout, and shower baths.

Remarks.—These springs, four in number, issue from the base of the Warm Springs Ridge. The mountain-side is clothed with a dense forest, which is permeated in every direction by enticing walks. The springs are respectively named the "Gentlemen's Spring," covered by a pavilion, supported by ten columns, and having a spacious lounging-room above for gentlemen; "Lord Fairfax's Spring," and the "Ladies' Spring," also surmounted by a pavilion and open above, for occupation by visitors or the band. The fourth spring is a small one.

These springs possess an historic interest. The original title was vested in Thomas, Lord Fairfax, who made a grant of a few acres of land, with the springs, to the State, reserving to his own use one spring, still known as "Lord Fairfax's Spring." In colonial times the gentry assembled here, and, in a rude way, enjoyed the pleasures of the wildwood and the luxury of the baths. Log-huts and tents formed the only shelter. The day was passed in horse-racing, hunting, fishing, rambles through the forests, and, at certain hours, in bathing. The pool was a hollow formed in the sand, and screened by a thatching of interwoven boughs of the pines. At a certain predetermined signal from a tin horn, the gentlemen retired while the ladies bathed; and by a similar device the gentlemen occupied the bath. "Peeping Toms" were dealt with unmercifully. At night, fiddling and dancing were indulged in by the young, under the cheerful illumination of pine-knots and tallow-dips; while the elders, under the exhilaration of pure "rye," recounted stories of the chase, arranged races for the coming day, and exchanged money at the magic call of the cards.

In 1777, by virtue of an act of the Assembly of the Commonwealth of Virginia, a town by the name of Bath was laid out, General George Washington being one of the purchasers. This property is named in his will in the following terms: "Two well-situated and handsome buildings, to the amount of £150;" and in a note thereto we find the following: "The lots in Bath (two adjoining) cost me, to the best of my recollection, between fifty and sixty pounds, twenty years ago. Whether property there has increased or decreased in value, and in what condition the houses are, I am ignorant, but suppose they are not valued too high."

ALLEGHANY SPRINGS.

Location and Post-Office.—Alleghany Springs, Montgomery County, Virginia.

Access.—From Washington, *via* Orange, Alexandria & Manassas Railroad, and Virginia & Tennessee Railroad, to Alleghany Station, two hundred and fifty-four miles southwest; thence, three and a half miles by stage to the springs. From the south and west, *via* Chattanooga, Knoxville & Virginia, and Tennessee Railroads, to Alleghany Station.

Hotel.—Alleghany Springs.

ANALYSIS.

One pint contains (53° Fahr. F. A. Genth, M. D.):

SOLIDS.	Grains.
Carbonate of magnesia	0.037
Carbonate of iron	0.016
Carbonate of manganese	0.006
Carbonate of lime	0.376
Carbonate of lithia	trace.
Carbonate of strontia	0.006
Carbonate of baryta	0.002
Chloride of sodium	0.028
Sulphate of potassa	0.385
Sulphate of soda	0.178
Sulphate of magnesia	5.299
Sulphate of lime	12.007
Phosphate of alumina	0.002
Nitrate of magnesia	0.335
Nitrate of ammonia	0.058
Fluoride of calcium	0.002
Silicate of alumina	0.021
Silicic acid	0.091
Organic matter	0.208
Total	19.057
GASES.	Cubic in.
Carbonic acid	1.20
Sulphuretted hydrogen	trace.

Dr. Genth also finds minute quantities of carbonate of copper, lead, zinc, and cobalt; also teroxide of antimony and crenic acid and epocrenic acid. These constituents were not derived directly from the spring-water, but were detected in the deposit which forms in the spring reservoir. The flow of the water is about one-fourth gallon per minute. The taste is pleasant, without odor or flavor of sulphuretted hydrogen.

Properties.—It will be seen from the analysis that the chief constituents of this water are the sulphates of lime and magnesia, a combination seldom met with. It is allied, by the large proportion of sulphate of magnesia, to purgative waters. As might be expected from this combination, the action of the water is both *purgative* and *diuretic*, when taken in considerable quantity. In moderate quantity, however, this action is not marked, the cathartic action of the sulphate of magnesia being controlled by the constipating tendency of the sulphate of lime. The play of the other constituents, of which Dr. Genth has found so great a number, cannot be estimated.

This water is very highly esteemed in the treatment of the various types of *dyspepsia*, and it is in this disease that it numbers the most important cures. It has also proved valuable in *engorgement of the liver*, *gall-stones*, and habitual constipation.

Remarks.—The Alleghany Springs are situated on the Roanoke River, at the eastern foot of the Alleghany Mountains. The hotel and principal cottages occupy smooth and undulating hills, while, on either hand, the lofty spurs of the Alleghanies present attractive mountain-scenery. In every direction the visitor finds opportunity for the enjoyment of mountain-climbing and mountain-air. Five miles from the springs is *Fisher's View*, where an extended panorama of mountain-summits is presented to the eye. Eight miles from the springs are *Puncheon Run Falls*, also a point of considerable interest.

BETHESDA SPRINGS.[1]

Location and Post-Office.—Waukesha, Waukesha County, Wisconsin.

Access.—Waukesha is a station on the Prairie du Chien division of the Milwaukee & St. Paul Railroad, twenty-one miles west of Milwaukee.

Hotels.—Exchange, American, Fox River House, National.

Properties.—It will be seen from the analysis that these waters contain 1.027 grain of carbonate of soda and magnesia, and 1.478 grain of carbonate of lime, to the pint. They are, therefore, closely allied to the alkaline waters, though the calcareous salt is slightly in excess. The waters, as is usual

[1] *See* Analysis, page 282.

with this class, are decidedly *diuretic*, and have proved exceedingly efficient in *diabetes mellitus*, *gravel*, calculus, and chronic inflammation and *catarrh of the bladder*. They are also palliative in *albuminuria* or Bright's disease, and by the increased flow of urine relieve dropsy.

The usual quantity taken is eight to ten glasses a day for the first three or four days, and then reduce the quantity according to the effect on the urine. In diabetes mellitus, the usual restrictions as to saccharine and amylaceous diet are to be observed.

ANALYSIS.

One pint contains (60° Fahr. C. F. Chandler):

SOLIDS.	Grains.
Carbonate of soda	0.109
Carbonate of magnesia	0.918
Carbonate of iron	0.004
Carbonate of lime	1.478
Chloride of sodium	0.145
Sulphate of potassa	0.057
Sulphate of soda	0.068
Phosphate of soda	trace.
Alumina	0.015
Silica	0.092
Organic matter	0.248
Total	3.134

Remarks.—Waukesha, an Indian name, signifying "Little Fox," is a pleasantly-shaded village on the banks of the Little Fox River. The population numbers about three thousand five hundred. The climate is cool and refreshing during the summer months. At a distance of six to ten miles from the village, at Pewaukee, Nashota, Delafield, Merton, and Oconomowoc, are several lakes much resorted to for delightful drives and fine sport.

HOLSTON SPRINGS.

Location and Post-Office.—Holston Springs, Scott County, Virginia.

Access.—From Washington *via* Orange, Alexandria & Manassas Railroad, and Virginia & Tennessee Railroad, to Abingdon, three hundred and sixty-eight miles southwest; thence forty miles northwest, by stage, to the springs.

Hotel.—Holston Springs.

ANALYSIS.

One pint contains (68½° Fahr. Prof. Hayden):

Solids.	Grains.
Carbonate of lime	.80
Chloride of sodium and muriate of ammonia	.19
Sulphate of soda	trace.
Sulphate of magnesia	1.59
Sulphate of lime	2.56
Sulphate of alumina	trace.
Phosphate of alumina	trace.
Total	5.14

CHAPTER XVI.

THERMAL WATERS.

All waters possessing an unvarying temperature of 85° Fahr., or above, are included under this designation. I use the term thermal in the sense of *heat as indicated by the sensations of the body;* although, geologically speaking, "all springs are considered warm, or thermal, the temperature of which exceeds, however little, the mean annual temperature of the place at which they rise." Accordingly, a spring of a certain degree would be called warm in Iceland and cold at the equator. Waters of 85° Fahr. will convey a sensation of warmth to the hand of most persons on first immersion, though if the entire body were placed in the water a feeling of chilliness might be experienced. Waters of from 70° to 85° Fahr. may be termed temperate, from 85° to 92° Fahr. they are tepid, from 92° to 98° they are warm, and from 98° Fahr. upward they are hot—all, except the first, included under the term thermal. In one or two instances springs below 85° Fahr. have been introduced in this class, being above the temperature of cold springs, 70° Fahr., and not possessing decided chemical constituents.

Thermal waters are chiefly used for bathing, and in this their efficacy mainly consists in the majority of instances. These waters sometimes contain considerable carbonic-acid gas, sulphuretted hydrogen, or even chloride of sodium, or the alkaline carbonates; but, as a rule, they yield but a very small proportion of mineral ingredients. The manner of using the different kinds of tepid, warm, and hot waters, is discussed in the chapter on baths, under the respective titles.

It has been questioned whether there is a difference between the heat of mineral waters and artificial heat. Formerly, many held the affirmative, and there are not wanting those who still hold this view. But there are no observations that show any actual difference, and those who have investigated the matter in late years have decided in the negative.[1] This being so, why are hot or warm mineral waters more active medicinal agents than artificially-heated water? In some instances the waters are highly charged with gases, or contain considerable mineral ingredients, but, aside from this, the uniform and continuous temperature of the water distinguishes it from ordinary hot water. The latter is often not uniformly heated throughout, and from the time it is passed into the tub is decreasing in temperature, or, if heated by steam in the tub, is alternating each moment from one degree of heat to another, while in large pools at the hot springs the water remains of the same temperature continually. It may be added that it is impossible to arrange hot spout and douche baths at home equal to those of the springs. Another advantage is that of specialty. The attendants, the physician, and every one connected with the springs' baths, acquire dexterity and precision in their application, which is of great advantage to the invalid. However we may explain their action, *the fact remains of their efficacy.*

These waters are exceedingly beneficial in the treatment of *chronic rheumatism* and *gout*, especially when associated with *stiffening of the joints* and *concretions.* In certain irritable conditions of the nervous system they produce a calming effect, and in *neuralgia* depending on injuries or inflammation of the nervous sheaths, they are often curative. In *paraplegia, not organic*, and in which the muscles are excitable by electricity, the use of these waters often wonderfully hastens a cure; and the same observation may be made of

[1] In a letter to the author, Prof. John Tyndall, of the Royal Institution of Great Britain, than whom there is no higher living authority on heat, writes as follows: "I am not acquainted with any difference between natural heat and artificial heat. I am not acquainted with any thermo-electric conditions that could cause any perceptible difference between the therapeutic action of natural hot water and artificial hot-water"

other forms of *paralysis*, excepting hemiplegia, for which saline waters are preferable. In many of the scaly *diseases of the skin*, such as *psoriasis*, *lichen*, etc., they are a most efficient auxiliary in the treatment. They also form a desirable adjuvant in the treatment of *syphilis* by the metamorphosis of tissue which they produce, aiding and rendering more certain the action of other remedies.

In treatment of affections of the joints the water must be quite warm, and local frictions should be used. Care should be taken that persons affected with organic diseases of the heart are not treated by hot baths.

HOT SPRINGS.

Location and Post-Office.—Hot Springs, Hot Springs County, Arkansas.

Access.—Go to Little Rock, one hundred and thirty-five miles west from Memphis, by Memphis & Little Rock Railroad, or by steamboat on the Mississippi and Arkansas Rivers during navigable seasons; thence, fifty miles west, by stage or private conveyance, to the springs. Also by steamboat on the Ouachita River to Arkadelphia; thence thirty-five miles' staging.

Hotels.—Hot Springs, Aikin, Earle, Hale, Rector, Warren.

ANALYSIS.

One pint contains (93°–150° Fahr.):

SOLIDS.	Grains.
Carbonate of magnesia	0.016
Carbonate of lime	0.496
Chloride of sodium	0.001
Sulphate of potassa	0.029
Sulphate of soda	0.047
Sulphate of lime	0.014
Sesquioxide of iron	0.013
Iodine	trace.
Bromine	trace.
Silicate of lime	0.058
Silica	0.233
Alumina	0.056
Organic matter	0.088
Water	0.018
Total	1.069

The above analysis is the result of calculating the following percentages as given by Prof. E. Hills Larkin, who analyzed the waters in 1859; and combination of the elements according to approved formulæ:

Mineral constituents, 8½ grains per gallon.

	Percentage.
Silicic acid	24.74
Sesquioxide of iron	1.21
Alumina	5.15
Lime	28.83
Magnesia	.73
Chlorine	.07
Carbonic acid	21.36
Organic matter	8.31
Water	1.72
Sulphuric acid	4.49
Potassa	1.46
Soda	2.01
Iodine and bromine	trace.
Total	100.08

These waters resemble the waters of Gastein, in Austria, and Pfäffers, in Switzerland.

Properties.—They are very highly esteemed, and deservedly so, in the treatment of *chronic rheumatism*, *gout*, *contractions of joints*, *secondary* and *tertiary syphilis*, and *neuralgia*. In *paralysis*, unaccompanied by organic lesions, they are of considerable utility. As auxiliaries, in dartrous diseases of the skin, functional diseases of the uterus, and chronic poisoning by metals—either lead or mercury—they are efficient. Experience proves them to be *positively injurious* in affections of the heart or brain, dropsies, and diseases of the lungs in any form; and persons laboring under diseases for which these waters are beneficial, but accompanied by such maladies, need not journey to the Hot Springs.

How do these waters act? Principally, if not altogether, by elevated temperature. Having a continuous flow of three hundred and sixty gallons per minute, and ranging in temperature from 93° to 150° Fahr., we would expect favorable results from their judicious use, and we are not surprised to learn of cures under their employment that have resisted all other modes of treatment. It is asked, "Why not use hot water at home?" Because it is *impossible* to procure it in sufficient quantity and of uniform temperature. Some consider that terrestrial heat possesses peculiar properties, rendering it more efficient than artificial heat. Dr. G. W. Lawrence, who has had ample opportunity for observation, holds that "a positive difference exists in the natural thermal waters of Arkansas and artificially-heated waters," which he attributes, among other causes, "to the thermo-electric properties of the thermal waters." He says, "The natural produces a *stimulating sweat;* the artificial waters a *relaxing diaphoretic action.*" These differences, however, if such exist, are not at present tangible.

In these waters, as in many thermal waters, there is a confervoid growth, or "moss," which is frequently used by patients as an external application to painful parts or ulcerated surfaces. It acts much like a poultice.

Remarks.—It was these waters that De Soto's companions passed in search of El Dorado, and thought the "fountain of youth." They are situated in a valley, on the western slope of the Hot Springs Mountain—one of the Ozark Mountains—at an elevation of thirteen hundred and sixty feet above the level of the sea. The climate is pleasant, the temperature seldom ranging as high as 98° Fahr. during the hottest days of summer, and the nights being always cool, so that blankets are desirable. The winters are usually mild and of short duration; and the "springs season" begins in April and continues till December.

The springs are fifty-seven in number, flowing, as I have said, three hundred and sixty gallons per minute. This large volume of water is utilized for all modes of bathing, by conduits, which convey it to the various establishments. The *Hot Springs Bath* consists of three compartments: First, a dressing-room, where, having disrobed, you enter the bath-room, the water in the tub having been previously prepared of the proper temperature; here you remain for a specified length of time, bathing in the water and using the hot spout-jet of water on any portion of the body, as may be required. From the bath you enter into the adjoining vapor-room, the floor of which is formed by narrow strips of wood, with spaces an inch and a half between. From these interstices a volume of vapor escapes from the hot water flowing beneath, filling the room, and giving it a temperature of about 110° Fahr. Here you remain from one to three minutes, drinking freely from the can of hot water previously placed in the room. After the vapor-bath you wipe the surface quickly, till dry, put on your *flannels*, dress rapidly, protect the person well with *warm over-garments*, *hasten* to bed, where you remain, *in your flannels* and *well blanketed*, usually twenty minutes, drinking the hot water at intervals. When the circulation has become tranquil and perspiration has ceased, the person may rise, but not to go out-of-doors immediately if the weather is at all chilly.

Within eight miles of the Hot Springs are good *sulphur-waters*, not, however, improved.

CALISTOGA HOT SPRINGS.

Location and Post-Office.—Calistoga Springs, Napa County, California.

Access.—From San Francisco, cross the bay by regular boat to Vallejo, connecting with Napa Valley Railroad direct for Calistoga, three and a half hours from San Francisco. From Sacramento, go by rail direct to Vallejo; thence, as above.

Hotels.—Calistoga Springs Hotel, Mountain House.

Analysis.—The principal ingredients are said to be sulphur, iron, and magnesia, sulphur largely predominating. Temperature, 100° to 195° Fahr. The waters have not been quantitatively analyzed.

Properties.—These springs, belonging to the sulphur class, and possessing, besides, the properties of thermal waters, are of decided efficacy in many diseases, such as *gout*, *paralysis*, *rheumatism*, *dartrous diseases of the skin*, *chronic lead-poisoning*, and, as an auxiliary, in tertiary syphilis.

Remarks.—The springs number about sixty, varying in temperature from lukewarm to boiling-hot, and distributed over an area of a hundred acres. The waters are used almost exclusively for bathing. For this purpose a commodious swimming-bath has been constructed, in which many persons may enjoy the pleasures of a plunge-bath at the same time. It is arranged with the usual conveniences of side-cabinets for disrobing and dressing. There are also well-arranged private baths. A hot-sulphur steam-bath is also arranged, so that the effects of the water in the form of hot vapor may be procured. Here also are found the *moor* or *mineral-mud baths*, similar to those of Franzensbad and Marienbad, in Bohemia.

Calistoga is one of the outgrowths of our rapid American civilization. A few years ago the area which it occupies was a waste; but, under the energetic management of the proprietor, Samuel Brannan, Esq., smooth lawns and inviting walks have succeeded the waste places, and embowered cottages allure the invalid. The name was formed by uniting the first two syllables of California with the last two of Saratoga though there is not the least analogy between the two as regards the properties of the water. Within the lands of the springs is a large vineyard of many acres, yielding tons of grapes of the choicest varieties. Here Californians are accustomed to try the efficacy of the "grape-cure," as practised at Vevay, in Switzerland.

About five miles southwest of Calistoga is the *Petrified Forest*, an object of exceeding interest to the geologist or tourist. There are found the prostrate remains of a vast forest of gigantic trees, similar to the towering conifers of the Pacific coast, all converted into solid stone. It is supposed to be the result of volcanic agency, the surface having been deluged with hot silicious-alkaline waters.

Calistoga is the point whence the stage is taken for the Geysers; also for Skagg's Springs, Harbine Springs, Seigler Springs, and the White Sulphur Springs.

THE GEYSERS.

Location.—Sonoma County, California.

Access.—From San Francisco, across the bay, by boat, to Vallejo; thence, by Napa Valley Railroad, three and a half hours, to Calistoga Springs; thence twenty-eight miles by stage.

Hotel.—Geyser Hotel.

Analysis.— ———.

Remarks.—"The Geyser Cañon [1] is half a mile long, the bottom from one to two rods in width, and the banks shoot up fourteen hundred feet at an angle of forty-five degrees. Their surface in most places is whitish, covered with the residuum of extinct geysers, . . . which has been bleached by the suns and rains of scores of summers and winters. Here and there, at wide intervals, are small jets of steam from springs which are yet bubbling and hissing. Large spots are completely honey-combed with these faintly-working relics of a once thickly-boiling section. As we walk over them, the ground occasionally gives way beneath our tread, and we sink shoe-deep into the chemical deposits.

"The first spring we meet going up the ravine is the 'Alum and Iron Spring,' which has a temperature of ninety-seven degrees. Incrustations of iron form around it in a single night. A few feet farther on is the 'Medicated Geyser Bath,' having a temperature a few degrees less. . . . Next is the 'Boiling Alum and Sulphur Spring,' with a temperature of over a hundred and fifty degrees.

"Close by is the 'Black Sulphur,' which has about the same degree of heat. Beyond these are the 'Epsom Salts Spring' and the 'Boiling Black Sulphur,' which boil, bubble, and roar constantly. The largest of all is the 'Witches' Caldron,' whose diameter exceeds seven feet, and is tossing continually with ebullition. When we saw it the water was thrown up four or five inches, but we are assured that sometimes it is thrown up two feet. The temperature is one hundred and ninety-five degrees. It is large enough to boil an ox, and the bottom is of an unknown depth. Large volumes of steam rise from it, as visible as the puffings from the smoke-stack of a locomotive. Twelve feet away is the 'Intermittent Scalding Spring,' which sends forth jets of water of a temperature of one hundred and seventy-five degrees. They sometimes rise to a height of fifteen feet, but the pressure varies at different times. It is the same with nearly all the springs,

[1] J. F. Manning, in *Lippincott's Magazine*, December, 1870.

and what is seen by one may be very different from what is seen by another. At no time, however, do the jets cease entirely. As the degree of pressure and the height to which the water is thrown vary, so does the sound. There are periods when it is heard at a considerable distance, and again the ear must be near by to distinguish it.

"The most wonderful and interesting of all the springs is the 'Steamboat Geyser,' the play of which resembles exactly the 'blowing off steam' in a high-pressure steamboat. A little beyond this singular spring the cañon divides or forks, smaller ones branching off to the right and left. Just at the fork a bold, lofty bluff rises up, which is surmounted by a tapering rock named 'The Pulpit.' . . . From the Pulpit a full, fine view is obtained of the entire cañon and the immediate surroundings. Besides the springs we have named, which are the largest and most valuable for medicinal purposes, there are numerous smaller ones, numbering, all counted, about a hundred. Among them is the 'Devil's Inkstand,' a small spring, whose product is as black as ink, and serves very well as a substitute for that article.

"Passing up the bank which forms the upper right-hand end of the cañon, and taking position on a knoll, we get the best view of the larger springs and their operation. About two hundred feet below us is the Witches' Caldron, black as ink, tossing and steaming: farther down are the minor ones, sending up into the scorching sunlight their gossamer vapors. We hear distinctly the Steamboat Geyser. It seems as if we were on the brink of Tartarus itself, while all around, on the sides and summits, excepting in the spots covered with the chemicals from extinct geysers, are wild-oats growing abundantly, beautiful flowers, and wide-spreading oaks, under whose deep-green shade grows luxuriantly a peculiar mountain-grass. All this vegetation borders closely on the most barren of all wastes.

"From this resting-place we pass over the 'Mountain of Fire,' a section filled with scores of orifices. . . . Then comes the 'Alkali Lake,' followed by other springs of boiling water impregnated with numberless chemicals. One is a white-sulphur spring, the water of which is of an amber purity. Another is the 'Boiling Eye-water Spring.' One of the guides, a very intelligent German, has put up ten different specimens of the most interesting and valuable chemicals, and spring-waters in small phials, for the convenience of visitors, that they may have in compact and portable form apt tokens of remembrance of one of earth's marvels. Near the hotel, in Pluton Cañon, is the 'Acid Spring.' . . . Sweetened with sugar, it makes a palatable lemonade. About a mile and a half from the inn is the 'Indian Spring,' so called because the Indians for many years carried their sick there to be healed. It is a chalybeate, the water being an inky blackness. . . . Steam or vapor-baths have been constructed by building sheds over the springs, so as to imprison the steam long enough to be used for sanitary and pleasure purposes. The principal one is in the bottom of Pluton Cañon, near the fresh-water brook, so that, after the warm douche and the vapor bath, the bather goes a few steps, and finds a plunge-bath of the most sparkling mountain-water, in an artificial reservoir so arranged that the contents are constantly renewed."

PASO ROBLES HOT SPRINGS.

Location and Post-Office.—Paso Robles Hot Springs, San Luis Obispo County, California.

Access.—From San Francisco by steamer, about one hundred and eighty miles south to San Luis Obispo; thence, twenty-seven miles north by stage, to the springs. Or, by San Francisco & St. José Railroad, to Sargent's Station; thence, one hundred and twenty miles south by stage, to the springs. From Los Angeles north, by steamer, to San Luis Obispo.

Hotel.—Paso Robles.

Properties.—From the following analysis it will very readily be seen that this is an exceedingly valuable thermal water, closely allied in chemical composition to the waters of Aix-la-Chapelle, in Rhenish Prussia. There is the unusual combination of thermality, considerable chloride of sodium, sulphuretted hydrogen, carbonic-acid gas, and an active amount of alkaline carbonates. A water such as this cannot fail to be of benefit in very many cases of *gout*, *chronic rheumatism*, and *dartrous skin-diseases*; also, in *contractions of the joints* and *old gunshot-wounds*. In fine, it is applicable to all those diseases especially benefited by a *thermal saline-sulphur water*. The immediate effect of the water is laxative and diuretic; the remote, alterative.

ANALYSIS.

One pint contains—	Main Spring, 112° Fahr. Prof. Thomas Price.	Mud Spring, 122° Fahr. Prof. Thomas Price.
SOLIDS.	Grains.	Grains.
Carbonate of soda	3.664	0.543
Carbonate of magnesia	0.057	0.323
Chloride of sodium	2.830	10.047
Sulphate of potassa	0.092	trace.
Sulphate of soda	0.818	4.281
Sulphate of lime	0.334	1.864
Protoxide of iron	0.037	....
Iodides and bromides	traces.	....
Alumina	0.023	....
Silica	0.046	0.116
Organic matter	0.171	0.361
Total	8.072	17.535
GASES.	Cubic in.	Cubic in.
Carbonic acid	2.31	10.53
Sulphuretted hydrogen	saturated.	saturated.

Remarks.—The name, Paso de Robles, means White-Oak Pass, so called from the white-oaks grown in the valley. Unfortunately, the immediate surroundings of the springs are not attractive, the valley in which they are situated being flat, and the mountains on either side low and of a monotonous uniformity. "But let the visitor go over a few miles to the southern slopes of the Santa Lucia Mountains, and his eyes shall be sated with color.

"I sat one October morning in a vast amphitheatre, between the Santa Lucia Mountains and the outer buttes, or foot-hills, and gazed upon a mosaic more enchanting than can be witnessed outside of California. The crest of the mountain bore a straggling row of pale-green California pines, while here and there a live-oak stood darkly in the unbroken sheet of gold. Directly before me there was a great sunny mountain, daintily crinkled and dimpled, and thus shadowing the wild grasses, here into a pale claret, there into a cinnamon, or a *cuir*, or a buff, or that exquisitely rich and satisfying tint often seen on California hills when they lie at a certain slope beneath the sun, and resembling nothing so much as a damson purple, all rimy crisp with a soft and sunny flush of violet haze. In another place, the ripened wild-oats had faded in the dewless summer days from their golden splendor to an inexpressibly subdued, tender, creamy tint, like the finest velvet-plush, which seemed to float over the slope as the merest nimbus, now creeping a little in the breeze, and now dying with a kind of lazy, delicious shudder."[1]

The conveniences at these springs are such as accompany the early stage of improvement. There are two swimming-pools—one for gentlemen, one for ladies.

SANTA BARBARA HOT SULPHUR SPRINGS.

Location and Post-Office.—Santa Barbara Springs, Santa Barbara County, California.

Access.—From San Francisco, two hundred and eighty miles south, by steamer, to Santa Barbara; thence, four miles by stage.

Hotel.—Sulphur Springs. (Good accommodations in Santa Barbara.)

Analysis.—No quantitative analysis has been made. They are hot sulphur-waters. Temperature, 60° to 130° Fahr.

Properties.—These waters are valuable in *chronic rheumatism, diseases of the skin, contractions of the joints, paralysis*, and, as an auxiliary, in the treatment of secondary and tertiary syphilis.

Remarks.—In this connection I insert a portion of a letter received March 22, 1872, from Dr. M. H. Biggs, of Santa Barbara:

"The Hot Sulphur Springs of Santa Barbara are situated at the head of a deep cañon, about five miles to the northeast of the town of Santa Barbara, at an elevation of fourteen hundred and fifty feet above the level of the sea. They number in all seven, and seem to be of two distinct varieties. Those nearest the head of the cañon escape from crevices in the rock,

[1] Stephen Powers, Esq.

and are four in number, all appearing to have the same properties, the most sensible of which are free sulphur and sulphuretted hydrogen; their temperature, 114° Fahr. Another spring is situated about one hundred yards off, in a westerly direction from the first mentioned; temperature, 117° Fahr. Its principal constituent is sulphate of alumina, evident from the thick incrustation of this salt on the under surface of the rock beneath which this water escapes; it also tastes strongly of sulphate of iron, and is said to contain soda and potash, and a trace of arsenic. The two remaining springs are located in a branch cañon, about one hundred rods in a northerly direction from the last one mentioned, and appear to possess the same qualities, with the exception of the temperature, which is only 112° Fahr. No thorough analysis of these mineral springs has ever been made, at least in our time.

"It is said that while this country was in possession of the King of Spain, a corps of scientific men was sent out to this coast, commissioned, among other things, to test the properties of the several mineral springs known to abound here; and that in their report they pronounced the Santa Barbara Hot Sulphur Springs to be the best and most medicinal, and superior to any other in California 'for the cure of many diseases.' Whether they came to this conclusion from actual analysis, or from simply witnessing their effect, is not known. Certain it is that at the present day they are becoming famous for their curative effects in many cases of rheumatism, paralysis, various diseases of syphilitic origin, and skin-diseases generally; and from a persistent use of the waters (drinking and bathing), many individuals have been cured of such affections."

The climate of Santa Barbara is delightful. It seems more nearly to resemble that of Monaco and Mentone, on the shores of the Mediterranean, than any other in America. Throughout the year the temperature is mild and equable, affording that opportunity for continual out-door exercise that is so important to consumptives. From a report by Dr. Thomas M. Logan, Permanent Secretary of the State Board of Health of California, we select the following:

"Santa Barbara is the county-seat and principal town of the county of the same name. It is built upon a beautiful slope, rising from the sea-beach, at the southeastern extremity of a gently-ascending valley, some fifteen miles in length and two in width, but gradually spreading out to five miles, as it extends into the interior. The beautiful harbor consists of a cove, or semi-ellipse, about one and a half mile wide from point to point, indented into the curving shore, and protected by the overlapping Santa Ynez and adjoining ranges. The gently-sloping beach for several miles affords safe sea-bathing at all seasons of the year. At low water an admirable and pleasing drive, equal to that of Newport, may here be had, and the interesting drawing of the seine, full of every variety of fishes, may be witnessed—a most important item in the dietary of the feeble, from the warmth-giving phosphorus contained in fish.

"As to the climate of Santa Barbara, it will be seen that, although lying in about the same latitude as Charleston, S. C., yet it is totally different, and that the isothermal line would be deflected toward St. Augustine, Fla. Nearly the same clothing is worn all the year round, and there is no day in the year in which the invalid may not sit out-of-doors. This covers the most essential indication in the treatment of consumption, by affording a continuous supply of pure, unadulterated air-food for the lungs. Still, as the climate possesses some latent peculiarities in its favor, too subtile for ordinary observation, I shall instance the remarkable phenomenon so philosophically noted by Dr. Brinkerhoff, who has resided here eighteen years:

"'Some ten miles from Santa Barbara, in a westerly direction, in the bed of the ocean, about one and a half mile from the shore, is an immense spring of petroleum, the product of which continually rises to the surface of the water and floats upon it over an area of many miles. This mineral oil may be seen any day from the deck of steamers plying between here and San Francisco, or from the high banks along the shore, its many-changing hues dancing upon the shifting waves of the sea, and affording various suggestions, both for the speculative and the speculator. Having read statements that, during the past few years, the authorities of Damascus and other plague-ridden cities of the East have resorted to the practice of introducing crude petroleum into the gutters of the streets to disinfect the air, and as a preventive of disease, which practice has been attended with the most favorable results, I throw out the suggestion, but without advancing any theory of my own, whether the prevailing westerly sea-breezes, passing over this wide expanse of sea-laden petroleum, may not take up from it and bear along with them to the places whither they go, some subtile power which serves as a disinfecting agent, and which may account for the infrequency of some of the diseases referred to, and probably for the superior healthfulness of the climate of Santa Barbara.'

"I would add that, during one week's sojourn here, my attention has been directed to the peculiar ambrosial influence pervading the air, so well described above, and that I indorse all that has been stated in this respect. That the climate of Santa Barbara possesses all the elements of general healthfulness in an eminent degree, is substantiated by the fact that the epidemics incident to childhood are almost unknown. Fevers and agues never originate here. Small-pox, frequently brought from abroad, never spreads, although hundreds of the native population, either from ignorance or prejudice, never allow themselves to be vaccinated.

"I have said, when speaking of the prolific yield of the soil, that it was due to the moist sea-air. On this depends the deliciousness of the climate. Moist air, either too hot or too cold, is injurious. The latter chills the surface and drives the blood in upon the internal organs. But the moist air in which we bathe in Santa Barbara is possessed of that happy combination of temperature with moisture, which, while it refreshes, also invigorates and vitalizes equally the whole system. The range between the wet and dry bulb thermometers, at two P. M., is usually about four degrees, except on foggy or rainy days, when they are often identical; and yet, strange to say, the feeling of chilliness is never experienced. During the prevalence of a high land wind, the range is occasionally extended to ten or even twenty degrees; but even then that feeling of irritation and dryness which attends the same wind in the more northern portions of California, is unknown. This occurrence, however, does not happen oftener than once or twice a year, and then only for a brief period about the equinoxes.

"The peculiar evenness of the climate is shown in the following tables, compiled from the meteorological register of the Rev. J. A. Johnson, the indefatigable editor of the *Santa Barbara Press:*

'MONTHLY MEAN.

April, Average of the three daily observations,	60.62° F.
May, " " " " "	62.35° F.
June, " " " " "	65.14° F.
July, " " " " "	71.49° F.
August, " " " " "	72.12° F.
Sept., " " " " "	68.08° F.
Oct., " " " " "	65.96° F.
Nov., " " " " "	61.22° F.
Dec., " " " " "	52.12° F.
Jan., " " " " "	54.51° F.
Feb., " " " " "	53.35° F.
March, " " " " "	58.12° F.
Average temperature for the year, . .	60.20° F.

COLDEST DAY.	WARMEST DAY.
April 12th, 60° F.	April 16th, 74° F.
May 15th, 66° F.	May 23d, 77° F.
June 1st, 69° F.	June 3d, 80° F
July 26th, 76° F.	July 11th, 84° F.
Aug. 11th, 77° F.	Aug. 8th, 86° F.
Sept. 23d, 66° F.	Sept. 27th, 90° F.
Oct. 23d, 60° F.	Oct. 20th, 92° F.
Nov. 7th, 64° F.	Nov. 20th, 87° F.
Dec. 15th, 52° F.	Dec. 28th, 71° F.
Jan. 11th, 56° F.	Jan. 3d, 76° F.
Feb. 22d, 42° F.	Feb. 28th, 71° F.
Mar. 13th, 56° F.	March 27th, 83° F.

Coldest day in the year, Feb 22d, 42° F.; warmest day in the year, Oct. 20th, 92° F. Variation, 50°.' "

From the date of Dr. Logan's report, I presume the table above was compiled from records of observations during 1870.

AGUA CALIENTE; OR, WARNER'S RANCH SPRINGS.

Location.—San Diego County, California.
Access.—From San Diego, about fifty miles northeast, in a direct line.
Hotel.— ———. (No improvements.)

Analysis.—Thermal sulphur-waters.

Remarks.—The following is the description of these springs as given by W. P. Blake, geologist of U. S. Exploring Expedition:

"The Thermal Springs, generally known as the 'Agua Caliente,' are situated on the slope of one of the ridges at the most eastern part of the valley (Warner's Ranch.) They have long been resorted to by the Indians for bathing, and the cure of various diseases. The water boils up from out of a granite ledge through a number of openings or cleavage-fissures, and in one place it appears to have enlarged the opening so that it has become nearly cylindrical. The water flows copiously from different apertures, and the united streams give a volume of water about equal to what would be delivered from a two-inch pipe under a pressure of one or two feet. These openings are in a slight ravine, which appears to have been the bed of a brook that is now deflected from its course by a dam built for the purpose by the Indians. In descending toward the spring the odor of sulphuretted hydrogen is at once perceptible, and a slight cloud of steam rises from the water. The temperature of the water was taken, and the following are the results:

Time, 9 A. M., November 30, 1853.

First, or principal spring	142° F.
Second spring	141° F.
Third spring	140° F.
Fourth spring	140° F.
Fifth spring, ten feet distant	136° F.
Stream below the springs	130° F.
Stream above the springs	58° F.
Air	74° F.

"Bubbles of sulphuretted hydrogen were constantly escaping, and the water was highly charged with it; and had an acid taste that was quite agreeable. There was only a slight deposit or incrustation on some of the rocks (consisting of sulphur). A small jet of steam was constantly issuing from a crevice near the main spring, producing a slight hissing sound like steam from a leak in a boiler."—(*Government Explorations for Pacific Railroad*, vol. v., p. 106.)

SAN BERNARDINO HOT SPRINGS.

Location.—San Bernardino County, California.

Access.—From the town of San Bernardino, about fifty miles northeast from Los Angeles; thence, about five miles distant.

Hotel.— ———. (No improvements.)

Analysis.—Pure and calcic thermal waters.

Remarks.—These springs are situated on the flanks of Mount San Bernardino. They are described as follows, by W. P. Blake, geologist of the U. S. Survey, who visited them between the 3d and 6th of November, 1853:

"The warm and hot waters gush out from the granitic rocks on the flanks of San Bernardino and adjacent heights. In one place the springs are so numerous, and the water rises in such volume, that a good-sized mill-stream of hot water is formed, which flows down into the valley, and is one of the principal tributaries of the Santa Anna River. This brook of hot water retains a temperature of 100° Fahr., three or four miles from its source.

"I visited several of the springs on the sides of the Sierra, between San Bernardino Mountain and the Cajon Pass, near the saw-mill road. . . . It was evident that the adjacent granite was very near the surface, as shown by one or two outcrops, from one of which the hot waters issued. Small springs rise at intervals of ten or twenty feet along a distance of thirty or forty rods. Their waters unite, and form a little stream that empties into the brook a short distance below. The banks of the stream were thickly overgrown with grass.

A dense mass of beautiful green confervæ grew from the bottom and sides of the channel, and floated in rich waving masses in the hot water. In the immediate vicinity of the springs, however, no vegetable growth was visible. The rocks and gravel in contact with the water were covered with a snow-white incrustation, and little twigs and leaves that had fallen into it were softened to a white, pulpy mass, and were partly incrusted. This was also the case with insects that were lying dead in the shallows of one of the springs, but I could not observe that in either case any petrifaction or internal deposit of mineral matter had taken place. The following temperatures were observed: 172, 169, 166, 130, 128, 108° Fahr. The temperature of the hot stream below all the springs was 130° Fahr., and the mountain-brook only 65° Fahr. Temperature of air, 76° Fahr.

"The white crust was not found in equal quantities at all the springs. It appeared to be most abundant at one of them. . . . An analysis of the crust (by J. D. Easter, Ph. D.) since the return of the expedition, gave the following results:

"The aqueous extract contained only a small proportion of chloride of sodium. In hot hydrochloric acid the mass dissolved with strong effervescence, leaving a residue of silica and alumina. The solution contained—

Lime (carbonate) chief constituent.
Silica (soluble in acid).
Magnesia.
Alumina and oxide of iron, traces.
Phosphoric acid, trace.

"The springs are estimated to be at least five hundred feet above the level of the Santa Anna, at the Mormon settlement, and thus nearly sixteen hundred and eighteen feet above the sea.

"These springs are not the source of the large stream of water first referred to. It takes its rise farther eastward, near the mountain of San Bernardino. I regret that I could not visit its source, as the springs must be of great volume and high temperature to send forth such a large stream of water retaining its temperature a long distance from the mountains. I was informed there are several other localities of hot springs along these mountains, and there are, no doubt, many that have not yet been discovered. The large stream of hot water appears to be nearly pure."—(*Government Explorations for Pacific Railroad*, vol. v., pp. 63, 64.)

SKAGGS'S HOT SPRINGS.

Location and Post-Office.—Sonoma County, California.

Access.—From San Francisco, by daily boat, to Petaluma; thence, by rail, to Healdsburg; thence, about twenty miles by stage, to springs. Time, about twelve hours.

Hotel.—Skaggs's Springs.

Analysis.—None.

Remarks.—"There are three springs open at present: That nearest the hotel is impregnated with sulphur, iron, and borax. . . . Temperature varies from 128° to 130° Fahr. The second spring, about one hundred yards distant, contains manganese, iron, sulphur, and soda; temperature, 138° to 140° Fahr. To the left, and nearly opposite the spring just described, is the iron spring situated on a knoll. The cañon in which the hotel is located contains several trout-streams affording excellent fishing. There is also an abundance of game, such as deer, quail, rabbits, etc." [1]

GILROY HOT SPRINGS.

Location.—Santa Clara County, California.

Post-Office.—Gilroy, Santa Clara County, California.

Access.—From San Francisco, by Central Pacific Railroad, forty-seven miles south to San José; thence, ——— miles south by Southern Pacific Railroad, to Gilroy; thence, ——— miles south by stage, to the springs.

Hotel.—Gilroy Springs.

Analysis.—None.

LAKE TAHOE HOT SPRINGS.

Location.—On the borders of Lake Tahoe. The lake is on the eastern boundary of California, and lies partly in Placer and partly in El Dorado County.

[1] Correspondence of a California paper.

Access.—Go to Truckee, a station on the Pacific Central Railroad, two hundred and fifty-eight miles east from San Francisco; thence, by stage, to the springs.

Hotel.— ——— (at Truckee, the Kennebec and the Truckee).

Analysis.— ———.

Remarks.—This is an interesting mountain resort, about six thousand five hundred feet above the sea. At the Hot Springs a steamer conveys passengers across the lake, and returns, in one day.

IDAHO HOT SPRINGS.

Location and Post-Office.—Idaho Springs, Clear Creek County, Colorado.

Access.—Go to Denver, *via* Kansas Pacific Railroad; thence, *via* Colorado Central Railroad and stage, to Central City, thirty-four miles west; thence, six miles by stage, to Idaho.

Hotels.—Beebe House, Springs House.

ANALYSIS.

One pint contains (85° to 115° Fahr. J. G. Dohle):

Solids.	Grains.
Carbonate of soda	3.85
Carbonate of magnesia	0.36
Carbonate of iron	0.52
Carbonate of lime	1.19
Chloride of sodium	0.52
Chloride of magnesium	trace.
Chloride of calcium	trace.
Sulphate of soda	3.67
Sulphate of magnesia	2.34
Sulphate of lime	0.43
Silicate of soda	0.51
Total	13.39

Flow, one hundred gallons per minute. (1870.)

Properties.—In chemical ingredients and temperature these waters are of the nature of the celebrated Carlsbad waters in Bohemia, though not equal in the amount of constituents, or height of temperature. They are valuable waters—especially useful in *rheumatism*, *cutaneous diseases*, *contractions of joints*, tertiary syphilis, etc.

Remarks.—Idaho, within the range of the Rocky Mountains, and seven thousand eight hundred feet above the sea, presents an altogether Alpine character. "The scenery is Swiss-like in every particular. Snow always in sight, cascades, the rushing roar of sparkling waters, rounded mountains, beetling crags, and grand, barren cliffs, 'rock-ribbed and ancient as the sun.' The town itself is built in a broad, fertile valley, irrigated with ditches and enlivened by the sound of waters. The hill-sides, cut by deep cañons, rise up gently in some places, in others abruptly; here, covered with grass, and there with pine-forests. The emerald of the valley, dotted with its white houses, is picturesquely succeeded by the deep green of the mountain-slopes, whose dense forests stand out clearly defined, mingling with a sky of an Italian blue, and transparently beautiful." [1]

There are two large bathing establishments, known as the Ocean Bath and the Mammoth Bath, having pools: one, twenty by forty, and four feet deep; the other, thirty by fifty, and five feet deep. There are also arrangements for private baths of any desired temperature.

MIDDLE PARK HOT SULPHUR SPRINGS.

Location.—Middle Park, Summit County, Colorado.

Access.—Go to Denver, *via* Kansas Pacific Railroad; thence, seventeen miles west, *via* Colorado Central Railroad, to Golden City; thence, thirty-two miles by stage, to Georgetown or Empire; thence, fifty miles horseback over Berthoud Pass. Or, from Denver, thirty-four miles west, *via* Colorado Central Railroad, to Central City; thence, fifty-five miles horseback over the James Peak route. Or, from Central City by wagon or carriage, fifty-five miles, over the South Boulder route. Camp out on the way

Hotel.—One in contemplation.

Analysis.—None has been made. They are, however, said to be of the sulphur class, and range in temperature from 111° to 116° Fahr. Flow, two hundred gallons per minute.

Remarks.—These springs are no doubt destined to be a very popular resort. Situated as they are, on a mountain-bound plateau eight thousand feet above the level of the sea,

[1] Correspondence of Rev. H. C. Waltz.

under a cloudless sky, and surrounded by the attractions of mountain scenery and the chase, they cannot fail to receive visitors.

The atmosphere is cool and exhilarating, and bathing in the water delightful. With all the inconvenience that attends a journey thither, and the necessity of camping out, over five hundred persons were there during the month of July, 1871.

The favorite route to the springs is by the way of Berthoud Pass. Having arrived at Georgetown, the tourist procures saddle and pack horses, and guides. The first day's journey will be over the summit of the range, eleven thousand feet above the sea, and through a dense forest of timber for fourteen miles beyond, to the "head of the park." Here camp is usually made. The next day's ride is down an open valley or arm of the park, following for some miles the course of Fraser's River. The route by South Boulder Pass is tedious and difficult, the road passing over the extreme summit of the range, more than 12,000 feet above the sea, where snow-storms are not unusual in July and August. The James Peak route is one of the most interesting, the road winding around the mountain, one of the highest points in the range; and the ascent easily made. All the roads, however, after crossing the mountains, meet together in the valley of the Fraser River. Thence the road is a pleasant carriage-drive along meadow-like valleys, with timbered ridges or table-lands, to the right and left. The grass is of luxuriant growth, and great variety. Clover of several kinds, and the blue flowering flax, are seen everywhere. All through late spring and early summer the prairies are bright with flowers, and the air laden with their fragrance. Delightful camping-places are seen all along the route, and days or weeks can be whiled away in Arcadian simplicity and enjoyment.

Arrived at the springs, there are several houses, a little trading establishment, and a primitive blacksmith-shop. The springs, many in number, are grouped together on an embankment, three hundred feet from Grand River, and about thirty feet above it. The stream, formed by the united overflow of the springs, is from three to five inches deep, and four to six feet wide. The flow is probably much greater than that recorded. The sources vary in temperature from 111° to 116° Fahr. Curiously enough, on the opposite side of the river is a *cold sulphur-spring.*

The bath is a natural basin in the rock, fifteen by thirty feet, and four feet deep. It has been housed and roofed. The temperature of this bath is about 109° Fahr.

In this distant region the sportsman readily gratifies his inclination. All the streams abound in trout, and the forests are frequented by elk, deer, antelope, and mountain-sheep. During the season, grouse and water-fowl shooting may be indulged.

Grand Lake, twenty-seven miles northeast from the springs, is another attraction. The road is up the valley, and is an exceedingly pleasant one. The lake is at the extremity of a deep cove in the main mountain-chain. On three sides it is overshadowed by frowning cliffs, while on the other is a narrow gap between high wooded hills, through which the river makes its exit, and the road enters. Thick forests of tall pines come down on all sides to the water's edge, separated therefrom only by a narrow beach of clean-washed white sand. The water is very deep, and clear as crystal. Most astonishing echoes are sent to and fro over its waters, the sound reverberating back and forth from cliff to cliff.

Near the springs are many patches of agate, where moss-agate, chalcedony, and amethyst, may be found.

WARM SPRINGS.

Location and Post-Office.—Warm Springs, Madison County, North Carolina.

Access.—Go to Morristown, a station on the Virginia & Tennessee Railroad, one hundred and fifty-four miles northeast from Chattanooga, and four hundred and seventy miles southwest from Washington; thence, *via* Cincinnati, Cumberland Gap & Charleston Railroad, thirty-nine miles, to Wolf Creek; thence, eight miles by stage or omnibus, to the springs. The Western North Carolina Railroad, from Salisbury *via* Asheville, will soon be completed to the springs.

Hotel.—Warm Springs.

ANALYSIS.

One pint contains—	Bathing Springs. 102° Fahr. E. Adelmarth, M. D.	Drinking Springs. 97° Fahr. E. Adelmarth, M. D.
SOLIDS.	Grains.	Grains.
Chloride of potassium	0.089	0.063
Chloride of sodium	0.114	0.187
Chloride of magnesium	0.027	0.046
Chloride of calcium	1.263	1.118
Sulphate of potassa	0.045	0.059
Sulphate of soda	1.128	1.113
Sulphate of magnesia	0.168	1.016
Sulphate of lime	5.110	5.067
Soluble silicates	1.121	1.192
Total	9.015	9.811
GASES.	Cubic in.	Cubic in.
Carbonic acid	1.87	1.84
Sulphuretted hydrogen	0.22	0.31

Properties.—Chemically considered, these are calcic-sulphur waters, bearing considerable resemblance to the well-known baths of Leuk, in the valley of the Rhone, Switzerland. They are valuable thermal waters and are efficacious in *chronic rheumatism*, *gout*, *paralysis*, *dartrous skin-diseases*, and irritable conditions of the urinary apparatus. They also are useful in certain cases of *amenorrhœa* and *dysmenorrhœa.*

Remarks.—The Warm Springs are at an elevation of seventeen hundred feet above the sea, surrounded on all sides by pine-covered mountain-summits, save the gorge and valley where the French Broad River has worn its pathway. The hotel and cottages are included in an area of about one hundred and fifty acres, well shaded, and interwoven with winding walks. The scenery of the region is exceedingly wild and beautiful. The banks of the river are precipitous in many places, at the springs being over one hundred feet in height. At a distance of some two miles from the hotel is Lover's Leap, an elevated point frequently visited by tourists, whence a far-extended view, for many miles, is had of the winding and turbulent river and the enclosing mountain-peaks. The climate is cool and bracing, the severe heats of summer being unknown.

The springs are near the banks of the river. One, the largest, is enclosed by a brick-wall laid in cement, and has a bath-house built over it. The bath is divided into two compartments — one for ladies, the other for gentlemen. The swimming-baths are about twenty by thirty feet, and four and a half feet deep. The mean temperature of the ladies' bath is 102° Fahr.; gentlemen's, 100° Fahr. The flow of water is constant, averaging nine gallons per minute.

AGUA CALIENTE.

Location.—Mesilla County, New Mexico.
Access.— ———.
Hotel.— ——— (Unimproved).

Remarks.—This spring is described as follows by T. Antisell, M. D., geologist of United States Exploring Expedition:

"Between the Mimbres and Ojo de la Vacca, and close to trail leading from the former to the copper-mines, is that remarkable spring known as the 'Agua Caliente.' It lies about five miles from the river.

"Where the springs issue out is a mound or bank of tufaceous deposit, formed by the overflow of the spring at some former time, previous to the side-channels being formed. This mound is twenty feet above the valley-level and two and one-half feet above the level of the water in the spring, showing that the spring, by deposit of carbonate of lime from its waters, has formed a basin-wall for itself, and allowed its level to be raised above the surrounding valley. This calcareous basin is twenty-five feet across and does not show bottom, except around the edges, which are rocky; a twelve-foot pole thrust into the middle did not find bottom. The temperature of the spring was 130° Fahr. at the surface. From one point below bubbles of gas arose in great abundance (carbonic acid). The water is agreeable to the taste." [1]

[1] "Government Explorations for Pacific Railroad," vol. vii., p. 156.

WARM SPRINGS.

Location and Post-Office.—Warm Springs, Merriwether County, Georgia.

Access.—From Macon, *via* Western Railway, one hundred miles west, to Columbus; thence, thirty-six miles by stage.

Hotel.—Warm Springs.

ANALYSIS.

One pint contains (90° Fahr. Prof. A. Means):

SOLIDS.	Grains.
Oxide of magnesium	11.68
Oxide of calcium	4.64
Protoxide of iron	2.14
Total	18.46
GASES.	Cubic in.
Carbonic acid	1.11
Sulphuretted hydrogen	trace.

The above bases are combined with carbonic acid, forming carbonates. A new analysis of this water is needed.

Remarks.—These springs are situated on a spur of the Pine Mountain. The flow is fourteen hundred gallons per minute; and, as a consequence of this large supply of water, every facility for bathing is offered. The height of the springs above the sea is eighteen hundred feet. Surrounding the springs are walks, terraces, and grottos, and the usual accompaniments of springs resorts. Within the enclosure there is a sulphur-spring; while three-quarters of a mile distant is the *cold spring*, an acidulous chalybeate, discharging, it is said, five thousand three hundred and forty-one cubic inches per hour of carbonic-acid gas, from a surface about five feet square. The drive thither is delightful—a fine pebbled road, leading through a skirt of wood, beneath the shade of mountain-oak, chestnut, and pine.

LEBANON SPRINGS.

Location and Post-Office.—Lebanon Springs, Columbia County, New York.

Access.—From New York, *via* Harlem Railroad, direct to the springs, one hundred and fifty-five miles north. Or take Hudson River day-boat to Hudson; thence, by Hudson & Boston Railroad, to Chatham Four Corners; thence, by Harlem Extension Railroad to the springs, twenty-seven miles north. From the east, take Boston & Albany Railroad to Chatham Four

Corners; thence as described. From the west, go to Albany; thence, by Boston & Albany Railroad, to Chatham Four Corners; thence as described. From the north, go to Rutland; thence, by Harlem Extension Railroad, to the springs, eighty-one miles south.

Hotel.—Columbia Hall.

ANALYSIS.

One pint contains (73° Fahr. Prof. H. Dussance):

Solids.	Grains.
Carbonate of soda	0.301
Carbonate of lime	0.506
Chloride of sodium	0.120
Sulphate of potassa	0.130
Sulphate of magnesia	0.132
Sulphuret of sodium	0.002
Oxide of iron	0.117
Alumina	0.056
Silicic acid	0.406
Organic compounds { Glairine	0.094
Organic compounds { Barégine	1.183
Total	3.047
Gases.	**Cubic in.**
Oxygen	0.25
Nitrogen	0.44
Carbonic acid	0.06
Total	0.75

This spring claims our attention as being the only thermal water in New York, or the New-England States. The temperature—73° Fahr.—is about the same as the old Sweet Springs of Virginia. The discharge from the spring is large, being estimated at five hundred gallons per minute. Elevation, one thousand feet above the level of the sea. The water is principally used for bathing.

But a short distance from Lebanon Springs is the village of the Brick-Yard Shakers, where there is a *chalybeate* spring which Prof. Briggs reports as highly charged with iron.

Remarks.—Lebanon Springs have been a favorite resort since the earliest settlement. It is related that one of our Revolutionary fathers stopped at the spring to water his horse, and, while there, carelessly thrust the end of his freshly-cut whip in the soft earth and rode away. Soon roots were formed, leaves appeared, and from that woodman's whip has grown the beautiful sycamore-tree that stands near the spring.

The salubrity of the climate, and beauty of scenery, combine to make this an exceedingly attractive resort. The valley is enclosed by gently-receding hills, from the summits of which extended views may be had. From a point on Gilbert Hill sail-boats may be seen on the Hudson in clear weather, and far beyond the blue outlines of the Catskill Mountains. Pleasure-drives are numerous. The valley roads to Queechy Lake, or the Williamstown or Nassau road, are exceedingly attractive. But the road from Lebanon to Pittsfield, over the Taghanic Mountains, is unsurpassed. From the summit there is a view of the entire country for sixty miles in every direction.

PUEBLA HOT SPRING.

Location.—Humboldt County, Nevada.
Access.— ———.
Hotel.— ———. (Unimproved.)

Analysis.— ———.

Remarks.—From the proceedings of the California Academy of Sciences I extract the following: "Dr. Blake made some remarks on the extent of the deposits that had been formed by the Hot Spring at Puebla, in Humboldt County, Nevada. He had caused specimens of the earth to be taken at different depths, and from spots situated in different directions and distances from the spring. The farthest spot at which these explorations had been made was at a distance of one hundred and fifteen yards from the spring, in a northwesterly direction, and here, to the depth of five feet, the earth contained a large number of diatoms of the same species as those obtained from the spring—in fact, a large portion of the soil was composed of diatoms, evidently formed in the water of the Hot Spring. From the earth obtained to the south of the spring few diatoms were found, and, in these, but two or three were of the same species as those growing in the

Hot Spring. The time in which a small surface like the outlet of the Puebla Hot Spring—about thirty yards long and two feet broad—would require to produce thousands of cubic yards of this infusorial earth, almost transcends the power of the imagination to conceive; and yet this process can only have been going on during the present geological epoch, or since the surface of this portion of the globe has been subject to any disturbance."

VOLCANO SPRINGS.

Location.—Lander County, Nevada.

Access.—From Beowawe, a station on the Central Pacific Railroad, four hundred and seventeen miles east of Sacramento, ride ——— miles south-east.

Analysis.— ———.

Remarks.—From a description by Colonel Albert S. Evans, in the *Overland Monthly*, February, 1869, I extract the following:

"Across the valley, some six miles to the southward, halfway up the western slope of a hill, perhaps six hundred feet in height, we saw a long table-land of *mesa*, white upon the top, and with long ribbon-like streaks of blue and white running down thence to the plain below. This had been designated as the locality of the Volcano Springs, but, beyond the discolorations mentioned, there was nothing to attract the attention of a traveller, and one might pass the point a dozen times without being made aware of their existence. 'There she blows,' exclaimed one of my companions after we had ridden on in sight of the place for some minutes. Looking up, I saw a long jet of white steam shoot far up into the air from the top of the *mesa*. Another and another followed, and in a few minutes a dozen or more were rising from different parts of the hill-side, and one or two from the plain at its foot. Half an hour's gallop brought us to the foot of the hill. Some time before we reached it we heard a noise as of many steam-engines working away in some huge factory, and as we forced our horses up the steep acclivity over ground that resounded beneath their tread, hollow and cavernous, we heard other sounds emanating from the deep bosom of the mountain. Dismounting, we hitched our panting, half-frighted horses to a huge honey-combed rock, and approached the opening in the earth from which the steam was escaping. The orifice might have been ten inches in diameter, and from it poured a stream of scalding water clear as crystal, while a column of steam rose forty or fifty feet into the air. The whole *mesa* appeared to be composed of lime, soda, and sulphur deposits, the gradual accretion of years, and was blistering with a fierce heat from the undying fires below. It was as if we were walking over the surface of a freshly-burned lime-kiln, on which rain had just been falling. The orifice was round, and had the appearance of having been artificially lined with coarse porcelain. It was higher than the hill around it, showing clearly that it was gradually rising steadily from below by the accumulation of its own deposits, as a brick chimney increases in height as brick after brick is added to it by the mason. A kind of basin several feet in width surrounded the orifice, and in this orifice were many curious lime-formations, some resembling coral, others round and polished, as if by the wheel of the lapidary; others still polished on one side, and on the other presenting the appearance of a basket of wax-flowers. We went on to another and still larger spring. There was a low rumbling sound accompanying the action of the first. The second worked, exactly like a steam-pump, with a steady, regular stroke, the water being thrown out, not in a continuous stream, but in jets corresponding with the regular strokes of a piston. As we stood over it, we could hardly divest ourselves of the impression that we were standing above a well-regulated steam-engine in full operation, as, in fact, we were. We timed the pulsations with our watches, and counted just one hundred in a minute. From many small orifices, some not larger round than one's finger, all around us the steam was escaping, and the whole *mesa* seemed a mere crust perforated like a cullender. We stamped with our boot-heels on the crumbling shell, and broke it through in one place. Below we found a mass of soft, coarse, granulated matter, red, white, and yellow, resembling in appearance rice-pudding well mixed with red-wine sauce, blistering hot as if fresh from the oven, and emitting a nauseating odor, of which a few sniffs were all-sufficient. We dug down into the mass with our hands, as long as we could stand the heat, and found it growing softer in proportion to its depth.

"Passing on to the southward over a small divide, we saw a number of springs which had been running at intervals during the night, but were then inactive, long ribbons of ice running out from them over the side of the *mesa*, and down into the plain three hundred feet below, where all the water sinks and disappears. Others, projecting, in some cases, three or four feet above the surface of the hill, appeared to have completely choked themselves up with their own deposits, and ceased to operate entirely, the water finding an escape elsewhere.

"Looking southward along the height extending over half a mile of space, we saw dozens of these hot-water volcanoes, if we may be permitted the expression, in full operation, and an immense number of others quiet for the moment, but bearing evidence of being in working order. The largest of those quiet for the moment had an orifice as large as a sugar-hogshead, and was filled to the surface with clear, sparkling water. The sun was now well up in the heavens, and the air, especially where affected by the clouds of steam, warm enough to make the temptation to indulge in a tepid bath almost irresistible. The water in the basin, though not boiling, was not quite cold enough for bathing purposes, and we concluded to wander on a little farther and wait for it to cool. . . . Finding, at last, a shallow pool of water which had run down from a spring then quiet, we sat down, and stripping our heated feet gave them a soaking, while we waited for the cooling of that in the basin of the great spring above us, and looked around on the strange scene about us. . . .

"While we were sitting with our feet in the tepid water, discussing the formation of the place, a low droning, moaning sound came up from the deep bosom of the hill, followed by a sharp 'Clap! clap! clap!' as if a pair of giant-hands had been struck together three times with force; then with a tremendous swash a torrent of scalding water flew into the air, scattering in all directions from the great spring in which we had just been proposing to bathe, and poured in a stream ten feet wide down the hill."

DES CHUTES HOT SPRINGS.

Location.—Wasco County, Oregon.
Access.— ———.
Hotel.— ———. (Unimproved.)

ANALYSIS.

One pint contains (143° and 145° Fahr. L. M. Dornbach and Prof. E. N. Horsford):

SOLIDS.	Grains.
Carbonate of soda	4.312
Chloride of potassium	0.250
Chloride of sodium	2.552
Chloride of magnesium	0.152
Sulphate of soda	1.183
Sulphate of lime	0.228
Silicate of soda	1.025
Iron	trace.
Total	9.702
GAS.	Cubic in.
Carbonic acid	2.82

Properties.—This is a valuable *muriated-alkaline* thermal water, according to the analysis, of which there are few in this country.

Remarks.—These springs are described by G. J. S. Newberry, M. D., geologist of the U. S. Exploring Expedition, as follows:

"At different points along the valley of the Wam-Chuck River, hot springs issue from the base of the cliffs which bound it. The number of these springs is large, and two or three of them quite copious. They issue from fissures in the rock, the water flowing from them collecting in basins of several feet in diameter, thence flowing into the Wam-Chuck

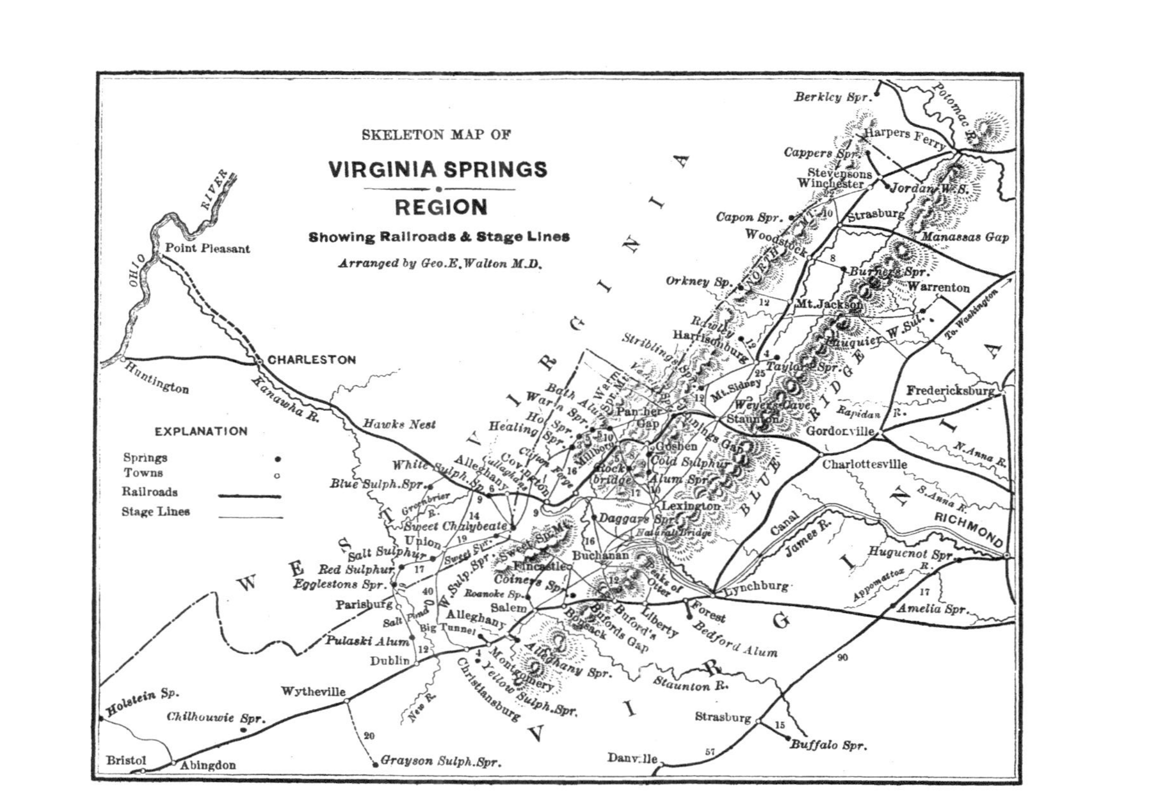
SKELETON MAP OF
VIRGINIA SPRINGS
REGION
Showing Railroads & Stage Lines
Arranged by Geo. E. Walton M.D.
EXPLANATION
Springs
Towns
Railroads
Stage Lines
OHIO RIVER
Point Pleasant
CHARLESTON
Huntington
Kanawha R.
Hawks Nest
WEST VIRGINIA
VIRGINIA
Berkley Spr.
Harpers Ferry
Potomac R.
Cappers Spr.
Stevensons
Winchester
Jordan W.S.
Capon Spr.
Strasburg
Woodstock
Manassas Gap
Orkney Sp.
Burners Spr.
Warrenton
Mt. Jackson
Harrisonburg
Fauquier W. Sul.
To Washington
Taylors Spr.
Mt. Sidney
Fredericksburg
Weyers Cave
Staunton
Rapidan R.
Gordonsville
N. Anna R.
Charlottesville
S. Anna R.
RICHMOND
BLUE RIDGE
Bath Alum
Warm Spr.
Hot Spr.
Healing Spr.
Panther Gap
Goshen
Millboro
Cold Sulphur
Rockbridge
Alum Spr.
Lexington
Daggars Spr.
Natural Bridge
Canal
James R.
Huguenot Spr.
Appomattox R.
Lynchburg
Amelia Spr.
White Sulph. Sp.
Alleghany
Covington
Clifton Forge
Blue Sulph. Spr.
Greenbrier R.
Sweet Chalybeate
Union
Salt Sulphur
Sweet Spr.
Red Sulphur
Egglestons Spr.
W. Sulp. Spr.
Buchanan
Fincastle
Coiners Spr.
Roanoke Sp.
Peaks of Otter
Parisburg
Salt Pond
Salem
Alleghany
Big Tunnel
Bonsack
Bufords Gap
Liberty
Forest
Bedford Alum
Pulaski Alum
Dublin
Montgomery
Alleghany Spr.
Yellow Sulph. Spr.
Christiansburg
New R.
Staunton R.
Wytheville
Holstein Sp.
Chilhouwie Spr.
Bristol
Abingdon
Grayson Sulph. Spr.
Danville
Strasburg
Buffalo Spr.

River, and giving it its name. The temperature of two of these springs was respectively 143° and 145° Fahr. The water holds large quantities of silica in solution, but has a bland and pleasant taste."—(*Government Explorations for Pacific Railroad*, vol. vi., p. 49.)

HOT SPRINGS.

Location and Post-Office.—Hot Springs, Bath County, Virginia.

Access.—From Washington, *via* Orange, Alexandria & Manassas, and Chesapeake & Ohio Railroads, to Millboro, one hundred and ninety-six miles southwest (Millboro Hotel); or to Covington, two hundred and twenty-five miles southwest (McCurdy's Hotel). From Millboro, twenty miles by stage. From Covington, nineteen miles by stage. The latter route is preferable for invalids. From Richmond, *via* Chesapeake & Ohio Railroad, one hundred and seventy-six miles to Millboro, and two hundred and five miles to Covington. From the west, *via* Cincinnati and Ohio River, to Huntington, one hundred and sixty-five miles east; thence, *via* Chesapeake & Ohio Railroad, to Covington, two hundred and fourteen miles southeast.

Hotel.—Hot Springs.

ANALYSIS.

One pint contains—	Ladies' Boiler-Bath, 110° Fahr. Prof. Wm. Gilham.	Ladies' Sulphur-Bath, 102° Fahr. Col. Wm. Gilham.	Gentlemen's Pleasure-Bath, 78° Fahr. Col. Wm. Gilham.
SOLIDS.	Grains.	Grains.	Grains.
Carbonate of magnesia	0.335	0.350	0.252
Carbonate of iron (protoxide)	0.014	0.008	0.010
Carbonate of lime	2.168	2.055	1.185
Chloride of potassium	0.200	0.021	0.020
Chloride of sodium	0.015	0.017	0.016
Sulphate of potassa	0.168	0.228	0.071
Sulphate of soda	0.128	0.126	0.106
Sulphate of magnesia	0.707	0.688	0.133
Sulphate of lime	0.217	0.263	0.378
Silica	0.218	0.171	0.086
Total	4.170	3.877	2.257

Properties.—As will be seen by the analyses, these waters contain but a small proportion of mineral constituents, not sufficient to be considered an active agent in curing the maladies that are relieved by them. Their efficacy is doubtless due to elevated temperature. Every convenience has been arranged for utilizing the water in the form of baths. For reference, we insert a table giving the temperatures of the various baths and capacity. The first column gives the temperature as published in the pamphlet issued by the springs company; the second column as found by myself in company with Prof. Cabell, on August 22, 1871:

TEMPERATURE AND CAPACITY OF BATHS.

NAME OF BATH.	Pamphlet. Temperature Fahrenheit.	The Author's. Temperature Fahrenheit.	Capacity.			
			Length feet.	Breadth feet.	Depth feet.	Gallons.
Ladies' pleasure-bath	86°	90°	15	15	4½	7,573
Gentlemen's pleasure-bath	78°	76°	32	21	5½	27,646
Ladies' boiler-baths (four pools)	108°	..	8	4	5	1,197
Gentlemen's boiler-baths (four pools)	..	102½° to 103½°	8	4	5	1,197
Ladies' sulphur-bath	102°	....	20	16	5	11,968
Gentlemen's sulphur-bath	..	98°	16	16	5½	10,532
Ladies' hot spout-bath	108°	..	12	8	4½	8,231
Gentlemen's hot spout-bath	..	106°	15	15	5	8,415
Warm baths (four)	92°	..	5	5	3	561
Octagon	..	99¾°	22	..	5½	16,500
Specific	..	102½°	..	..	..	....
No. 5	..	97°	..	..	..	....
Mud-bath: Mud-vat	100°	100°	10	4	3½	1,047
Mud-bath: Warm pool			12	12	5	5,386
Mud-bath: Cold pool	48°	..	12	8	5	8,590

The spout and boiler baths are worthy of especial mention. The first consists of a large quadrangular room. On entering, you find yourself on a raised platform, surrounding a deep, cistern-like-looking vat, fifteen feet square and as many deep. From one side of the wall, on a level with the platform, the steaming water spouts out in a full stream, two inches in diameter, and falls in a graceful curve into the water below. The bather descends a pair of stairs into the water and places himself under the descending stream, which, by change of his position, may be made to fall on any part of the body. The temperature of the spout at the point of emergence varies from 106° to 108° Fahr., but some degrees of heat are lost in its fall, so that it is not quite that temperature when it strikes the body.

The boiler-baths, eight in number, vary in temperature from 102° to 108° Fahr. They are eight feet by four, and five feet deep. For the convenience of infirm and crippled patients, two of each are arranged with chairs suspended by rope and pulley. The patient is placed in the chair, and then it is permitted gradually to descend into the hot water. At the end of the required time the chair is elevated and the person assisted in dressing, or he may recline for some time on a cot, close at hand, until rested and desirous of returning to the hotel.

The mud-bath consists of a thick mixture of earth from the adjacent valley, with water from the springs at a temperature of about 100° Fahr. After having remained in this mixture for some time, the patient passes under a small spout-bath, in an adjoining compartment, and the mud is thus quickly removed. This bath is supposed to be of especial value in rheumatic affections and diseases of the skin.

These waters are a most valuable therapeutic agent in the treatment of the following diseases: *Chronic rheumatism*, *gout*, *diseases of the liver*, associated with *congestion* and *engorgement*, *neuralgia*, *contractions of joints* (false anchylosis), and secondary and tertiary syphilis which has proved rebellious to the usual modes of treatment. In cases of paralysis and paraplegia, unaccompanied by organic lesions and in which there is *no inflammatory* action, they have given favorable results. *Concretions* and *enlargements of joints*, the result of the rheumatic or gouty diathesis, are sometimes resolved under their use.

In conversation with Prof. Cabell, of the University of Virginia, resident physician, he said he found cases of chronic rheumatism, accompanied with contractions of the joints, quite rebellious to treatment when the patients are *anæmic;* but that, on the contrary, most marked benefit is derived in plethoric cases. In gout of an adynamic type similar difficulty is met with. He also said he had treated several cases of seven and twenty-one day *intermittent fever*, that had proved rebellious to nine months' treatment at Charlottesville, Virginia, a place where intermittent fever is unknown as an endemic disease. They were students at the university from southern climates. On coming to the Hot Springs the first effect of the baths was to change the fever into a tertian, which then very readily yielded to the usual medicines, associated with the baths, and permanent relief obtained.

Remarks.—These springs are located in a most charming valley, at the summit of the mountains. Five miles distant are the Warm Springs. The Healing Springs are three miles away. On an elevated plateau, on the banks of what may be called the Hot Springs Creek, are the hotel buildings. The baths are in the valley. From the piazza of the hotel a beautiful mountain-view is had to the northwest, through a niche in the ridge. The hotel is open through the entire year.

The prevailing temperature is similar to that at the Healing Springs, which *see*.

SALT LAKE HOT SPRINGS.

Location and Post-Office.—Salt Lake City, Salt Lake County, Utah.
Hotels.—Walker's, Salt Lake, Revier.

ANALYSIS.

One pint contains—

Solids.	Grains.
Carbonate of lime and magnesia	0.447
Chloride of sodium	2.443
Chloride of magnesium	0.066
Chloride of calcium	0.566
Sulphate of soda	0.692
Peroxide of iron	0.021
Total	4.235

The above combinations have been arranged by J. G. Rogers, M. D., from an analysis in elements given by C. T. Jackson, M. D., of Boston.

Properties.—This water belongs to the group of thermal sulphur-waters. Unlike the majority of warm waters, it contains a considerable proportion of mineral constituents. It is valuable in diseases of the skin, chronic rheumatism, etc.

Remarks.—These springs are situated one mile north of the North Gate of the city, and supply the city baths. They are much resorted to by invalids.

Two miles farther north another group of hot springs occur, of a still higher temperature—128° Fahr. They break forth at the base of a rock where the mountain rises from the plain. The waters flow into a lake near by, known as the Hot Springs Lake, three miles long and one mile wide.

WARM SPRINGS.

Location and Post-Office.—Bath Court-House, Bath County, Virginia.

Access.—From Washington, *via* Orange, Alexandria & Manassas Railroad, and Chesapeake & Ohio Railroad, one hundred and ninety-six miles southwest, to Millboro Depot (Millboro Hotel); thence, fifteen miles by stage. From the west, *via* Cincinnati and the Ohio River, to Huntington, one hundred and sixty-five miles east; thence, *via* Chesapeake & Ohio Railroad, two hundred and fourteen miles southeast, to Covington (McCurdy's Hotel); thence, by stage, twenty-two miles.

Hotel.—Springs.

ANALYSIS.

One pint contains (96° to 98° Fahr. A. H. Hayes, M. D.):

SOLIDS.	Grains.
Carbonate of lime	0.653
Sulphate of lime	1.816
Crenate of iron	0.312
Silicates of magnesia and alumina	0.216
Total	2.997
GASES.	Cubic in.
Carbonic acid	1.80
Sulphuretted hydrogen [1]	0.04
Nitrogen [1]	0.41

Properties.—This water is limpid, has a slight styptic taste, some odor of sulphuretted hydrogen, and the temperature is 98° Fahr. The flow has been estimated at six thousand gallons per minute, forming a stream sufficient to move a mill. The temperature of these baths, as taken by myself, August 24, 1871, was as follows: Gentlemen's swimming-bath, 97.4° Fahr. at the south steps, undoubtedly 98° Fahr. at the centre; gentlemen's spout, 96.4° Fahr.; temperature of ladies' baths about the same; drinking-fountain, 96.8° Fahr. The large swimming-bath is forty feet in diameter, and contains forty-

[1] From an analysis by another chemist.

three thousand gallons of water. There are four other baths, of which two are spout-baths.

The action of these waters is *sedative* in most instances. Immersion in the bath gives rise to a sense of voluptuous repose; and, as the hand is passed over the body, the surface presents a velvet smoothness, as though anointed with some delicate ointment. On emerging from the bath this smoothness is still retained, and continues for twelve hours after. This bath may justly be compared to the "Bains des délices" of Molitg, France, or the Serpent Bath of Schlangenbad, Nassau, of which a Frenchman said, "One becomes absolutely in love with himself in this bath." The water has also been appropriately compared with those of Wildbad, near Stuttgart. The unctuous quality of this water, which is also possessed by the waters named, has not been made note of heretofore. It is very peculiar, the cause therefor not being known. This quality of certain waters has been variously ascribed, by European writers, to the presence of silicates, the monosulphuret of sodium, or an organic matter, the latter with most probability. The duration of the bath should be from fifteen minutes to half an hour. Many remain longer, but the last-named period is sufficient for securing all the remedial action of the water, and guards against too great relaxation.

The diseases to which these waters are applicable are *chronic* and *subacute rheumatism* (in subacute cases preferable), *gout*, *neuralgia*, congestive *amenorrhœa* and *dysmenorrhœa*, and in *nephritic* and *calculous* diseases, by its soothing effects. The spout-bath, arranged with an ascending douche, is especially useful in dysmenorrhœa of the type named. From analogy, we should expect these waters to prove useful in psoriasis, lichen, pityriasis, and other squamous eruptions, but data are wanting. As a warm pleasure-bath these waters are unsurpassed, and will always be sought with especial favor by ladies.

Remarks.—The natural surroundings of these springs are exceedingly attractive. They lie in a beautiful valley at the summit of the Warm Springs Mountain. From the springs an easy and most delightful road leads up to *Flag Rock*, two thousand four hundred feet above the sea, a point in the mountain-crest which gives a far-extended view, over verdant hill and vale, of fifty or sixty miles in every direction. To the eastward, in the distance, is House Mountain. and the Blue Ridge reaching far away to the northeast. To the southward, the Peaks of Otter may be seen on a clear day. Far to the northwest and west are the Alleghanies; while, looking down into the valley, we behold the hotel and outlying cottages, charmingly nestled amid the trees.

On the road from Millboro to the springs the *Blowing Cave* is passed. It was thus described by Thomas Jefferson: "It is in the side of a hill, is of about one hundred feet in diameter, and emits constantly a current of air of such force as to keep the weeds prostrate to the distance of twenty yards before it. This current is strongest in dry, frosty weather, and, in long spells of rain, weakest." At the time I passed (August, 1871), the outward current was exceedingly strong, and of a coolness to render one chilly if he remained in it for any time.

HEALING SPRINGS.[1]

Location and Post-Office.—Healing Springs, Bath County, Virginia.

Access.—From Washington, *via* Orange, Alexandria & Manassas Railroad, and Chesapeake & Ohio Railroad, two hundred and twenty-five miles southwest, to Covington (McCurdy's Hotel); thence, sixteen miles by stage, to the springs. From Richmond, two hundred and five miles by Chesapeake & Ohio Railroad, to Covington. From the west, *via* Cincinnati and the Ohio River, to Huntington, one hundred and sixty-five miles east; thence, *via* Chesapeake and Ohio Railroad, two hundred and fourteen miles southeast, to Covington.

Hotel.—Healing Springs.

Properties.—This water corresponds very nearly in temperature to the Schlangenbad of Nassau, though in chemical constituents and therapeutic value it differs. It has been well named, as it finds appropriate application to all *ulcerated* conditions, whether of the skin or mucous membrane. In

[1] *See* Analysis, page 824.

ANALYSIS.

One pint contains—	Old Spring. 85° Fahr. Prof. Wm. E. A. Aikin, M. D.	New Spring. 88° Fahr. Prof. Wm. E. A. Aikin, M. D.
SOLIDS.	Grains.	Grains.
Carbonate of magnesia	0.156	0.246
Carbonate of iron	0.009	0.084
Carbonate of lime	2.238	2.340
Chloride of potassium	0.029	0.082
Chloride of sodium	0.034	0.036
Sulphate of potassa	0.276	0.316
Sulphate of magnesia	0.906	0.924
Sulphate of iron	0.022	0.018
Sulphate of lime	0.165	0.158
Sulphate of ammonia	0.029	0.029
Iodine	trace.	trace
Bromine	trace.	trace.
Silicic acid	0.237	0.228
Organic acid, probably crenic	0.107	0.109
Total	4.208	4.465
GAS.	Cubic in.	Cubic in.
Carbonic acid	0.58	0.60

many such cases its efficacy is undoubted. In this class are embraced all *scrofulous ulcers*, *scrofulous ophthalmia*, *ozœna*, *chronic diarrhœa* and *dysentery*, and many forms of *secondary and tertiary syphilis* and diseases of the skin known as *scrofulides.* It has also given relief in cases of gout and neuralgia. It should be stated that the forms of chronic diarrhœa and dysentery to which it is applicable are those accompanied with *great irritability* and *hyperœmia* of the mucous membrane as shown by a red tongue. In the opposite condition, other waters will prove more useful. M. H. Houston, M. D., of Richmond, Va., who has given considerable attention to the study of these waters, in an article in the *Richmond and Louisville Medical Journal* testifies as follows: "The Healing-Spring water will be found to be slightly hypnotic, sedative, diuretic, diaphoretic, and alterative. Unless it be in exceptional cases of very rare occurrence it produces no cathartic effect—indeed, in a majority of cases it rather tends to produce constipation. Nor is it possessed of any very direct tonic effect, the small quantity of iron it contains being scarcely adequate to this purpose. The invigoration which follows its use is mainly due to its alterative power, and by alterative I mean a rapid transformation of the tissues in every part of the body;

a transformation which, by absorbing and eliminating the old tissues, creates a keen demand for the materials to supply the deficiency in the organism. The alterative effect is secondary, the primitive being sedative and hypnotic. In ordinary cases, the properly regulated use of the water is followed by a decided inclination to sleep. . . . In general terms, it may be safely stated that benefit is not to be expected from the use of this water in disease of whatever kind attended by relaxed fibre and impaired sensibility, unless these have been caused by morbid deposits; and that it may be recommended with confidence for all curable chronic diseases accompanied or not by constitutional irritation, and attended by local hyperæmia and exalted or perverted sensibility."

In these springs there is a confervoid growth, no doubt depending on the presence of soluble organic matter for its development. It is a soft, green, silken moss, about an inch to two inches in length, and found clinging to the walls of the reservoirs, pools, and baths. It is formed with much rapidity, for, if all the moss be removed from a surface on the wall of the reservoir, on the next day it will be found to have been reproduced. This moss is used in the form of an epithem as a dressing for ulcerated surfaces, having been previously saturated with the spring's water. It acts as an irritant, retaining the water in contact with the diseased surface, and probably containing some of the active ingredients of the water within its structure, by which it cleanses the ulcer. Persons using the moss should distinguish between it and the large and coarse growth which forms in great abundance in the reservoir.

The external use of the water in most cases should be combined with the internal, and for this purpose there are swimming-baths, private baths, and facilities for heating the water to any required temperature, though the natural temperature of the swimming-baths—80° to 84° Fahr.—is best adapted to the majority of cases.

Remarks.—These springs are situated in the valley running along the summit of the Warm Springs Mountain, sixteen miles from Covington by stage. The road up the mountain presents exceedingly fine views of the valley of Jackson's River, while within a few miles of the springs is the beautiful cataract of the *Falling Springs*, a sheet of water one hundred yards in breadth, which is precipitated over a perpendicular cliff to the depth of one hundred and fifty feet. A short walk from the springs are the *Cascades*, well worth a visit.

The following table gives the averages of temperature at these springs for the years and months named. It will apply almost equally well to the climate of the Hot Springs and Warm Springs on the same mountain:

AVERAGES OF TEMPERATURE AT HEALING SPRINGS.

1868.	6 A. M.	12 M.	6 P. M.	10 P. M.	11 P. M.
July, . .	68.2° F.	81.7° F.	74.8° F.	69.1° F.	66.8° F.
August, . .	64.5	75.9	67.9	....	62.8
September, .	57.6	79.4	60.7	....	57.2
October, to 8th,	54.5	65.3	55.3	....	5.27
1870.					
July, . .	66.2	81.6	....	69.1	....
August, .	62.7	79.2	....	66.8	....
September, .	55.	73.9	....	60.7	....
October, to 8th,	50.7	68.9	....	44.	....
1871.					
June, from 19th,	63.2	79.	....	66.2	....
July,	61.	77.7	....	64.8	....
August, to 21st,	63.3	83.	....	68.5	....

On October 8, 1870, there was frost. On October 20, 1868, there was snow.

These observations were taken with an ordinary thermometer; nevertheless they answer a good purpose till more accurate observations are made.

AMERICAN GEYSERS.

Location.—Wyoming Territory.

Access.—From St. Paul, Minnesota, to Fort Benton, Montana, eight hundred and seventy-five miles northwestwardly in a direct line; thence to Helena, one hundred and ten miles south (direct line); thence, *via* Gallatin City, to Fort Ellis, one hundred and twenty miles southeast; thence several days' journey southward.

In this distant and almost inaccessible country a series of geysers have lately been discovered which, according to descriptions, surpass any in the world. Although frequently seen by trappers, their tales were regarded as the idle extravagances in which that class so frequently indulge. In the autumn of 1870, however, an exploring party of adventurous gentlemen, under General H. D. Washburn, ventured into the unknown region, and there found some of the most wonderful natural phenomena. They saw a water-fall, in one continuous, compact, glistening sheet, one hundred and fifty feet broad and *three hundred and fifty feet* in descent, by actual measurement. They passed—amid volcanoes and boiling-springs of colored waters—places where the earth was hot under foot, and shook under the tread. But, most wonderful of all were the geysers. From a report of the expedition, in *Scribner's Monthly*, we extract the following:

"Our search for new wonders leading us across the Fire-Hole River, we ascended a gentle incrusted slope, and came suddenly upon a large oval aperture with scalloped edges, the diameters of which were eighteen and twenty-five feet, the sides corrugated and covered with a grayish-white silicious deposit, which was distinctly visible at the depth of one hundred feet below the surface. No water could be discovered, but we could distinctly hear it gurgling and boiling at a great distance below. Suddenly it began to rise, boiling and spluttering, and sending out huge masses of steam, causing a general stampede of our company, driving us some distance from our point of observation. When within about forty feet of the surface it became stationary, and we returned to look down upon it. It was foaming and surging at a terrible rate, occasionally emitting small jets of hot water nearly to the mouth of the orifice. All at once it seemed seized with a fearful spasm, and rose with incredible rapidity, hardly affording us time to flee to a safe distance, when it burst from the orifice with terrific momentum, rising in a column the full size of this immense aperture to the height of sixty feet; and through and out of the apex of this vast aqueous mass, five or six lesser jets or round columns of water, varying in size from six to fifteen inches in diameter, were projected to the marvellous height of two hundred and fifty feet. These lesser jets, so much higher than the main column, and shooting through it, doubtless proceed from auxiliary pipes leading into the principal orifice near the bottom, where the explosive force is greater. If the theory that water by constant boiling becomes explosive when freed from air be true, this theory rationally accounts for all irregularities in the eruptions of the geysers.

"This grand eruption continued for twenty minutes, and was the most magnificent sight we ever witnessed. We were standing on the side of the geyser nearest the sun, the gleams of which filled the sparkling column of water and spray with myriads of rainbows, whose arches were constantly changing —dipping and fluttering hither and thither, and disappearing only to be succeeded by others, again and again, amid the aqueous column, while the minute globules into which the spent jets were diffused when falling sparkled like a shower of diamonds, and around every shadow which the denser clouds of vapor, interrupting the sun's rays, cast upon the column, could be seen a luminous circle radiant with all the colors of the prism, and resembling the halo of glory represented in paintings as encircling the head of Divinity. All that we had previously witnessed seemed tame in comparison with the perfect grandeur and beauty of this display. Two of these wonderful eruptions occurred during the twenty-two hours we remained in the valley. This geyser we named 'The Giantess.'

"A hundred yards distant from 'The Giantess' was a silicious cone, very symmetrical but slightly corrugated upon its exterior surface, three feet in height and five feet in diameter at its base, and having an oval orifice twenty-four by thirty-six and one-half inches in diameter, with scalloped edges. Not one of our company supposed that it was a geyser; and among so many wonders it had almost escaped notice. While we were at breakfast upon the morning of our departure a column of water, entirely filling the crater, shot from it, which, by actual triangular measurement, we found to be two hundred and nineteen feet in height. The stream did not deflect more than four or five degrees from a vertical line, and the eruption lasted eighteen minutes. We named it 'The Beehive.'"

Five other geysers were observed by the exploring party, which were variously named according to the degree of activity, the shape of the column of water, or the form of the silicious deposit about the orifice.

"Old Faithful" was the first geyser observed by the party, and was so named from its continuous activity, not having intermitted more than an hour during their stay, and spouting for fifteen or twenty minutes each time. The crater is five feet by three, and elevated five or six feet above the surrounding earth. The column of water was eighty or ninety feet high.

"The Fan" was named from the fan-shaped column of water which it throws out. The height of the stream was about sixty feet, and it continued in action from ten to twenty minutes.

"The Grotto" received its name from the form of the crater, which is about ten feet high, and twenty feet through the base, with several large openings. Connected with this, by a ridge of incrustations, was a smaller mound, about five feet high. Through one of the side-openings one of the party crawled to the discharging orifice—about four feet in diameter—from which, a few hours afterward, a column of boiling-water shot to the height of sixty feet. The discharge continued for half an hour.

"The Castle" is situated on the summit of an incrusted mound, and has a turret-shaped crater, with an orifice about three feet in diameter. The water issues from this geyser to a height of about fifty feet.

"The Giant" has a rugged crater ten feet in diameter on the outside, with an irregular orifice five or six feet in diameter. It resembles a miniature model of the Coliseum. The column of water, which shot upward from it, was five feet in diameter and one hundred and forty-five feet in height. It continued to flow for nearly three hours.

The party did not analyze the waters. The sinter was both carboniferous and silicious, the latter characteristic predominating; and we may with confidence conclude that the waters contain considerable silica in solution.

The springs observed in this region, which resembled boiling mud, deposited a sediment of various colors—some white, some delicate lavender, and others of a brilliant pink. An analysis of specimens of this sediment, by Prof. Augustus Steitz, gave the following result:

ANALYSIS.

SOLIDS.	White Sediment. Per cent.	Lavender Sediment. Per cent.	Pink Sediment. Per cent.
Silica	42.2	28.2	32.6
Magnesia	33.4	....	....
Lime	17.8	4.2	8.3
Alkalies	6.6	....	....
Alumina	....	58.6	52.4
Boracic acid	....	3.2	....
Oxide of iron	....	0.6	....
Soda and potassa	....	....	4.2
Water and loss	....	5.2	2.5
Total	100.0	100.0	100.0

CHAPTER XVII.

UNCLASSIFIED WATERS.

ALABASTER CAVE SPRING.

Location.—El Dorado County, California.

Access.—Go to Folsom, a station on the Sacramento Valley Railroad, twenty miles east from Sacramento; thence by stage, ten miles.

Hotel.—Cave Hotel.

Analysis.—None.

Remarks.—This spring is in a cave, known as Alabaster Cave. The cave was discovered in 1860, by William Gwynn, whose workmen were engaged in quarrying stone near by. It is not large, but is said to be even more beautiful than Mammoth Cave. Mr. Gwynn says: "On our first entrance we descended about fifteen feet to the centre of the room, which is about one hundred by thirty feet. At the north end there is a magnificent pulpit in the Episcopal Church style. It is completed by beautiful drapery of alabaster stalactites of all colors, varying from white to pink-red, which overhang the beholder. Immediately under the pulpit is a lake of water, extending an unknown distance. On arriving at the centre of the first room we saw another still more splendid, two hundred by thirty feet, with the most beautiful alabaster overhanging us in every possible shape." There are several apartments, known respectively as Crystal Chapel, Dungeon of Enchantment, Julia Bower, and Picture Gallery.

Within this cave is a *spring*, which, according to S. Powers, Esq., is "literally freezing over with alabaster ice, about as thick as window-glass." He says: "I put my hand under it, and found it of the same thickness all over, and graining on the edges with particles not yet attached."

Visitors so wishing, may have the entire cave illuminated, thus adding to the beauty of the scene.

SUMMIT SODA SPRINGS.

Location.—Alpine County, California.

Access.—From San Francisco to Summit Station, on the Central Pacific Railroad, two hundred and forty-three miles east; thence by private conveyance.

Hotel.—Summit Hotel, at the station.

Analysis.—None. The water is said to possess a chalybeate taste, and precipitate a red deposit. It is highly charged with gas, supposed to be carbonic acid.

Remarks.—This is an exceedingly desirable resort for those who wish to breathe mountain-air, obtain a large amount of exercise, and enjoy camp-life. Summit Station is seven thousand and forty feet above the sea, and the surrounding mountain-tops attain a height of fifteen thousand and eighty-six feet. At the Summit Hotel horses are procured, and a delightful ride of some miles awaits the traveller. The road winds through dense forests of pines, cedars, firs, and tamarack; gay-colored wild-flowers deck the earth in profusion, while the openings in the wood disclose magnificent views of valleys and mountain-peaks.

Near the springs is abundance of sport; grouse, quail, ground-hogs, badger, and deer, are plenty, and easily secured.

A correspondent states that $100 or $150 would pay the entire expense of a party of three or four, for two or even four weeks.

TUSCAN SPRINGS.

Location.—Shasta County, California.

Access.—From Sacramento, *via* Oregon Division Central Pacific Railroad, north to Tehama, six hours; thence by stage.

Hotel.— ———.

Analysis.—No quantitative analysis has been made.

Remarks.—"The waters of the Tuscan Springs have considerable repute for their medicinal qualities, especially in the cure of rheumatic and syphilitic diseases. The temperature (October, 1862) was 76° Fahr. They contain common salt, carbonate of soda, borate of soda, salts of lime, and evolve some sulphuretted hydrogen and a large quantity of carburetted hydrogen, which is collected, partially purified, and burned for heating the water under the steam-baths."[1]

VICHY SPRINGS.

Location and Post-Office.—New Almaden, Santa Clara County, California.

Access.—From San Francisco, forty-seven miles south, to San José; thence twelve miles by stage.

Hotel.—Vichy Springs.

Analysis.— ———.

BARTLETT SPRINGS.

Location.—Colusa County, California.

Access.—Go to Lockport, Lake County; thence, by mountain-road, over a range several thousand feet high.

Hotel.— ———.

Analysis.— ———.

Remarks.—These springs first became known during the summer of 1871, and were one of the California sensations. Thousands underwent the fatiguing journey across the mountain in search of this new-found spring, which, like that which De Leon sought, was to restore them to youth and vigor. The rush thither shows there are numbers in every community ready for a Quixotic chase after the fountain of eternal youth.

ADAMS SPRINGS.

Location and Post-Office.—Adams Springs, Lake County, California.

Access.— ———.

Hotel.— ———.

Analysis.—None.

Remarks.—These springs were located in 1871. They are situated about two miles from Cobb Valley, between the Gey-

[1] "Geological Survey of California," vol. i., p. 208.

sers and Seigler's. The water is said to resemble that of the Vichy Springs, Santa Clara County.

NAPA SODA SPRINGS.

Location.—Napa County, California.

Access.—From San Francisco, by steamer, to Vallejo; thence, by Napa Valley Railroad, to Napa City; thence by stage.

Hotel.—Napa Springs.

Analysis.—None.

Remarks.—These waters are bottled, and consumed in the State in considerable quantities.

HARBINES SPRINGS.

Location.—Lake County, California.

Access.—From San Francisco, by Napa Valley Railroad, to Calistoga; thence by stage.

Hotel.—Harbines Springs.

Analysis.—None.

SAN RAFAEL SPRINGS.

Location and Post-Office.—San Rafael Springs, Marin County, California.

Access.—From San Francisco across the bay by steamboat.

Hotel.—San Rafael Springs.

Analysis.—None.

CRYSTAL SPRINGS.

Location.—San Mateo County, California.

Access.—Go to San Mateo, a station on the San José branch of the Central Pacific Railroad, about twenty miles south of San Francisco; thence by stage.

Hotel.—Crystal Springs.

Analysis.—None.

ST. LEON SPRINGS.

Location.—St. Leon, Three Rivers, Quebec, Canada.

Access.—By steamer, on the St. Lawrence, to Three Rivers; thence, twenty-six miles, by stage.

Hotel.— ———.

Analysis.— ———.

ROCKY MOUNTAIN SPRINGS.

Location.—Boulder County, Colorado.

Post-Office.—Jamestown, Boulder County, Colorado.

Access.—Go to Denver; thence, *via* Denver City & Boulder Valley Railroad, to Erie, thirty-four miles; thence twenty miles, by private conveyance (until the railroad is finished) to Boulder City; thence ten miles by private conveyance.

Hotel.—Mountain House.

Analysis.—A quantitative analysis states that the waters contain carbonate of soda, carbonate of magnesia, carbonate of iron, and free carbonic-acid gas.

Remarks.—These springs are located two miles from Jamestown, amid the mountains, at an elevation of six thousand five hundred feet above the sea.

VARENNES SPRINGS.

Location and Post-Office.—Varennes, Verchères County, Quebec, Canada.

Access.—By steamboat, from Montreal down the St. Lawrence, fifteen miles.

Hotel.— ———.

Analysis.—None.

ORANGE SPRING.

Location and Post-Office.—Orange Spring, Marion County, Florida.

Access.—Go by coast steamers to Pilatka, on the St. John's River; thence, by steamboat on Thursdays and Saturdays, about twenty-five miles south. Or go to Jacksonville, Florida; thence about sixty miles south, by boat, to Pilatka.

Hotel.—Ocklawaha House.

Analysis.—None.

BERKSHIRE SODA SPRING.

Location.—Berkshire County, Massachusetts.

Post-Office.—Great Barrington, Berkshire County, Massachusetts.

Access.—From Great Barrington, a station on the Housatonic Railroad, two and a half miles by carriage or stage.

Hotel.—Soda Springs House.

Analysis.—No quantitative analysis. Said to contain chlorine, carbonic acid, soda, and alumina.

Remarks.—These waters have been highly praised in dartrous eruptions.

The hotel is situated amid the mountains and hills of Berkshire—so celebrated for their quiet beauty.

BETHESDA SPRINGS.

Location.—Lumpkin County, Georgia.

Post-Office.—Dahlonega, Lumpkin County, Georgia.

Access.—Go to Atlanta; thence, *via* Atlanta & Richmond Airline Rail-way, fifty-three miles to Gainesville; thence twenty-nine miles, by stage, to the springs.

Hotel.—Bethesda Hotel.

Analysis.—None.

Remarks.—These springs, three in number, arise at the base of a spur of Cedar Mountain. The town of Dahlonega is nine miles distant.

TOGUS SPRINGS.

Location.—Kennebec County, Maine.

Post-Office.—National Asylum, Kennebec County, Maine.

Access.—By Rockland stage, from Augusta; distance, five miles.

Hotels.—None.

These springs—at one time quite a resort—were purchased by the Board of Managers of the National Asylum for Disabled Volunteer Soldiers. The place is now known as the Eastern Branch of the National Asylum.

FLINT'S SPRINGS.

Location and Post-Office.—Three Rivers, St. Joseph County, Michigan.

Access.—Go to White Pigeon, a station on the Lake Shore & Michigan Southern Railroad, one hundred and twenty miles east of Chicago; thence, twelve miles north by railroad, to Three Rivers.

Hotels.—Hatch, Three Rivers.

Analysis.—None has been made.

Remarks.—The town is pleasantly situated at the confluence of the St. Joseph, Rocky, and Portage Rivers. The population is over three thousand. There are good accommodations for bathing.

LATONIA SPRINGS.

Location and Post-Office.—Latonia Springs, Kenton County, Kentucky.

Access.—From Covington, Kentucky, opposite Cincinnati, four miles south by carriage.

Hotel.—Latonia Springs.

Analysis.—None has been made. The mineral ingredients are in feeble proportion.

GRAND LEDGE WELLS.

Location and Post-Office.—Grand Ledge, Eaton County, Michigan.

Access.—Grand Ledge is a station on the Detroit, Lansing & Lake Michigan Railroad, ninety-nine miles west of Detroit.

Hotel.— ———.

Analysis.—None has been made.

Remarks.—Grand Ledge is a town on the Grand River. The population is about one thousand. There are two wells here, and a bath-house.

BIRCH-DALE SPRINGS.

Location and Post-Office.—Concord, Merrimac County, New Hampshire.

Access.—The springs are nearly four miles from the State-house.

Hotel.—Birch-Dale Springs.

Analysis.—Extracts from an analysis by C. T. Jackson, M. D., of Boston, show these waters to contain salts of lime, sodium, phosphates, silicates, crenates, and a portion of iron and organic matter. The result as published, however, does not give the amount of each salt, and it is not possible to assign the water a place in the proper classification. There are four springs, named the Concord, Merrimac, Granite, and Penacook.

ABENAQUIS SPRINGS.

Location.—Walpole, Cheshire County, New Hampshire.

Post-Office.—Bellows Falls, Vermont.

Access.—From Boston, go to Bellows Falls, *via* Fitchburg Railroad and Cheshire Railroad, one hundred and twelve miles northwest; thence, by carriage, to the springs.

Hotel.—Fall Mountain.

Analysis.—None.

Remarks.—The springs are located at the base of Fall Mountain. From the hotel, there is a path to Table Rock, on the summit of the Mountain, from which there is an extended view of the valley of the Connecticut.

AMHERST SPRINGS.

Location.—Amherst, Hillsborough County, New Hampshire.

Access.—From Boston, *via* Boston, Lowell & Nashua Railroad, forty-eight miles north, to Amherst.

Hotel.—Amherst Spring.

Analysis.—None.

BRADFORD SPRINGS.

Location.—Merrimac County, New Hampshire.

Post-Office.—Bradford, Merrimac County, New Hampshire.

Access.—From Concord, New Hampshire, *via* Concord & Claremont Railroad, to Bradford, twenty-seven miles west; thence, by stage, to the springs.

Hotel.—Bradford Springs.

Analysis.—None.

VALLONIA SPRINGS.

Location and Post-Office.—Vallonia Springs, Broome County, New York.

Access.—From Albany, *via* Albany & Susquehanna Railroad, to Afton, one hundred and fourteen miles southwest; thence by stage.

Hotel.—Spring House.

Analysis.— ———.

Remarks.—This is a pleasant, quiet resort, surrounded by wild and romantic scenery, and affording fine opportunity for hunting and fishing.

PIEDMONT SPRINGS.

Location.—Grimes County, Texas.

Post-Office.—Millican, Brazos County, Texas.

Access.—Go to Houston; thence, *via* Houston & Texas Central Railroad, eighty miles northwest, to Millican; thence, six and a half miles, by stage, to the springs.

Hotel.—Piedmont Hotel.

Analysis.— ———.

ELGIN SPRING.

Location.—Addison County, Vermont.

Post-Office.—Vergennes, Addison County, Vermont.

Access.—Vergennes is a station on the Rutland Division of the Vermont Central Railroad, ninety-nine miles northwest of Bellows Falls.

Hotel.— ———.

Analysis.— ———.

CAPPERS SPRINGS.

Location.—Frederick County, Virginia.

Access.—From Baltimore to Harper's Ferry, eighty-one miles west; thence, *via* Winchester Branch, to Winchester, thirty-two miles; thence, seventeen miles west, to springs.

Hotel.—Cappers Springs.

Analysis.— ———.

BLUE RIDGE SPRINGS.

Location.—Botetourt County, Virginia.

Access.—From the line of the Virginia & Tennessee Railroad.

Hotel.—Blue Ridge.

Analysis.—No accurate quantitative analysis has been made. They are said to closely resemble the Alleghany Springs of Virginia.

Remarks.—These springs are situated near the summit of the Blue Ridge, at an elevation of thirteen hundred feet above the level of the sea.

PARKERSBURG MINERAL WELLS.

Location and Post-Office.—Mineral Wells, Wood County, West Virginia.

Access.—Go to Parkersburg, a terminus of the Baltimore & Ohio Railroad, on the Ohio River, either by Baltimore & Ohio Railroad or Marietta & Cincinnati Railroad; thence six and a half miles by stage.

Hotel.—Parshall's.

Analysis.—A very imperfect analysis shows this water to contain, as the principal constituents, sulphate of magnesia, sulphate of soda, with some iron. The water is also charged with carbonic-acid gas, according to the analysis. Temperature, 46° Fahr. The water is agreeable to the taste.

Remarks.—The wells are very pleasantly located on high, dry, and rolling land, on the margin of a beautiful valley, through which runs Tygart's Creek. The surrounding country affords the sportsman many opportunities for recreation.

ORKNEY SPRINGS.

Location and Post-Office.—Orkney Springs, Shenandoah County, Virginia.

Access.—From Washington, *via* Orange, Alexandria & Manassas Railroad, to Mount Jackson, one hundred and twelve miles; thence, twelve miles west, by stage.

Hotel.—Orkney Springs.

Analysis.— ———.

SHANNONDALE SPRINGS.

Location.—Jefferson County, West Virginia.

Access.—From Baltimore, *via* Baltimore & Ohio Railroad, and Winchester & Strasburg Branch, to Charlestown, ninety-one miles west; thence five and a half miles.

Hotel.— ———

Analysis.—An examination of one hundred grains of the solid contents, by Dr. De Butts, of Baltimore, showed these waters to be similar in composition to the Alleghany Springs, though it is impossible to say whether the substances exist in the same degree of concentration.

EUROPEAN SPAS.

CHAPTER XVIII.

ALKALINE WATERS.

Vichy.—France, department of Allier, one hundred and sixteen miles south of Paris.

Ems.—Germany, duchy of Nassau, three and three-quarter miles east of Coblentz.

Fachingen.—Germany, duchy of Nassau.

ANALYSIS.

One pint contains—	VICHY. Grande Grille. 105.8° Fahr. Bouquet.	FACHINGEN. 50° Fahr. Fresenius.	EMS. Kesselbrunnen. 115° Fahr. Fresenius.
SOLIDS.	Grains.	Grains.	Grains.
Carbonate of potassa	2.04	....	....
Carbonate of soda	26.00	19.4763	10.5379
Carbonate of magnesia	1.38	1.3580	0.8510
Carbonate of iron	0.02	0.0801	0.0202
Carbonate of manganese	trace.	....	0.0085
Carbonate of lime	2.31	2.0110	1.2591
Carbonate of lithia	....	0.0004	....
Carbonate of strontia	0.01	0.0007	} 0.0080
Carbonate of baryta	....	....	
Chloride of sodium	4.10	4.5574	7.7705
Chloride of calcium	.. .	0.0034	....
Sulphate of potassa	....	....	0.3937
Sulphate of soda	2.29	0.1372	0.0061
Phosphate of soda	0.78	0.0506	....
Phosphate of alumina	....	0.0003	0.0096
Phosphate of lime	....	0.0004	....
Phosphate of lithia	....	0.0002	....
Phosphate of silica	....	0.2610	....
Fluoride of calcium	....	0.0027	....
Borate of soda	trace.	....	....
Arseniate of soda	0.01	....	....
Silica	0.05	....	0.3648
Total	38.99	27.9397	21.2194
GASES.	Cubic in.	Cubic in.	Cubic in.
Carbonic acid	14.74	32.975	6.788
Nitrogen	....	0.025	....

Vichy.—This is probably the best known of all mineral waters, the fame of its baths and its cures having penetrated to every portion of the globe. Its essential power consists in the unusual combination of a high degree of thermality, with an exceedingly large amount of alkali, and sufficient carbonic-acid gas to render it palatable. The springs—of which there are nine in use—are not all of the same temperature. They range from 53° to 110° Fahr. In the analysis given the bi-carbonates are reduced to carbonates. The original analysis shows thirty-seven and a half grains of bicarbonate of soda in each pint of water, and the total solids amount to fifty-four grains, nearly one drachm. In chemical constitution the different sources vary but little.

The action of the Vichy waters varies with the individual. In many cases they are diuretic, while some persons are always purged while using them. Perspiration if absent is usually developed, but seldom excited in a high degree. One fact, however, is well established, that, in the medical administration of these waters, their efficacy in no wise depends on the production of their physiological effects. Like all alkaline waters, they render the urine alkaline.

This water is especially applicable to *dyspepsia*—simple dyspepsia—characterized by laborious digestion, by disgust of food, by vertigo, acidity, and constipation. In dyspepsias accompanied by catarrh, or in gastralgia, other waters prove more efficacious. *Diseases of the liver* are most satisfactorily influenced by these waters, the bile is liquefied, and flows more freely, and biliary calculi (gall-stones) are discharged without pain. In the case of *gall-stones*, one or two seasons at the waters frequently correct the morbid conditions that produce them, so that the patient is free from attacks for years. In *regular gout*, presenting in plethoric subjects, these waters have achieved a world-wide reputation. The treatment of this disease, however, by these waters, requires close circumspection, lest the regular form of the disease be converted into irregular or metastatic gout.

These waters have long constituted one of the admitted

remedies in *diabetes*, and the combination of thermal baths found there favors the action of the waters in a marked degree. Under the use of Vichy waters all trace of sugar sometimes disappears from the urine, the appetite and strength are restored, sleep becomes natural, thirst diminishes, and constipation ceases. In this way life is frequently prolonged for years. The water and baths have also proved of exceeding value in that grave condition known as *paludal cachexia*, resulting from prolonged exposure to miasma.

The Vichy bath is usually formed one-half of mineral water and one-half of ordinary water, this combination proving, according to Durand-Fardel, superior to the mineral water alone. Of private baths there are three hundred, so that from two thousand five hundred to three thousand baths per day may be given.

The surroundings of Vichy are thus described by Constantin James: "Those who arrive at Vichy to-day (1869)—having not seen the place for ten years—feel the same surprise that those do who visit Paris after having been absent for an equal time. Old Vichy is lost in the midst of beautiful villas and splendid hotels, which surround it on every side. And there, where the river Allier overflowed its banks and deposited insalubrious soil, has appeared a delightful park, with its sanded walks, verdant shade, and magnificent lake. And the assembly halls, yesterday so humble and so modest, are replaced to-day by a *casino* which rivals, if it does not surpass, the most beautiful in Germany."

The popularity of Vichy is attested by the fact that twenty-three thousand persons visited the resort in 1868.

Ems.—The waters of Ems are limpid, soft, and unctuous to the touch. They deposit large quantities of solid incrustations, and a brown-and-green confervoid growth forms in the reservoirs. As many as twenty-one springs have been counted at Ems.

When these waters are taken in moderate quantity they cause an increased urinary secretion, and augment perspiration. The urine becomes promptly alkaline. They tend, as a rule, to cause constipation. If taken in considerable quantity they readily produce gastro-intestinal irritation, a result which is to be guarded against.

The Ems water is especially adapted, according to Spengler, to the treatment of *all chronic catarrhal affections.* In this class we have *chronic bronchitis*, of the form accompanied by exacerbations of the cough morning and night. Cases of this kind are cured by this water. If the water alone proves too exciting, it is usual to mix it with milk or whey. In those cases of bronchitis accompanying gout, Ems is the best resort. *Granular pharyngitis*, or clergyman's sore-throat as it is often called, is peculiarly influenced in a favorable manner by this water. For the treatment of this condition it is usual to mix the water with whey, and also to apply the gas from the springs—carbonic acid and nitrogen—directly to the diseased surfaces by means of tubes. In *catarrh of the stomach*, and also *catarrh of the hepatic ducts*, the water is exceedingly serviceable. Chronic *catarrh of the bladder*, accompanied by renal calculi, or gravel, is equally subject to favorable action.

These waters have a well-established reputation in *uterine catarrh.* For this purpose the internal use of the water is combined with the ascending douche. The arrangements for the use of the douche, in this disease, are of the most perfect kind. Althaus thus describes the condition of the uterus in which the waters are especially successful: "The vaginal portion, and the cervix uteri, are in such instances generally dark red, hyperæmic, hypertrophied, and either painful to the touch or not; the whole tissue of the uterus being harder and firmer than it is in healthy women. In many cases there is also displacement of this organ, and dysmenorrhœa or amenorrhœa is mostly present. The mucous membrane of the uterus secretes a considerable quantity of puriform mucus, and the cervix uteri is filled with transparent mucus. Sterility, cardialgia, habitual sickness and vomiting, constipation, and various hysterical symptoms, are generally the consequence of this condition of the womb. All these symptoms are often relieved bv the Ems waters."

Ems is an exceedingly attractive watering-place, possessing all the comforts to which the wealthy are accustomed, and without the incessant commotion that characterizes many of these resorts. The beautiful Gothic castle of Stolzenfels, on the Rhine, and the fortress of Ehrenbreitstein, are not far distant.

Fachingen.—These waters are used in the diseases to which the Vichy waters are applicable. The spring is not a resort. The water is bottled and sold largely throughout Europe, as much as half a million bottles being consumed annually.

SALINE WATERS.

Homburg.—Germany, Hesse-Homburg, nine miles north from Frankfort.

Kissingen.—Bavaria, twenty-eight miles north of Würtzburg.

Wiesbaden.—Germany, duchy of Nassau, five and a half miles northwest from Mayence.

Bourbonne.—France, department of Haute-Marne, one hundred and seventy-three miles west from Paris.

Selters.—Germany, duchy of Nassau, twenty-five miles north of Mayence.

Homburg.—This is one of the most popular of German watering-places, having been sought, however, more for the attractions of society, and the gaming-table, than the waters. But since gaming is now forbidden, it is probable the waters will receive more attention. The water taken in doses of three or four glasses usually proves cathartic, but without causing debility of the intestines. These effects are readily explained by the ingredients. The Homburg waters are strongly saline, with a considerable quantity of iron. They are especially applicable to *catarrhal dyspepsia* in anæmic subjects, etc., cases of *abdominal plethora* and *engorgement of the liver*, occurring in weak, irritable, and scrofulous persons, and to whom the use of purging-waters might prove detrimental—to cases of *tumid spleen*, arising from ague, or suppression of the hemorrhoidal or catamenial flow—to cases of *chlorosis* and *anœmia* in scrofulous patients, for whom the pure chalybeates might prove too constipating, or too exciting to the circulation.

[1] *See* Analysis, page 346.

ANALYSIS.

One pint contains—	HOMBURG. Elizabethbrunnen. 50° Fahr. Liebig.	KISSINGEN. Ragoczi. 51° Fahr. Liebig.	WIESBADEN. Kochbrunnen. 155.75° Fahr. Fresenius.	BOURBONNE. Fontaine Chaude. 149° Fahr. Chevallier.	SELTERS. 62¼° Fahr. Hastner.
SOLIDS.	Grains.	Grains.	Grains.	Grains.	Grains.
Carbonate of soda	....	....	....	....	6.778
Carbonate of magnesia.	2.01	....	0.08	....	1.516
Carbonate of iron	0.46	0.24	0.04	....	0.079
Carbonate of manganese	....	....	0.004	....	0.002
Carbonate of lime......	10.99	8.14	3.21	2.264	1.852
Chloride of potassium..	....	2.20	1.12	....	0.289
Chloride of sodium	79.15	44.71	52.50	46.110	17.228
Chloride of magnesium.	7.79	2.33	1.57	....	....
Chloride of calcium....	7.77	....	3.62	5.683	....
Chloride of ammonium.	....	....	0.13	....	....
Chloride of lithium	....	0.15	0.001	....	....
Sulphate of soda	0.38	....	....	....	0.261
Sulphate of magnesia ..	....	4.50	....	....	....
Sulphate of lime.......	....	2.99	0.69	5.993	0.261
Phosphate of soda.....	....	....	....	....	0.0002
Phosphate of alumina..	....	....	....	....	0.0004
Phosphate of lime......	....	0.04	0.003	....	....
Iodide of sodium......	....	trace.	....	....	....
Bromide of potassium.	....	....	....	0.384	0.0002
Bromide of sodium....	....	0.06	....	....	....
Bromide of magnesium	....	....	0.03	....	....
Fluoride of calcium....	....	....	....	....	0.0016
Nitrate of soda........	....	0.07	....	....	....
Arseniate of lime......	....	....	0.001	....	....
Silicate of alumina	....	....	0.004	....	....
Silica.................	0.82	0.09	0.46	....	0.250
Total..............	108.87	65.52	63.463	60.484	28.5184
GASES.	Cubic in.	Cubic in.	Cubic in.		Cubic in.
Carbonic acid	48.46	41.77	16.7	....	30.
Oxygen..............	....	....	....	....	0.0046
Nitrogen..............	....	....	0.10	....	0.0285
Ammonia..............	....	0.007	....	....	....

Homburg is a small village situated on the declivity of a hill at the eastern extremity of the chain of the Taunus. The Kursaal is without contradiction one of the most beautiful establishments of the kind. The interior is ornamented with marble columns, beautiful frescos, and elegant paintings. The springs are five in number, and vary in temperature from 50° to 53½° Fahr. The *Kaiserbrunnen* contains 104 grains of chloride of sodium, one-half grain of carbonate of iron, and 109 cubic inches of carbonic-acid gas, in each pint.

Kissingen.—There is a close resemblance between the waters of Kissingen and Homburg. Kissingen, however, has a far more decided reputation in the cure of disease, and much more attention is given to medical treatment. These waters, according to Prof. Seegen, slightly increase secretion from all the mucous surfaces, particularly those of the digestive tract; they increase the appetite, accelerate the circulation of the blood, and revive the nutritious functions. They are at once aperient, tonic, and exciting.

The waters of Kissingen are adapted to *catarrhal dyspepsia*, accompanied with constipation in anæmic subjects. In cases of this kind they are excellent. At Kissingen, much attention is given to the treatment of *gout*, and for certain conditions of the disease the waters are valuable. Plethoric persons suffering from this malady, are favorably influenced by a combination of Ragoczi and the bitter water. Those suffering from irregular gout, with structural lesions of the joints, the bones, the heart and blood-vessels, are better treated by the waters of Wiesbaden or Töplitz. In plethoric persons of middle age, and sedentary habits, suffering from *hyperœmia of the liver*, the Ragoczi and bitter waters of Kissingen, combined, frequently effect a cure. These waters are also favorable in *icterus* due to catarrh of the mucous membrane of the duodenum. It should be mentioned that if in catarrhal dyspepsia there is any inflammatory condition of the stomach, the cold acidulous saline waters, such as Homburg and Kissingen, should not be employed, but the waters of Wiesbaden in small doses. Many maladies are favorably treated at Kissingen that are not amenable to the saline waters alone, because of the bitter water, which adds to the resources. This is a purgative water, and in one pint contains—46 grains sulphate of soda, 39 grains sulphate of magnesia, 61 grains chloride of sodium, 30 grains chloride of magnesium, and 6 cubic inches carbonic-acid gas.

Kissingen is located in a fertile valley on the banks of the rapid river Saal. The climate is salubrious, and all the necessities of the invalid are well provided for. Neither are social attractions wanting. The Bavarian Government for many years annually added improvements, until Kissingen became one of the most popular watering-places.

Wiesbaden.—Here are the best thermal-saline waters in Europe. The waters are peculiar, tasting like warm highly-salted chicken-broth, and, when collected in reservoirs, presenting a somewhat yellowish color. Besides the ingredients given in the analysis, they contain a small proportion of organic matter, which has not been closely studied. The physiological action of the waters, according to Dr. Braun, is as follows: In a moderate dose, about a pint, they increase the flow of saliva, give a sense of warmth to the stomach, and produce moderate alvine evacuation; in quantities of a quart to three pints, and taken but slightly warm, they prove decidedly purgative. From one to three hours after drinking even small quantities of the water, the flow of urine is increased, and its chemical composition altered; more considerable quantities of chloride of sodium, uric acid, and urea, are eliminated, than if a corresponding quantity of ordinary water were taken. Under the influence of these waters the fæces are fluidified, and contain more biliary constituents, menstruation becomes more abundant, and the flow of milk is promoted, perspiration is increased, and the pulse accelerated. The effect of the waters on the urinary secretion was closely investigated by Drs. Neubauer and Genth. They first determined the quantity of urine and urinary solids, under usual habits of life, for periods of five and eight days. Then for five days they took baths of the water at 95° Fahr., and examined the urine, and then for eight days they took the same baths, and drank four hundred and five hundred cubic centimetres respectively. The quantity of urine under ordinary circumstances—1,414 in one, and 1,252 in the other—rose, while taking the baths alone, to 1,707 in the one, and 1,305 in the other. While taking baths and drinking the water, it rose to 2,050 and 1,547 respectively; the urea rose from 33 to 39.6 and 42.8 grains; chloride of sodium, from 14.742 to 16.467 and 23.678; chloride of ammonium, from 2.072 to 2.344 and 2.722, and in similar ratio for the other constituents. During the course of the experiments, the weight of the body did not undergo any particular change.

The waters and baths of Wiesbaden are especially employed in *gout*, and *rheumatism*. They are advantageously used in all forms of gout, unless inflammatory symptoms be present at the time, but are especially adapted to cases of anomalous or irregular gout. When external manifestations have almost ceased, and the disease tends to attack internal organs, it is said these waters will recall it to the point of external attack. For action on the kidneys, the water is taken in doses of two to four tumblersful, and cooled before drinking, but little exercise being taken in the mean time; but if diaphoresis is desired it should be taken hot, and considerable exercise in the intervals of drinking.

In chronic rheumatism, *facial neuralgia*, and *sciatica*, these waters are frequently curative, and cases of *paralysis* also improve under their use. In these cases baths and douches are freely employed. *Deforming rheumatism* (*rhumatisme noueux*) is also very much relieved by this treatment. Wiesbaden also enjoys a deserved reputation for the relief of *contraction* of the joints, and old *gunshot-wounds* complicated by the presence of the ball, or necrosis.

Wiesbaden is situated on the southerly exposure of the Taunus, in a valley enclosed by opposing spurs of the chain. The climate is notably temperate, so that treatment may be pursued in the early spring, and late in autumn, and even through the winter months. There are twenty-nine springs at Wiesbaden supplying a volume of hot water that is utilized for bathing in every conceivable form. The mineral mud-bath is also employed. This is also a station where the whey-cure is administered.

Wiesbaden was known to the ancient Romans under the name of Aquæ Mattiacæ, and is described by Pliny. At the present day it is probably the most popular resort in Germany; sixty-three thousand persons are said to have visited there during the present year—1872.

Baden-Baden.—The waters of this spa are mild thermal-saline waters of 155° Fahr., and containing sixteen grains chloride of sodium to the pint. They are chiefly used for bathing, the waters of other springs, as Homburg and Kissingen, being drunk. There is a *muriated-lithia* spring at Baden containing, according to Bunsen, two and three-tenths grains chloride of lithium in the pint. It does not appear, however, to have justified expectations as a curative in gout and lithiasis. Baden-Baden is charmingly located on the banks of the Oos, just at the entrance of the Black Forest. The valley is exceedingly picturesque. Heretofore, the principal attractions have been the gaming-tables and *fêtes*. This resort was frequented by the Romans, and was known to them by the name of Civitas Aurelia Aquensis. Numerous relics of sculpture, of piscinæ, and of vapor-baths, testify to this fact.

Bourbonne.—This water is mildly laxative when taken cold or tepid. At the natural temperature it does not prove cathartic unless taken in large doses, and even then this effect is only temporary, and succeeded by constipation. As a rule, the purgative effect is not sought in treatment.

There is a decided analogy between the application of these waters and those of Wiesbaden. They prove valuable in *chronic rheumatism*, accompanied with contractions, with enlargement of the joints, and deposits; also in *paralysis*. Especially are the waters suitable to these maladies when they are allied to a scrofulous diathesis. So certain are these waters as a remedy in *false anchylosis*, in *contractions*, in old *gunshot-wounds* and *necrosis*, that the French Government has erected a military hospital capable of accommodating one hundred officers and three hundred soldiers.

Bourbonne is agreeably situated at an altitude of nine hundred feet, on the brow of a gently-inclined hill which commands a distant view of the range of the Vosges. There are three springs supplying a large number of baths of every description. The mineral mud-bath is also a resource of Bourbonne. Its principal constituents in 100 parts are silicic acid 64 parts, oxide of iron 5, lime 6, and vegetable and animal matter 15.

Selters.—This water is cool and refreshing in taste, with a slight trace of iron, alkali, and salt in the flavor. It is chiefly employed as a table-drink, and under the name *seltzer* is known and imitated (*inferiorly*, as a rule) the world over. There are no establishments at the spring. Two million bottles are sold annually.

BRINE-BATHS.

Kreuznach.—Rhenish Prussia, seven miles south of Bingen.

Nauheim.—Germany, Hesse-Cassel, fifteen miles north from Frankfort.

ANALYSIS.

One pint contains—	KREUZNACH.		NAUHEIM.
	Elisenquelle. 54.5° Fahr. Löwig.	Oranienquelle. 54.5° Fahr. Liebig.	Kurbrunnen. 71.3° Fahr. Bromeis.
SOLIDS.	Grains.	Grains.	Grains.
Carbonate of magnesia	0.106	0.180	....
Carbonate of iron	....	0.356	0.145
Carbonate of manganese	....	....	0 021
Carbonate of lime	1.693	0.255	8.028
Chloride of potassium	0.624	0.460	4.047
Chloride of sodium	72.883	108.705	109.923
Chloride of magnesium	4.071	....	2.155
Chloride of calcium	13.889	22.749	8.215
Chloride of lithium	0.613	....	...
Sulphate of lime	....	....	0.740
Phosphate of alumina	0.025	0.095	....
Iodide of magnesium	0.035	0.012	....
Bromide of magnesium	0.278	1.780	0.295
Silica	0.129	0.999	0.115
Total	93.846	135.541	133.684
GAS.			Cubic in.
Carbonic acid	....	....	31.2

Kreuznach.—These were the first waters of the kind to be medicinally employed in Germany, and the success which attended their use has caused the development of numerous waters of similar character. The Elisenquelle is the only spring used internally. When taken in small doses, it tends to constipation, at the same time diuretic; but in large doses it is purgative.

These waters have been used in *scrofula* with the most decided success, especially the forms accompanied with infiltration of the glands. Scrofulous diseases of the skin, such as lupus and sycosis, are also favcrably influenced. The water is also said to possess a resolutive action in fibroid tumors of the uterus. According to Scanzoni, the good results in these cases are chiefly due to the reduction of the size of the womb, thus controlling hæmorrhage, uterine colic, and other symptoms. In ovarian tumors, Scanzoni discountenances the use of these waters when symptoms of congestion are present, and the tumor is rapidly enlarging. In other conditions, however, the growth of the tumor may be decidedly retarded. In certain cases of tertiary syphilis, associated with scrofula, this water proves exceedingly efficacious. Besides the spring-water, graduated brine and mother-lye are employed. The following is the composition of these solutions:

One pint contains—	Graduated Brine. Dr. Wiesbaden.	Mother-lye. Polsdorf.
SOLIDS.	Gra'ns.	Grains.
Chloride of potassium	11.28	168.31
Chloride of sodium	1,311.89	226.37
Chloride of magnesium	73.22	230.81
Chloride of aluminum	....	1.56
Chloride of calcium	241.00	1,789.97
Chloride of lithium	....	7.95
Perchloride of iron	....	traces.
Sulphate of soda	....	traces.
Iodide of sodium	....	0.05
Iodide of magnesium	0.68	....
Bromide of sodium	....	59.14
Bromide of magnesium	5.00	....
Total	1,642.97	2,484.16

The following is the usual method of Kreuznach treatment. The patient drinks daily from twenty to thirty ounces of the Elisenquelle; children less, according to age. An hour after drinking the water, a bath is taken at from 86° to 92° Fahr. in temperature. In the beginning of the treatment, the simple brine-bath is used, but gradually, as the system becomes accustomed, the mother-lye is employed. From one to fifty, and even a hundred quarts of the mother-lye are added to the bath; but, as soon as symptoms of excitement and saturation occur, the quantity is diminished, or even entirely withdrawn. The duration of the bath is from a quarter to three-quarters of an hour, and, in severe cases of scrofula and skin-disease, two baths per day are sometimes given. It is customary while in the bath to rub the diseased parts with a soft sponge or brush. Cloths soaked in brine are also applied, especially to enlarged lymphatic glands.

Kreuznach is situated in the valley of the Nahe, on the

left side of the Rhine. The principal wells and baths are on a wooded island in the Nahe. Pleasant excursions may be made in the vicinity.

Nauheim.—The waters of Nauheim, like strong saline waters in general, tend in small quantities to produce constipation, and in large quantities to cause purgation. The baths readily produce the phenomena of eruptions, known as *la poussée.* The large quantity of carbonic acid in these waters renders them more palatable than saline waters of equal strength usually are, and the temperature, ranging as high as 99°.9 Fahr., makes them especially applicable for bathing purposes. There are five springs, yielding a large volume of water. Similar method of treatment is pursued here to that of Kreuznach, graduated brines and mother-lye being employed. In addition, there is an establishment especially devoted to administration of the carbonic-acid bath.

The application of this water is like that of Kreuznach, especially adapted to scrofula, and diseases allied to scrofulous conditions, declaring themselves in young persons. Catarrh of the vagina in scrofulous and anæmic persons, and scrofulous diseases of the bones, are frequently cured by these baths. Brine-baths are also of utility for the purpose of promoting absorption of rheumatic exudations. Indeed, the rheumatic diathesis seems sometimes to be overcome by their use.

Nauheim is situated on the northeast slope of the Taunus, and is a pleasant drive from Homburg. It is comparatively a newly-developed resort, only dating back some eighteen years; neverthelesss, every arrangement for securing the full benefits of the warm salt-water has been made, and the facilities for social enjoyment are quite complete.

SULPHUR-WATERS.

Aix-la-Chapelle.—Rhenish Prussia, forty-seven miles west from Cologne.

Aix-les-Bains.—Savoy, ten and a half miles north from Chambéry.

Barèges.—France, department of Hautes-Pyrénées, one hundred and twelve miles south of Bordeaux.

Bagnères-de-Luchon.—France, department of Haute-Garonne, one hundred and twenty-five miles south of Bordeaux.

Nenndorf.—Germany, principality of Hesse, 12 miles west from Hanover.

Meinberg.—Germany, principality of Lippe-Detmold, thirty-eight miles south of Hanover.

ANALYSIS.

One pint contains—	AIX-LA-CHAPELLE. Kaiserquelle. 131° Fahr. Liebig.	NENNDORF. Trinkquelle. 53.6° Fahr. Bunsen.	MEINBERG. Schwefelquelle. 48° Fahr. Brandes.
SOLIDS.	Grains.	Grains.	Grains.
Carbonate of soda	4.995	....	....
Carbonate of magnesia	0.895	....	0.172
Carbonate of iron	0.078	....	0.008
Carbonate of lime	1.217	8.881	2.149
Carbonate of lithia	0.002	....	....
Carbonate of strontia	0.002	....	....
Chloride of sodium	20.271	....	....
Choride of magnesium	....	1.851	1.035
Sulphate of potassa	1.186	0.339	0.005
Sulphate of soda	2.171	4.549	5.844
Sulphate of magnesia	....	2.818	1.733
Sulphate of lime	....	8.121	8.835
Sulphate of strontia	....	....	0.008
Sulphuret of sodium	0.073	....	0.067
Sulphuret of calcium (hydrated)	....	0.555	....
Phosphate of alumina	....	....	0.010
Iodide of sodium	0.004	....	....
Bromide of sodium	0.028	....	....
Silica	0.508	0.162	0.120
Organic matter	0.577	....	....
Total	31.502	21.276	19.486
GASES.	Per cent.[1]	Cubic in.	Cubic in.
Carbonic acid	30.89	5.25	2.31
Sulphuretted hydrogen	0.31	1.28	0.61
Carburetted hydrogen	1.82	0.05	....
Nitrogen	66.98	0.61	0.40
Oxygen	....	....	0.02

Aix-la-Chapelle.—The waters of these famous thermals possess an alkaline, saltish, and sulphurous taste. Taken internally, they are especially diuretic and diaphoretic.

The treatment at Aix-la-Chapelle consists both in drinking the water—that of the Kaiserquelle being chiefly used—and bathing, to which the waters are eminently adapted by their temperature. The bathing arrangements are excellent, and the attendants have an unsurpassed reputation for dexterity in application of douches and shampooing. The douches have a fall of from twenty-five to thirty feet, and range in temperature from 89° to 100° Fahr. The bath is usually given at from 92° to 96° Fahr.

These waters possess a high reputation in the treatment

[1] Percentage of gases ascending from the water.

of *chronic rheumatism, chronic metallic poisoning*, and *diseases of the skin*. Of the latter, it is especially to humid dartrous diseases that they are applied.

ANALYSIS.

One pint contains—	AIX-LE-BAINS. Eaux de Soufre. 108°–111° Fahr. Bonjean.	BARÉGES. Boucheries. 64.4° Fahr.[1] Latour.	BAGNÈRES-DE-LUCHON. La Reine. 131° Fahr. Filhol.
SOLIDS.	Grains.	Grains.	Grains.
Carbonate of soda	....	....	traces.
Carbonate of magnesia	0.188	....	....
Carbonate of iron	0.064	....	....
Carbonate of lime	1.084	0.014	....
Carbonate of strontia	traces.	....	....
Chloride of sodium	0.057	0.234	0.492
Chloride of magnesium	0.125	0.292	....
Sulphate of potassa	....	....	0.068
Sulphate of soda	0.701	0.147	0.162
Sulphate of magnesia	0.257	....	....
Sulphate of alumina	0.400	....	....
Sulphate of iron	traces.	[2] 0.080	....
Sulphate of lime	0.117	....	0.286
Sulphuret of sodium	....	0.116	0.401
Sulphuret of iron	....	....	0.020
Sulphuret of manganese	....	....	0.024
Sulphuret of copper	....	....	traces.
Hyposulphite of soda	....	....	traces.
Phosphates of lime and alumina and fluoride of calcium	0.017	....	....
Iodide of potassium	traces.	....	....
Iodide of sodium	....	0.007	traces.
Silicate of soda	....	0.146	traces.
Silicate of magnesia	..	....	0.060
Silicate of alumina	....	} 0.080 {	0.180
Silicate of lime	....		0.086
Silica	0.036	....	traces.
Alumina	....	....	traces.
Phosphates	....	....	traces.
Bituminous matter and glairine.	Undetermined.	} 0.087	
Loss	0.087		....
Total	8.133	1.203	1.724
GASES.	Cubic in.		
Carbonic acid	0.89	....	....
Sulphuretted hydrogen	0.82	....	traces.
Nitrogen	19.04	....	....

Aix-la-Chapelle was an early resort of the Romans, and known to them by the name of Aquæ Grani. Numerous remains of ancient thermal establishments are found. Subsequently it was the favorite abode of the great Charlemagne. It is said that he luxuriated in the thermal baths, and was accustomed to bathe in public with the officers of his court, and even held councils of state in the baths. The city, which has

[1] Some of the Barèges springs reach 111° Fahr.

[2] With carbonate of iron.

now shrunk into small compass compared with its former limits, shows outward evidence in many portions of the former presence of the great Frank, now dead a thousand years. His remains are sacredly guarded in the treasury of the ancient cathedral, and are shown to the public once in seven years. One of the principal baths—that which he frequented, and which was a favorite with the great Napoleon—is known as the Kaiserbad. This establishment is veritably a "thermal palace."

Aix-les-Bains.—The use of these waters is almost exclusively external. For the employment of the waters in this way there are unsurpassed facilities. The flow of the water is exceedingly large, and the grand bath establishment, built in 1773 by Victor-Amédée III., received such additions in 1854 that it is now one of the most complete in Europe. The number and variety of douches are said to be unequalled.

The application of these waters is to all those diseases which are benefited by thermal baths, such as chronic rheumatism, diseases of the skin, syphilis, paralysis, independent of organic lesion of the nerve-centres, etc.

Aix is quite a pretty village, situated in an agreeable valley, bounded to the south and north by mountains. The climate is exceedingly salubrious.

This resort again reminds us of the pleasure taken by the Romans in thermal baths. Many relics of their residence here are found in the village, and the place was known to them as Aquæ Gratianæ. To-day the resort equals, if it does not surpass, its ancient splendor, and offers many attractions to the valetudinarian.

Barèges.—These waters, taken internally, possess an exciting action. The effect is upon the nervous system, and especially on the circulation, compared by Borden to that of strong coffee, but easily developing, both in the well and in the sick, a febrile condition. Although these waters have given name to the soluble organic principle of mineral waters, they contain but a small proportion according to analyses. The naming of the substance was but accidental, Longchamp being engaged with these waters at the time he made the discovery.[1] The analysis of the waters has not been as exact as the science of hydrology demands, that of the spring given in the table being only less imperfect than others. The composition of l'Entrée (103° Fahr.), according to Henry, is as follows, in one pint: Sulphuret of sodium, 0.262 grains; sulphate of soda, 0.219; carbonate and silicate of soda, 0.175; organic matter (iodine, lime, and magnesia), traces.

The waters of Barèges enjoy a celebrity in the treatment of *gunshot-wounds*, and bringing to the surface *unextracted balls* and pieces of *shell*, that has penetrated every corner of Europe, so much so that they have been termed *les Eaux d'Arquebusade.* Says Constantin James: "One should not despair of the curative action of the water because the foreign body appears too voluminous, or too deeply imbedded in the tissues; nothing seems to limit their power." The French Government has a military hospital at this resort. The waters are used internally, and in the form of douches and baths. The douche having a fall of only three feet, the effect cannot be attributed to percussion. The water is also efficacious in certain *scrofulous conditions*, such as diseases of the bones, caries, chronic ostitis, fistulous tracts, abscess, and ulcers. It is not to young scrofulous subjects that these waters are adapted, but, says Durand-Fardel, "if the scrofula is already an old disease, if the patient approaches the age when the disease tends to become extinct, if the capital indication is to treat an old manifestation, born of the diathesis and persisting less because of the early impulsion than by inability of the organism to produce resolution, then the waters of Barèges appear to us the most efficacious of all sulphur-waters." In dartrous diseases of the skin, and in syphilis, they prove of utility. Because of the excessive excitement usually produced by the baths and douches, the patient frequently can take them only every other day, and the duration of treatment is from five to eight weeks.

Barèges is situated near the summit of the Pyrenees, at an

[1] "Chimie Hydrologique," par Lefort, Paris, 1859, p. 203.

elevation of four thousand two hundred feet, surrounded by wild and unattractive scenery, and overhung by ice-crowned peaks. The climate is exceedingly changeable, in the midst of summer a suffocating heat in the morning being sometimes succeeded by icy cold in the afternoon. Only invalids frequent the place.

Bagnères-de-Luchon.—The waters of Luchon, taken in doses of two to four glasses, augment the appetite, and often produce constipation, rendering the excrementitious matter black or brown. The internal functions are excited even in the absence of baths, the secretion of urine being augmented. They frequently do not rest well on the stomach, producing nausea and sulphurous eructations. Some persons cannot take them without the addition of syrups or infusions. The baths even, at moderate temperature, act decidedly upon the skin. After a quarter of an hour's immersion the cutaneous surface is swollen, and severe itching is felt. Sometimes the irritation is sufficient to produce slight eruptions, which, however, disappear soon afterward. Baths of elevated temperature often determine severe eruptions, *la poussée.*

These waters are celebrated for the cure of dartrous diseases of the skin. Of these diseases they prove of especial service in *pustulous eczema*, in *psoriasis*, *pityriasis*, *ichthyosis*, etc. For the treatment of secondary and tertiary *syphilis*, with the various *syphilides*, they are perhaps superior to any other European sulphur-waters. The waters also prove efficacious in scrofulous eruptions, classed by some authors as *scrofulides.* They are also applicable to chronic *rheumatism*, in persons of lymphatic constitution. For the cure of *old wounds*, and elimination of balls and foreign bodies, they are efficacious, but not equal to the waters of Barèges.

Luchon is situated in the midst of one of the most magnificent valleys of the Pyrenees, at an elevation of two thousand feet above the sea, and is the most frequented resort of this region, as many as twenty thousand persons going there during the season. The *Cours d'Etigny* is a long avenue, shaded by four rows of linden-trees and bordered by buildings, in which visitors lodge. At the southerly extremity of this avenue the springs—forty-eight in number—issue at the base of the mountain Super-Bagnères. A sojourn at Luchon offers many attractions. The *Cours d'Etigny* is animated by the movement of visitors, and inviting excursions are made to the Lake d'Oo, to the valley of the Lys, and to the *Pont de Vénasque*, whence grand views are obtained of the Maladetta, with its immense glaciers.

Nenndorf.—These cold sulphur-springs are much frequented by North-Germans. The arrangements are good. There are hot baths and douches, and an excellent inhalation-house. Mineral mud-baths and saline baths are also administered. Opportunities for the whey-cure are offered. This resort is chiefly visited by those suffering from gout, rheumatism, paralysis, neuralgia, and diseases of the skin.

Meinberg.—This resort offers an unusual variety of curative agencies. There are carbonic-acid inhalations, baths and douches of carbonic acid, mineral mud-baths, and, besides the sulphur-waters, a good saline water. The resort has considerable repute in the treatment of chronic articular rheumatism, certain forms of paralysis, scrofula, when exhibited in the lymphatic ganglions, and irregularities of menstruation. Meinberg is pleasantly situated, on a wooded hill-side, in a pleasing country.

CHALYBEATE WATERS.[1]

Schwalbach.—Germany, duchy of Nassau, five miles southeast from Ems.

Pyrmont.—Germany, principality of Waldeck, twenty-eight miles southwest of Hanover.

Spa.—Belgium, province of Liége, seventy miles east of Brussels.

St.-Moritz.—Switzerland, canton of Grisons.

Schwalbach.—These may be termed pure chalybeate waters, containing nearly half a grain of carbonate of iron per pint, and but a small proportion of other constituents, together with a large quantity of carbonic-acid gas.

The action of these waters is that of chalybeates in general, tending to produce constipation, rendering the fæces dark

[1] *See* Analysis, page 360.

in color, and restoring the red color to impoverished blood-globules. Under their use the appetite and digestion are improved. The waters are applicable to *anæmic conditions* and *chlorosis*, and form an admirable succedaneum to a course of alterative mineral-water treatment.

ANALYSIS.

One pint contains—	SCHWALBACH. Stahlbrunnen. 46°–61° Fahr. Fresenius.	PYRMONT. Trinkbrunnen. 54.5° Fahr. Wiggers.	SPA. Pouhon. 50° Fahr. Monheim.	SAINT-MORITZ. Grande Source. 42° Fahr. Planta & Kekulé.
SOLIDS.	Grains.	Grains.	Grains.	Grains.
Carbonate of soda	0.110	....	0.700	1.364
Carbonate of magnesia	0.966	0.740	0.241	0.827
Carbonate of alumina	....	....	0.024	....
Carbonate of iron	0.467	0.310	.677	0.173
Carbonate of manganese	0.108	0.024	....	0.080
Carbonate of lime	1.181	7.276	0.580	5.303
Carbonate of ammonia	....	0.002	....	....
Chloride of sodium	0.052	3.752	0.157	0.282
Chloride of magnesium	....	0.508	....	....
Chloride of lithium	....	0.019	....	....
Sulphate of potassa	0.029	0.170	....	0.119
Sulphate of soda	0.061	....	....	1.967
Sulphate of magnesia	....	2.838	....	....
Sulphate of lime	....	6.609	....	....
Phosphate of soda	traces.	....	....	....
Nitrate of soda	....	traces.	....	....
Borate of soda	traces.	....	....	....
Phosphoric acid	....	....	....	0.003
Bromine, iodine, and fluorine	....	....	....	traces.
Alumina	....	0.008	....	0.002
Silica	0.246	0.019	0.217	0.278
Organic matter	traces.	traces.	....	....
Loss	....	....	0.012	....
Total	3.215	22.275	2.608	10.848
GASES.	Cubic in.	Cubic in.	Cubic in.	Cubic in.
Carbonic acid	50.27	47.10	71. 6	39.29
Sulphuretted hydrogen	0.003	....	....	....

Schwalbach lies in a pleasant valley surrounded by wooded hills. It is one of the most popular chalybeate waters in Europe. The large quantity of carbonic acid discharged is utilized in baths, which are so arranged that the gas does not escape when the water is heated.

Pyrmont.—This water is not equal to Schwalbach or Spa. It is not a pure chalybeate, as will be seen by the analysis, containing a considerable quantity of sulphate of lime and other salts, in all twenty-two grains to the pint, and not quite one-third of a grain of carbonate of iron.

This resort does not attract so large a number of visitors

as formerly, though the arrangements are excellent, and a saline water adds to the resources.

Spa.—This is the type of pure chalybeate waters, and is not equalled in Europe. As will be seen by the analysis, the Pouhon Spring—the most used—contains two-thirds of a grain of carbonate of iron to the pint, and seventy cubic inches of carbonic-acid gas, with less than two grains of other constituents. These waters, like iron-waters in general, are especially applicable to *anæmic conditions* and *chlorosis.* In many cases of dyspepsia, with decided anæmia, the results are exceedingly satisfactory. In all those chlorotic conditions depending on impoverished blood and irregularity of the menses they are a most valuable remedy. Patients subject to *passive hæmorrhage* are also relieved by these waters. The water also possesses reputation for the cure of sterility, a result, however, only due to the invigoration and stimulation of the uterine function resulting from the iron contained.

Spa is situated at the base of a miniature mountain, and is protected from the north winds by a similar mountain. The surroundings are exceedingly agreeable, and recreations of every kind invite the pleasure-seeker. A most beautiful bathing-establishment has been erected within a few years. The resort has been renowned since the commencement of the seventeenth century.

Saint-Moritz.—This is a fair chalybeate water, but the curative effects may, in great measure, be attributed to the fresh mountain-air that surrounds. It is situated in a valley of the Haute-Engadine, at an elevation of six thousand and eighty-eight feet above the level of the sea.

Within a few years, Saint-Moritz has become quite a popular place of resort. The waters are chiefly used for drinking, but there are arrangements for bathing, and the carbonic-acid gas is applied in the way of inhalations and local douches. These springs are said to have been brought into notice by Paracelsus during the sixteenth century.

This resort is convenient to the saline purgative springs of Tarasp and Wyh, in the Lower Engadine.

PURGATIVE WATERS.

Püllna.—Bohemia, thirty-two miles northwest of Prague.

Friedrichshall.—Germany, duchy of Saxe-Meiningen, eight miles from Coburg.

Carlsbad.—Bohemia, sixty-nine miles west of Prague.

Marienbad.—Bohemia, seventy-three miles west of Prague, and twenty-two miles south of Carlsbad.

ANALYSIS.

One pint contains—	PÜLLNA. — Strüve.	FRIEDRICH-SHALL. 46.5° Fahr. Bauer.	CARLSBAD. Sprudel. 162.5° Fahr. Göttl.	MARIENBAD. Kreuzbrunnen. 53.3° Fahr. Kersten.
SOLIDS.	Grains.	Grains.	Grains.	Grains.
Carbonate of soda	....	....	9.062	8.594
Carbonate of magnesia	6.406	3.53	0.399	3.200
Carbonate of iron	....	....	0.031	0.350
Carbonate of manganese	....	....	....	0.039
Carbonate of lime	0.770	0.11	2.020	4.605
Carbonate of lithia	....	....	....	0.049
Carbonate of strontia	....	....	....	0.014
Chloride of sodium	....	67.37	8.724	11.166
Chloride of magnesium	16.666	31.08	....	....
Chloride of aluminum	....	0.07	....	....
Chloride of ammonium	....	0.06	....	....
Sulphate of potassa	4.800	0.02	0.370	0.449
Sulphate of soda	123.800	41.73	19.960	36.269
Sulphate of magnesia	93.086	39.55	....	....
Sulphate of lime	2.600	11.24	....	....
Phosphate of alumina	....	....	0.215	0.054
Phosphate of lime	0.003	....	....	0.018
Bromide of magnesium	....	0.02	....	....
Silica	0.176	0.21	1.052	0.679
Total	248.307	194.99	41.833	65.486
GASES.		Cubic in.	Cubic in.	Cubic in.
Carbonic acid	....	5.32	7.80	15.7
Nitrogen	....	....	0.03	....

Püllna.—This is an exceedingly strong purgative water, and of the class known in Germany as *Bitterwasser.* It is indicated in such cases as demand a saline purgative; its action, however, is milder than ordinary Epsom salts. The water should only be used as an evacuant, as continuous use causes derangement of digestion, and decidedly impoverishes the blood.

The manner in which this water is collected is peculiar. There is no spring, properly speaking, but several pits sunk in the earth. The water which enters them is that which falls directly in rain and filters through the surrounding earth. In dry weather the supply is considerably diminished. The surrounding soil is composed of basalt and phonolite, containing large quantities of sulphate of soda and sulphate of magnesia.

There are no bath-buildings at Püllna, the water only being used in the bottled form.

Friedrichshall.—This is a more agreeable purgative water than Püllna, and very popular at the various German spas. Its action is much less liable, it is said, to be followed by constipation, and it may be used for considerable time without producing injurious effects.

There are no accommodations for visitors at the spring, but the bottled water is consumed in considerable quantities.

Sedlitz.—This purgative water contains, in the pint, 75 grains sulphate magnesia, 17 sulphate of soda, 4 sulphate of potassa, 4 sulphate of lime, 5 carbonate of lime, and 1 grain chloride of magnesium.

It is this water which gives the name to the familiar *sedlitz-powder*, composed of tartrate of soda and potassa, carbonate of soda, and tartaric acid, and *not containing a single constituent of the water from which it is named.*

Sedlitz is in Bohemia, not far distant from Püllna. The water is exported in bottles.

Carlsbad or Karlsbad.—These waters contain the very unusual combination of a considerable proportion of carbonate of soda, salt, and Glauber's salt, together with a high degree of heat. They may, therefore, be termed *alkaline-saline purgative* waters. The taste of the water is said to resemble weak mutton-broth. The water produces, according to Kreysig, "slight purgation and liquid motions, but without colic. It is rare that it produces nausea, unless the person is exceedingly delicate, or the digestive organs much diseased. The urinary and cutaneous secretions are favored in a marked degree, but at the same time the circulation is excited and the water disposes to congestion toward the head." Prof. Seegen says of the water: "The effect upon the kidneys is only trifling. The function of the intestine is moderately excited, and a really laxative effect is very rare. . . . The secretion of the bile is increased, and the composition of this liquid is probably altered. The high temperature facilitates the absorption of the water, and at the same time prevents loss of animal heat." The water is said to have produced ptyalism when no mercurials have been taken.

Prof. Seegen has made a special study of the action of this water. He experimented on seven persons whose condition was carefully noted for seven days previous to drinking the water, and for from seven to nine days during the administration of the water. From the results, as given by Althaus, I have formed the following table:

EXCRETIONS EXAMINED.	RESULTS.			
	Increased.	Unaltered.	Diminished.	Total.
Fæces	2	3	2	7
Urine	5	1	1	7
Urine, urea in	1	2	4	7
Urine, phosphoric acid in	6	..	..	6
Urine, chloride of sodium in	3	..	4	7
Body weight	7	..	..	7

The *acidity of the urine* was affected thus: continued acid in three, became alkaline in three, rendered neutral after taking the water in one, but became acid by night.

The *specific gravity* of the urine was diminished in some cases, and increased in others, always inversely proportional to the quantity of urine discharged.

Although the urine was increased in five out of seven, the increase was not proportional to the additional quantity of water ingested.

The waters of Carlsbad possess a reputation above all others in *diseases of the liver.* Of these diseases, *hyperæmia,* from whatever cause, whether the congestion be active or passive, is most frequently cured. Those cases arising from prolonged exposure to paludal poison, are often relieved in a remarkable manner. It is also said that *fatty degeneration* of the liver is cured by their use. The proof of this must, however, be exceedingly difficult to determine. In cases of gallstone they are also exceedingly efficient, and in icterus arising from catarrh of the hepatic ducts. In each of the conditions named, no less an authority than Frerichs testifies to their utility. The waters have also considerable reputation for the relief of *diabetes*, when associated with disease of the liver or gout. *Gout* is also frequently amenable to these waters when the liver or abdominal organs are in a turgid condition. *Gastric catarrh* is most especially subject to cure by these waters. Prof. Niemeyer is exceedingly explicit on this point.

Carlsbad is situated in a profound valley, surrounded on either side by immense masses of overhanging granitic rock. Being one of the most renowned resorts in Europe for those diseases which most frequently attack those who lead an easy and luxurious life, it possesses all the requirements for persons of that class. The name of the place is due to Charles IV., who erected an establishment there in the fourteenth century.

The Sprudel is the spring most frequently employed. Constantin James says: "This source, the queen, without contradiction, of all the mineral waters of Europe, jets forth, bounding and boiling from beneath the earth by a large orifice, then falls back in foam. A cloud of vapor envelops it on all sides, and, united to the noise made by the rushing water, announces its presence from afar." Large quantities of incrustations form about the reservoir, and green confervoid growths appear. There are many springs at Carlsbad, varying in temperature, but differing little in constitution. The high temperature of the water affords ample facilities for baths, which are frequently employed in conjunction with the internal use of the water for the treatment of the diseases named. Bathing, however, is of secondary importance at this resort.

Marienbad.—The waters of these springs do not differ essentially from those of Carlsbad, except in containing a larger proportion of sulphate of soda, carbonic acid, and iron; and being cold in temperature. The difference in the effects can readily be traced to this difference in constitution. They are much more readily purgative, and, if large quantities are taken, the excretion of urine is decidedly augmented. The secretions of the mucous membrane are increased, perspiration is more free, and in some instances eruptions appear on the surface. The appetite and digestion usually improve under their use, and, owing to the presence of carbonic acid and iron, the prolonged use of the water does not prove as debilitating as otherwise would be anticipated.

The waters are recommended in the same diseases as Carlsbad. They are preferable to Carlsbad in those cases in which free purgation is advisable, but, in subacute gastric catarrh, the large amount of carbonic acid contained would prove injurious.

A specialty at Marienbad is the *mineral mud-bath.* The dried moor from which these baths are made, contains, besides purging sulphates, humic acid, and organic matter, a large amount of the salts of iron, as much as two hundred and sixty-eight grains in a thousand.

Marienbad is beautifully situated at an altitude of two thousand feet above the sea-level. The country is open and inviting, and the arrangements for entertainment and for bathing are superior.

Franzensbad.—These springs are situated in Bohemia, three and a half miles from Eger. In chemical characteristics they very much resemble Marienbad—the Wiesenquelle (51° Fahr.,) containing in the pint 25 grains sulphate of soda, 9 of chloride of sodium, 0.376 carbonate of iron, traces of bromides and iodides, and 45 cubic inches of carbonic-acid gas. Their therapeutic application also resembles Marienbad, except that, containing but a very small proportion of alkaline carbonates, they act much more decidedly as an *iron tonic.*

The specialty of Franszensbad is the *mineral mud-bath,* which possesses a reputation above every other in Germany. The composition of the dried moor, of which this bath is composed, is given under the title mud-baths. These baths are especially recommended in cases of paralysis, rheumatism, and gout.

CALCIC WATERS.

Contrexville.—France, department of Vosges, two hundred and thirty-five miles east of Paris.

Bagnères-de-Bigorre.—France, department of Hautes-Pyrénées, eighty-five miles west of Toulouse.

Leuk.—Switzerland, canton of Valais, twenty-two miles east of Sion.

Wildungen.—Germany, principality of Waldeck, eighteen miles south-west of Cassel.

ANALYSIS.

One pint contains—	CONTREX-VILLE. Pavillon. 53.6° Fahr. Henry.	BAGNÈRES-DE-BIGORRE. La Reine. 115.7° Fahr. Ganderax and Rosière.	LEUK. Lorenzquelle. 123° Fahr. Brunner.	WILDUNGEN. Stadtbrunnen. 50° Fahr.
SOLIDS.	Grains.	Grains.	Grains.	Grains.
Carbonate of soda	1.438	....	....	0.492
Carbonate of magnesia	1.606	0.821	0.002	2.408
Carbonate of iron	0.066 [1]	0.584	0.024	0.139
Carbonate of manganese	....	....	....	0.053
Carbonate of lime	4.927	1.942	0.357	8.778
Carbonate of strontia	traçes.	....	....	....
Chloride of potassium	1.022	....	0.020	....
Chloride of sodium		0.453	0.055	0.071
Chloride of magnesium	0.292	0.949	0.027	....
Sulphate of potassa	traces.	....	....	....
Sulphate of soda	0.949	2.891	0.509	0.919
Sulphate of magnesia	1.887		1.991	0.289
Sulphate of lime	8.395	12.264	12.712	....
Sulphate of strontia	....	....	0.081	....
Phosphate of lime	0.511	....	....	....
Organic matter and arsenic		....	....	....
Loss		0.394	....	....
Alumina	....	....	....	0.008
Silica	0.876 [2]	0.263	0.102	0.279
Residue, fatty matter	....	0.050	....	....
Total	21.469 [3]	20.111	15.830	8.431
GASES.	Cubic in.		Cubic in.	Cubic in.
Carbonic acid	0.29	undetermined.	0.26	42.70
Oxygen	undetermined.	....	0.19	....
Nitrogen	....	....	0.85	....

Contrexville.—The prominent effect of this water is diuretic, and the quantity of urine passed seems more than in proportion to the water ingested. When taken in large quantities, and it is readily tolerated, there is frequently slight diarrhœa, abundant perspiration, and phenomena of general excitement.

These waters are distinguished for the relief given in cases

[1] And carbonate of manganese.

[2] And alumina.

[3] This spring also contains traces of iodine, bromine, and nitrates.

of *catarrh of the bladder, nephritic colic, calculus, and gravel.* The value of the waters in gravel, says Durand-Fardel, is "neither contested nor contestable." The effect of the waters in this disease, according to his view, depends on their diuretic action, on the washing out of the urinary organs, and not on any decided effect on the organism by which the diathesis is destroyed. The relief given, however, is immediate, and continues for a considerable time after the use of the water is suspended. In catarrh of the bladder, however, the waters exercise a decidedly curative effect.

This is comparatively a recent resort, but within a few years has received considerable patronage, and possesses the requisites for a comfortable abode.

Bagnères-de-Bigorre.—These waters are reputed sedative to all conditions of over-excitement or sensitiveness of the nervous system, and find especial application in disorders of the genito-urinary apparatus, and menstruation in females. They also prove useful in the atonic and nervous condition of students, and men who lead a sedentary life. These good effects are attributable almost, if not altogether, to the baths and fresh mountain-air. The waters, however, contain a considerable proportion of iron, which proves valuable in the conditions named, and in certain dyspepsias.

The number of springs at Bigorre is upward of thirty, and the supply of water is abundant. The bathing arrangements are superior.

Besides the calcic waters, there is a fine sulphur-spring not far distant, the waters of which have been brought into the village.

Bagnères-de-Bigorre is one of the most popular resorts in the Pyrenees, as many as eighteen thousand persons going there during the season. It is delightfully situated amid the heights of the mountains, at an elevation of eighteen hundred feet. Every opportunity for pleasure and recreation is afforded.

Leuk.—These waters are chiefly appropriated to the bath. For this purpose they are used in common by both sexes, after the manner described in another chapter. The patient remains in the water from one to five hours, with the object of producing the phenomenon known as *la poussée*, or the bath-eruption. This mode of treatment is especially applicable to dry dartrous diseases of the skin, such as *psoriasis*, *lichen*, and *pityriasis*, accompanied with want of vital action in the integument. The bath-eruption seems to remove this inertia, and cure by substitution. The application of the waters, in these diseases and conditions, is recommended by Hardy and other specialists of equal note.

The village of Leuk is situated at the foot of the Gemmi Pass, at an elevation of four thousand six hundred feet above the sea. On either hand glacier-crowned summits tower five thousand feet above, and the entire region possesses a wild and sterile grandeur.

Wildungen.—The waters of this spa are readily tolerated by the stomach, and prove decidedly efficacious in *gravel* and the lithic-acid diathesis. They exercise a happy effect on the mucous membrane of the urinary passages, and under their use gravel and renal calculi are passed without pain, and the formation of new concretions is prevented. The water also proves curative in *catarrh of the bladder.*

Wildungen is a quiet resort, situated in a pleasant valley, and offers attractions to those who desire to avoid the confusion of the larger watering-places.

THERMAL WATERS.[1]

Gastein.—Austria, duchy of Salzburg, seventy-four miles south of Salzburg.

Töplitz.—Bohemia, circle of Leitmeritz, forty miles south of Dresden.

Schlangenbad.—Germany, duchy of Nassau, four miles south of Schwalbach Springs.

Plombières.—France, department of the Vosges, two hundred and fifty-one miles east of Paris.

Gastein.—These waters are devoted almost exclusively to bathing. There are eight springs varying little in composi-

[1] *See* Analysis, page 370.

tion, but ranging in temperature from 87° to 160° Fahr. The effects of the waters are in great measure those of the warm and hot bath. Prof. Seegen regards the curative agency as due only to this action and the mountain-air. However, Constantin James affirms that a bath in these waters, unlike one in ordinary warm or hot water, produces contraction and rigidity of the skin, and that when a number of baths are taken, they especially stimulate the genital organs and the nervous system. The temperature of the bath is from 98° to 100° Fahr.

ANALYSIS.

One pint contains—	GASTEIN. 87°–160° Fahr. Wolf.	TÖPLITZ. Hauptquelle. 120° Fahr. Wolf.	SCHLANGENBAD. 82.4°–89.6° Fahr. Fresenius.	PLOMBIÈRES. Source des Dames. 125° Fahr. Lhéritier.
SOLIDS.	Grains.	Grains.	Grains.	Grains.
Carbonate of soda..........	0.04	2.635	0.079	....
Carbonate of magnesia......	0.02	0.088	0.047	....
Carbonate of iron...........	0.05	0.019	....	....
Carbonate of manganese	0.02	0.021	....	....
Carbonate of lime...........	0.36	0.330	0.250	....
Carbonate of strontia........	....	0.027	....	....
Chloride of potassium.......	....	....	0.004	} 0.275
Chloride of sodium..........	0.86	0.438	1.825	
Chloride of calcium..........	....	....	....	....
Sulphate of potassa.........	0.01	0.098	0.091	....
Sulphate of soda............	1.51	0.290	....	0.627
Phosphate of soda..........	....	0.014	0.004	....
Phosphate of alumina.......	0.04	0.020	....	....
Fluoride of calcium.........	traces.	....	....	....
Fluoride of silicium.........	....	0.351	....	....
Arseniate of soda...........	....	....	....	0.005
Silicate of potassa...........	....	....	....	0.008
Silicate of soda.............	....	....	....	0.626
Silicate of lime and magnesia..	....	....	....	0.158
Crenic acid.................	....	0.084	....	....
Alumina.....................	....	....	....	0.076
Strontia....................	traces.	....	....	....
Silica......................	0.24	0.443	0.258	0.089
Organic matter.............	traces.	....	....	0.153
Total................	2.65	4.803	2.558	2.012
GASES.	In 100 parts.	In 100 parts.	Cubic in.	
Carbonic acid..............	....	4.74	0.67	....
Oxygen.....................	30.89	0.66	....	....
Nitrogen...................	69.11	94.59	....	....

These baths possess especial reputation in cases of *paralysis*, both *hemiplegia* and *paraplegia*, provided the originating attack has been some time passed, and organic degeneration of the nerve-tissues has not occurred. They are also said to be of service in restoring virility. It is almost needless to add that they prove valuable in *chronic rheumatism.* Gastein is situated in a romantic valley of the Noric Alps, at an elevation of three thousand five hundred and twenty feet above the sea. The journey thither is a most delightful one to the tourist, passing by the charming *châteaux* of Hellbrunn, through the narrow defile of Pass-Leug, and the perilous passage of the Klamm, with the pathway cut in the solid rock.

Töplitz.—The waters of this resort are devoted to the bath, for which they are especially adapted. It is this resort which has added most to the reputation of indifferent thermal waters. The effect of the baths is that of warm or hot bathing. When skilfully administered, according to Prof. Seegen, they increase the function of the skin, stimulate the circulation and peripheric innervation, and in certain cases facilitate the depletion of engorged organs.

Paralysis and *neuralgia* are successfully treated at Töplitz, also chronic muscular and articular rheumatism. *Atonic gout* is frequently improved under the treatment.

There are five springs at Töplitz, and the system of baths, consisting of swimming-baths, private baths, douches, and vapor-baths, is unsurpassed. We should not omit naming the mud-bath. *Schönau*, a suburb, where there are six springs, is included in this statement. The surroundings of this resort are agreeable, and visitors or patients have every opportunity for passing time agreeably. Ten thousand persons visit Töplitz during the summer.

Schlangenbad.—This is exclusively a tepid bath, but a tepid bath possessing peculiar properties. The water is characterized in a high degree by *unctuosity*, so that, when passed between the fingers and rubbed, there is a sense of oiliness, or velvety sensation. When immersed in the water, the entire integument presents the same soft and velvet-like feeling. The bath is delightful. The resort is known throughout Europe as *the ladies' bath.*

The baths prove sedative, and are especially applicable to *hysteria*, and *erethism of the nervous system*, depending on functional derangements of the sexual organs in females. They also prove valuable in certain cases of gout and rheumatism, and, by virtue of their calming action on the integument, prove of utility in *diseases of the skin*, accompanied by hyperæsthesia. The waters also have a reputation as a cosmetic.

Schlangenbad is situated in a pleasant valley nine hundred feet above the sea-level, on the road between Wiesbaden and Schwalbach, and not distant from either place. The surroundings are agreeable. The *whey-cure* adds to the resources of Schlangenbad.

Plombières.—These waters, like the indifferent thermals in general, are largely employed in the form of baths. The Source des Dames and du Crucifix are, however, used for drinking. They are distinguished from other thermal waters by the large proportion of silicates, and an appreciable amount of arsenic. They present, however, no characteristic effect when taken internally, or employed externally. The water is transparent, without taste or odor, and soft to the touch.

As a remedy, they prove exceedingly efficacious in *gastralgia*, also in *chronic enteritis*, associated with much abdominal pain. In *articular and muscular rheumatism*, unaccompanied by exudation, they are also of decided utility. In the dry dartrous *diseases of the skin*, such as *psoriasis* and *lichen*, they have proved efficacious. *Paraplegia* is also treated at this resort with considerable success.

Plombières is situated in a valley of the Vosges Mountains, at an elevation of fourteen hundred feet above the sea. The surroundings are agreeable. The place was largely patronized by the Emperor Louis Napoleon, and the Bain Napoléon is one of the most complete in Europe. Every convenience for swimming-baths and douches is afforded. This resort was a favorite with the Romans, as numerous remains testify. One of the ancient thermæ is in an excellent state of preservation.

SEA-SIDE RESORTS.

CHAPTER XIX.

ONE who has passed his early life in an inland city or village can well remember how frequently he has desired to see the heaving waters of the ocean, to hear its tempestuous roar; and, on visiting a seaboard city for the first time, he may not have been content to look upon the waters of the bay, but may have journeyed to some exposed portion of the coast-line, where the waves roll in from across the broad waste of waters. To every one there are majesty and beauty in the sea.

The air at the sea-side has a peculiar freshness and life, that, as we breathe, seems to penetrate every portion of our frame, and impart to us renewed vitality. And we shall not have breathed this air long before we shall experience a keen appetite, and, if vigorous, feel inclined to athletic exercise. Exactly what it is in the constitution of *sea-air* that produces these effects has not been discovered. We, however, know that the air is purer than that of the land, less contaminated by miasm, by vegetable exhalations and noxious gases, though in the component oxygen it differs but little. The air of the ocean is always highly charged with watery vapor, bearing with it a perceptible amount of chloride of sodium. When we have been exposed to the sea-air for a long time we detect this in the salt taste experienced when the tongue touches the outer borders of the lips. Experiment has shown that this saline vapor is much more freely diffused when the ocean is agitated, and it is then carried inland for several miles. Besides containing chloride of sodium, it is quite probable that the atmosphere of the sea also contains a proportion of iodides and bromides—a conclusion, however, which is not based on direct experiment. And, although chemistry has not revealed the minute differences between ocean air and that of the land, still, whoever is familiar with its odor can recognize it miles inland from the sea-shore. Many persons sojourn at the sea-shore more for the purpose of breathing the sea-air than for bathing in the surf. Breathing sea-air affects the organism by the change wrought in the blood, and thus in the entire system. How quickly medical agents act through the lungs is shown by the rapidity with which anæsthesia may be produced by chloroform.

Sea-air is deemed especially applicable to chronic bronchitis accompanied with considerable expectoration. If the patient, on the contrary, has dry cough and great irritability of the lungs and larynx, it will not prove beneficial. In the chronic cough of old age—senile bronchitis—it is also advantageous, if the patient is not a sufferer from asthma and emphysema. Phthisis in its early stages is favorably influenced by a residence at the sea-side, or repeated ocean-voyages. Indeed, the last-named remedy has been a favorite in all ages. Pliny, Celsus, and Galen, have all testified to its virtues. Care, however, is recommended that those cases only seek the sea in which the cough is moist, and there is very little tendency to hæmoptysis.

The *water* of the sea is exceedingly complex in constitution, and contains several medical substances in active proportion. The analysis of sea-water, on page 375, will illustrate this statement.

From the analysis it is seen that chloride of sodium is the chief constituent, and next is chloride of magnesium, then sulphate of potassa, sulphate of lime, sulphate of magnesia, etc. It will also be noticed that the composition varies in different seas. The waters of northern seas are less saline, because of the small amount of surface evaporation. The waters of the Dead Sea are very heavily charged, because of the continual access from surrounding rivers without any corresponding outflow.

ANALYSIS.

One pint contains—	Atlantic Ocean. Herepath.	Mediterranean Sea. Usiglio.	North Sea. Duménil.	Caspian Sea. Gobel.	Dead Sea. Herepath.
SOLIDS.	Grains.	Grains.	Grains.	Grains.	Grains.
Carbonate of magnesia	....	....	....	0.94	....
Carbonate of lime	trace.	0.86	....	12.45	trace.
Chloride of potassium	....	3.78	2.42	5.56	85.33
Chloride of sodium	208.92	220.41	149.68	268.23	837.84
Chloride of magnesium	24.96	24.12	12.38	46.18	557.15
Chloride of aluminum	....	....	....	....	3.92
Chloride of iron	trace.	....	....	....	0.19
Chloride of calcium	....	....	2.72	....	172.09
Chloride of ammonium	....	....	....	....	0.42
Chloride of manganese	....	....	....	....	0.42
Sulphate of potassa	13.56	....	....	....	....
Sulphate of magnesia	4.37	13.55	17.34	90.47	....
Sulphate of lime	11.66	10.16	....	85.80	4.76
Phosphate of soda	trace.	....	....	....	....
Iodide of sodium	trace.	....	....	....	trace.
Bromide of sodium	3.89	4.16	....	....	19.57
Bromide of magnesium	....	....	....	trace.	....
Oxide of iron	....	0.02	....	....	....
Bromine	....	....	trace.	....	....
Silver	trace.	....	....	....	....
Copper	trace.	....	....	....	....
Lead	trace.	....	....	....	....
Silica	trace.	....	0.66	....	trace.
Organic matter	trace.	....	....	....	4.82
Bitumen	....	....	....	....	trace.
Resin and extractive matter	....	....	0.39	....	....
Total	267.36	282.06	185.59	459.63	1686.01

The accumulation of solid matter in the water of the sea occurs as follows: The pure clear drops of water descend from the heavens, and, as they pass to the stream, dissolve and carry from the rocks and loam many of their constituents, though in exceedingly small proportion. These myriads of drops of water, each freighted with its little burden, meet in the rivers and pass on to the ocean. Arriving here they are heated by the sun and arise in vapor, depositing the burden they have borne. Again this vapor, wafted across the land, meets a cold stratum of air and descends once more in rain, again to bear a portion of the earth's surface to the ocean. This aggregation for ages of dissolved salts has, in great part, caused the saline condition of the ocean. But, in addition, there are large beds of salt on the shores and in the depths of the ocean which, doubtless, contribute to its saltness.

We find, then, that sea-water is exceedingly complex in constitution. Besides, it possesses various *colors*, due, however, in great measure to its varied surroundings—the color of the sky, the disposition of the coast-line, whether bold and precipitous, or low and receding. From the varied colors we have the names White, Red, and Black Sea, etc. One characteristic, however, which has been the subject of a number of theories, is its *phosphorescence*. When, on a steamer far out in the ocean, we look back at night over the ship's track we see, just bordering the crest of the wave, a line of faint sparkles appearing and disappearing with the changes of the wave—now they flash out in peculiar brilliance, then are lost in the dark surge. Some consider that this effect is due to a peculiar chemical combustion, others to myriads of animalcules capable of luminosity, like the glow-worm, and another theory attributes it to electrical conditions.

The *temperature* of the sea, like that of rivers, is never constant, varying according to the seasons. The mean temperature of the surface of the Mediterranean Sea, near the coast of France, is found to be 59° Fahr. But, beneath the surface, the temperature decreases downward, and in mid-ocean the temperature has been found as high as 83.4° Fahr. at the surface, while at the depth of six thousand feet it marked but 45.5° Fahr. Aimé has shown that the lowest temperature of the depths of the ocean is equal to the mean temperature of the surface during the winter. At the sea-side resorts the temperature ranges between 60° and 70° Fahr. during the season. The *sea-bath* is a cold bath, and its effects may almost all be deduced from this fact. But it is a cold bath under the most favorable conditions. The fascination of the sea, the attraction of many bathers in the water at the same time, the excitement attendant on the rolling in of the waves, and the exercise required in meeting them, contribute to the salutary effect that is experienced. Here the person makes no conscious effort to exercise, but the entire surroundings lead him to do so, and often so vigorous is this exercise that reaction commences while in the water, to be followed by complete redness of the surface, and a feeling of renewed energy when he retires to the dressing-room and is thoroughly rubbed and dried. That the mineral constituents of the water have any part in the result, is exceedingly doubtful, for, on the one hand, the temperature of the water is so low that the skin is unprepared for absorption, and, on the other, the period of immersion is usually so short that, under the most favorable conditions, little absorption could occur. However, it must be remembered that, during the entire time, the lungs are continually filled with the aroma of the sea, and the blood much more highly charged with its medical properties than when at the hotel on the shore. The time passed in the bath varies from five to twenty minutes, and, where the water is unusually warm, it may be extended beyond these limits. One bath a day is sufficient, and two each day as many as should be indulged by the most vigorous. In some instances reaction is not readily established on coming from the bath, and, in such cases, in addition to rubbing with the coarse towel, it will be advantageous to immerse the feet in warm water. It is almost unnecessary to say that morning is the preferable time for the bath, and that the stomach should be empty when it is taken. The rules given under the title of "The Cold Bath" are also applicable to sea-bathing.

The effect of a course of sea-bathing, according to Durand-Fardel, is as follows: The first baths cause excitement, excessive fatigue, pain in the muscles and course of the nerves, especially if the sea has been rough; sometimes the appetite is lost. But, in five or six days, these conditions disappear, and a feeling of *bien-être*, of vigor and joyousness, succeeds; at the same time the appetite is increased, and the secretions are more active, especially those of the kidneys, skin, and lungs. But, if the baths are too long continued, after fifteen, twenty, or thirty days—according to the individual—the excitement, fatigue, and the pain reappear, and, if the baths are not discontinued, all the advantage gained may be lost.

Sea-baths are especially applicable to persons of lymphatic constitutions. In these classes they favorably influence a number of diseases by the tonicity wrought in the system. They have been highly lauded as a remedy at the age of puberty, in both sexes, when there is a want of development, an apparent failure of the vital force; they then stimulate to a renewed effort, the pale youth develops into a vigorous boy, and the cheek of the anæmic girl assumes the rosy hue of health. In cases of delayed or difficult menstruation, accompanied with chlorosis in the young girl, sea-baths are of peculiar benefit. Indeed, so decided is their influence upon the uterine functions that, in women who have ceased to menstruate, the flow has reappeared, and those always sterile have become *enceinte.* The beneficial effects to the scrofulous of a residence at the sea-side are generally known.

Sea-bathing is not without *danger* to those who are reckless, or do not observe the rules which are given for the guidance of bathers. Those who, in a strong sea, quit the lines of rope are never without danger, for, in those seemingly small waves, there is a power that can only be appreciated by those who have felt their force; and those who wander beyond the prescribed limits, recklessly peril their lives.

Marshall Hall's ready method for resuscitating persons asphyxiated from drowning, may prove useful to those at the sea-side. It is as follows:

1. Treat the patient *instantly on the spot* in the *open air*, freely exposing the face, neck, and chest to the breeze, except in severe weather.

2. In order to *clear the throat*, place the patient gently on the face, with one wrist under the forehead, that all fluid and the tongue itself may fall forward, and leave the entrance into the windpipe free.

3. *To excite respiration*, turn the patient slightly on his side, and apply some irritating or stimulating agent to his nostrils, as *ammonia*, *camphor*, etc.

4. Make the face warm by brisk friction; then dash cold water upon it.

5. If not successful, lose no time; but, to *imitate respiration*, place the patient on his face, and turn the body gently but completely *on the side, and a little beyond;* then again on the face, and so on alternately. Repeat these movements deliberately and perseveringly, *fifteen times only* in a minute. When the patient lies on the chest, this cavity is *compressed*, and *ex*piration takes place. When he is turned on the side, this pressure is removed and *in*spiration occurs.

6. When the patient is in the prone position, make a uniform and efficient pressure *along the spine*, removing the pressure immediately before rotation on the side. The pressure augments the *ex*piration; the rotation commences *in*spiration. Continue these measures *without tiring*, for restoration often results when hope is entirely lost.

7. Rub the limbs *upward*, with *firm pressure* and with *energy;* the object being to aid the return of venous blood to the heart.

8. Substitute for the patient's wet clothing, if possible, such other covering as can instantly be procured, each bystander supplying a coat or cloak. Meantime, and from time to time, to *excite inspiration*, let the surface of the body be *slapped* briskly with the hand.

Avoid the immediate removal of the patient, as it involves a *dangerous loss of time;* also the use of the bellows, or any forcing instrument.

SEA-SIDE RESORTS.

Portland, Maine.—Three miles distant from this city is *Cushing's Island*, which contains about two hundred and fifty acres. It commands magnificent ocean-views. The beach, on either side of the island, is exceedingly good, and every facility, including bathing-houses, dresses, etc., are at hand. This resort is popular with Canadians, and those who prefer a quiet retreat to the excessive excitement of more noted places. Fishing of all kinds is abundant.

Portsmouth, New Hampshire.—Near this city is *Rye Beach*, growing in popularity. The bathing is good. It may be reached by carriage-drive of seven miles, over an excellent road, from Portsmouth, or by train to Greenland, four miles from Portsmouth; thence by stage. *Hampton Beach* is also near by; not so fashionable as Rye, but celebrated many years ago. To good fishing and bathing it adds the attraction of charming scenery. Access by railroad, seven miles southwest from Portsmouth, to Hampton Station; thence, by stage, to the beach.

Boston, Massachusetts.—The fashionable sea-side resort of Boston is *Swampscott.* It is twelve miles north of the city, on the coast-line of railroad to Portsmouth. The bathing is excellent, with no undertow. Its popularity seems, however, to be entirely fortuitous, as the beaches are not large and the scenery not peculiarly attractive.

The best beach in the immediate vicinity of Boston is *Nahant.* It is approached by the coast-line of railroad. The passenger leaves the train at Lynn, eleven miles north of Boston; thence four miles by stage. It is a charming peninsula of rocky islands, connected with each other by a series of unsurpassed beaches. Many Cambridge professors choose this for their summer home. *Chelsea Beach* is situated in the town of Chelsea, four miles north of Boston by rail. The beach is three miles long. It is a pleasant resort.

Newport, Rhode Island.—This is the most elegant watering-place in the United States, and the facilities for bathing are unsurpassed. The beaches are known as *Easton's*, *Sachuset's*, and *Smith's*, the first-named being the most popular. The location of Easton's is admirable, the waves rolling in in majestic succession, and, at the same time, the bather is without danger from undercurrents.

Besides the attraction of Newport as a resort, it is interesting to those who delight in studying the early history of America.

The drives about Newport are delightful, the new one—ten miles long—giving an unobstructed view of the ocean almost the entire distance.

Narragansett Pier, about one hour's sail from Newport,

has been known over twenty years as a watering-place; within a few years it has become quite a popular resort. The beach is at the mouth of Narragansett Bay. It slopes gradually, and there is an absence of strong undercurrents. The Pier is also reached by the Shore-line Railroad from New York to Boston, leaving the train at Kingston, a station twenty-seven miles southwest from Providence, whence stages convey to the hotels.

New York City.—The most fashionable resort in the vicinity of New York is *Long Branch.* It is about thirty-two miles distant from the city, by steamer to Port Monmouth, or Sandy Hook, New Jersey; thence by rail. Within a few years many commodious hotels have been erected, and throngs of visitors have gathered during the summer season. Long Branch is famed for its bathing, its sea-breezes, its shell-fish, and its hotels. Its nearness to New York and Philadelphia, and its ease of access, are its chief claims to popularity.

Coney Island was once a fashionable resort, but it is now only sought by those of moderate means. During the summer season large numbers go over for a day's pleasure, by steamboat from New York. The distance is ten miles. Or, it is reached from Fulton Ferry, Brooklyn, by street-cars. The beach is exceedingly fine.

Rockaway is also one of the once fashionable resorts which have fallen into decay, because of their immediate proximity to the city. It is accessible during the summer season by steamboat from New York, or from Brooklyn by Long Island Railway and South Side Railway.

Philadelphia, Pennsylvania.—The sea-side resort of Philadelphia is *Cape May, New Jersey.* It is the extreme southern point of the State, having on the one side the Atlantic Ocean, and on the other Delaware Bay. It has long been one of the most fashionable and elegant sea-side watering-places, patronized by the inhabitants of every portion of the United States, but especially from Philadelphia, Baltimore, Washington, and the West and South. The beach is over five miles long, exceedingly firm and solid, and offers every facility for the enjoyment of sea-bathing. Here the hotels are built almost on the beach, in full view of the ocean, giving easy access to the baths, and affording the amplest opportunity for breathing sea-air. Cape May is reached by cars from Philadelphia on the West Jersey Railroad, distance eighty-one miles south. Passengers from New York change cars at Camden; thence southward.

Atlantic City is on the eastern coast of New Jersey, about sixty miles southeast by rail, *via* the Camden & Atlantic Railroad. There are fine accommodations for bathing.

GENERAL INDEX.

A.

B.

O.

P.

R.

S.

T.

AMERICAN SPRINGS.

EUROPEAN SPAS.

THE END.

GETTYSBURG KATALYSINE WATER.

THE United States Dispensatory classes this water with the most renowned of the Alkaline or Carbonated Waters of Europe. It far excels any other known, in the Old or New World, in its self-preserving qualities. It does not deteriorate by bottling and keeping. While we believe it will be difficult to find, if at all, a well-authenticated cure of Chronic Disease by any other water away from its source, the most remarkable results have been effected by the Katalysine Water, after it had been bottled and sent from the spring. It certainly is not claimed for any other mineral water, the power to dissolve the Urates or so-called Chalk Formations in the body or on the limbs and joints. This the Gettysburg Katalysine Water has done in nearly every case where the patient has taken and continued its use according to directions.

Gout, Rheumatism, Neuralgia, Dyspepsia, Gravel, Diabetes, Kidney and Urinary Diseases generally, have all yielded to its influence.

It has restored muscular power to the paralytic, cured Abdominal Dropsy, and given to the torpid liver healthy action. It has cured Chronic Diarrhœa, Piles, Constipation, Asthma, Catarrh, Bronchitis, Diseases of the Skin, General Debility, and Nervous Prostration from mental and physical excesses. All of these results have been effected by the bottled water away from the spring, and are attested by eminent physicians and medical writers.

It is a powerful antidote to the effects of excessive eating or drinking. It corrects the stomach, promotes digestion, and relieves the head, almost immediately.

The Gettysburg Water is now for sale by all respectable Druggists.

Pamphlets containing a history of the spring, reports from eminent physicians and medical writers, certificates of marvellous cures, and recommendations from distinguished citizens, will be furnished, and sent by mail, to all who apply to

WHITNEY BROTHERS,

General Agents Gettysburg Spring Co.,

227 South Front Street, Philadelphia.

CHESAPEAKE & OHIO RAILROAD.

Richmond, Va., to Huntington, W. Va. (Ohio River).

CONNECTIONS.

At Richmond.—R. D. & P. R. R., for Greensboro, Charlotte, Columbia, and all points South.
" R. F. & P. R. R., for Fredericksburg and the North.
" R. & Y. R. R. R., for West Point, and Steamer to Baltimore.
" R. & P. R. R., for Petersburg, Weldon, Wilmington, and the South.
" Steamships of the Old Dominion Line, for New York, tri-weekly.
" Steamers for Norfolk, daily.
Gordonsville.—O. A. & M. R. R., for Alexandria, Washington, and the North.
Charlottesville.—O. A. & M. R. R., for Lynchburg, Bristol, and the South.
Huntington.—Express Steamers for Portsmouth and Cincinnati, and with Steamers for Wheeling, Parkersburg, Gallipolis, Pomeroy, &c.

STAGES CONNECT.

Staunton.—For Harrisburg, Weyer's Cave, and Stribbling's Springs.
Goshen.—For Lexington, Rockbridge Alum Springs, Cold Sulphur, Jordan's Alum Springs, and Rockbridge Baths.
Millboro.—For Bath Alum and Warm Springs.
Covington.—For Healing and Hot Springs.
Alleghany.—For Sweet Chalybeate and Sweet Springs.

This road passes through the magnificent scenery of the Blue Ridge and Alleghanies and down the Greenbrier River, through the wonderful cañon of the New River, giving the traveller such a variety of scenery as is not surpassed in this country. The world-renowned

WHITE SULPHUR SPRINGS,

the "Saratoga of the South," are situated on this road, 227 miles from Richmond and 193 from Huntington.

For time of trains, see Travellers' Official and Appletons' Railway Guide.

A. H. PERRY,
Gen. Sup't.

J. F. NETHERLAND,
G. T. A., Richmond, Va.

UPPER

Blue Lick Water,

The Best Saline Sulphur Water in the World.

See Analysis in this work, page 191.

MAYSVILLE, KY. **STANTON & PIERCE, Proprietors.**

CATOOSA SPRINGS, GEORGIA.

In a beautiful and lovely vale, twenty-five miles southeast of Chattanooga, and within two miles of the railroad leading to Atlanta, lie the celebrated and world-renowned Catoosa Springs, noted for the great variety and curative properties of their waters. There are fifty-two distinct springs within this magic vale, comprising almost every variety of water found in the famous mountains of Virginia—Red, Black, and White Sulphurs; Alum, All-healing, Red Sweet, Montvale, and all the Chalybeate Waters known to the medical world. A balm of Gilead and cure for all diseases that human flesh is heir to. Will be opened on the 1st day of June, 1873, by

W. C. HEWITT.

MONTVALE SPRINGS.

This favorite summer-resort is situated in Blount County, East Tennessee, twenty-five miles south of Knoxville, in a sequestered valley almost encircled by mountain-spurs of the Alleghany, known as the Chilhowee, which rise up on every side and embosom a valley of surpassing loveliness. Their elevation is 1,400 feet above the level of the sea. The marked beneficial results attending the use of these waters, in functional derangements of the **Liver, Bowels, Kidneys,** and **Skin,** and the cure of **Chronic Diseases,** attest their medical properties. Will be opened for the reception of visitors on the 15th of May, and maintained in a style worthy the patronage of a discriminating public.

All the accessories for enjoyment and recreation, at the best watering-places, will be found here. ROUTE.—Visitors to Montvale necessarily pass over the East Tennessee, Georgia & Virginia Railroad, making the city of Knoxville a point; thence, *via* Knoxville & Charleston Railroad, to Maryville, sixteen miles, whence passengers are conveyed in mail-stages, running in connection with the trains, to the springs, nine miles distant.

Address, for the pamphlet containing analysis and description of the waters, etc.,

JOS. L. KING,

Montvale Springs, East Tennessee.

D. APPLETON & CO.'S NEW WORKS.

MAN AND HIS DWELLING-PLACE. By James Hinton, author of the "Mystery of Pain" and "Life in Nature." 1 vol., 12mo. Cloth. Price, $1.75.

The author of this work holds a unique position among the thinkers of the age. He brings to the discussion of man and Nature, and the higher problems of human life, the latest and most thorough scientific preparation, and constantly employs the later dynamic philosophy in dealing with them. But he is broader than the scientific school which he recognizes, but with him the moral and religious elements of man are supreme. He conjoins strict science with high spirituality of view. "Man and his Dwelling-Place" is here rewritten and compressed, and presents in a pointed and attractive style original aspects of the most engaging questions of the time.

A MANUAL OF THE ANATOMY OF VERTEBRATED ANIMALS. By Thomas H. Huxley, LL. D., F. R. S. 1 vol., 12mo. Illustrated. Price, $2.50.

"This long-expected work will be cordially welcomed by all students and teachers of Comparative Anatomy as a compendious, reliable, and, notwithstanding its small dimensions, most comprehensive guide on the subject of which it treats. To praise or to criticise the work of so accomplished a master of his favorite science would be equally out of place. It is enough to say that it realizes in a remarkable degree the anticipations which have been formed of it; and that it presents an extraordinary combination of wide, general views, with the clear, accurate, and succinct statement of a prodigious number of individual facts."—*Nature.*

THE WORLD BEFORE THE DELUGE. By Louis Figuier. The Geological portion newly revised by H. W. Bristow, F. R. S., of the Geological Survey of Great Britain, Hon. Fellow of King's College, London. With 235 Illustrations. Being the first volume of the new and cheaper edition of Figuier's works. 1 vol., small 8vo. Price, $3.50.

The *Athenæum* says: "We find in 'The World before the Deluge' a book worth a thousand gilt Christmas volumes, and one most suitable as a gift to intellectual and earnestly inquiring students."

N. B.—In the new edition of "The World before the Deluge," the text has been again thoroughly revised by Mr. Bristow, and many important additions made, the result of the recent investigations of himself and his colleagues of the Geological Survey.

The other volumes of the new and cheaper edition of Figuier's Works will be issued in the following order:

THE VEGETABLE WORLD. From the French of Louis Figuier. Edited by C. O. G. Napier, F. G. S. With 471 Illustrations. Cloth. Price, $3.50.

THE INSECT WORLD. A Popular Account of the Orders of Insects. From the French of Louis Figuier. Edited by E. W. Jansen. With 570 Illustrations. Cloth. Price, $3.50.

THE OCEAN WORLD. A Descriptive History of the Sea and its Inhabitants. From the French of Louis Figuier. Edited by C. O. G. Napier, F. G. S. With 427 Illustrations. Cloth. Price, $3.50.

REPTILES AND BIRDS. From the French of Louis Figuier. Edited by Parker Gilmore. With 307 Illustrations. Cloth. Price, $3.50.

DESCHANEL'S NATURAL PHILOSOPHY.

NATURAL PHILOSOPHY:

AN ELEMENTARY TREATISE.

By PROFESSOR DESCHANEL, of Paris.

Translated, with Extensive Additions,

BY J. D. EVERETT, D. C. L., F. R. S.,

PROFESSOR OF NATURAL PHILOSOPHY IN THE QUEEN'S COLLEGE, BELFAST.

1 vol., medium 8vo. Illustrated by 760 Wood Engravings and 3 Colored Plates. Cloth, $. Published, also, separately, in Four Parts. Limp cloth, each $1.75.

Part I. MECHANICS, HYDROSTATICS, and PNEUMATICS. Part II. HEAT. Part III. ELECTRICITY and MAGNETISM. Part IV. SOUND and LIGHT.

Saturday Review.

"Systematically arranged, clearly written, and admirably illustrated, showing no less than than 760 engravings on wood and three colored plates, it forms a model work for a class of experimental physics. Far from losing in its English dress any of the qualities of matter or style which distinguished it in its original form, it may be said to have gained in the able hands of Professor Everett, both by way of arrangement and of incorporation of fresh matter, without parting in the translation with any of the freshness or force of the author's text."

Athenæum.

"A good working class-book for students in experimental physics."

Westminster Review.

"An excellent handbook of physics, especially suitable for self-instruction. . . . The work is published in a magnificent style; the woodcuts especially are admirable."

Quarterly Journal of Science.

"We have no work in our own scientific literature to be compared with it, and we are glad that the translation has fallen into such good hands as those of Professor Everett. . . . It will form an admirable text-book."

Nature.

"The engravings with which the work is illustrated are especially good, a point in which most of our English scientific works are lamentably deficient. The clearness of Deschanel's explanations is admirably preserved in the translation, while the value of the treatise is considerably enhanced by some important additions. . . . We believe the book will be found to supply a real need."

D. APPLETON & CO., New York.

www.ingramcontent.com/pod-product-compliance
Lightning Source LLC
LaVergne TN
LVHW011156110826
845150LV00006B/1233

* 9 7 8 1 4 2 5 5 4 5 7 9 6 *